Outside the Catholic Church No Salvation

By Bro. Peter Dimond, O.S.B.

Listing of Sections

INTRODUCTION

The dogma Outside the Catholic Church There is No Salvation and the necessity of the Sacrament of Baptism can actually be covered in <u>one page</u> (see section 1 and section 8). This is because this truth is exactly the same as defined by our first Pope:

> "… *the name of Our Lord Jesus Christ*… **Nor is there salvation in any other**. *For there is no other name, under heaven, given to men, whereby we must be saved*." (Acts 4:12).

There is no salvation outside of Jesus Christ, and the Catholic Church is His Mystical Body. And because there is no entering into the Catholic Church of Christ without the Sacrament of Baptism, this means that only baptized Catholics who die in the state of grace (and those who become baptized Catholics and die in the state of grace) can hope to be saved – *period*.

> "*If anyone abideth not in me, he shall be cast forth as a branch, and shall wither, and they shall gather him up, and cast him into the fire, and he burneth.*" (John 15:6)

The only reason that this document that you are looking at is approximately 300 pages long, and delves into a variety of issues in great detail, is simply because of **the almost unceasing attacks against – and almost universal denial of – these otherwise simply expressed truths in our day.**

The reader will notice that I've gone out of my way to answer every single significant objection raised against the true meaning of Outside the Church There is No Salvation and the necessity of the Sacrament of Baptism, while the people who write books and articles against these truths almost never address any of the arguments from the teaching of the Church that we bring forward, simply because they cannot refute the facts.

Some of the liberals who read this document will also make the objection that it is "bitter" or "uncharitable." But this is not true. The "foundation of charity is <u>faith pure and undefiled</u>" (Pope Pius XI, *Mortalium Animos*, #9). The statements in this document relating to Outside the Church There is No Salvation are made out of a desire to be faithful to Jesus Christ and His truth. A Catholic tells his neighbor the truth on this issue without compromise simply because he loves his neighbor.

> Pope Pius XI, *Mortalium Animos* #9, Jan. 6, 1928: "**Everyone knows that John himself, <u>the Apostle of love</u>, who seems to reveal in his Gospel the secrets of the Sacred Heart of Jesus, and who never ceased to impress on the memories of his followers the new commandment 'Love one another,' <u>altogether forbade any intercourse with those who professed a mutilated and corrupt form of</u>**

Christ's teaching: 'If any man come to you and bring not this doctrine, receive him not into the house nor say to him: God speed you.' (II John 10)."

A Catholic who refuses to denounce heresy and heretics (when necessary) is not acting charitably, but uncharitably.

Pope Leo XIII, *Sapientiae Christianae* #14, Jan. 10, 1890: "St. Thomas maintains: 'Each one is under obligation to show forth his faith, either to instruct and encourage others of the faithful, or to repel the attacks of unbelievers.' To recoil before an enemy, or to keep silence when from all sides such clamors are raised against truth, is the part of a man either devoid of character or who entertains doubt as to the truth of what he professes to believe."

The reader will also notice that each numbered section of this document was intended to be, for the most part, complete in itself; that is to say, one can read an individual section of this document and find the relevant citations from the teaching of the Church re-quoted for him without having to find them in a different part of the document.

I strongly encourage the reader to read the entire document, because the subjects dealt with in this document are all important; but, in my opinion, the most important sections of this document that the reader definitely does not want to miss are: 1, 2, 3, 4, 5, 7, 8, 13, 14, 15, 16, 18, 21, 24, 25, 26, 27, 31, 32, 33 and 34.

The reader will see that the conclusions that are formed in this document are formed on the basis of the infallible teaching of the Chair of St. Peter. Those who reject these facts, therefore, are not simply rejecting my opinions; they are rejecting the teaching of the Chair of St. Peter (the dogmatic teachings of the Catholic Church).

Pope Gregory XVI, *Mirari Vos* (# 13), Aug. 15, 1832: "With the admonition of the apostle that 'there is one God, one faith, one baptism' (Eph. 4:5) may those fear who contrive the notion that the safe harbor of salvation is open to persons of any religion whatever. They should consider the testimony of Christ Himself that 'those who are not with Christ are against Him,' (Lk. 11:23) and that they disperse unhappily <u>who do not gather with Him</u>. **Therefore, 'without a doubt, they will perish forever, unless they hold the Catholic faith whole and inviolate" (Athanasian Creed).**

-Bro. Peter Dimond, O.S.B. (May 3, 2004)

1. The Chair of St. Peter on Outside the Catholic Church There is No Salvation

The following statements on Outside the Catholic Church There is No Salvation are from the highest teaching authority of the Catholic Church. They are *ex cathedra* Papal decrees (decrees from the Chair of St. Peter). Therefore, they constitute the teaching given to the Catholic Church by Jesus Christ and the Apostles. Such teachings are unchangeable and are classified as part of the solemn Magisterium (the extraordinary teaching authority of the Catholic Church).

Pope Innocent III, *Fourth Lateran Council*, Constitution 1, 1215, *ex cathedra*:
"There is indeed one universal Church of the faithful, outside of which nobody at all is saved, in which Jesus Christ is both priest and sacrifice."[1]

Pope Boniface VIII, *Unam Sanctam*, Nov. 18, 1302, *ex cathedra*:
"With Faith urging us we are forced to believe and to hold the one, holy, Catholic Church and that, apostolic, and we firmly believe and simply confess **this Church outside of which there is no salvation nor remission of sin… Furthermore, we declare, say, define, and proclaim to every human creature that they by absolute necessity for salvation are entirely subject to the Roman Pontiff."**[2]

Pope Clement V, *Council of Vienne*, Decree # 30, 1311-1312, *ex cathedra*:
"Since however there is for both regulars and seculars, for superiors and subjects, for exempt and non-exempt, *one universal Church, outside of which there is no salvation*, for all of whom there is *one Lord, one faith, and one baptism*…"[3]

Pope Eugene IV, *Council of Florence*, Sess. 8, Nov. 22, 1439, *ex cathedra*:
"Whoever *wishes* to be saved, needs above all to hold the Catholic faith; unless each one preserves this whole and inviolate, he will without a doubt perish in eternity."[4]

Pope Eugene IV, *Council of Florence*, "Cantate Domino," 1441, *ex cathedra*:
"The Holy Roman Church firmly believes, professes and preaches that all those who are outside the Catholic Church, not only pagans but also Jews or heretics and schismatics, cannot share in eternal life and will go into the everlasting fire which was prepared for the devil and his angels, unless they are joined to the Church before the end of their lives; that the unity of this ecclesiastical body is of such importance that only those who abide in it do the Church's sacraments contribute to salvation and do fasts, almsgiving and other works of piety and practices of the Christian militia productive of eternal rewards; and that **nobody can be saved, no matter how much he has given**

away in alms and even if he has shed blood in the name of Christ, unless he has persevered in the bosom and unity of the Catholic Church."[5]

Pope Leo X, *Fifth Lateran Council*, Session 11, Dec. 19, 1516, *ex cathedra*: "For, regulars and seculars, prelates and subjects, exempt and non-exempt, belong to the **one universal Church, outside of which no one at all is saved**, and they all have *one Lord and one faith*."[6]

Pope Pius IV, Council of Trent, *Iniunctum nobis*, Nov. 13, 1565, *ex cathedra*: *"This true Catholic faith, outside of which no one can be saved*… I now profess and truly hold…"[7]

Pope Benedict XIV, *Nuper ad nos*, March 16, 1743, Profession of Faith: **"This faith of the Catholic Church, without which no one can be saved**, and which of my own accord I now profess and truly hold…"[8]

Pope Pius IX, *Vatican Council I*, Session 2, Profession of Faith, 1870, *ex cathedra*: **"This true Catholic faith, outside of which none can be saved**, which I now freely profess and truly hold…"[9]

2. The Keys of St. Peter and his Unfailing Faith

It is a fact of History, Scripture and Tradition that Our Lord Jesus Christ founded His Universal Church (the Catholic Church) upon St. Peter.

Matthew 16:17-18-"And I say to thee: **That thou are Peter: and upon this rock I will build my Church, and the gates of hell shall not prevail against it. And I will give to thee the keys of the kingdom of heaven.** And whatsoever thou shalt bind upon earth, it shall be bound also in heaven: and whatsoever thou shalt loose upon earth, it shall be loosed also in heaven."

Our Lord made St. Peter the first Pope, entrusted to him His entire flock, and gave him supreme authority in the Universal Church of Christ.

John 21:15-17-"**Jesus saith to Simon Peter:** Simon, son of John, lovest thou me? He saith to him: Yea, Lord, thou knowest that I love thee. **He saith to him: <u>Feed my lambs</u>.** He saith to him again: Simon, son of John, lovest thou me? He saith to him: Yea, Lord, thou knowest that I love thee. **He saith to him: <u>Feed my lambs</u>.** He saith to him a third time: Simon, son of John, lovest thou me? Peter was grieved, because he had said to him the third time: Lovest thou me? And he said to him: Lord, thou knowest all things: thou knowest that I love thee. **He said to him: <u>Feed my sheep</u>**."

And with the supreme authority that Our Lord Jesus Christ conferred upon St. Peter (and his successors, the Popes) comes what is called Papal Infallibility. Papal Infallibility is inseparable from Papal Supremacy – there was no point for Christ to make St. Peter the head of His Church (as Christ clearly did) if St. Peter or his successors, the Popes, could err <u>when exercising that supreme authority to teach on a point of Faith</u>. The supreme authority must be unfailing on binding matters of Faith and morals or else it is no true authority from Christ at all.

Papal Infallibility does not mean that a Pope cannot err at all and it does not mean that a Pope cannot lose his soul and be damned in Hell for grave sin. It means that the successors of St. Peter (the Popes of the Roman Catholic Church) cannot err <u>when authoritatively teaching on a point of Faith or morals to be held by the entire Church of Christ</u>. We find the promise of the unfailing faith for St. Peter and his successors referred to by Christ in Luke 22.

> Luke 22:31-32- "And the Lord said: Simon, Simon, behold Satan hath desired to have all of you, that he may sift you as wheat: **But I have prayed for thee, <u>that thy faith fail not</u>:** and thou being once converted, confirm thy brethren."

Satan desired to sift all the apostles (plural) like wheat, but Jesus prayed for Simon Peter (singular), that his <u>faith fail not.</u> Jesus is saying that St. Peter and his successors (the popes of the Catholic Church) have an unfailing faith when authoritatively teaching a point of faith or morals to be held by the entire Church of Christ.

> Pope Pius IX, *Vatican Council I*, 1870, *ex cathedra*:
> **"<u>SO, THIS GIFT OF TRUTH AND A NEVER FAILING FAITH WAS DIVINELY CONFERRED UPON PETER AND HIS SUCCESSORS IN THIS CHAIR</u>...**"[10]

> Pope Pius IX, *Vatican Council I*, 1870, *ex cathedra*:
> "... **<u>the See of St. Peter always remains unimpaired by any error</u>**, according to the divine promise of our Lord the Savior made to the chief of His disciples: '**<u>I have prayed for thee [Peter], that thy faith fail not</u>** ...'"[11]

And this truth has been held since the earliest times in the Catholic Church.

> Pope St. Gelasius I, epistle 42, or Decretal *de recipiendis et non recipiendis libris*, 495:
> "Accordingly, **the see of Peter** the Apostle of the Church of Rome is first, *having neither spot, nor wrinkle, nor anything of this kind* (Eph. 5:27)."[12]

The word "infallible" actually means "cannot fail" or "unfailing." Therefore, the very term *Papal Infallibility* comes directly from Christ's promise to St. Peter (and His successors) in Luke 22, that Peter has an unfailing Faith. Though this truth was believed since the beginning of the Church, it was specifically defined as a dogma at the First Vatican Council in 1870.

> Pope Pius IX, *Vatican Council I*, 1870, Session 4, Chap. 4:
> "...the Roman Pontiff, when he speaks *ex cathedra* [from the Chair of Peter], that is, when carrying out the duty of the pastor and teacher of all Christians in accord with his supreme apostolic authority he explains a doctrine of faith or morals to be held by the universal Church... **operates with that infallibility** with which the divine Redeemer wished that His Church be instructed in defining doctrine on faith and morals; **and so such definitions of the Roman Pontiff from himself, but not from the consensus of the Church, are unalterable.**"[13]

But how does one know when a Pope is exercising his unfailing Faith to infallibly teach from the Chair of St. Peter? The answer is that we know from the language that the Pope uses or the manner in which the Pope teaches. Vatican I defined two requirements which must be fulfilled: 1) when the Pope is carrying out his duty as Pastor and Teacher of all Christians in accord with his supreme apostolic authority; 2) when he explains a doctrine on faith or morals to be held by the entire Church of Christ. A Pope can fulfill both of these requirements in just one line, by anathematizing a false opinion (such as many dogmatic Councils) or by saying "By our apostolic authority we declare..." or by saying "We believe, profess, and teach" or by using words of similar importance and meaning, which indicate that the Pope is teaching the whole Church on Faith in a definitive and binding fashion.

So, when a Pope teaches from the Chair of Peter in the manner stipulated above he cannot be wrong. If he could be wrong, then the Church of Christ could be officially led into error, and Christ's promise to St. Peter and His Church would fail (which is impossible). That which is taught from the Chair of Peter by the Popes of the Catholic Church is the teaching of Jesus Christ Himself. To reject that which is taught by the Popes from the Chair of Peter is simply to despise Jesus Christ Himself.

> Luke 10:16- "He that heareth you, heareth me: and he that despiseth you despiseth me..."

> Matthew 18:17 -"And if he will not hear the church, let him be to thee as the heathen and publican."

> Pope Leo XIII, *Satis Cognitum*, 1896:

"… Christ instituted a living, authoritative and permanent Magisterium… **If it could in any way be false, an evident contradiction follows; for then God Himself would be the author of error in man."[14]**

THE CHAIR OF PETER SPEAKS THE TRUTH THAT CHRIST HIMSELF DELIVERED

The truths of faith which have been proclaimed by the Popes speaking infallibly from the Chair of Peter are called dogmas. The dogmas make up what is called the deposit of Faith. And the deposit of Faith ended with the death of the last Apostle.

> Pope St. Pius X, *Lamentabile*, The Errors of the Modernists #21:
> "<u>Revelation</u>, constituting the object of Catholic faith, <u>was not completed with the apostles</u>."[15] - **Condemned**

This means that when a Pope defines a dogma from the Chair of Peter he does not <u>make</u> the dogma true, but rather he proclaims what is already true, what has <u>already been revealed by Christ and delivered to the Apostles</u>. The dogmas are therefore unchangeable, of course. One of these dogmas in the deposit of Faith is that Outside the Catholic Church There is No Salvation. Since this is the teaching of Jesus Christ, one is not allowed to dispute this dogma or to question it; one must simply accept it. It does not matter if one doesn't like the dogma, doesn't understand the dogma, or *doesn't see justice in the dogma*. If one doesn't accept it as infallibly true then one simply does not accept Jesus Christ, because the dogma comes to us from Jesus Christ.

> Pope Leo XIII, *Satis Cognitum* (# 9), June 29, 1896:
> **"… can it be lawful for anyone to reject any one of those truths without by that very fact falling into heresy? – without separating himself from the Church? – without repudiating in one sweeping act the whole of Christian teaching?** For such is the nature of faith that nothing can be more absurd than to accept some things and reject others. **Faith,** as the Church teaches, **<u>is that supernatural virtue by which… we believe what He has revealed to be true, not on account of the intrinsic truth perceived by the natural light of human reason [author: that is, not because it seems correct to us], but because of the authority of God Himself, the Revealer, who can neither deceive nor be deceived</u>… But he who dissents even in one point from divinely revealed truth absolutely rejects all faith,** since he thereby refuses to honor God as the supreme truth and the *formal motive of faith*."[16]

Those who refuse to believe in the dogma Outside the Church There is No Salvation until *they* understand how there is justice in it <u>are simply withholding their Faith in Christ's Revelation</u>. Those with the true Faith in Christ (and His Church) accept His teaching <u>first</u> and understand the truth in it (i.e., *why* it is true) second. A Catholic does

Also, those who insist that infallible DEFINITIONS must be interpreted by non-infallible statements (e.g., from theologians, catechisms, etc.) are also denying the whole purpose of the Chair of Peter. They are subordinating the dogmatic teaching of the Chair of Peter (*truths from heaven*) to the re-evaluation of fallible human documents, thereby inverting their authority, perverting their integrity and denying their purpose.

> Pope Gregory XVI, *Mirari Vos* (#7), Aug. 15, 1832: "… nothing of the things appointed ought to be diminished; nothing changed; nothing added; **but they must be preserved both as regards expression and meaning.**"[21]

Thus, there is no "strict" or "loose" interpretation of Outside the Church There is No Salvation, as the liberal heretics like to emphasize; there is only what the Church has once declared.

4. Other Popes on Outside the Church There is No Salvation

In addition to the *ex cathedra* (from the Chair of Peter) proclamations of the Popes, a Catholic must also believe what is taught by the Catholic Church *as divinely revealed* in her ordinary and universal Magisterium (Magisterium = the teaching authority of the Church).

> Pope Pius IX, *Vatican I*, Sess. III, Chap. 3, ex cathedra: "Further, by divine and Catholic faith, all those things must be believed which are contained in the written word of God and in tradition, and those which are proposed by the Church, either in a solemn pronouncement or in her ordinary and universal teaching power, to be believed *as divinely revealed.*"[22]

The teaching of the Ordinary and Universal Magisterium consists of those doctrines which Popes, by their common and universal teaching, propose to be believed *as divinely revealed*. For instance, in their common and universal teaching, approximately 10 Popes have denounced the heretical concept of liberty of conscience and worship as contrary to Revelation. A Catholic cannot reject that teaching. The teaching of the Ordinary and Universal Magisterium can never contradict the teaching of the Chair of Peter (the dogmatic definitions), of course, since both are infallible. Thus, the Ordinary and Universal Magisterium does not actually have to be considered at all in regard to Outside the Church There is No Salvation, because this dogma has been defined from the Chair of Peter and nothing in the Ordinary and Universal Magisterium can possibly contradict the Chair of Peter. So beware of those heretics who try to find ways to deny the Church's dogmatic teaching on Outside the Church There is No Salvation by calling fallible, non-Magisterial statements which contradict this dogma, part of the "Ordinary and Universal Magisterium," when they aren't. This is a clever ploy of the heretics.

But the following quotations from many Popes are reaffirmations of the dogma Outside the Church There is No Salvation. These teachings of the Popes are part of the Ordinary and Universal Magisterium – and are therefore infallible – since they reiterate the teaching of the Chair of St. Peter on the Catholic dogma Outside the Church There is No Salvation.

Pope St. Gregory the Great, quoted in *Summo Iugiter Studio,* 590-604:
"The holy universal Church teaches that it is not possible to worship God truly except in her **and asserts that all who are outside of her will not be saved."**[23]

Pope Innocent III, *Eius exemplo*, Dec. 18, 1208:
"By the heart we believe and by the mouth we confess the one Church, not of heretics, but **the Holy Roman, Catholic, and Apostolic Church outside of which we believe that no one is saved."**[24]

Pope Clement VI, *Super quibusdam*, Sept. 20, 1351:
"In the second place, we ask whether you and the Armenians obedient to you believe that **no man of the wayfarers outside the faith of this Church**, and outside the obedience to the Pope of Rome, **can finally be saved."**[25]

Pope Leo XII, *Ubi Primum* (# 14), May 5, 1824:
"It is impossible for the most true God, who is Truth itself, the best, the wisest Provider, and the Rewarder of good men, **to approve all sects who profess false teachings** which are often inconsistent with one another and contradictory, **and to confer eternal rewards on their members**… by divine faith we hold one Lord, one faith, one baptism… **This is why we profess that there is no salvation outside the Church."**[26]

Pope Leo XII, *Quod hoc ineunte* (# 8), May 24, 1824: **"We address all of you who are still removed from the true Church and the road to salvation.** In this universal rejoicing, one thing is lacking: that having been called by the inspiration of the Heavenly Spirit and having broken every decisive snare, you might sincerely agree with **the mother Church, outside of whose teachings there is no salvation."**[27]

Pope Gregory XVI, *Mirari Vos* (# 13), Aug. 15, 1832: "With the admonition of the apostle, that 'there is one God, one faith, one baptism' (Eph. 4:5), may those fear who contrive the notion that the safe harbor of salvation is open to persons of any religion whatever. They should consider the testimony of Christ Himself that 'those who are not with Christ are against Him,' (Lk. 11:23) and that they disperse unhappily who do not gather with Him. **Therefore, 'without a doubt,** they will perish forever, unless they hold the Catholic faith whole and inviolate (Athanasian Creed)."[28]

Pope Gregory XVI, *Summo Iugiter Studio* (# 2), May 27, 1832:
"Finally some of these misguided people attempt to persuade themselves and others that men are not saved only in the Catholic religion, but that even heretics may attain eternal life."[29]

Pope Pius IX, *Ubi primum* (# 10), June 17, 1847: **"For 'there is one universal Church outside of which no one at all is saved**; it contains regular and secular prelates along with those under their jurisdiction, **who all profess one Lord, one faith and one baptism."**[30]

Pope Pius IX, *Nostis et Nobiscum* (# 10), Dec. 8, 1849: "In particular, **ensure that the faithful are deeply and thoroughly convinced of the truth of the doctrine that the Catholic faith is necessary for attaining salvation.** (This doctrine, received from Christ and emphasized by the Fathers and Councils, is also contained in the formulae of the profession of faith used by Latin, Greek and Oriental Catholics)."[31]

Pope Pius IX, *Syllabus of Modern Errors*, Dec. 8, 1864 - Proposition 16: "Man may, in the observance of any religion whatever, <u>find the way of eternal salvation</u>, and <u>arrive</u> at eternal salvation."[32] – **Condemned**

Pope Leo XIII, *Tametsi futura prospicientibus* (# 7), Nov. 1, 1900: "Christ is man's 'Way'; the Church also is his 'Way'… **Hence all who would find salvation apart from the Church, are led astray and strive in vain."**[33]

Pope St. Pius X, *Iucunda sane* (# 9), March 12, 1904: "Yet at the same time We cannot but remind all, great and small, as Pope St. Gregory did, of **the absolute necessity of having recourse to this Church in order to have eternal salvation**…"[34]

Pope St. Pius X, *Editae saepe* (# 29), May 26, 1910: **"The Church alone** possesses together with her magisterium the power of governing and sanctifying human society. Through her ministers and servants (each in his own station and office), she **confers on mankind suitable and necessary means of salvation."**[35]

Pope Pius XI, *Mortalium Animos* (# 11), Jan. 6, 1928: "**The Catholic Church** is alone in keeping the true worship. This is the fount of truth, this is the house of faith, this is the temple of God: **if any man enter not here, or if any man go forth from it, he is a stranger to the hope of life and salvation."**[36]

5. The Sacrament of Baptism is the only Way into the Church

The Catholic Church has always taught that receiving the Sacrament of Baptism is the only way into Christ's Church, outside of which there is no salvation.

> Pope Julius III, *Council of Trent*, On <u>the Sacraments of Baptism</u> and Penance, Sess. 14, Chap. 2, *ex cathedra*: "But in fact this sacrament [Penance] is seen to differ in many respects from baptism. For, apart from the fact that the matter and form, by which the essence of a sacrament is constituted, are totally distinct, there is certainly no doubt that the minister of baptism need not be a judge, **since the Church exercises judgment on no one who has not previously <u>entered it by the gate of baptism</u>. *For what have I to do with those who are without* (1 Cor. 5:12), says the Apostle. It is otherwise with those of the household of the faith, whom Christ the Lord <u>by the laver of baptism has once made 'members of his own body</u>' (1 Cor. 12:13)."**[37]

This definition is particularly significant because it proves that only through water baptism is one incorporated into the *Body of the Church*. The significance of this will become clearer in the later sections where it is proven that Body membership is necessary for salvation.

> Pope Eugene IV, *The Council of Florence*, "Exultate Deo," Nov. 22, 1439, *ex cathedra*: "<u>**Holy baptism**</u>**, which is the gateway to the spiritual life, holds the first place among all the sacraments; <u>through it we are made members of Christ and of the body of the Church</u>. And since death entered the universe through the first man, 'unless we are born again of water and the Spirit, we cannot,' as the Truth says, 'enter into the kingdom of heaven' [John 3:5]. The matter of this sacrament is real and natural water."**[38]

> Pope Pius XII, *Mystici Corporis* (# 22), June 29, 1943: **"Actually only those are to be numbered among the members of the Church who have received the laver of regeneration [water baptism] and profess the true faith."**[39]

> Pope Pius XII, *Mystici Corporis* (# 27), June 29, 1943: "He (Christ) also determined that **through Baptism (cf. Jn. 3:5) those who should believe would be incorporated in the Body of the Church."**[40]

Pope Pius XII, *Mediator Dei* (# 43), Nov. 20, 1947: "In the same way, actually that **baptism is the distinctive mark of all Christians, and serves to differentiate them from those who have not been cleansed in this purifying stream and consequently are not members of Christ**, the sacrament of holy orders sets the priest apart from the rest of the faithful who have not received this consecration."[41]

6. The One Church of the Faithful

Pope Innocent III, *Fourth Lateran Council*, Constitution 1, 1215, *ex cathedra*: **"THERE IS INDEED ONE UNIVERSAL CHURCH OF THE FAITHFUL, outside of which nobody at all is saved, in which Jesus Christ is both priest and sacrifice."**[42]

The first dogmatic definition from the Chair of Peter on Outside the Church There is No Salvation (from Pope Innocent III) taught that the Catholic Church is the one Church "of the faithful," outside of which *no one at all* is saved. But who are "the faithful"? Can one who has not been baptized be considered part of "the faithful"? If we look to Catholic Tradition, the answer is a resounding "no."

As many of you know, the Catholic Mass is divided into two parts: the Mass of the catechumens (those preparing to be baptized) and the Mass of the faithful (those baptized).

In the early Church, the unbaptized catechumens (i.e., those who had not received <u>the Sacrament</u> of Baptism) had to leave after the Mass of the catechumens, when the faithful professed the Creed. **The unbaptized were not allowed to stay for the Mass of the faithful**, because it is only by receiving the Sacrament of Baptism that one becomes one of the faithful. <u>This is the teaching of Tradition.</u>

Casimir Kucharek, *The Byzantine-Slav Liturgy of St. John Chrysostom:*
"In Canon 19 of the Synod of Laodicea (A.D. 343-381), for example, we read: 'After the sermons of the bishops, the prayer for the catechumens is to be said by itself first; **when the catechumens have gone out**, the prayer for those who are doing penance; and after these… there should then be offered *the three prayers of the faithful*…'"[43]

Here we see the 4th century Synod of Laodicea affirming the tradition that unbaptized catechumens were to depart from the Liturgy before the Mass of the Faithful began.

And this distinction between the Mass of the Catechumens and the Mass of the Faithful was a staple in the ancient rites of the Catholic Church. Hence, Fr. Casimir Kucharek, in his large work on the *Byzantine-Slav Liturgy of St. John Chrysostom*, says that the Liturgy of the Catechumens is "**present in <u>all</u> Rites**…"[44] In other words, <u>all</u> of the ancient Catholic rites testified to the fact that no unbaptized person could be considered part of *the faithful* **because they *all* dismissed unbaptized catechumens before the Mass of the Faithful began!**

Hence Fr. Casimir Kucharek further writes,

> "[St.] Athanasius mentions that they (catechumens) were not allowed to be present at the mysteries, while Cyril of Alexandria speaks of their departure before the more solemn parts of the service."[45]

The Catholic Encyclopedia acknowledges the same teaching of Tradition.

> The Catholic Encyclopedia, "Faithful," Vol. 5, p. 769: "St. Augustine (says): '*Ask a man: are you a Christian? If he be a pagan or Jew, he will reply: I am not a Christian. But if he say: I am a Christian, ask him again*: **are you a catechumen, or one of the faithful?**'"[46]

In the third century, the early Church father Tertullian criticized the custom of certain heretics who disregarded this crucial distinction between the unbaptized and *the faithful*.

> The Catholic Encyclopedia, "Catechumen," Vol. 3, p. 430: "Tertullian reproaches the heretics with disregarding it; among them, he says, '**one does not know which is the catechumen and which the faithful**, *all alike come [to the mysteries], all hear the same discourses, and say the same prayers*."[47]

Finally, I will quote a prayer from the ancient Byzantine-Slav Liturgy of St. John Chrysostom. The prayer was recited at the dismissal of the catechumens before the Mass of the faithful began.

> Byzantine-Slav Liturgy of St. John Chrysostom, *Dismissal of the Catechumens*: "**Let us, <u>the faithful</u>, pray for the catechumens**, that the Lord have mercy on them… Lord and God, Jesus Christ, as the salvation of mankind: *look down upon your servants, the catechumens, who bow their heads before you.* **In due time make them worthy of the waters of regeneration, the forgiveness of their sins, and the robe of immortality. Unite them to your holy, catholic, and apostolic church**, *and number them among your chosen floc*k."[48]

Here we see that the ancient eastern rite liturgy of St. John Chrysostom makes a forceful distinction between the unbaptized (the catechumens) and *the faithful*. **It** confirms that because the catechumens are not baptized into *the faithful*, **they are not forgiven their sins or united to the Catholic Church.** The unbaptized do not belong to the one Church of the faithful. This is part of the ancient Catholic Faith. And obviously this fact is not proven to be part of the ancient Catholic Faith simply because an early Church father stated it – for a statement from a given early Church father doesn't prove this definitively; but rather it is proven because the testimonies of the aforementioned saints are in perfect harmony with the clear teaching of Catholic liturgical worship, which divides the Mass of Catechumens from the Mass of the Faithful. It is, therefore, the teaching and rule of Catholic worship that no unbaptized person is to be considered part of *the faithful*. **And this is why all who died without the Sacrament of Baptism were refused Christian burial everywhere in the universal Church since the beginning.**

And because this was the universal rule of worship in the Catholic Church, it was the expression of the universal Faith and Tradition of the Catholic Church.

Pope Pius XI, *Quas Primas* (# 12), Dec. 11, 1925: "The perfect harmony of the Eastern liturgies with our own in this continual praise of Christ the King shows once more the truth of the axiom: *Legem credendi lex statuit supplicandi.* **The rule of faith is indicated by the law of our worship."**[49]

Therefore, it would be contrary to Tradition to assert that a person who has not received the Sacrament of Baptism is part of *the faithful*.

St. John Chrysostom (*Hom. in Io. 25, 3*), (4th Century):
"For the Catechumen is a stranger to the Faithful… One has Christ for his King; the other sin and the devil; the food of one is Christ, of the other, that meat which decays and perishes… Since then we have nothing in common, in what, tell me, shall we hold communion?… Let us then give diligence that we may become citizens of the city above… **for if it should come to pass (which God forbid!) that through the sudden arrival of death we depart hence uninitiated [unbaptized], though we have ten thousand virtues, our portion will be none other than hell,** and the venomous worm, and fire unquenchable, and bonds indissoluble."

St. Ambrose, (4th Century) Bishop and Doctor of the Church:
"I shall now begin to instruct you on the sacrament you have received; of whose nature it was not fitting to speak to you before this; **for in the Christian what comes first is faith. *And at Rome for this reason those who have been baptized are called the faithful (fideles)."*[50]**

This teaching of Tradition is why in the Traditional Rite of Baptism, the unbaptized catechumen is asked what he desires from holy Church, **and he answers "Faith."** The unbaptized catechumen does not have "the Faith," so he begs the Church for it in the "Sacrament of Faith" (Baptism), which alone makes him one of "the faithful." This is why the Sacrament of Baptism has been known since apostolic times as "the Sacrament of Faith."

> *Catechism of the Council of Trent*, On Baptism – Effects of Baptism:
> "… Baptism …. **the Sacrament of faith**…."[51]

> *Catechism of the Council of Trent*, On Baptism – Second Effect: Sacramental Character: "… **Baptism**… **By it we are qualified to receive the other Sacraments, and the Christian is distinguished from those who do not profess the faith.**"[52]

> Pope Clement VI, *Super quibusdam*, Sept. 20, 1351:
> "… **all those who <u>in baptism have received the same Catholic faith</u>**…"[53]

> Pope Paul III, *Council of Trent*, Session 6, Chap. 7 on Justification, *ex cathedra*:
> "… **THE SACRAMENT OF BAPTISM, <u>WHICH IS 'THE SACRAMENT OF FAITH</u>… THIS FAITH**, IN ACCORDANCE WITH APOSTOLIC TRADITION, **CATECHUMENS BEG OF THE CHURCH BEFORE THE SACRAMENT OF BAPTISM**, when they ask for 'faith which bestows life eternal,' (Rit. Rom., Ordo Baptismi)."[54]

And with these facts in mind (that a catechumen "begs" for the faith because he isn't part of the faithful), remember the definition of Pope Innocent III at the Fourth Lateran Council: "There is indeed one universal Church of **the faithful**, outside of which nobody at all is saved…" The original Latin reads: "*Una vero est fidelium universalis ecclesia, extra quam <u>nullus omnino</u> salvatur…*" The Latin words *nullus omnino* mean "absolutely nobody." Absolutely nobody outside the one Church of the faithful is saved. Since the one Church of "the faithful" only includes those who have received the Sacrament of Baptism – as apostolic tradition, liturgical tradition and Church dogma show – this means that absolutely nobody is saved without the Sacrament of Baptism.

7. Subjection to the Church/Roman Pontiff

The second definition from the Chair of Peter on Outside the Church There is No Salvation came from Pope Boniface VIII in the Bull *Unam Sanctam*.

> Pope Boniface VIII, *Unam Sanctam*, Nov. 18, 1302, *ex cathedra*:
> "With Faith urging us we are forced to believe and to hold the one, holy, Catholic Church and that, apostolic, and we firmly believe and simply confess this Church outside of which there is no salvation nor remission of sin…
> **Furthermore, we declare, say, define, and proclaim to <u>every human creature</u>**

that they by absolute necessity for salvation are entirely subject to the Roman Pontiff."[55]

This means infallibly that *every human creature* must be subject to the Roman Pontiff for salvation. Obviously, this does not mean that one must be subject to an Antipope for salvation, which is what we have today. It means that everyone must be subject to the true Pope, if and when we have one.

But how are infants subject to the Roman Pontiff? This is a good question. Notice that Pope Boniface VIII did not declare that every human creature must *know* the Roman Pontiff, but that every human creature must *be subject* to the Roman Pontiff. Infants become subject to the Roman Pontiff by their baptism into the one Church of Christ, of which the Roman Pontiff is the head.

> Pope Leo XIII, *Nobilissima* (# 3), Feb. 8, 1884:
> "The Church, guardian of the integrity of the Faith – which, in virtue of its authority, deputed from God its Founder, has to call all nations to the knowledge of Christian lore, and which is consequently bound to watch keenly over the teaching and upbringing of **the children placed under its authority by baptism**…"[56]

Children are placed under the authority of the Church by baptism. Thus, by their baptism *they are made subject* to the Roman Pontiff, since the Roman Pontiff possesses supreme authority in the Church (First Vatican Council, *de fide*). This proves that **baptism is actually the first component in determining whether or not one is subject to the Roman Pontiff. If one has not been baptized, then one cannot *be subject* to the Roman Pontiff, because the Church exercises judgment (i.e., jurisdiction) over no one who has not entered the Church through the Sacrament of Baptism (*de fide*).**

> Pope Julius III, *Council of Trent*, On the Sacraments of Baptism and Penance, Sess. 14, Chap. 2, *ex cathedra*: "… since **the Church exercises judgment on no one who has not previously entered it by the gate of baptism**. *For what have I to do with those who are without* (1 Cor. 5:12), says the Apostle. It is otherwise with those of the household of the faith, whom Christ the Lord by the laver of baptism has once made 'members of his own body' (1 Cor. 12:13)."[57]

It is not possible, therefore, to be subject to the Roman Pontiff without receiving the Sacrament of Baptism, since the Church (and the Roman Pontiff) cannot exercise judgment (jurisdiction) over an unbaptized person (*de fide, Trent*). **And since it is not possible to be subject to the Roman Pontiff without the Sacrament of Baptism, it is not possible to be saved without the Sacrament of Baptism, since every human creature must be subject to the Roman Pontiff for salvation** (*de fide, Boniface VIII*).

8. The Sacrament of Baptism is Necessary for Salvation

To further show that the Sacrament of Baptism is necessary for salvation, I will quote numerous other infallible statements from the Chair of St. Peter.

Pope Paul III, *The Council of Trent*, Sess. 7, Can. 5 on the Sacrament of Baptism, *ex cathedra*: **"If anyone says that baptism [the Sacrament] is optional, that is, not necessary for salvation (cf. Jn. 3:5): let him be anathema."**[58]

This infallible dogmatic definition from the Chair of St. Peter condemns anyone who says that the Sacrament of Baptism is not necessary for salvation. The Sacrament of Baptism is necessary for all for salvation, first of all, because, as the Council of Trent defines, all men (except the Blessed Virgin Mary) were conceived in a state of original sin as a result of the sin of Adam, the first man. The Sacrament of Baptism is also necessary for all for salvation because it is the means by which one is marked as a member of Jesus Christ and incorporated into His Mystical Body. And in defining the truth that all men were conceived in the state of Original Sin, the Council of Trent specifically declared that the Blessed Virgin Mary was an exception to its decree on Original Sin.[59] But in defining the truth that the Sacrament of Baptism is necessary for salvation, the Council of Trent made no exceptions at all.

Pope Eugene IV, *The Council of Florence*, "Exultate Deo," Nov. 22, 1439, *ex cathedra*: "Holy baptism, which is the gateway to the spiritual life, holds the first place among all the sacraments; through it we are made members of Christ and of the body of the Church. **And since death entered the universe through the first man, 'unless we are born again of water and the Spirit, we cannot,' as the Truth says, 'enter into the kingdom of heaven' [John 3:5].** The matter of this sacrament is real and natural water."[60]

Pope Innocent III, *Fourth Lateran Council*, Constitution 1, 1215, *ex cathedra*: **"But the sacrament of baptism is consecrated in water at the invocation of the undivided Trinity – namely, Father, Son and Holy Ghost – and brings salvation to both children and adults** when it is correctly carried out by anyone in the form laid down by the Church."[61]

Pope Benedict XIV, *Nuper ad nos*, March 16, 1743, Profession of Faith: **"Likewise (I profess) that baptism is necessary for salvation, and hence, if there is imminent danger of death, it should be conferred at once and without delay,** and that it is valid if conferred with the right matter and form and intention by anyone, and at any time."[62]

Pope Pius XI, *Quas Primas* (# 15), Dec. 11, 1925 : "Indeed this kingdom is presented in the Gospels as such, into which men prepare to enter by doing penance; **moreover, they cannot enter it except through** faith and baptism, which, although **an external rite**, yet signifies and effects an interior regeneration."[63]

We see here that one cannot enter the kingdom of heaven without faith and the external rite of baptism (i.e., the Sacrament of Baptism).

9. Water is Necessary for Baptism and John 3:5 is literal

"JESUS ANSWERED: AMEN, AMEN, I SAY TO THEE, UNLESS A MAN BE BORN AGAIN OF WATER AND THE HOLY GHOST, HE CANNOT ENTER INTO THE KINGDOM OF GOD." (JOHN 3:5)

The Catholic Church is the guardian and interpreter of the Sacred Scriptures. She alone has been given the power and authority to infallibly determine the true sense of the sacred texts.

Pope Pius IX, *First Vatican Council*, Sess. 3, Chap. 2 on Revelation, 1870: "… We, renewing the same decree, declare this to be its intention: that, in matters of faith and morals pertaining to the instruction of Christian Doctrine, **that must be considered as the true sense of Sacred Scripture which Holy Mother Church has held and holds, whose office it is to judge concerning the true understanding and interpretation of the Sacred Scriptures**; and, for that reason, no one is permitted to interpret Sacred Scripture itself contrary to this sense, or even contrary to the unanimous consent of the Fathers."[64]

But not every scripture is understood by the Catholic Church in the literal sense. For example, in Matthew 5:29, Our Lord Jesus Christ tells us that if our eye scandalizes us we should pluck it out, for it is better that it should perish than our whole body in Hell.

Matt. 5:29- "And if thy right eye scandalize thee, pluck it out and cast it from thee. For it is expedient for thee that one of thy members should perish, rather than thy whole body be cast into hell."

But Our Lord's words here are not to be understood literally. His words are spoken figuratively to describe an occasion of sin or something in life that may scandalize us and be a hindrance to our salvation. We must pluck it out and cut it off, says Our Lord, because it is better to be without it than to perish altogether in the fires of Hell.

On the other hand, other verses of scripture are understood by the Church in the literal sense. For example:

> Matt. 26:26-28 "And whilst they were at supper, Jesus took bread, and blessed, and broke: and gave to his disciples, and said: Take ye, and eat. **This is my body**. And taking the chalice, he gave thanks, and gave to them, saying: Drink ye all of this. **For this is my blood** of the new testament, which shall be shed for many unto remission of sins."

When Our Lord Jesus Christ says in Matthew 26:26: "This is My Body," and in Matthew 26:28: "This is My Blood," His words are understood by the Catholic Church exactly as they are written, for we know that Our Lord Jesus Christ was indeed referring to His actual Body and Blood, not a symbol or a figure.

So the question is: How does the Catholic Church understand the words of Jesus Christ in John 3:5- *Amen, amen, I say to thee, unless a man be born again of water and the Holy Ghost, he cannot enter into the kingdom of God*? Does the Catholic Church understand these words as they are written or in some other way? Does the Catholic Church understand these words to mean that <u>every man must be born again of water and the Holy Ghost to be saved</u>, as Our Lord says? The answer is clear: every single dogmatic definition that the Catholic Church has issued dealing with Our Lord's words in John 3:5 understands them literally, exactly as they are written.

Pope Eugene IV, *The Council of Florence*, "Exultate Deo," Nov. 22, 1439, *ex cathedra*: "Holy baptism, which is the gateway to the spiritual life, holds the first place among all the sacraments; through it we are made members of Christ and of the body of the Church. **And since death entered the universe through the first man, '<u>unless we are born again of water and the Spirit, we cannot</u>,' as the Truth says, '<u>enter into the kingdom of heaven</u>' [John 3:5].** The matter of this sacrament is real and natural water."[65]

This means that Our Lord Jesus Christ's declaration that no man can be saved without being born again of <u>water and the Holy Ghost</u> is a literal dogma of the Catholic Faith.

Pope Paul III, *The Council of Trent*, Can. 2 on the Sacrament of Baptism, Sess. 7, 1547, *ex cathedra*: **"If anyone shall say that real and natural water is not necessary for baptism, <u>and on that account those words of Our Lord Jesus Christ: 'Unless a man be born again of water and the Holy Spirit' [John 3:5], are distorted into some sort of metaphor</u>**: let him be anathema."[66]

Pope Paul III, *The Council of Trent*, Can. 5 on the <u>Sacrament</u> of Baptism, Sess. 7, 1547, *ex cathedra*: **<u>"If anyone says that baptism [the sacrament] is optional, that is, not necessary for salvation (cf. Jn. 3:5): let him be anathema."</u>**[67]

Pope Paul III, *The Council of Trent*, On Original Sin, Session V, *ex cathedra*: "By one man sin entered into the world, and by sin death... so that in them there may be washed away by regeneration, what they have contracted by generation, '*<u>For unless a man be born again of water and the Holy Ghost, he cannot enter into the kingdom of God</u>* [John 3:5]."[68]

Pope St. Zosimus, *The Council of Carthage XVI*, on Original Sin and Grace: **"For when the Lord says: 'Unless a man be born again of water and the Holy Ghost, he shall not enter into the kingdom of God' [John 3:5],** what Catholic will doubt that he will be a partner of the devil who has not deserved to be a coheir of Christ. For he who lacks the right part will without doubt run into the left."[69]

Pope Gregory IX, *Cum, sicut ex*, July 8, 1241, to Sigurd of Nidaros: "Since as we have learned from your report, it sometimes happens because of scarcity of water, that infants of your lands are baptized in beer, we reply to you in the tenor of those present that, **since according to evangelical doctrine it is necessary 'to be reborn from water and the Holy Spirit' (Jn. 3:5) they are not to be considered rightly baptized who are baptized in beer."**[70]

10. Infants Cannot Be Saved Without Baptism

The teaching of the Catholic Church already cited shows that no one can be saved without the Sacrament of Baptism. Obviously, therefore, this means that children and infants also cannot get to heaven without Baptism because they are conceived in a state of Original Sin, which cannot be removed without the Sacrament of Baptism. But this truth of the Catholic Church is denied by many people today. They look at the horrible tragedy of abortion – the millions of slaughtered children – and they conclude that these children must be headed to heaven. But such a conclusion is heretical. The worst part of abortion is the fact that these children are barred from entrance into heaven, not that they don't get to live in this pagan world. Satan delights in abortion because he knows that these souls can never get to heaven without the Sacrament of Baptism. If aborted children went straight to heaven without the Sacrament of Baptism, as many today believe, then Satan would not be behind abortion.

The Church teaches that aborted children and infants who die without baptism descend immediately into Hell, but that they do not suffer the fires of Hell. They go to a place in Hell called the limbo of the children. The most specific definition of the Church proving that there is no possible way for an infant to be saved without the Sacrament of Baptism is the following one from Pope Eugene IV.

> Pope Eugene IV, *Council of Florence*, Session 11, Feb. 4, 1442, *ex cathedra*: "**Regarding children**, indeed, because of danger of death, which can often take place, **when no help can be brought to them by another remedy than through the sacrament of baptism, through which they are snatched from the domination of the Devil [original sin] and adopted among the sons of God**, it advises that holy baptism ought not be deferred for forty or eighty days, or any time according to the observance of certain people…"[71]

Pope Eugene IV here defines *from the Chair of Peter* that there is <u>no other remedy</u> for infants to be snatched away from the dominion of the devil (i.e., original sin) other than the Sacrament of Baptism. This means that anyone who obstinately teaches that infants can be saved without receiving the Sacrament of Baptism is a heretic, for he is teaching that there is *another remedy* for original sin in children other than the Sacrament of Baptism.

Pope Martin V, *Council of Constance*, Session 15, July 6, 1415 - Condemning the articles of John Wyclif - Proposition 6: "**Those who claim that the children of the faithful dying without sacramental baptism will not be saved, are stupid and presumptuous in saying this**."[72] - **Condemned**

This is a fascinating proposition from *The Council of Constance*. Unfortunately, this proposition is not found in Denzinger, which only contains some of the Council's decrees, but it is found in a full collection of the Council of Constance. The arch-heretic John Wyclif was proposing that those (such as ourselves) are stupid for teaching that infants who die without *water* (*i.e., sacramental*) baptism cannot possibly be saved.   He was anathematized for this assertion, among many others. And here is what *The Council of Constance* had to say about John Wyclif's anathematized propositions, such as #6 above.

> Pope Martin V, *Council of Constance*, Session 15, July 6, 1415: "The books and pamphlets of John Wyclif, of cursed memory, were carefully examined by the doctors and masters of Oxford University… **This holy synod, therefore, in the name of our Lord Jesus Christ, repudiates and condemns, by this perpetual decree, the aforesaid articles and each of them in particular; and it forbids each and every Catholic henceforth, under pain of anathema, to preach, teach, or hold the said articles or any one of them.**"[73]

So those who criticize Catholics for affirming the dogma that no infant can be saved without the Sacrament of Baptism are actually proposing the anathematized heresy of John Wyclif. Here are some other dogmatic definitions on the topic.

> Pope St. Zosimus, *The Council of Carthage*, Canon on Sin and Grace, 417 A.D.- "**It has been decided likewise that if anyone says** that for this reason the Lord said: '*In my Father's house there are many mansions*' [John 14:2]: **that it might be understood that in the kingdom of heaven there will be some middle place or some place anywhere where the blessed infants live who departed from this life without baptism, without which they cannot enter into the kingdom of heaven, which is life eternal, let him be anathema.**"[74]

> Pope Paul III, *The Council of Trent*, On Original Sin, Session V, *ex cathedra*: "If anyone says that recently born babies should not be baptized even if they have been born to baptized parents; **or says that they are indeed baptized for the remission of sins, but incur no trace of the original sin of Adam needing to be cleansed by the laver of rebirth for them to obtain eternal life**, with the necessary consequence that in their case there is being understood a form of

baptism for the remission of sins which is not true, but false: **let him be anathema.**"[75]

This means that anyone who asserts that infants don't need the "laver of rebirth" (water baptism) to attain eternal life is teaching heresy.

11. Those who Die in Original Sin or Mortal Sin descend into Hell

As I have proven above, there is no possible way for children to be freed from original sin other than through the Sacrament of Baptism. This, of course, proves that there is no way for infants to be saved other than through the Sacrament of Baptism. So the following definitions merely affirm what has already been established: that no child can possibly enter the kingdom of Heaven without receiving water baptism, but will rather descend into Hell.

> Pope Eugene IV, *Council of Florence*, "Letentur coeli," Sess. 6, July 6, 1439, *ex cathedra*: "We define also that… **the souls of those who depart this life in actual mortal sin, or in original sin alone, go straightaway to hell**, but to undergo punishments of different kinds."[76]

> Pope Pius VI, *Auctorem fidei*, Aug. 28, 1794:
> "26. **The doctrine which rejects as a Pelagian fable, that place of the lower regions (which the faithful generally designate by the name of the limbo of the children) in which the souls of those departing with the sole guilt of original sin are punished with the punishment of the condemned, exclusive of the punishment of fire**, just as if, by this very fact, that these who remove the punishment of fire introduced that middle place and state free of guilt and of punishment between the kingdom of God and eternal damnation, such as that about which the Pelagians idly talk" – **Condemned** as false, rash, injurious to Catholic schools.[77]

Here Pope Pius VI condemns the idea of some theologians that infants who die in original sin suffer the fires of Hell. At the same time, he confirms that these infants do go to a part of the lower regions (i.e., Hell) called the limbo of the children. They do not go to Heaven, but to a place in Hell where there is no fire. This is perfectly in accord with all of the other solemn definitions of the Church, which teach that infants who die without water baptism descend into Hell, but suffer a punishment different from those who die in mortal sin. Their punishment is eternal separation from God.

> Pope Pius XI, *Mit brennender Sorge* (# 25), March 14, 1937: "'**Original sin**' is the hereditary but impersonal fault of Adam's descendants, who have sinned in him

(Rom. v. 12). **It is the loss of grace, and therefore eternal life**, together with a propensity to evil, which everybody must, with the assistance of grace, penance, resistance and moral effort, repress and conquer."[78]

12. There is only One Baptism, Not Three

It is defined Catholic dogma that there is only one baptism. This is why the dogmatic Nicene Creed, historically professed every Sunday in the Roman Rite, reads: *"I confess one baptism for the remission of sins."* And this dogma that there is one baptism for the remission of sins comes from Our Lord and the apostles. It is affirmed by St. Paul in Ephesians 4:5: *"One Lord, one faith, one baptism."* Could it be possible that there is more than one baptism for the remission of sins when Catholics have prayed and believed for 2000 years that there is only one? No.

> Pope Pius XI, *Quas Primas* (# 12), Dec. 11, 1925: "The perfect harmony of the Eastern liturgies with our own in this continual praise of Christ the King shows once more the truth of the axiom: *Legem credendi lex statuit supplicandi*. **The rule of faith is indicated by the law of our worship."**[79]

Throughout history many Popes have expressly reaffirmed this rule of faith: that there is only one baptism for the remission of sins.

> *The Nicene-Constantinople Creed*, 381, *ex cathedra*: "We confess **one baptism for the remission of sins**."[80]

> Pope St. Celestine I, *Council of Ephesus*, 431: "Having read these holy phrases and finding ourselves in agreement (for 'there is one Lord, one faith, **one baptism'** [Eph. 4:5]), we have given glory to God who is the savior of all…"[81]

> Pope St. Leo IX, *Congratulamur Vehementer*, April 13, 1053: "I believe that the one true Church is holy, Catholic and apostolic, **in which is given one baptism** and the true remission of all sins."[82]

> Pope Boniface VIII, *Unam Sanctam*, Nov. 18, 1302, *ex cathedra*: "One is my dove, my perfect one… which represents the one mystical body whose head is Christ, of Christ indeed, as God. And in this, 'one Lord, one faith, **one baptism'** (Eph. 4:5)."[83]

> Pope Clement V, *Council of Vienne*, Decree # 30, 1311-1312, *ex cathedra*: "Since however there is for both regulars and seculars, for superiors and subjects, for exempt and non-exempt, *one universal Church, outside of which there is no salvation*, for all of whom there is *one Lord, one faith, and **one baptism**…"[84]

Pope Pius VI, *Inscrutabile* (# 8), Dec. 25, 1775: "… We exhort and advise you to be all of one mind and in harmony as you strive for the same object, **just as the Church has** one faith, **one baptism**, and one spirit."[85]

Pope Leo XII, *Ubi Primum* (# 14), May 5, 1824: "**By it we are taught, and by divine faith we hold** one Lord, one faith, **one baptism**, and that no other name under heaven is given to men except the name of Jesus Christ in which we must be saved. **This is why we profess that there is no salvation outside the Church.**"[86]

Pope Pius VIII, *Traditi Humilitati* (# 4), May 24, 1829: "Against these experienced sophists the people must be taught that **the profession of the Catholic faith is uniquely true**, as the apostle proclaims: one Lord, one faith, **one baptism (Eph. 4:5).**"[87]

Pope Gregory XVI, *Mirari Vos* (# 13), Aug. 15, 1832: "With the admonition of the apostle that 'there is one God, one faith, **one baptism**' (Eph. 4:5) may those fear who contrive the notion that the safe harbor of salvation is open to persons of any religion whatever."[88]

Pope Leo XIII, *Graves de communi re* (# 8), Jan. 18, 1901: "**Hence the doctrine of the Apostle**, who warns us that 'We are one body and spirit called to the one hope in our vocation; one Lord, one faith and **one baptism**…"[89]

To say that there are "three baptisms," as many unfortunately do, is heretical. There is only one baptism, which is celebrated in water (*de fide*).

Pope Clement V, *Council of Vienne*, 1311-1312, *ex cathedra*: "Besides, **one baptism** which regenerates all who are baptized in Christ **must be faithfully confessed by all** just as 'one God and one faith' [Eph. 4:5], **which celebrated in water** in the name of the Father and of the Son and of the Holy Spirit we believe to be commonly the perfect remedy for salvation for adults as for children."[90]

Here Pope Clement V defines as a dogma that ONE BAPTISM must be faithfully confessed by all, **which is celebrated in water**. This means that all Catholics must profess one baptism of water, not three baptisms: of water, blood and desire. To confess "three baptisms," and not one, is to contradict defined Catholic dogma. Did those who believe that there are three baptisms (water, blood and desire) ever wonder why countless Popes have professed that there is only one baptism, and not a single one of them bothered to tell us about the so-called "other two"?

13. The Athanasian Creed

The Athanasian Creed is one of the most important Creeds of the Catholic Faith. It contains a beautiful summary of a Catholic's belief in the Trinity and the Incarnation, which are the two fundamental dogmas of Christianity. Before the 1971 changes in the Liturgy, the Athanasian Creed, consisting of 40 rhythmic statements, had been used in the Sunday Office for over a thousand years. The Athanasian Creed sets forth the necessity of believing the Catholic Faith for salvation. It closes with the words: "This is the Catholic Faith, which, except a man believe faithfully and firmly, he cannot be saved." The Athanasian Creed was composed by the great St. Athanasius himself, as the Council of Florence confirms.

Pope Eugene IV, *Council of Florence*, Sess. 8, Nov. 22, 1439, *ex cathedra*:

"Sixthly, we offer to the envoys that compendious rule of the faith composed by most blessed Athanasius, which is as follows:

"**Whoever *wishes* to be saved, needs above all to hold the Catholic faith; unless each one preserves this whole and inviolate, he will without a doubt perish in eternity.**– But the Catholic faith is this, that we worship one God in the Trinity, and the Trinity in unity; neither confounding the persons, nor dividing the substance; for there is one person of the Father, another of the Son, another of the Holy Spirit, their glory is equal, their majesty coeternal...and in this Trinity there is nothing first or later, nothing greater or less, but all three persons are coeternal and coequal with one another, so that in every respect, as has already been said above, both unity in Trinity, and Trinity in unity must be worshipped. **Therefore let him who wishes to be saved, think thus concerning the Trinity.**

"**But it is necessary for eternal salvation that he faithfully believe also in the incarnation of our Lord Jesus Christ...the**

Son of God is God and man... This is the Catholic faith; unless each one believes this faithfully and firmly, he cannot be saved."[91]

The above definition of the Athanasian Creed at the ecumenical Council of Florence means that this Creed qualifies as a pronouncement from the Chair of St. Peter (an *ex cathedra* pronouncement). To deny that which is professed in the Athanasian Creed is to cease to be Catholic. The Creed declares that whoever <u>wishes</u> to be saved needs to hold the Catholic Faith and believe in the Trinity and the Incarnation. Notice the phrase, "whoever <u>wishes</u> to be saved" (*quicunque **vult** salvus esse*).

This phrase is without question the product and inspiration of the Holy Ghost. It tells us that everyone who can *"wish"* must believe in the mysteries of the Trinity and the Incarnation in order to be saved. This does not include infants and those below the age of reason, **since they cannot wish**! Infants are numbered among the Catholic faithful, since they receive the habit of Catholic Faith at the Sacrament of Baptism. But, being below the age of reason, they cannot make any act of faith in the Catholic mysteries of the Trinity and the Incarnation, an act which is absolutely necessary for the salvation of all above the age of reason (for all who *wish* to be saved). Is it not remarkable how God worded this infallible Creed's teaching on the necessity of belief in the mysteries of the Trinity and the Incarnation in a way that would not include infants? The Creed, therefore, teaches that everyone above the age of reason must have a knowledge and belief in the mysteries of the Trinity and Incarnation to be saved – no exceptions. **This creed, therefore, *eliminates* the theory of invincible ignorance** (that one above the age of reason can be saved without knowing Christ or the true Faith) and further renders those who preach it unable to profess this creed with honesty.

And the fact that no one who *wishes* to be saved can be saved without a knowledge and belief in the mysteries of the Trinity and the Incarnation is the reason why the Holy Office under Pope Clement XI responded that a missionary must, before baptism, explain these **absolutely necessary** mysteries to an adult who is at the point of death.

Response of the Sacred Office to the Bishop of Quebec, Jan. 25, 1703:
"Q. Whether a minister is bound, before baptism is conferred on an adult, to explain to him all the mysteries of our faith, especially if he is at the point of death, because this might disturb his mind. Or, whether it is sufficient, if the one at the point of death will promise that when he recovers from the illness, he will take care to be instructed, so that he might put into practice what has been commanded him.

"A. **A promise is not sufficient, but a missionary is bound to explain to an adult,** even a dying one who is not entirely incapacitated, **the mysteries of faith**

which are necessary by a necessity of means, as are especially the mysteries of the Trinity and the Incarnation."[92]

Another question was posed at the same time and answered the same way.

> Response of the Sacred Office to the Bishop of Quebec, Jan. 25, 1703:
> "Q. Whether it is possible for a crude and uneducated adult, as it might be with a barbarian, to be baptized, if there were given him only an understanding of God and some of His attributes… although he does not believe explicitly in Jesus Christ.
>
> "A. **A missionary should not baptize one who does not believe explicitly in the Lord Jesus Christ, but is bound to instruct him about all those matters which are necessary, by a necessity of means**, in accordance with the capacity of the one to be baptized."[93]

The dogma that belief in the Trinity and Incarnation is absolutely necessary for salvation for all those above the age of reason is also the teaching of St. Thomas Aquinas, Pope Benedict XIV and Pope St. Pius X.

> St. Thomas Aquinas, *Summa Theologica*: "<u>After grace had been revealed</u>, **both the learned and simple folk are bound to <u>explicit faith in the mysteries of Christ</u>**, chiefly as regards those which are observed throughout the Church, and publicly proclaimed, **such as** the articles which refer to **the Incarnation**, of which we have spoken above."[94]

> Saint Thomas Aquinas, *Summa Theologica*: "And consequently, when once grace had been revealed, **all were bound to explicit faith in the mystery of the Trinity.**"[95]

> Pope Benedict XIV, *Cum Religiosi* (# 1), June 26, 1754:
> "We could not rejoice, however, when it was subsequently reported to Us that in the course of religious instruction preparatory to Confession and Holy Communion, it was very often found that these people were **ignorant of the mysteries of the faith, even those matters which must be known by** *necessity of means*; consequently they were ineligible to partake of the Sacraments."[96]

> Pope Benedict XIV, *Cum Religiosi* (# 4):
> "See to it that every minister performs carefully the measures laid down by the holy Council of Trent… that confessors should perform this part of their duty whenever anyone stands at their tribunal who does not know **what he must by** *necessity of means* **know to be saved…**"[97]

Those above the age of reason who are ignorant of these absolutely necessary mysteries of the Catholic Faith – these mysteries which are a *"necessity of means"* – cannot be numbered among the elect, as Pope St. Pius X confirms.

> Pope St. Pius X, *Acerbo Nimis* (# 2), April 15, 1905:
> "And so Our Predecessor, Benedict XIV, had just cause to write: 'We declare that **a great number of those who are condemned to eternal punishment suffer that everlasting calamity because of <u>ignorance</u> of <u>those mysteries of faith which must be known and believed in order to be numbered among the elect</u>.'"**[98]

So let those who believe that salvation is possible for those who don't believe in Christ and the Trinity (which is "the Catholic Faith" if defined in terms of its simplest mysteries) change their position and align it with Catholic dogma. *There is no other name under all of heaven whereby a man is saved other than the Lord Jesus* (Acts 4:12). Let them cease contradicting the Athanasian Creed and let them confess that knowledge of these mysteries is absolutely necessary for the salvation of all who wish to be saved. And let those who think that Protestants (i.e., those who reject the fullness of Catholic Faith or one or more articles of it) can be saved also change their heretical position and align it with this Creed, which declares that whoever does not preserve this Catholic Faith will, without any doubt, perish eternally. This means that all who die as Protestants will go to Hell. Catholics must firmly hold this so they can themselves possess the Catholic Faith and profess this creed with honesty and as our Catholic forefathers did.

14. Baptism of Blood and Baptism of Desire – Erroneous Traditions of Man

In this document, I have shown that the Catholic Church infallibly teaches that the Sacrament of Baptism is necessary for salvation. I have also shown that it is only through receiving the Sacrament of Baptism that one is incorporated into the Catholic Church, outside of which there is no salvation. I have also shown that the Catholic Church infallibly teaches that the words of Jesus Christ in John 3:5 – *Amen, amen I say unto thee, unless a man be born again of water and the Holy Ghost, he cannot enter into the kingdom of God* – are to be understood literally: as they are written. **This is the infallible teaching of the Church and it excludes any possibility of salvation without being born again of water and the Holy Ghost.** However, throughout the history of the Church, many have believed in the theories called baptism of desire and baptism of blood: that one's desire for the Sacrament of Baptism or one's martyrdom for the faith supplies for the lack of being born again of water and the Holy Ghost. Those who believe in baptism of blood and baptism of desire raise certain objections to the absolute necessity of receiving the Sacrament of Baptism for salvation. So, in order to be complete, I will respond to all of the major objections made by baptism of desire and blood advocates; and in the process, I will give an overview of the history of the errors of baptism of desire and baptism of blood. In doing this I will demonstrate that neither baptism of blood nor baptism of desire is a teaching of the Roman Catholic Church.

THE FATHERS ARE UNANIMOUS FROM THE BEGINNING

In the first millennium of the Church there lived hundreds of holy men and saints who are called "Fathers of the Church." Tixeront, in his *Handbook of Patrology*, lists over five hundred whose names and writings have come down to us.[99] The Fathers (or prominent early Christian Catholic writers) are unanimous from the beginning that no one enters heaven or is freed from original sin without water baptism.

In the letter of Barnabas, dated as early as 70 A.D., we read:

"… *we descend into the water full of sins and foulness*, and we come up bearing fruit in our heart…"[100]

In 140 A.D., the early Church Father Hermas quotes Jesus in John 3:5, and writes:

"They had need to come up through the water, so that they might be made alive; **for they could not otherwise enter into the kingdom of God**."[101]

This statement is obviously a paraphrase of John 3:5, and thus it demonstrates that from the very beginning of the apostolic age it was held and taught by the fathers that no one enters heaven without being *born again of water and the Spirit* based specifically on Our Lord Jesus Christ's declaration in John 3:5.

In 155 A.D., St. Justin the Martyr writes:

"… they are led by us to a place where there is water; and there they are reborn in the same kind of rebirth in which we ourselves were reborn… in the name of God… they receive the washing of water. For Christ said, '***Unless you be reborn, you shall not enter into the kingdom of heaven.***' **The reason for doing this we have learned from the apostles**."[102]

Notice that St. Justin Martyr, like Hermas, also quotes the words of Jesus in John 3:5, and based on Christ's words he teaches that it is from apostolic tradition that no one at all can enter heaven without being born again of water and the Spirit in the Sacrament of Baptism.

In his dialogue with Trypho the Jew, also dated 155 A.D., St. Justin Martyr further writes:

"… hasten to learn in what way forgiveness of sins and a hope of the inheritance… may be yours. **There is no other way than this**: acknowledge Christ, be washed in the washing announced by Isaias [Baptism]…"[103]

In <u>180 A.D.</u>, St. Irenaeus writes:

"… giving the disciples the power of regenerating in God, He said to them: 'Go teach all nations, **and baptize**… Just as dry wheat without moisture cannot become one dough or one loaf, so also, **we who are many cannot be made one in Christ Jesus, <u>without the water from heaven</u>**…Our bodies achieve unity through the washing… our souls, however, through the Spirit. **Both, then, are necessary.**"[104]

Here we see again a clear enunciation of the constant and apostolic Tradition that no one is saved without the Sacrament of Baptism, from no less than the great apostolic father St. Irenaeus in the 2nd century. St. Irenaeus knew St. Polycarp and St. Polycarp knew the Apostle John himself.

In <u>181 A.D.</u>, St. Theophilus continues the Tradition:

"… those things which were created from the waters were blessed by God, so that this might also be a sign that **<u>men would at a future time receive repentance and remission of sins through water and the bath of regeneration</u>**…"[105]

In <u>203 A.D.</u>, Tertullian writes:

"… it is in fact prescribed that no one can attain to salvation without Baptism, especially in view of that declaration of the Lord, who says: *'Unless a man shall be born of water, he shall not have life* [John 3:5]…"[106]

Notice how Tertullian affirms the same apostolic Tradition that no one is saved without water Baptism based on the words of Jesus Himself.

Tertullian further writes in <u>203 A.D.</u>:

"A treatise on our sacrament of water, by which the sins of our earlier blindness are washed away … **<u>nor can we otherwise be saved, except by permanently abiding in the water</u>**."[107]

Baptism has also been called since apostolic times the Seal, the Sign and the Illumination; for without this Seal, Sign or Illumination no one is forgiven of original sin or sealed as a member of Jesus Christ.

"… he that confirmeth us with you in Christ, and that hath anointed us, is God: Who also hath **sealed** us, and given the pledge of the Spirit in our hearts." (2 Cor. 1:21-22)

As early as 140 A.D., Hermas had already taught this truth – that Baptism is the Seal – which was delivered by the Apostles from Jesus Christ.

Hermas, 140 A.D.: "… before a man bears the name of the Son of God, he is dead. **But when he receives the seal, he puts mortality aside and again receives life. The seal, therefore, is the water. They go down into the water dead, and come out of it alive.**"[108]

St. Ephraim, c. 350 A.D.: "… we are anointed in **Baptism, whereby we bear His seal**."[109]

St. Gregory Nyssa, c. 380 A.D.: "Make haste, O sheep, towards **the sign of the cross and the Seal [Baptism] which will save you from your misery!**"[110]

St. Clement of Alexandria, 202 A.D.:

"When we are baptized, we are enlightened. Being enlightened, we are adopted as sons… This work is variously called grace, illumination, perfection, washing. It is a washing by which we are cleansed of sins…"[111]

Origen, 244 A.D.:

"The Church received from the Apostles the tradition of giving baptism even to infants… there is in everyone the innate stains of sin, **which must be washed away through water and the Spirit**."[112]

St. Aphraates, the oldest of the Syrian Fathers, writes in 336 A.D.:

"This, then, is faith: that a man believe in God … His Spirit …His Christ… Also, that a man believe in the resurrection of the dead; **and moreover, that he believe in the Sacrament of Baptism. This is the belief of the Church of God.**"[113]

The same Syrian Father further writes:

"For from baptism we receive the Spirit of Christ… **For the Spirit is absent from all those who are born of the flesh, until they come to the water of re-birth**."[114]

Here we see in the writings of St. Aphraates the same teaching of Tradition on the absolute necessity of water baptism for salvation based on the words of Christ in John 3:5.

St. Cyril of Jerusalem, 350 A.D.:

"He says, '*Unless a man be born again*' – and He adds the words '*of water and the Spirit*' – *he cannot enter into the Kingdom of God*…..if a man be virtuous in his deeds, but does not receive the seal by means of the water, shall he enter into the kingdom of heaven. **A bold saying, but not mine; for it is Jesus who has declared it**."[115]

We see that St. Cyril continues the apostolic Tradition that no one enters heaven without being born again of water and the Spirit, based again on an absolute understanding Our Lord's own words in John 3:5.

St. Basil the Great, c. 355 A.D.:

"Whence is it that we are Christians? Through faith, all will answer. **How are we saved? By being born again in the grace of baptism… For it is the same loss for anyone to depart this life unbaptized, as to receive that baptism from which one thing of what has been handed down has been omitted.**"[116]

St. Gregory of Elvira, 360 A.D.:

"Christ is called Net, because through Him and in Him **the diverse multitudes of peoples are gathered from the sea of the world, through the water of Baptism** and into the Church, where a distinction is made between the good and the wicked."[117]

St. Ephraim, 366 A.D.:

"This the Most Holy Catholic Church professes. **In this same Holy Trinity She baptizes unto eternal life**."[118]

Pope St. Damasus, 382 A.D.:

"**This, then, is the salvation of Christians**: that believing in the Trinity, that is, in the Father, and in the Son and in the Holy Spirit, **and baptized in it**…"[119]

St. Ambrose, 387 A.D.:

"… **no one ascends into the kingdom of heaven except through the Sacrament of Baptism.**"[120]

St. Ambrose, 387 A.D.:

"'**Unless a man be born again of water and the Holy Spirit, he cannot enter the kingdom of God.**' No one is excepted: not the infant, not the one prevented by some necessity."[121]

St. Ambrose, *De mysteriis*, 390-391 A.D.:

"You have read, therefore, that the three witnesses in Baptism are one: water, blood, and the spirit; and if you withdraw any one of these, the Sacrament of Baptism is not valid. For what is water without the cross of Christ? A common element without any sacramental effect. **Nor on the other hand is there any mystery of regeneration without water: for 'unless a man be born again of water and the Spirit, he cannot enter the kingdom of God.' [John 3:5]** Even a catechumen believes in the cross of the Lord Jesus, by which also he is signed; but, unless he be baptized in the name of the Father and of the Son and of the Holy Spirit, *he cannot receive the remission of sins* nor be recipient of the gift of spiritual grace."[122]

St. John Chrysostom, 392 A.D.:

"Weep for the unbelievers; weep for those who differ not a whit from them, those **who go hence without illumination, without the seal!** … They are outside the royal city…. with the condemned. '**Amen, I tell you, if anyone is not born of water and the Spirit, he shall not enter into the kingdom of heaven.**"[123]

St Augustine, 395 A.D.:

"… **God does not forgive sins except to the baptized.**"[124]

Pope St. Innocent, 414 A.D.:

"But that which Your Fraternity asserts the Pelagians preach, **that even without the grace of Baptism infants are able to be endowed with the rewards of eternal life, is quite idiotic.**"[125]

Pope St. Gregory the Great, c. 590 A.D.:

"**Forgiveness of sin is bestowed on us only by the baptism of Christ.**"[126]

Theophylactus, Patriarch of Bulgaria, c. <u>800 A.D.</u>:

> "*He that believeth and is baptized, shall be saved.* **It does not suffice to believe; he who believes, and is not yet baptized, but is only a catechumen**, has not yet fully acquired salvation."[127]

Many other passages could be quoted from the fathers, but it is a fact that the Fathers of the Church are unanimous from the beginning of the apostolic age that no one at all can be saved without receiving the Sacrament of Baptism, based on the words of Jesus Christ in John 3:5. The eminent Patristic Scholar Fr. William Jurgens, <u>who has literally read thousands of texts from the fathers</u>, was forced to admit the following in his three volume set on the Fathers.

> Fr. William Jurgens: **"If there were not <u>a constant tradition</u> in the Fathers that the Gospel message of *'Unless a man be born again of water and the Holy Ghost he cannot enter into the kingdom of God'* is to be taken absolutely,** it would be easy to say that Our Savior simply did not see fit to mention the obvious exceptions of invincible ignorance and physical impossibility. **<u>But the tradition in fact is there</u>; and it is likely enough to be found <u>so constant as to constitute revelation</u>.**"[128]

The eminent scholar Fr. Jurgens is admitting here three important things:

1) The Fathers are <u>constant</u> in their teaching that John 3:5 is absolute with no exceptions; that is, no one at all enters heaven without being born again of water and the Spirit;
2) The Fathers are so constant on this point that it likely constitutes divine revelation, without even considering the infallible teaching of the Popes;
3) The constant teaching of the Fathers that all must receive water baptism for salvation in light of John 3:5 excludes exceptions for the "invincibly ignorant" or "physically impossible" cases.

And based on this truth, declared by Jesus in the Gospel (John 3:5), handed down by the Apostles and taught by the fathers, the Catholic Church has infallibly defined as a dogma (as we have seen already) that no one at all enters heaven without the Sacrament of Baptism.

> Pope Paul III, *The Council of Trent*, Canon 5 on <u>the Sacrament</u> of Baptism, *ex cathedra*: **"If anyone says that baptism is optional,**

that is, not necessary for salvation (John. 3:5): let him be anathema."[129]

But, as is the case with many other matters, not all of the fathers remained consistent with their own affirmation of the absolute necessity of water baptism for salvation.

NOT ALL OF THE FATHERS REMAINED CONSISTENT WITH THEIR OWN AFFIRMATION

Despite the fact that there is a constant tradition from the beginning that no one at all is saved without water baptism, not all of the fathers always remained consistent with their own affirmation on this point. **And that is where we come across the theories of "baptism of blood" and "baptism of desire,"** each of which will be discussed in turn. But it must be understood that the fathers of the Church were mistaken and inconsistent with their own teaching and the apostolic Tradition on <u>many points</u> – since they were fallible men who made many errors.

> Fr. William Jurgens: "… we must stress that **a particular patristic text [a particular statement from a father] is in no instance to be regarded as a 'proof' of a particular doctrine. Dogmas are not 'proved' by patristic statements, but by the infallible teaching instruments of the Church. The value of the Fathers and writers is this: that in the aggregate [that is, in totality], they demonstrate what the Church believes and teaches;** and again, in the aggregate [that is, in totality], they provide a witness to the content of Tradition, that Tradition which is itself a vehicle of revelation."[130]

The fathers of the Church are only a definite witness to Tradition when expressing a point held <u>universally</u> and constantly or when expressing something that is in line with defined dogma. Taken individually or even in multiplicity, they can be dead wrong and even dangerous. St. Basil the Great said that the Holy Ghost is second to the Son of God in order and dignity, in a horrible and even heretical attempt to explain the Holy Trinity.

> St. Basil (363): "The Son is not, however, second to the Father in nature, because the Godhead is one in each of them, and plainly, too, in the <u>Holy Spirit, even if in order and dignity He is second to the Son (yes, this we do concede!</u>), though not in such a way, it is clear, that He were of another nature." [131]

When St. Basil says above that the Godhead is One in Father, Son and Holy Spirit, he is correctly affirming the universal, apostolic Tradition. But when he says that the Holy Spirit is second in *dignity* to the Son he ceases to remain consistent with this Tradition and falls into error (material heresy, in fact). And the fathers made countless errors in attempting to defend or articulate the Faith.

St. Augustine wrote <u>an entire book of corrections</u> and was writing a second when he died. St. Fulgentius and a host of others, including St. Augustine, held that it was certain that infants who die without *baptism descend into the fires of hell,* a position that was later condemned by Pope Pius VI. As Pope Pius VI confirmed, unbaptized infants go to hell, but to a place in hell where there is no fire.[132]

But St. Augustine was so outspoken in favor of this error that it became the common and basically unchallenged teaching for more than 500 years, according to *The Catholic Encyclopedia.*

> The Catholic Encyclopedia, Vol. 9, "Limbo," p. 257: **"On the special question, however, of the punishment of original sin after death, <u>St. Anselm was at one with St. Augustine in holding that unbaptized infants share in the positive sufferings of the damned; and Abelard was the first to rebel against the severity of the Augustinian tradition on this point</u>."**[133]

This is why Catholics don't form definite doctrinal conclusions from the teaching of a father of the Church or a handful of fathers; a Catholic goes by the infallible teaching of the Church proclaimed by the Popes; and a Catholic assents to the teaching of the fathers of the Church when they are in <u>universal and constant agreement</u> from the beginning and in line with Catholic dogmatic teaching.

> Pope Benedict XIV, *Apostolica* (# 6), June 26, 1749: **"The Church's judgment is preferable to that of a Doctor** renowned for his holiness and teaching."[134]

> *Errors of the Jansenists,* #30: **"When anyone finds a doctrine clearly established in Augustine, he can absolutely hold it and teach it, disregarding any bull of the pope."- <u>Condemned by Pope Alexander VIII</u>**[135]

> Pope Pius XII, *Humani generis* (# 21), Aug. 12, 1950: **"This deposit of faith our Divine Redeemer has given for authentic interpretation not to each of the faithful, <u>not even to theologians</u>, but only to the Teaching Authority of the Church.'"**[136]

The Catholic Church recognizes infallibility in no saint, theologian or early Church father. It is only a Pope operating with the authority of the Magisterium who is protected by the Holy Ghost from teaching error on faith or morals. So, when we examine and show how Churchmen have erred on the topics of baptism of desire and blood this is 100% consistent with the teaching of the Church, which has always acknowledged that any Churchman, no matter how great, can make errors, even significant ones. **Finally, after dealing with baptism of desire and blood, I will quote a Pope, who is also an early Church father, whose teaching ends all debate on the subject**. I will now proceed to discuss baptism of blood and baptism of desire.

THE THEORY OF BAPTISM OF BLOOD - A TRADITION OF MAN

A small number of the fathers – **approximately 8 out of a total of hundreds** – are quoted in favor of what is called "baptism of blood," the idea that a catechumen (that is, one preparing to receive Catholic Baptism) who shed his blood for Christ could be saved without having received Baptism. It is crucial to note at the beginning that **none of the fathers considered anyone but a catechumen as a possible exception to receiving the Sacrament of Baptism; they would all condemn and reject as heretical and foreign to the teaching of Christ the modern heresy of "invincible ignorance"** saving those who die as non-Catholics. So, out of the fathers, approximately 8 are quoted in favor of baptism of blood for catechumens. And, **only 1 father out of hundreds, St. Augustine, can be quoted as clearly teaching what is today called "baptism of desire":** the idea that a catechumen could be saved by his explicit desire for water baptism. This means that with the exception of St. Augustine, all of the few fathers who believed in baptism of blood actually rejected the concept of baptism of desire. Take St. Cyril of Jerusalem, for example.

> St. Cyril of Jerusalem, 350 A.D.: "**If any man does not receive baptism, he does not receive salvation**. The only exception is the martyrs..."[137]

Here we see that St. Cyril of Jerusalem believed in baptism of blood, but rejected baptism of desire. St. Fulgence expressed the same.

> St. Fulgence, 523: "From that time at which Our Savior said: "*If anyone is not reborn of water and the Spirit, he cannot enter into the kingdom of heaven,*' no one can, without the sacrament of baptism, except those who, in the Catholic Church, without Baptism pour out their blood for Christ..."[138]

Here we see that St. Fulgence believed in baptism of blood but rejected the idea of baptism of desire. And what's ironic and particularly dishonest is that the baptism of desire apologists (such as the priests of the Society of St. Pius X) will quote these patristic texts (such as the two above) in books written to prove *baptism of desire,* without pointing out to their readers that these passages actually deny baptism of desire; for we can see that St. Fulgence, while expressing belief in baptism of blood, rejects baptism of desire, only allowing martyrs as a possible exception to receiving baptism. (What would St. Fulgence say about the modern version of the heresy of baptism of desire, also taught by such priests of the SSPX, SSPV, CMRI, etc. whereby Jews, Muslims, Hindus and pagans can be saved without Baptism?)

> St. Fulgence, *On the Forgiveness of Sins*, 512 A.D.: "**Anyone who is outside this Church**, which received the keys of the kingdom of heaven, **is walking a path not to heaven but to hell**. He is not approaching the home of eternal life; rather, he is hastening to the torment of eternal death."[139]

> St. Fulgence, *The Rule of Faith*, 526 A.D.: "Hold most firmly and never doubt in the least that not only **all the pagans but also all the Jews and all the heretics and schismatics who end this present life outside the Catholic Church are about to go into the eternal fire that was prepared for the devil and his angels**."[140]

We can see that St. Fulgence would have – like all of the other fathers – sternly condemned the modern heretics who hold that those who die as non-Catholics can be saved.

But what is most interesting about this is that *in the same document* in which St. Fulgence expresses his error on baptism of blood (quoted already), he makes a different and significant error.

> St. Fulgence, 523: "**Hold most firmly and never doubt** in the least that not only men having the use of reason but **even infants who… pass from this world without the Sacrament of holy Baptism**… <u>**are to be punished in the everlasting torment of eternal fire**</u>."[141]

St. Fulgence says "*Hold most firmly and never doubt*" that infants who die without baptism are "*to be punished in the everlasting torment of eternal fire.*" This is wrong. Infants who die without baptism descend into hell, but to a place in hell where there is no fire (Pope Pius VI, *Auctorem Fidei*).[142] St. Fulgence therefore shows that his opinion in favor of baptism of blood is <u>quite fallible</u> by making a different error <u>in the same document</u>. It is quite remarkable, in fact, **that in almost every instance when a father of the Church or someone else expresses his error on baptism of blood or baptism of desire that same person makes another significant error in the same work, as we will see.**

It is also important to point out that some of the fathers use the term "baptism of blood" to describe the Catholic martyrdom of one already baptized, **<u>not as a possible replacement for water baptism</u>**. This is the only legitimate use of the term.

St. John Chrysostom, *Panegyric on St. Lucian*, 4th Century AD:
"Do not be surprised that I call martyrdom a Baptism; for here too the Spirit comes in great haste and there is a taking away of sins and a wonderful and marvelous cleansing of the soul; and just as those being baptized are washed in water, so too those being martyred are washed in their own blood."[143]

St. John is here describing the martyrdom of <u>a priest St. Lucian</u>, a person already baptized. He is not saying that martyrdom replaces baptism. St. John Damascene describes it the same way:

St. John Damascene:
"These things were well understood by our holy and inspired fathers --- thus they strove, **after Holy Baptism**, to keep... spotless and undefiled. Whence some of them also thought fit to receive **another** Baptism: I mean that which is by blood and martyrdom."[144]

This is important because many dishonest scholars today (such as the priests of the Society of St. Pius X) will distort the teaching on this point; they will quote a passage on baptism of blood where St. John is simply speaking of baptism of blood as a Catholic martyrdom for one already baptized, and they will present it as if the person were teaching that martyrdom can replace baptism – when such is not stated anywhere.

Some may wonder why the term *baptism of blood* was used at all. I believe that the reason the term "baptism of blood" was used by some of the fathers was because Our Lord described His coming passion as a baptism in Mark 10:38-39.

[Mark 10:38-39]: *"And Jesus said to them: You know not what you ask. Can you drink the chalice that I drink of: or be baptized with the baptism wherewith I am baptized? But they said to him: We can. And Jesus saith to them: You shall indeed drink of the chalice that I drink of: and with the baptism wherewith I am baptized, you shall be baptized."*

We see in the aforementioned passage that Our Lord, although already baptized by St. John in the Jordan, refers to another baptism which He must receive. This is His martyrdom on the cross, not a substitute for baptism of water. It is His "second baptism," if you will, not his first. Thus, baptism of blood is described by Our Lord in the same way as St. John Damascene, not to mean a substitute baptism for an unbaptized person, but rather a Catholic martyrdom which remits all the fault and punishment due to sin.

The term *baptism* is used in a variety of ways in the Scriptures and by the Church Fathers. The baptisms: of water, of blood, of the spirit, of Moses, and of fire are all terms that have been implemented by Church Fathers to characterize certain things, but not necessarily to describe that an unbaptized martyr can attain salvation. Read the verse of scripture in which the term *baptism* is used for the Old Testament forefathers:

> [1Cor. 10:2-4]: *"And all in Moses were BAPTIZED, in the cloud, and in the sea: And did all eat the same spiritual food, And all drank the same spiritual drink: (and they drank of the spiritual rock that followed them, and the rock was Christ.)"*

I believe this explains why a number of fathers **erred** in believing that baptism of blood supplies the place of baptism of water. They recognized that Our Lord referred to His own martyrdom as a baptism, and they erroneously concluded that martyrdom for the true faith can serve as a substitute for being born again of water and the Holy Ghost. But the reality is that there are no exceptions to Our Lord's words in John 3:5, as the infallible teaching of the Catholic Church confirms. **Anyone of good will who is willing to shed his blood for the true faith will not be left without these saving waters. It is not our blood, but Christ's blood on the Cross, communicated to us in the Sacrament of Baptism, which frees us from the state of sin and allows us entrance into the kingdom of heaven (more on this later).**

Pope Eugene IV, "Cantate Domino," *Council of Florence, ex cathedra*: **"No one, whatever almsgiving he has practiced, <u>even if he has shed blood for the name of Christ</u>, can be saved, unless he has persevered within the bosom and unity of the Catholic Church."**[145]

THE TWO EARLIEST STATEMENTS ON BAPTISM OF BLOOD

Out of the few fathers that can be quoted in favor of baptism of blood being a possible replacement to actual Baptism, the two earliest statements supporting the idea come from St. Cyprian and Tertullian.

> St. Cyprian, *To Jubaianus* (254): **"Catechumens who suffer martyrdom before they have received Baptism with water <u>are not deprived of the Sacrament of Baptism</u>. Rather, they are baptized with the most glorious and greatest Baptism of Blood…"**[146]

Let's examine this passage. While teaching baptism of blood, notice that St. Cyprian makes a significant error in the same sentence. He says:

> *"catechumens who suffer martyrdom before they have received Baptism are not deprived of <u>the Sacrament of Baptism</u>."*

This is completely wrong, even from the point of view of the baptism of blood/desire advocates. All baptism of desire and blood advocates readily admit that neither is a sacrament, because neither confers the indelible character of the Sacrament of Baptism. Hence, even the staunchest advocates of baptism of blood would admit that St. Cyprian's statement here is wrong. Therefore, in the very SENTENCE in which St. Cyprian teaches the error of baptism of blood, he makes a significant error in explaining it – he calls it "the Sacrament of Baptism." What more proof is necessary to demonstrate to the liberals that the teaching of individual fathers is not infallible and does not represent the universal Tradition and can even be dangerous, if held obstinately? Why do they quote such erroneous passages to attempt to "teach" the faithful when they do not even agree with them?

Furthermore, St. Cyprian's errors in this very document (*To Jubaianus*) don't end here! In the self-same document, St. Cyprian teaches that heretics cannot administer valid baptism.

> St. Cyprian, *To Jubaianus* (254): "… *in regard to what I might think in the matter of the baptism of heretics… This baptism we cannot reckon as valid*…"[147]

This is also wrong, as the Council of Trent defined that heretics, provided they observe the correct matter and form, confer valid baptism. But St. Cyprian actually held that it was from apostolic Tradition that heretics could not confer a valid baptism! And this false idea was opposed by the then Pope (St. Stephen) and later condemned by the Catholic Church. So much for the claim that St. Cyprian's Letter *To Jubaianus* is a sure representation of apostolic Tradition! In fact, St. Cyprian and 30 other bishops declared in a regional council in 254 A.D.:

> "We… judging and holding it as certain that no one beyond the pale [that is, outside the Church] is able to be baptized…"[148]

This again proves the point: Jesus Christ only gave infallibility to St. Peter and his successors (the Popes).

> "And the Lord said: **Simon, Simon**, behold Satan hath desired to have all of you, that he may sift you as wheat: **But I have prayed for thee, that thy faith fail not:** and thou being once converted, confirm thy brethren." (Luke 22:31-32)

Jesus Christ did not give unfailing faith to bishops, theologians or fathers of the Church; He only gave it to Peter and his successors when speaking from the Chair of Peter or when proposing a doctrine for the faithful to be believed as divinely revealed.

> Pope Pius IX, *Vatican Council I, ex cathedra*:
> "So, this gift of truth **AND A NEVER FAILING FAITH WAS DIVINELY**

CONFERRED UPON PETER AND HIS SUCCESSORS IN THIS CHAIR…"[149]

Another early father who is frequently quoted in favor of baptism of blood is Tertullian.

> Tertullian, *On Baptism*, 203 A.D.: "If they might be washed in water, they must necessarily be so by blood. This is the Baptism which replaces that of the fountain, when it has not been received, and restores it when it has been lost."[150]

But guess what? In the same work in which Tertullian expresses his opinion in favor of baptism of blood, he also makes a different and significant error. He says that infants should not be baptized until they are grown up!

> Tertullian, *On Baptism*, 203 A.D.: "According to circumstance and disposition and even age of the individual person, *it may be better to delay baptism; and especially so in the case of little children…Let them come, then, while they grow up…*"[151]

This contradicts the universal Catholic Tradition, received from the apostles, and the later infallible teaching of the Popes, that infants should be baptized as soon as possible.

> Pope Eugene IV, *Council of Florence, ex cathedra*: **"Regarding children… holy baptism ought not be deferred…"[152]**

But in addition to this, in the same work *On Baptism*, Tertullian actually affirms the universal teaching of Tradition on the absolute necessity of water baptism, contrary to the idea of baptism of blood.

> Tertullian, *On Baptism*, 203: **"… it is in fact prescribed that no one can attain to salvation without Baptism, especially in view of that declaration of the Lord, who says: '*Unless a man shall be born of water, he shall not have life* [John 3:5]…"[153]**

Thus, those who think that baptism of blood is a teaching of the Catholic Church simply because this error was expressed by a small number of fathers are simply mistaken. As many or more fathers held that unbaptized infants suffer the fires of hell and that heretics cannot validly baptize. The theory of baptism of blood was not held universally or constantly in Catholic Tradition and it has never been taught or mentioned by any Pope, any Council or in any Papal Encyclical.

UNBAPTIZED SAINTS?

One of the biggest objections from baptism of desire/blood advocates is the claim that the Catholic Church recognizes saints who never received the Sacrament of Baptism. The answer to this is that **the Catholic Church has never recognized that there are saints in heaven who were not baptized.** Some historians have written _accounts_ of the lives of certain saints in which these saints died without baptism of water – by "baptism of blood"; but the assertions of these historians prove nothing.

Not all of the information surrounding the deaths of martyrs is accurate. For instance, "_According to St. Ambrose, Prudentius and Father Butler, Saint Agnes was beheaded. Others had said she [St. Agnes] was burned to death._ Our point is that not all of the information given in the martyrdom narrative is necessarily accurate, consistent, or complete."[154]

> Pope St. Gelasius, _Decretal_, 495: **"Likewise the deeds of the holy martyrs… [which] with remarkable caution are not read in the holy Roman Church… <u>because the names of those who wrote them are entirely unknown… lest an occasion of mockery might arise</u>."**[155]

Pope St. Gelasius is saying here that the acts and deeds recorded of the martyrs are uncertain. Their authors are unknown, the accounts may contain error and they were not even read out in the holy Roman Church to avoid possible scandal or mockery which might arise from any false statements contained therein. In fact, in his work _The Age of Martyrs_, the renowned Church historian Abbot Giuseppe Ricciotti says: "_For guides we have appropriate documents. These, however, as we have already seen, **are often uncertain and would lead us completely astray. Especially unreliable are the Acts or Passions of martyrs.**_"[156] The infallible teaching of the Catholic Church, on the other hand, is absolutely reliable, and it has never taught that souls can be saved without the Sacrament of Baptism by "baptism of blood." Thus, in short, there is no proof that any saint martyred for the Catholic Faith never received the Sacrament of Baptism.

THE FORTY MARTYRS OF SEBASTE

An example of how the baptism of blood advocates err in this matter is their assertion that the fortieth martyr of Sebaste was unbaptized. They say that he was unbaptized, but that he joined himself with the other thirty-nine martyrs and froze to death for Christ on the lake. The fact is that there is no proof that the fortieth martyr of Sebaste was unbaptized, whose identity is unknown. The accounts of the story reveal that he "cried out with a loud voice that he was a Christian," probably because he was already a baptized Catholic who was spurred on to martyrdom by the example of the other thirty-nine. Further, in the Roman Martyrology under the date of September 9, we read:

"As Sebaste in Armenia, St. Severian, a soldier of Emperor Licinius. **For frequently visiting the Forty Martyrs in prison**, he was suspended in the air with a stone tied to his feet by order of the governor Lysias…"

It is certain that Severian was not the fortieth martyr (from the date and circumstances of his death), but we see from this account that other people and soldiers were able to visit the Forty in prison. Thus, the Forty Martyrs easily could have baptized any soldiers who showed interest and sympathy with their cause, *including the one who joined himself to them eventually* (if he wasn't already baptized). Thus, there is nothing that proves that the fortieth martyr was unbaptized, and *we know that he was* from the truth of our Faith. The same can be said about all of the approximately 20 cases which are brought forward by the baptism of blood advocates.

Pope Eugene IV, *The Council of Florence*, "Exultate Deo," Nov. 22, 1439, *ex cathedra*: "**And since death entered the universe through the first man, 'unless we are born again of <u>water and the Spirit</u>, we cannot,' as the Truth says, 'enter into the kingdom of heaven' [John 3:5].** The matter of this sacrament is real and natural water."[157]

I will quote verbatim from Brother Robert Mary, in *Father Feeney and The Truth About Salvation (pp. 173-175),* who clears up some of the confusion which swirls around this topic:

"We will now examine the historical evidence put forth by those who claim that 'baptism of blood' is a substitute for, even superior to, the sacrament of baptism. This evidence is found in the many writings that have been handed down to us over the centuries as recorded in various martyrologies, acts of the martyrs, lives of the saints and similar sources. The most concise information on martyrs is found in martyrologies.

"The present *Roman Martyrology* is a catalogue of saints honored by the Church, not only those martyred for the Faith. It first appeared in 1584, and was derived from ancient martyrologies that existed in the fourth century, plus official and non-official records taken from acts of the martyrs that date back to the second century. <u>It has been revised several times</u> since its first compilation. When he was assigned to revise the ancient accounts, Saint Robert Bellarmine himself had to be restrained from overly skeptical editorial deletions.

"**First, it was not the intent of those who first reported the circumstances of the deaths of the martyrs to provide information from which 'baptismal registers' could later be compiled. If the chronicler makes no mention of the martyr's Baptism, it does not necessarily mean that he was never baptized. A case in point is Saint Patrick. He was not a martyr, but his Baptism was never**

recorded. Yet, we know positively that he received the sacrament since he was a bishop.

"Next, even if a chronicler states positively that a martyr had not been baptized, it should be understood to mean that he was 'not recorded' as having been baptized. In those times especially, no person could hope to know with certainty that another had not been baptized.

"Third, if a chronicler says that a martyr was 'baptized in his own blood', this does not automatically preclude (rule out) prior reception of the sacrament by water. When Christ referred to His coming Passion as a 'Baptism', He had already been baptized by Saint John in the Jordan.

"Fourth, 'baptism of blood' should be understood as the greatest act of love of God that a man can make. God rewards it with direct entrance into heaven for those who are already baptized and in the Church: no purgatory --- it is a perfect confession. **If it were capable of substituting for any sacrament, it would be the sacrament of Penance, because Penance does not oblige with a necessity of means, but precept only**.

"In his book *Church History*, Father John Laux, M. A., writes:

> 'If he [the Christian] was destined to lose his life, he had been taught that martyrdom was a <u>second</u> Baptism, which washed away every stain, and that the soul of the martyr was secure in immediate admission to the perfect happiness of heaven.'

"Fifth, when a martyr is referred to as a 'catechumen,' it does not always mean he was not yet baptized. A catechumen was a person learning the Faith, as a student in a class called a catechumenate, under a teacher called a catechist. That students continued in their class even after they were baptized is confirmed conclusively by these words of Saint Ambrose to his catechumens: "I know very well that many things still have to be explained. It may strike you as strange that you were not given a complete teaching on the sacraments before you were baptized. However, the ancient discipline of the Church forbids us to reveal the Christian mysteries to the uninitiated. For the full meaning of the sacraments cannot be grasped without the light which they themselves shed in your hearts." (*On the Mysteries* and *On the Sacraments*, Saint Ambrose)

Whereas the unbaptized were never considered part of *the faithful* until they were baptized (they were always required to leave before the Mass of the Faithful), Bro. Robert Mary is pointing out that some recently baptized persons, who were still undergoing instruction, were occasionally referred to as "catechumens."

Pope St. Sylvester I, *First Council of Nicaea*, 325 A.D., Can. 2: **"For a catechumen needs time and further probation after baptism..."**[158]

In Tradition, the Church did not reveal certain things except to the initiated (the baptized). So, after a person was baptized he or she frequently continued catechetical instruction, and was therefore sometimes referred to as a "catechumen." The fact that there is a distinction between *unbaptized* catechumens and *baptized* catechumens is implicit in the following quotation from the Council of Braga in 572.

> Council of Braga, 572, Canon xvii: **"Neither the commemoration of Sacrifice** [*oblationis*] **nor the service of chanting** [*psallendi*] **is to be employed <u>for catechumens who have died without baptism</u>.**"[159]

If those described as "catechumens" were always unbaptized, then there would be no need for the Council to say that no chanting or sacrifice is to be employed for catechumens "who have died <u>without baptism</u>." Thus, the fact that the Roman Martyrology describes a few Saints as "catechumens" does not prove that they were unbaptized, even though the term "catechumen" usually means unbaptized. Besides, the Roman Martyrology is not infallible and contains historical errors.

> Donald Attwater, *A Catholic Dictionary*, p. 310: **"An historical statement in the 'Martyrology' as such has <u>no authority</u>... A number of entries in the Roman Martyrology are found to be unsatisfactory** when so tested."[160]

I continue with the quotation from Bro. Robert Mary:

> "Sixth, in those days, a formal Baptism was a very impressive ceremony conducted by the bishop. However, the Church has always taught that, in case of necessity, any person of either sex who has reached the use of reason, Catholic or non-Catholic, may baptize by using the correct words and intending to do what the Church intends to be done by the sacrament. Therefore, in the early Church, baptized Christians and unbaptized catechumens were instructed to administer the sacrament to each other, if and as needed, whenever persecutions broke out.
>
> "Seventh, salvation was made possible for us when, on the Cross on Calvary, Our Lord Jesus Christ sacrificed His Sacred Body and Blood in atonement for our sins. **Hence, a man is saved, not by sacrificing his own human blood, but by the sacrifice of the Most Precious Divine Blood of Our Holy Savior.**
>
> "Let us put it another way: In our opinion, the absolutely certain remission of original sin and incorporation into Christ and His Church are accomplished only by the water to which, alone, Christ has given that power. **A man's blood has no such power.** Martyrdom is the greatest act of love of God a man can make, but it cannot substitute for the sacrament of baptism." - end of quotation

There is no need to examine all of the <u>less than 20</u> individual cases of saints' martyrdoms (out of thousands) which some have said occurred without baptism. All that is necessary to prove this false is to show that the Church has infallibly taught that *no one can get to heaven without being born again of water and the Holy Ghost* in the Sacrament of Baptism.

> Pope Paul III, *The Council of Trent*, Canon 5 on <u>the Sacrament</u> of Baptism, *ex cathedra*: **"If anyone says that baptism [the sacrament] is optional, that is, not necessary for salvation (John. 3:5): let him be anathema."**[161]

However, one alleged case of "baptism of blood" is particularly interesting.

ST. ALBAN AND HIS CONVERTED GUARD

St. Alban was the protomartyr of England (303 A.D.) The account of his martyrdom is particularly interesting and instructive on this topic. On the way to his martyrdom, one of the guards who led him to execution was converted to Christ. The Roman Martyrology (a fallible document), as well as *Butler's Lives of the Saints*, says that the guard was "baptized in his own blood." St. Bede the Venerable, a Church historian, who also has an account of the story (and who was one of the approximately 8 fathers who are quoted in favor of baptism of blood), says that the guard's martyrdom occurred without "the purification of Baptism." But watch this: in recounting the story of the martyrdoms of St. Alban and his guard, St. Bede and Butler's lives of the Saints reveal a very important point.

> St. Bede: **"As he reached the summit, <u>holy Alban asked God to give him (Alban) water, and at once a perennial spring bubbled up at his feet</u>**…" <u>Butler</u>: "The sudden conversion of the headsmen occasioned a delay in the execution. In the meantime the holy confessor (Alban), with the crowd, went up the hill… **There Alban falling on his knees, <u>at his prayer a fountain sprung up, with water</u>** whereof *he refreshed his thirst*… Together with St. Alban, the soldier, who had refused to imbrue (stain) his hands in his blood, and had declared himself a Christian, was also beheaded, being baptized in his own blood."[162]

The reader may be confused at this point, and rightly so, so let me explain. We have two (fallible) accounts of the martyrdom of St. Alban and his guard, from St. Bede and Bulter's Lives of the Saints. **They both record that just before the martyrdom of St. Alban and his guard, St. Alban prayed for "water" which he miraculously received!** St. Bede then goes on to say that the guard died unbaptized! Butler's says that the water was merely to "refresh" Alban's thirst! With all due respect to St. Bede and the good things in Butler's, how obvious does it have to be? A Saint, who had a few minutes to live and who had a convert wanting to enter the Church of Christ, would not call for miraculous water in order to "refresh his thirst"! My goodness, he obviously called for the miraculous water <u>to Baptize the converted guard</u>, and God provided it for the sincere convert, since "*unless a man is born again of water and the Holy Ghost, he cannot enter* *into the Kingdom of God."* This is a prime example of how the errors of baptism of blood and desire have been perpetuated – by passing down the fallible conclusions of fallible men. **And this example of St. Alban and his guard,** *which actually shows the absolute necessity of the Sacrament of Baptism,* **is frequently and falsely used against the necessity of the Sacrament of Baptism.**

SUMMARIZING THE FACTS ON BAPTISM OF BLOOD

As stated already, the theory of baptism of blood <u>has never been taught by one Pope, one Council or in any Papal Encyclical</u>. At least 5 dogmatic Councils of the Catholic Church issued detailed definitions on Baptism, and not one ever mentioned the concept or the term Baptism of Blood. The Council of Trent had 14 canons on Baptism, and Baptism of blood is mentioned nowhere. And, in fact, various infallible statements from the Popes and Councils exclude the idea.

> Pope Eugene IV, "Cantate Domino," *Council of Florence, ex cathedra*: **"No one, whatever almsgiving he has practiced, <u>even if he has shed blood for the name of Christ</u>, can be saved, unless he has persevered within the bosom and unity of the Catholic Church."[163]**

Pope Eugene IV explicitly excludes from salvation even those who "shed blood for the name of Christ" unless they are living within the bosom and unity of the Church! And, as proven already, the unbaptized are not living within the bosom and unity of the Church (*de fide*)! The unbaptized are not subjects of the Catholic Church (*de fide, Council of Trent*, Sess. 14, Chap. 2);[164] the unbaptized are not members of the Catholic Church (*de fide, Pius XII, Mystici Corporis # 22);*[165] and the unbaptized do not have the mark of Christians (*de fide, Pius XII, Mediator Dei # 43*).[166]

If "baptism of blood" truly served as a substitute for the Sacrament of Baptism, God would never have allowed the Catholic Church to understand John 3:5 *as it is written* in its infallible decrees, as He has (Pope Eugene IV, *The Council of Florence*, "Exultate Deo," Nov. 22, 1439, etc.). This is certain, because the Church's official understanding of the scriptures cannot err.

Furthermore, God would never have allowed the infallible Council of Trent to completely pass over any mention of this "exception" in its canons on baptism and its chapters on justification as an alternative way of achieving the state of grace. He would never have allowed all of the infallible definitions from Popes on *only one baptism* to avoid any mention of "the baptism of blood."

And God would not have allowed Pope Eugene IV to define that nobody, even *if he has shed blood in the name of Christ, can be saved unless he is in the bosom and unity of the Catholic Church*, without mentioning the exception of "baptism of blood." **God has never allowed the theory of baptism of blood to be taught in one Council, by one Pope, or in one infallible decree, but only by fallible theologians and fallible early Church fathers**. All of this is because baptism of blood is not a teaching of the Catholic Church, but the erroneous speculation of a handful of fathers who also erred frequently in the same documents.

MIRACULOUS BAPTISMS

There would be no need for God to save anyone by baptism of blood (or "baptism of desire"), since He can keep any sincere souls alive until they are baptized, as we saw with the case of St. Alban and the converted guard. **St. Martin of Tours brought back to life a catechumen who had died so that he could baptize him.**[167] St. Joan of Arc brought back to life a dead infant so that she could baptize him.[168] There were many similar miracles. One striking example is said to have occurred in the life of St. Peter himself. While he was chained to a pillar in the Mamertine prison in Rome, he baptized two of his guards, Processus and Martinian, **with water which miraculously sprang up from the ground within hands distance from St. Peter**. These guards were also jailed with St. Peter and were to undergo execution the next day because they were converts. Their desire for baptism (baptism of desire) and their martyrdom for the faith (baptism of blood) weren't going to be enough. They needed to be baptized with "water and the Holy Ghost" (Jn. 3:5). And God saw that they truly desired the Sacrament, so He provided it miraculously.

History also records that St. Patrick – who himself raised over 40 people from the dead – raised a number of people from the dead specifically in order to baptize them, something which was totally unnecessary if one can be saved without baptism. **As one scholar notes,**

> **"In all, St. Patrick brought to life some forty infidels in Ireland**, one of whom was King Echu… On raising him from the dead, St. Patrick instructed and baptized him, asking what he had seen of the other world. **King Echu told how he had actually beheld the throne prepared for him in Heaven because of his life of being open to the grace of Almighty God, but that he was not allowed to enter *precisely because he was as yet unbaptized*.** After receiving the sacraments… (he) died instantly and went to his reward."[169]

The same scholar further notes:

> "Many such saints have been recorded as resurrecting grown-ups specifically and exclusively for the Sacrament of Baptism, including St. Peter Claver, St.

Winifred of Wales, St. Julian of Mans, St. Eleutherius, and others. But even more have raised up little infants for the sacrament of salvation: St. Gregory Nazianz… St. Hilary… St. Elizabeth… St. Colette… St. Frances of Rome… St. Joan of Arc… St. Philip Neri… St. Francis Xavier… St. Gildas… St. Gerard Majella… to name a few."[170]

One of the more interesting cases is the story of Augustina, the slave girl, which is related in the life of St. Peter Claver, a Jesuit missionary in 17th century Colombia.

"When Father Claver arrived at her deathbed, Augustina lay cold to the touch, her body already being prepared for burial. He prayed at her bedside for one hour, when suddenly the woman sat up, vomited a pool of blood, and declared upon being questioned by those in attendance: *'I have come from journeying along a long road. After I had gone a long way down it, I met a white man of great beauty who stood before me and said: Stop! You can go no further.'* … On hearing this, Father Claver cleared the room and prepared to hear her Confession, thinking she was in need of absolution for some sin she may have forgotten. But in the course of the ritual, St. Peter Claver was inspired to realize that *she had never been baptized*. He cut short her confession and declined to give her absolution, calling instead for water with which to baptize her. Augustina's master insisted that she could not possibly need baptism since she had been in his employ for twenty years and had never failed to go to Mass, Confession, and Communion all that time. Nevertheless, **Father Claver insisted on baptizing her, after which Augustina died again joyfully** and peacefully in the presence of the whole family."[171]

The great "Apostle of the Rocky Mountains," Fr. Pierre De Smet, who was the extraordinary missionary to the American Indians in the 19th century, was also a witness – as were his fellow Jesuit missionaries – of many people coming to baptism under miraculous circumstances.

Fr. De Smet, Dec. 18, 1839: "I have often remarked that many of the children seem to await baptism before winging their flight to heaven, **for they die almost immediately after receiving the Sacrament**." [172]

Fr. De Smet, Dec. 9, 1845: "… over a hundred children and eleven old people were **baptized**. Many of the latter [the old people], who were carried on buffalo hides, **seemed only to await this grace before going to rest in the bosom of God**."[173]

On this point the reader will also want to look at the section on St. Isaac Jogues and St. Francis Xavier later in this document.

In the life of the extraordinary Irish missionary St. Columbanus (+ 543-615 A.D.), we read of a similar story of God's providence getting all good willed souls to baptism.

> "[Columbanus said]: '**My sons, today you will see an ancient Pictish chief, who has faithfully kept the precepts of the Natural Law all his life, arrive on this island; he comes to be baptized and to die.**' Immediately, a boat was seen to approach with a feeble old man seated in the prow who was recognized as chief of one of the neighboring tribes. Two of his companions brought him before the missionary, to whose words he listened attentively. **The old man asked to be baptized, and immediately thereafter breathed out his last breath** and was buried on the very spot."[174]

Father Point, S.J. was a fellow Jesuit Missionary to the Indians with Fr. De Smet in the 19th century. He tells a very interesting story about the miraculous resuscitation for Baptism of a person who had been instructed in the Faith but apparently died without receiving the Sacrament.

> Father Point, S.J., quoted in *The Life of Fr. De Smet*, pp. 165-166: "One morning, upon leaving the church I met an Indian woman, who said: 'So-and-so is not well.' She [the person who was not well] was not yet a catechumen and I said I would go to see her. An hour later the same person [who came and told him the person is not well], who was her sister, **came to me saying she was dead. I ran to the tent, hoping she might be mistaken, and found a crowd of relatives around the bed, repeating, 'She is dead – she has not breathed for some time.' To assure myself, I leaned over the body; there was no sign of life.** I reproved these excellent people for not telling me at once of the gravity of the situation, adding, 'May God forgive me!' Then, rather impatiently, I said, 'Pray!' and all fell on their knees and prayed devoutly.
>
> "I again leaned over the supposed corpse and said, 'The Black Robe is here: do you wish him to baptize you?' **At the word baptism I saw a slight tremor of the lower lip; then both lips moved, making me certain that she understood. She had already been instructed, so I at once baptized her, and she rose from her bier**, making the sign of the cross. Today she is out hunting and is fully persuaded that she died at the time I have recounted."[175]

This is another example of a person who had already been instructed in the Faith but had to be miraculously resuscitated specifically for the Sacrament of Baptism, and the miraculous resuscitation occurred at the moment that the priest pronounced the word "Baptism."

In the life of St. Francis De Sales we also find a child miraculously raised from the dead specifically for the Sacrament of Baptism.

"**A baby, the child of a Protestant mother, had died without Baptism**. St. Francis had gone to speak to the mother about Catholic doctrine, **and prayed that the child would be restored to life long enough to receive Baptism. His prayer was granted**, and the whole family became Catholic."[176]

St. Francis De Sales himself summed up the beautifully simple truth on this issue in the following manner, when he was discoursing against the Protestant heretics.

St. Francis De Sales (Doctor of the Church), *The Catholic Controversy*, c. 1602, pp. 156-157: "The way in which one deduces an article of faith is this: **the Word of God is infallible; the Word of God declares that Baptism is necessary for salvation; <u>therefore Baptism is necessary for salvation</u>**."[177]

Here is another description of an infant child who died without the Sacrament of Baptism and was raised from the dead through the intercession of St. Stephen.

"**At Uzale, a woman had an infant son… Unfortunately, he died before they had time to baptize him**. His mother was overwhelmed with grief, **more for his being deprived of Life Eternal than because he was dead to her**. Full of confidence, she took the dead child and publicly carried him to the Church of St. Stephen, the first martyr. **There she commenced to pray for the son she had just lost. Her son moved, uttered a cry, and was suddenly restored to life**. She immediately brought him to the priests; and, after receiving the Sacraments of Baptism and Confirmation, he died anew."[178]

In the Acts of the Apostles alone we find three miraculous interventions involving Baptism – Cornelius the Centurion, the Eunuch of Candace, and Saul of Tarsus. And in each case not only is God's Providence evident, but the individuals involved are obliged to be baptized with water even though their intention to do the will of God is clear.

The fact is that God will keep any sincere soul alive until Baptism; He is <u>Almighty</u> and He has decreed that no one enters heaven without Baptism.

Pope Pius IX, *Vatican I, ex cathedra*: "**God protects and governs by His providence all things which He has created, 'reaching from end to end mightily and ordering all things sweetly'**…"[179]

In fact, the first infallible definition stating that the elect see the Beatific Vision immediately after death was from Pope Benedict XII in *Benedictus Deus*. It is interesting to examine what he infallibly declares about the saints and <u>martyrs</u> who went to heaven.

Pope Benedict XII, *Benedictus Deus*, 1336, ***ex cathedra***, on the souls of the just receiving the Beatific Vision: "By this edict which will prevail forever, with apostolic authority we declare… the holy apostles, <u>the martyrs</u>, the confessors, virgins, and the other faithful **who died after the holy baptism of Christ had been received by them**, in whom there was nothing to be purged… and the souls of children departing before the use of free will, **reborn and baptized in the same baptism of Christ, when all have been baptized**… have been, are, and will be in heaven…"[180]

In defining that the elect in whom nothing is to be purged are in heaven, Pope Benedict XII mentions <u>three times</u> that they have been baptized. Obviously, no apostle, <u>martyr</u>, confessor or virgin could receive the Beatific Vision without having received Baptism according to this infallible dogmatic definition.

THE THEORY OF BAPTISM OF DESIRE – A TRADITION OF MAN

Those who have been brainwashed by apologists for the theory of baptism of desire may be surprised to learn that of all the fathers of the Church, **only 1 can even be brought forward by baptism of desire advocates as having taught the concept.** That's correct, only one, St. Augustine. The baptism of desire advocates will make a feeble attempt to bring forward a second father, St. Ambrose, as we will see; but even if that were true, that would make only two fathers out of hundreds who can be quoted as ever having speculated on the concept of baptism of desire. So then, what is one to say about the following statements of the priests of the Society of St. Pius X (SSPX), who have written three separate books on "baptism of desire"?

> Fr. Jean-Marc Rulleau (SSPX), *Baptism of Desire*, p. 63: "This baptism of desire makes up for the want of sacramental baptism… The existence of this mode of salvation is a truth taught by the Magisterium of the Church and held from the first centuries **<u>by all the Fathers</u>. No Catholic theologian has contested it.**"[181]

> Fr. Francois Laisney (SSPX), *Is Feeneyism Catholic?*, p. 79, on Baptism of desire: "**It is not only the common teaching, but <u>unanimous</u> teaching**; it is not only since the early part of this millennium, but rather from the beginning of the Church…"[182]

These statements are totally false and grievous <u>lies</u> which completely misrepresent the teaching of Tradition and corrupt peoples' faith, as we will see. **The fathers are unanimously** *against* the concept that anyone (including a catechumen) could be saved without water baptism, as I have shown. But let us examine the teaching of the *one* father, St. Augustine, who did express belief (at least at times) in the idea that a catechumen could be saved without the Sacrament of Baptism by his desire for it.

ST. AUGUSTINE (354-430)

St. Augustine is quoted in favor of the concept of baptism of desire, but he admittedly struggled with the issue, sometimes clearly opposing the idea that unbaptized **catechumens** could achieve salvation, and other times supporting it.

> St. Augustine, 400: "That the place of Baptism is sometimes supplied by suffering is supported by a substantial argument which the same Blessed Cyprian draws…**Considering this over and over again**, <u>I find</u> that not only suffering for the name of Christ can supply for that which is lacking by way of Baptism, but even faith and conversion of heart, if… recourse cannot be had to the celebration of the Mystery of Baptism."[183]

There are two interesting points about this passage. The first relates to baptism of blood: notice that Augustine says that his belief in baptism of blood is supported by an inference or an argument that St. Cyprian made, not anything rooted in the Tradition of the Apostles or the Roman Pontiffs. As we saw already, many of the inferences of St. Cyprian showed themselves to be quite wrong, to put it nicely, such as his "inference" that it was from "apostolic Tradition" that heretics cannot confer baptism. Thus, St. Augustine is revealing by this statement a very important point: **that his belief even in baptism of blood is rooted in fallible human speculation, not in divine revelation or infallible Tradition. He is admitting that he could be wrong and, in fact, he is wrong**.

Secondly, when Augustine concludes that he also believes that faith (that is, faith in Catholicism) and a desire for baptism could have the same effect as martyrdom, he says: *"Considering this over and over again…"* By saying that he considered this over and over again, St. Augustine is admitting that his opinion on *baptism of desire* is also something that he has come to from <u>his own consideration</u>, not through infallible Tradition or Teaching. It is something that he admittedly struggled with, and contradicted himself on, as will be shown. All of this serves to prove again that baptism of desire, like baptism of blood, <u>is a tradition of man</u>, born in erroneous and fallible human speculation (albeit from some great men), and not rooted in or derived from any Tradition of the Apostles or of the Popes.

Interestingly, <u>in the same set of works on Baptism quoted already, St. Augustine made a different error</u>, which he later corrected in his *Book of Corrections*. In this set of works he had originally stated his opinion that the Good Thief who died on the Cross next to Our Lord was an example of Baptism of Blood. He later corrected this, by noting that the Good Thief could not be used as an example of Baptism of Blood because we don't know if the Good Thief was ever baptized. But actually, the Good Thief cannot be used as an example of baptism of blood primarily because the Good Thief died under the Old Law, not the New Law; he died before the Law of Baptism was instituted by Jesus Christ after the Resurrection. For that reason, the Good Thief, like the Holy Innocents, constitutes no argument against the necessity of receiving the Sacrament of Baptism for salvation.

> Catechism of the Council of Trent, *Baptism made obligatory after Christ's Resurrection*, p. 171: "Holy writers are unanimous in saying that after the Resurrection of our Lord, when He gave His Apostles the command to go and teach all nations: *baptizing them in the name of the Father, and of the Son, and of the Holy Ghost,* **the law of Baptism became obligatory on all who were to be saved.**"[184]

In fact, when Our Lord said to the Good Thief, *"This day you will be with Me in paradise,"* Jesus was not referring to heaven, but actually to hell. As Catholics know, no one entered heaven until after Our Lord did, after His Resurrection. On the day of the Crucifixion, Christ descended into hell, as the Apostles' Creed says. He did not descend to the hell of the damned, but to the place in hell called the *Limbo of the Fathers*, the waiting place of the Just of the Old Testament, who could not enter heaven until after the Savior came.

> 2 Peter 3:18-19- "Christ also died once for our sins… **In which also coming he preached to those spirits that were in prison**…"

To further prove the point that the Good Thief did not go to heaven on the Day of the Crucifixion, there is the fact that on Easter Sunday, when Mary Magdalene met the Risen Lord, He told her, *"Do not touch Me, for I have not yet ascended to My Father."*

> John 20:17- "**[On the Day of the Resurrection]** Jesus saith to her; Mary. She turning, saith to him; Rabboni, (that is to say, Master). Jesus saith to her; Do not touch me, **for I have not yet ascended to my Father**…"

Our Lord hadn't even yet ascended to Heaven on the Sunday of the Resurrection. It is therefore a fact that Our Lord and the Good Thief were not in heaven together on Good Friday; they were in the Limbo of the Fathers, the prison described in 2 Peter 3:18-19. Jesus called this place Paradise because He would be there with the just of the Old Testament. So, as St. Augustine later admitted, he erred in trying to use the Good Thief as an example for his point. This proves again that only the dogmatic teaching of the Popes are infallible, as well as the universal and constant Tradition. **But St. Augustine** himself in many, many places affirms the universal Tradition of the Apostles that no one is saved without the Sacrament of Baptism; and, in fact, he denied the concept that a catechumen could be saved without the Sacrament of Baptism by his desire for it numerous times.

St Augustine, 395: "… **God does not forgive sins except to the baptized.**"[185]

St. Augustine, 412: "… the Punic Christians call Baptism itself nothing else but salvation… Whence does this derive, except from an ancient and, as I suppose, apostolic tradition, **by which <u>the Churches of Christ hold inherently that without Baptism and participation at the table of the Lord it is impossible for any man to attain either to the Kingdom of God or to salvation and life eternal</u>?** This is the witness of Scripture, too."[186]

St. Augustine, 391: "When we shall have come into His [God's] sight, we shall behold the equity of God's justice. Then no one will say:… '*<u>Why was this man led by God's direction to be baptized, while that man, though he lived properly as a catechumen, was killed</u> in a sudden disaster, and was not baptized?*' **Look for rewards, and you will find nothing except punishments.**"[187]

Here we see St. Augustine completely rejecting the concept of baptism of desire. Nothing could be more clear! He says that God keeps sincere catechumens alive until their baptism, and that those who look for rewards in such <u>unbaptized catechumens</u> will find nothing but punishments! St. Augustine even makes it a special point to affirm that the Almighty doesn't allow unbaptized catechumens to be killed except for a reason! Those who say that St. Augustine held to baptism of desire are, therefore, simply not being complete with the facts. They must add the qualification that he many times <u>rejected the idea</u> and was on both sides of the issue. Thus, **the only father that the baptism of desire advocates can clearly quote in favor of the concept (Augustine) actually denied the concept of baptism of desire many times.**

St. Augustine: **"However much progress the catechumen should make,** he still carries the load of his iniquity: **nor is it removed from him unless he comes to Baptism."**[188]

Here we see St. Augustine again affirming the apostolic truth that no one enters heaven without water baptism <u>and again explicitly denying the concept of baptism of desire</u>, by denying that any catechumen can be freed from sin without baptism. All of this shows that baptism of desire is not the universal Tradition of the Apostles; rather,

the exact opposite is the universal Tradition of the Apostles and Fathers – that no catechumen can be saved without water baptism.

ST. AMBROSE (340-397)

Out of the hundreds of fathers of the Church, the only other one that the baptism of desire advocates *even try* to quote is St. Ambrose. They think that in his funeral speech for his friend (the Emperor Valentinian) he taught that the Emperor (who was only a catechumen) was saved by his desire for baptism. But St. Ambrose's funeral speech for Valentinian is extremely ambiguous and could be interpreted in a variety of ways. It is thus gratuitous for them to assert that it clearly teaches the idea of "baptism of desire."

> St. Ambrose, *Funeral Oration of Valentinian*, 4th century: "But I hear that **you grieve** because he did not receive the sacraments of baptism. Tell me: What else is in your power other than the desire, the request? But he even had this desire for a long time, that, when he should come to Italy, he would be initiated… Has he not, then, the grace which he desired; has he not the grace which he requested? And because he asked, he received, and therefore it is said: 'By whatsoever death the just man shall be overtaken, his soul shall be at rest' (Wis. 4:7)… Or if the fact disturbs you that the mysteries have not been <u>solemnly</u> celebrated, **then you should realize that <u>not even martyrs are crowned if they are catechumens, for they are not crowned if they are not initiated</u>.** But if they are washed in their own blood, his piety and desire have washed him, also."[189]

Let us reflect for a moment on what he just said. All of the faithful assembled for the memorial service are grieving and mourning. Why are they grieving? They are grieving because there is no evidence that Valentinian, a known catechumen, had been baptized. But if "baptism of desire" were something contained in the Deposit of Faith and part of apostolic Tradition, why should they grieve? Did not Valentinian earnestly desire baptism? Yet, these faithful were grief stricken because they had all been taught, and therefore believed, that *"unless a man is born again of water and the Holy Ghost, he cannot enter into the Kingdom of God"* (John 3:5). They had all been taught that no one is saved without the Sacrament of Baptism. Their teacher was their Bishop, St. Ambrose.[190]

Furthermore, St. Ambrose's funeral speech for Valentinian is extremely ambiguous, as is obvious to anyone who reads the above. In the speech, St. Ambrose clearly says that **"martyrs are not crowned [that is, not saved] if they are catechumens,"** a statement which directly denies the idea of baptism of blood and is perfectly consistent with his other statements on the issue, which will be quoted. Ambrose then emphasizes the same point, **by stating again that catechumens "are not crowned if they are not initiated."** "Initiation" is a term for baptism. Thus, St. Ambrose is repeating the apostolic truth that catechumens who shed their blood for Christ cannot be saved if they are not baptized. He then proceeds to say that if they are washed in their own blood, his (Valentinian's) piety and desire have washed him also, which seems to directly contradict what he just said and seems to teach baptism of desire and blood, although it is not clear, since he did not say that Valentinian was saved without baptism. But if that is what St. Ambrose means, then his funeral speech is nonsensical, since he just clearly denied two times that martyrs can be crowned if they are catechumens. And *this* is the oldest "text" quoted in favor of the idea of baptism of desire! It is, first of all, contradictory; secondly, it is ambiguous; and thirdly, if interpreted to mean that a catechumen is saved without water baptism, is opposed to every other statement St. Ambrose formally made on the issue.

But perhaps there is another explanation. St. Ambrose states that the faithful were grieving because Valentinian did not receive the sacrament**s** of baptism? Why did he use the term "sacrament**s**" instead of "sacrament"? Was he lamenting the fact that Valentinian was not able to receive Confirmation and the Eucharist, which were commonly administered together with baptism in the early Church? This would correspond to his statement about the crowd being disturbed because the mysteries were not "solemnly" celebrated, in other words, with all of the formal ceremonies which precede the solemn celebration of baptism. Exactly what St. Ambrose meant in this speech, we may never know in this world, but we are permitted to assume that it was not his intention to contradict in an emotionally charged eulogy what he had written with much thought and precision in *De Mysteriis* and elsewhere.[191]

Interestingly, the famous 12th century theologian Peter Abelard, whose orthodoxy was nevertheless suspect on other points, points out that **if St. Ambrose taught baptism of desire at any time he "contradicts tradition in this matter,"**[192] not to mention his own repeated teaching on the necessity of the Sacrament of Baptism, as we will see below.

And here is what St. Ambrose wrote with much thought and precision, which eliminates the very concept of baptism of desire and affirms the universal Tradition of all the fathers that no one (including catechumens) is saved without water baptism.

> St. Ambrose, *De mysteriis*, 390-391 A.D.:
> "You have read, therefore, that the three witnesses in Baptism are one: water, blood, and the spirit; and if you withdraw any one of these, the Sacrament of Baptism is not valid. For what is water without the cross of Christ? A common element without any sacramental effect. **Nor on the other hand is there any mystery of regeneration without water: for 'unless a man be born again of water and the Spirit, he cannot enter the kingdom of God.' [John 3:5] Even a *catechumen* believes in** the cross of the Lord Jesus, by which also he is signed; but,

unless he be baptized in the name of the Father and of the Son and of the Holy Spirit, *he cannot receive the remission of sins* nor be recipient of the gift of spiritual grace."[193]

Here we see St. Ambrose clearly denying the concept of baptism of desire. Nothing could be more clear!

St. Ambrose, *The Duties of Clergy*, 391 A.D.:
"The Church was redeemed at the price of Christ's blood. Jew or Greek, it makes no difference; but if he has believed he must circumcise himself from his sins so that he can be saved;...**for no one ascends into the kingdom of heaven except through the Sacrament of Baptism.**"[194]

St. Ambrose, *The Duties of Clergy*, 391 A.D.:
"Unless a man be born again of water and the Holy Spirit, he cannot enter the kingdom of God.' No one excepted: not the infant, **not the one prevented by some necessity.**"[195]

As opposed to St. Cyril of Jerusalem and St. Fulgence, who at one time mentioned their belief that there were exceptions to John 3:5 in the case of martyrs only, St. Ambrose acknowledges no exceptions, **thereby excluding baptism of desire *and* baptism of blood**.

And with *that* we come to the extent of the fathers' teaching on the so-called "baptism of desire"! That's right, one or at the most two fathers out of hundreds, St. Augustine and St. Ambrose, can even be quoted. St. Augustine admitted that he struggled with this issue, contradicted himself on it, and most importantly, frequently affirmed the universal Tradition that no one – including a catechumen – enters heaven without water baptism. And St. Ambrose clearly and repeatedly denied the concept of baptism of desire numerous times, by denying that any person – including a catechumen – could be saved without rebirth of water and the Spirit in the Sacrament of Baptism.

And when these facts are known, one can see how deceived and misled are many so-called Catholics and Traditional Catholics today who are listening to those lying teachers, many of whom claim to be "traditional" priests, who search land and sea to attempt to pervert the teaching of Tradition and get people into heaven without baptism. These lying teachers are convincing many of the ridiculous lie that "the fathers were unanimous in favor of baptism of desire." Such a claim is pure nonsense and a mortally sinful perversion of Catholic Tradition. As one author correctly put it:

"The Fathers of the Church, therefore, taken as a whole, can only be said to have verified definitively the official and

authentic teaching of the one true Church that it is absolutely necessary for the salvation of every human creature to be baptized in the water of the actual sacrament instituted by Our Lord Jesus Christ. On the other hand, it is intellectually dishonest to suggest otherwise. **And to exalt the personal theological opinions of a handful – even an impressive and well-known handful – to the rank of ecclesiastical Tradition or even magisterial infallibility is not only an exercise in sophomoric legerdemain [verbal sleight of hand], but also a brand of facile short-sightedness unconscionable in any serious study of Patristic Theology.**"[196]

The universal Tradition of the apostles on the absolute necessity of water baptism for regeneration and salvation, affirmed by Hermas as early as the 1st century, and repeated by all the rest, including St. Justin Martyr, St. Theophilus, Origen, Tertullian, St. Basil, St. Cyril, St. Augustine, St. Ambrose, etc., etc., etc. is summed up by the statement quoted already from Ambrose.

St. Ambrose: **"Nor on the other hand is there any mystery of regeneration without water: for 'unless a man be born again of water and the Spirit, he cannot enter the kingdom of God.' [John 3:5]** Even a _catechumen_ believes in the cross of the Lord Jesus, by which also he is signed; but, unless he be baptized in the name of the Father and of the Son and of the Holy Spirit, _he cannot receive the remission of sins_ nor be recipient of the gift of spiritual grace."[197]

This is the unanimous teaching of the fathers of the Church on this issue.

Fr. William Jurgens: **"If there were not <u>a constant tradition</u> in the Fathers that the Gospel message of** _'Unless a man be born again of water and the Holy Ghost he cannot enter into the kingdom of God'_ **is to be taken absolutely**, it would be easy to say that Our Savior simply did not see fit to mention the obvious exceptions of invincible ignorance and physical impossibility. **But the tradition in fact is there; and it is likely enough to be found so constant as to constitute revelation.**"[198]

ST. GREGORY NAZIANZ (329-389)

It is fitting also to look at the teaching of some of the other fathers. St. Gregory Nazianz is one of the four Great Eastern Doctors of the Catholic Church. He explicitly rejected the concept of baptism of desire.

St. Gregory Nazianz, 381 AD: "Of those who fail to be baptized some are utterly animal and bestial, according to whether they are foolish or wicked. This, I think, they must add to their other sins, that they have no reverence for this gift, but regard it as any other gift, to be accepted if given them, or neglected if not given them. Others know and honor the gift; but they delay, some out of carelessness, some because of insatiable desire. Still others are not able to receive it, perhaps because of infancy, **or some perfectly involuntary circumstance** **which prevents them from receiving the gift, even if they desire it**…

"If you were able to judge a man who intends to commit murder, solely by his intention and without any act of murder, then you could likewise reckon as baptized one who desired Baptism, without having received Baptism. But, since you cannot do the former, how can you do the latter? **I cannot see it**. If you prefer, we will put it like this: **if in your opinion desire has equal power with actual Baptism**, then make the same judgment in regard to glory. You will then be satisfied to long for glory, as if that longing itself were glory. Do you suffer any damage by not attaining the actual glory, as long as you have a desire for it?"[199]

So much for the claim that "the fathers are unanimous" in favor of baptism of desire! When the priests of the SSPX publicly assert such they are stating exactly the opposite of the truth and are lying through their teeth. And what makes this lie all the more incredible is the fact that the SSPX quotes the above statement from St. Gregory on pages 64-65 of their book, *Is Feeneyism Catholic?*!

But here is what the liturgy has to say about the teaching of the great St. Gregory Nazianz, who clearly rejected baptism of desire. A reading for the feast of St. Gregory Nazianz (May 9) states:

> "He wrote much, both in prose and verse, of an admirable piety and eloquence. **In the opinion of learned and holy men, there is nothing to be found in his writings which is not conformable to true piety and Catholic faith, or which anyone could reasonably call in question.**"[200]

St. Gregory was actually the only doctor in the entire history of the Church who was surnamed *"the theologian."* I will quote the famous Benedictine Dom Prosper Gueranger:

> "It is Gregory of [Nazianz]… **the one of all the Gregories who has merited and received the glorious name of Theologian,** on account of the soundness of his teachings, the sublimity of his ideas, and the magnificence of his diction."[201]

So much for the lie that "the theologians" are unanimous in favor of baptism of desire. The only Doctor in Church history surnamed "the theologian" explicitly rejected it!

ST. JOHN CHRYSOSTOM (347-407)

Besides St. Gregory and the others, **St. John Chrysostom** provides us with a plethora of quotations explicitly against the idea of salvation for unbaptized catechumens (those preparing to be baptized) by baptism of desire. **That anyone else besides unbaptized catechumens could qualify for salvation without first receiving the Sacrament of Baptism was not even considered a possibility worth refuting in this context**. (How horrified would these fathers be by the modern version of the theory of baptism of desire, which saves pagans, Jews, heretics and schismatics?)

> St. John Chrysostom, *The Consolation of Death*: "**And well should the pagan lament, who not knowing God, dying goes straight to punishment. Well should the Jew mourn, who not believing in Christ, has assigned his soul to perdition.**"[202]

It should be noted that since *the term* "baptism of desire" was not in use at the time, one won't find St. John Chrysostom or any other father explicitly rejecting *that term*. They reject baptism of desire when they reject *the concept* that unbaptized catechumens can be saved without Baptism, as St. John Chrysostom repeatedly does.

> St. John Chrysostom, *The Consolation of Death*: "**And plainly must we grieve for our own catechumens, should they**, either through their own unbelief or through their own neglect, **depart this life without the saving grace of baptism.**"[203]

This statement clearly rejects the concept of baptism of desire.

> St. John Chrysostom, *Hom. in Io. 25, 3*:
> "**For the Catechumen is a stranger to the Faithful**… One has Christ for his King; the other sin and the devil; the food of one is Christ, of the other, that meat which decays and perishes… Since then we have nothing in common, in what, tell me, shall we hold communion?… Let us then give diligence that we may become citizens of the city above… <u>**for if it should come to pass** (which God forbid!) **that through the sudden arrival of death we depart hence uninitiated**</u>, **though we have ten thousand virtues, <u>our portion will be none other than hell</u>**, and the venomous worm, and fire unquenchable, and bonds indissoluble."[204]

This statement totally rejects the concept of baptism of desire.

St. John Chrysostom, *Homily III. On Phil. 1:1-20:*
"Weep for the unbelievers; weep for those who differ in nowise from them, those **who depart hence without the illumination, without the seal!** They indeed deserve our wailing, they deserve our groans; they are outside the Palace, with the culprits, with the condemned: for, '**Verily I say unto you, Except a man be born again of water and the Spirit, he shall not enter into the kingdom of Heaven.**"[205]

The "seal" is the fathers' term for the <u>mark</u> of the Sacrament of Baptism. And here we see St. John affirming the apostolic truth held by all the fathers: that no one – including a catechumen – is saved without being born again of water and the Spirit in the Sacrament of Baptism.

St. John Chrysostom, *Homily XXV*: "Hear, ye as many as are unilluminated, shudder, groan, fearful is the threat, fearful is the sentence. '**It is not possible,**' He [Christ] saith, '**for one not born of water and the Spirit to enter into the Kingdom of heaven**'; because he wears the raiment of death, of cursing, of perdition, he hath not yet received his Lord's token, he is a stranger and an alien, he hath not the royal watchword. '**Except,**' He saith, '**a man be born again of water and the Spirit, he cannot enter into the Kingdom of heaven.**"[206]

St. John Chrysostom clearly rejected any possibility of salvation for one who has not received the Sacrament of Baptism. He affirmed the words of Christ in John 3:5 with an unequivocally literal understanding, which is the unanimous teaching of Tradition and the teaching of defined Catholic dogma.

LITURGICAL TRADITION AND APOSTOLIC BURIAL TRADITION

Besides these clear testimonies of the fathers against the theory of baptism of desire, perhaps most striking is the fact that in the history of the Catholic Church **there is not a single tradition that can be cited for praying for – or giving ecclesiastical burial to – catechumens who died without baptism.** *The Catholic Encyclopedia* (1907) had the following to say about the actual Tradition of the Church in this regard:

"A certain statement in the funeral oration of St. Ambrose over the Emperor Valentinian II has been brought forward as a proof that the Church offered sacrifices and prayers for catechumens who died before baptism. **There is not a vestige of such a custom to be found anywhere**… <u>The practice of the Church is more correctly shown in the canon (xvii) of the Second Council of Braga</u> (572 AD): '**Neither the commemoration of Sacrifice** *[oblationis]* **nor the service of chanting** *[psallendi]* **is to be employed for catechumens who have died without baptism.'"**[207]

There you have the teaching of Catholic Tradition! No catechumen who died without the Sacrament of Baptism received prayer, sacrifice or Christian burial! The Council of Braga, in 572 A.D., forbade prayer for catechumens who died without baptism. Pope St. Leo the Great and Pope St. Gelasius had earlier confirmed the same Church discipline – which was the universal practice – forbidding Catholics to pray for unbaptized catechumens who had died.[208] **This means that the belief in the early Church was that there was no such thing as baptism of desire**. The theory of baptism of desire didn't become a widespread belief until the middle ages, when St. Thomas Aquinas and some other eminent theologians made it their own, which caused many theologians to subsequently adopt that position out of deference to them, a position on the possible salvation of catechumens who died without baptism which was contrary to the overwhelming belief and liturgical tradition of the early Church, not to mention the Church's later infallible teaching on the scripture John 3:5.

The true teaching of apostolic and Catholic tradition on this topic is also seen from the teaching of the Catholic Liturgy, which all worshipping Catholics in the early Church acknowledged and believed: namely, that no unbaptized catechumen or unbaptized person was considered part of *the faithful* (see Section on "The One Church of the Faithful."). That unbaptized catechumens are not part of the faithful was held by all of the fathers, because it was taught to all Catholics in the liturgy.

> Dr. Ludwig Ott, *Fundamentals of Catholic Dogma*, Membership in the Church, p. 309: "3. The Fathers <u>draw a sharp line of separation</u> between Catechumens and 'the faithful.'"[209]

This means that no unbaptized person can be saved, because Catholic dogma has defined that no one is saved outside the one Church of the faithful.

> Pope Gregory XVI, *Summo Iugiter Studio*, May 27, 1832, on no salvation outside the Church: "Official acts of the Church proclaim the same dogma. Thus, in the decree on faith which Innocent III published with the synod of Lateran IV, these things are written: *'There is one universal Church of all <u>the faithful</u> outside of which no one is saved.'"*[210]

POPE ST. SIRICIUS (384-398)

In his letter to the Bishop of Tarragona in the year 385, Pope St. Siricius also shows how the belief in the early Church rejected any concept of baptism of desire.

Pope St. Siricius, *Letter to Himerius*, 385:

"As we maintain that the observance of the holy Paschal time should in no way be relaxed, in the same way we desire that infants who, on account of their age, cannot yet speak, or those who, in any necessity, <u>are in want of **the water** of holy baptism</u>, be succored with all possible speed, for fear that, **if those who leave this world should be deprived of the life of the Kingdom <u>for having been refused the source of salvation which they desired</u>**, this may lead to the ruin of our souls. **If those threatened with shipwreck, or the attack of enemies, or the uncertainties of a siege, or those put in a hopeless condition due to some bodily sickness, <u>ask for what in their faith is their only help</u>, let them receive at the very moment of their request the reward of regeneration they beg for. Enough of past mistakes! From now on, let all the priests observe the aforesaid rule if they do not want to be separated from the solid apostolic rock on which Christ has built his universal Church.**"[211]

This quotation from Pope St. Siricius is striking in that it again clearly shows how the early Church rejected belief in the concept of baptism of desire. He begins by affirming that the observance of Paschal time should not be relaxed. (He is referring to the fact that Baptisms were historically performed during Paschal time.) After affirming that this tradition should be maintained, he warns that infants and those in any necessity or danger should be baptized immediately, lest they are "deprived of the life of the Kingdom for having been refused the source of salvation *which they desired*." In other words, **the man who desires water baptism and begs for regeneration will still be denied heaven if he does not receive it!** Nothing could more clearly reject the concept of baptism of desire! (This also proves that the delay in baptizing adults is for the instruction and the testing of the catechumens, not because it was held that these catechumens could be saved without baptism.)

This point is made again by the Pope in the second half of the quotation, where he says that when those unbaptized persons "<u>**ask for what in their faith is their only help, let them receive at the very moment of their request the reward of regeneration they beg for.**</u>" This means that receiving water Baptism is the *only help to salvation* for such persons who earnestly desire to receive Baptism! There is no help to salvation for such persons in their desire or martyrdom, but only in receiving the Sacrament of Baptism!

THE MIDDLE AGES

Now that we have shown that the teaching of Tradition is definitely not in favor of baptism of desire, where did this baptism of desire furor that we now see come from? Why did it become such a widespread belief later on? It has never been taught by any Council, dogmatic definition or Papal Encyclical to the Church. But most people today think that it is a teaching of the Catholic Church. As stated already, the theory comes from the erroneous teaching of St. Augustine and an ambiguous passage in St. Ambrose in the 4th century. But due to St. Augustine's tremendous stature as a theologian, many *in the middle ages* adopted his <u>fallible</u> opinion on baptism of desire, despite the fact that it was contrary to the overwhelming belief in the early Church. And when the illustrious St. Bernard and St. Thomas Aquinas made baptism of desire their own position based on passages in St. Augustine and the ambiguous one in St. Ambrose, this caused hosts of theologians in the middle ages and down to our day to subsequently adopt baptism of desire out of deference to their great learning (particularly St. Thomas'), a position on the possible salvation of catechumens who died without baptism which was contrary to the overwhelming belief and liturgical tradition of the early Church, not to mention the Church's later infallible teaching on the Sacrament of Baptism, John 3:5 and One Baptism, as we will see.

ST. BERNARD

> St. Bernard, *Tractatus de baptismo*, II, 8, c. 1130: "So, believe me, it would be *difficult* to turn me aside from these two pillars – I mean Augustine and Ambrose. I confess that, **<u>whether in error or knowledge</u>**, I am with them; **for I believe that a man can be saved by faith alone, provided he desires to receive the sacrament,** in a case where death overtakes the fulfillment of his religious desire, or some other <u>invincible</u> power stands in his way."[212]

There are a number of very important points in this passage: <u>First</u>, we see St. Bernard explicitly admitting that his belief in baptism of desire is based <u>solely on what *he thinks* St. Augustine and St. Ambrose</u> taught, lending further credence to our point that baptism of desire is a tradition of man, not a teaching of God. And as we have already seen, even the two fathers that he quotes (Augustine and Ambrose) clearly denied the concept by affirming **many times** that no catechumen can be saved without the Sacrament of Baptism. In fact, as stated already – and it's worth repeating – Fr. Jean-Marc Rulleau (of the SSPX) is forced to admit in his book *Baptism of Desire* (p. 37) that during St. Bernard's period, when the idea of baptism of desire really began to gain momentum based on the passages in Augustine and Ambrose's funeral speech for Valentinian, the well-known Peter Abelard (whose orthodoxy nevertheless was suspect on other points) stated that **any idea of baptism of desire based on St. Ambrose "contradicts tradition in this matter."**[213] So, St. Bernard is not only basing his opinion on two fallible doctors, but he is positing an opinion which is clearly contrary to the overwhelming testimony of Tradition, as I have shown.

Second, and perhaps most importantly, in expressing his belief in baptism of desire, St. Bernard explicitly admits that he may be wrong!

> St. Bernard: "I mean Augustine and Ambrose. I confess that, **whether in error or knowledge**, I am with them; **for I believe that a man can be saved by faith alone, provided he desires to receive the sacrament…"**

But when Fr. Francois Laisney of the Society of St. Pius X quotes this passage of St. Bernard in his book *Is Feeneyism Catholic* (p. 67) he deliberately omits St. Bernard's statement, "whether in error or in knowledge…" Here is how the passage reads in *Is Feeneyism Catholic* (the book of the Society of St. Pius X):

> "Believe me, it will be difficult to separate me from these two columns, by which I refer to Augustine and Ambrose… believing with them that people can be saved by faith alone and the desire to receive the sacrament…"

The words *"whether in error or in knowledge"* are removed by Fr. Laisney and replaced with ellipses (…). Now, of course, it is perfectly justifiable to use ellipses (…) when quoting texts, in order to pass over parts of the quotation that are not crucial or necessary in the discussion. But, in this case, the readers of Fr. Laisney's book would have been well served to see this short, crucial admission by St. Bernard that he could have been right or wrong about baptism of desire. Fr. Laisney deliberately removed it because he knows that *it is devastating to his contention that baptism of desire is a teaching of the Church based on the opinions of saints*. This admission of St. Bernard, in fact, blows away the thesis of Fr. Laisney's book, so it had to go. But despite the attempt of Fr. Laisney of the SSPX to hide this from his readers, the fact is out: St. Bernard admits that he wasn't even sure about baptism of desire since the idea is not rooted in any teaching of the Church or infallible tradition, but only in **the opinion of man**.

Third, as I have pointed out, it is an incredible fact that in almost every instance in which a Saint or theologian expresses his opinion on baptism of desire or blood, he almost always makes a different error in the same document (thus proving his fallibility). In the document quoted above, **St. Bernard uses the phrase "faith alone" three times** (which was condemned approximately 13 times by the Council of Trent in the 16th century).

> St. Bernard, *Tractatus de baptismo*, II, 8, c. 1130: "So, believe me, it would be difficult to turn me aside from these two pillars – I mean Augustine and Ambrose. I confess that, **whether in error or knowledge**, I am with them; **for I believe that a man can be saved by faith alone**, provided he desires to receive

the sacrament, in a case where death overtakes the fulfillment of his religious desire, or some other <u>invincible</u> power stands in his way… This intimated that sometimes <u>faith alone</u> would suffice for salvation… In the same way, <u>faith alone</u> and turning the mind to God, without the spilling of blood or the pouring of water, doubtlessly brings salvation to one who has the will but not the way… to be baptized."[214]

Pope Paul III, *Council of Trent*, Session 6, Can. 9: "**If anyone shall say that by <u>faith alone</u> the sinner is justified**, so as to understand that nothing else is required to cooperate in the attainment of the grace of justification, and that it is in no way necessary that he be prepared and disposed by the action of his will: **let him be anathema.**"

Pope Paul III, *Council of Trent*, Session 7, Can. 8: "If anyone shall say that by the said sacraments of the New Law, grace is not conferred from the work which has been worked [*ex opere operato*], **but that <u>faith alone</u> in the divine promise suffices to obtain grace: let him be anathema.**"

Pope Paul III, *Council of Trent*, Session 6, Can. 19: "**If anyone shall say that nothing except faith is commanded in the Gospel… let him be anathema.**"

Pope Paul III, *Council of Trent*, Session 6, Chap. 11: "**And so no one should flatter himself because of faith alone, thinking that by <u>faith alone</u> he is made an heir and will obtain the inheritance,** even though he suffer not with Christ 'that he may be also glorified' (Rom. 8:17)."

Pope Paul III, *Council of Trent*, Session 6, Chap. 10: "'"You see, that by works a man is justified **and not by <u>faith alone</u>**' (Jas. 2:24)."

I'm sure that St. Bernard did not really believe that faith alone justifies and saves (Luther's heretical doctrine); but this is the phrase he uses above three times! This brings home the point with crystal clarity: that if one is going to dogmatize the teachings of saints (as many baptism of desire advocates like to do) and quote them as proof texts, then one is going to wind up with a lot of error and even heresy. And it proves again that St. Bernard's utterances are not teachings of the Catholic Church, but fallible opinions about which he could be wrong (as he himself admits) and, in this case, about which he is definitely wrong.

<u>Fourth</u>, in expressing his opinion on baptism of desire, St. Bernard says that one can be prevented from receiving baptism through some "invincible power." This is also theologically incorrect. God is Almighty; He alone is the "invincible power"! Nothing can prevent Him from getting a good willed soul to Baptism.

Pope Pius IX, *Vatican I*, ex cathedra: "**God protects and governs by His providence all things which He has created, 'reaching from end to end mightily and ordering all things sweetly'**…"[215]

And, ironically, by making the aforementioned statement on a catechumen being prevented from receiving baptism by some "invincible power," St. Bernard is also directly contradicting St. Augustine, the one he tries to use for his fallible opinion on baptism of desire.

> St. Augustine, 391: "When we shall have come into His [God's] sight, we shall behold the equity of God's justice. Then no one will say:… '**_Why was this man led by God's direction to be baptized, while that man, though he lived properly as a catechumen, was killed_** in a sudden disaster, and was not baptized?' **Look for rewards, and you will find nothing except punishments**."[216]

All of this proves that St. Bernard's endorsement of baptism of desire was flawed, contradictory, admittedly fallible and based solely on what he deemed to be the opinions of men. It holds no weight even for a moment against the flawless, perfectly consistent, infallible dogma, which proclaims that no man can be saved without the Sacrament of Baptism.

Pope Eugene IV, *The Council of Florence*, "Exultate Deo," Nov. 22, 1439, *ex cathedra*: "Holy baptism, which is the gateway to the spiritual life, holds the first place among all the sacraments; through it we are made members of Christ and of the body of the Church. **And since death entered the universe through the first man, 'unless we are born again of water and the Spirit, we cannot,' as the Truth says, 'enter into the kingdom of heaven' [John 3:5].** The matter of this sacrament is real and natural water."[217]

And this tradition of man (baptism of desire) gained more momentum after St. Bernard, when St. Thomas Aquinas unfortunately made it his own, based again on the few passages in St. Augustine, the one in St. Ambrose and his own speculative theological reasoning.

ST. THOMAS AQUINAS

St. Thomas Aquinas, despite all of his fabulous writing and learning about the Catholic faith, being a fallible human being, was wrong on many points, including his explicit statement in the *Summa Theologica* that "*The flesh of the Virgin was conceived in Original Sin.*"[218] One scholar noted that the book St. Thomas was writing when he died was called *The Compendium of Theology*, in which are found at least nine explicit errors.[219] In fact, "over thirty years ago, Dr. Andre Daignes, Professor of Philosophy in Buenos Aires, Argentina, pointed out twenty-four formal errors in the Summa of St. Thomas."[220] This simply proves again that the theological speculations of even our greatest sainted theologians are just that – fallible speculations. Only St. Peter and his successors, <u>the Popes</u>, when speaking from the Chair of Peter, have the unfailing faith.

> Pope Pius IX, *Vatican Council I, ex cathedra*:
> "So, this gift of truth AND **<u>A NEVER FAILING FAITH WAS DIVINELY CONFERRED UPON PETER AND HIS SUCCESSORS</u> IN THIS CHAIR**…"[221]

In *Summa Theologica* III, Q. 66, Art. 11, St. Thomas tries to explain his belief in baptism of desire and blood. He tries to explain how there can be "three baptisms" (water, blood and desire) when St. Paul declares in Ephesians 4:5 that there is only one. He says:

> "*<u>The other two Baptisms are included in the Baptism of Water</u>, which derives its efficacy, both from Christ's Passion and of the Holy Ghost.*"

With all due respect to St. Thomas, this is a feeble attempt to answer the objection as to how there can be three baptisms when God reveals that there is only one. It is feeble because St. Thomas says that the other two baptisms, desire and blood, are *included* in the baptism of water; but this is false, as one who receives baptism of water doesn't receive baptism of desire and baptism of blood, even according to the baptism of desire advocates. Therefore, it is false to say, as St. Thomas does, that the other two baptisms are *included* in the baptism of water; they most certainly are not.

Furthermore, in teaching the theory of baptism of desire, St. Thomas repeatedly admitted that neither is a Sacrament.

> St. Thomas Aquinas, *Summa Theologica* III, Q. 66, A. 11, Answer 2: "As stated above, a sacrament is a kind of sign. The other two [baptism of desire and blood], however, are like the Baptism of Water, not, indeed, in the nature of sign, but in the baptismal effect. **Consequently <u>they are not sacraments</u>**."

The fierce baptism of desire advocate, Fr. Laisney, admits the same in his book, *Is Feeneyism Catholic?*, p. 9:

> Fr. Laisney, *Is Feeneyism Catholic?*, p. 9: "<u>Baptism of Desire is not a sacrament</u>; it does not have the exterior sign required in the sacraments. The theologians, following St. Thomas… call it 'baptism' only because it produces the grace of baptism… yet it does not produce the sacramental character."[222]

But the Council of Trent (a few centuries after St. Thomas, in 1547) infallibly defined as a dogma that <u>THE SACRAMENT</u> OF BAPTISM is necessary for salvation!

Pope Paul III, *The Council of Trent*, Can. 5 on the <u>**Sacrament**</u> of Baptism, *ex cathedra*: **"If anyone says that baptism [the sacrament] is optional, that is, not necessary for salvation (cf. Jn. 3:5): let him be anathema."**[223]

So, who does one follow, St. Thomas or the infallible Council of Trent? Compare the two:

St. Thomas Aquinas, *Summa Theologica* III, Q. 68, Art. 2: "… it *seems* that a man can obtain salvation <u>**without the sacrament of Baptism,**</u> by means of the invisible sanctification…"

Pope Paul III, *The Council of Trent*, Can. 5 on the <u>**Sacrament**</u> of Baptism, Sess. 7, 1547, *ex cathedra*: **"If anyone says that baptism [the sacrament] is optional, that is, not necessary for salvation (cf. Jn. 3:5): let him be anathema."**[224]

There is an obvious contradiction here. The fallible St. Thomas Aquinas says that it is possible to obtain salvation <u>without the Sacrament</u> of Baptism, while the infallible Council of Trent defines that <u>the Sacrament is necessary for salvation</u>. And what does "necessary" mean? According to Part III, Q. 68, A. 2, Obj. 3 in St. Thomas' *own Summa Theologica, "<u>that is necessary without which something cannot be</u>* (Metaph. V)." Thus, "necessary" means without which something cannot be. Thus, salvation cannot be – it is impossible – without the Sacrament of Baptism (*de fide, Council of Trent*). Catholics must accept this truth and reject St. Thomas' fallible opinion in the *Summa Theologica* on baptism of desire.

Pope Benedict XIV, *Apostolica* (# 6), June 26, 1749: **"The Church's judgment is preferable to that of a Doctor** renowned for his holiness and teaching."[225]

Pope Pius XII, *Humani generis* (# 21), Aug. 12, 1950: **"This deposit of faith our Divine Redeemer has given for authentic interpretation not to each of the faithful, <u>not even to theologians,</u> but only to the Teaching Authority of the Church.'"**[226]

Pope St. Pius X, *Pascendi dominic gregis* (#45), Sept. 8, 1907: "It goes without saying that **if anything is met with among the scholastic doctors** which may be regarded as an excess of subtlety, or which is altogether destitute of probability, **We have no desire whatever to propose it for the imitation of present generations."**[227]

And just in case anyone argues that one can receive the Sacrament of Baptism without <u>water</u>, I will quote the Council of Trent's definition in Can. 2.

Pope Paul III, *The Council of Trent*, Can. 2 on <u>the Sacrament</u> of Baptism, Session 7, 1547, *ex cathedra*: **"If anyone shall say that real and natural water is not necessary for baptism,** and on that account those words of Our Lord Jesus Christ: 'Unless a man be born again of water and the Holy Spirit' [John 3:5], **are distorted into some sort of metaphor: let him be anathema."**[228]

THE DOGMATIC COUNCIL OF VIENNE (1311-1312)

It would have been interesting to see, however, what St. Thomas would have said if he had lived until the dogmatic *Council of Vienne* in 1311. St. Thomas died in 1274, 37 years <u>before</u> the Council. *The Council of Vienne* infallibly defined as a dogma that there is only one baptism that must be confessed by all Catholics, and that the one baptism is water baptism.

Pope Clement V, *Council of Vienne*, 1311-1312, *ex cathedra*: "Besides, **<u>one baptism</u>** which regenerates all who are baptized in Christ **<u>must be faithfully confessed by all</u>** just as 'one God and one faith' [Eph. 4:5], **<u>which celebrated in water</u>** in the name of the Father and of the Son and of the Holy Spirit we believe to be commonly the perfect remedy for salvation for adults as for children."[229]

This definition is crucial to this discussion, because one cannot affirm one baptism of water and at the same time obstinately cling to the belief that there are "three baptisms," two of which are not of water. That is a clear contradiction. Those who understand and comprehend this dogma must repudiate the so-called "three baptisms."

ST. THOMAS REJECTED "INVINCIBLE IGNORANCE"

It is also very important to point out that while St. Thomas Aquinas was wrong on baptism of desire, he held the dogma Outside the Church There is No Salvation and rejected the modern day heresy that persons can be saved who are "invincibly ignorant" of Jesus Christ. In numerous places St. Thomas explicitly addressed the question of persons in so-called invincible ignorance.

St. Thomas Aquinas, *De Veritate*, 14, A. 11, ad 1: Objection- **"It is possible that someone may be brought up in the forest, or among wolves; such a man cannot explicitly know anything about the faith. St. Thomas replies- It is the**

characteristic of Divine Providence to provide every man with what is necessary for salvation… provided on his part there is no hindrance. In the case of a man who seeks good and shuns evil, by the leading of natural reason, **God would either reveal to him through internal inspiration what had to be believed, or would send some preacher of the faith to him**…"[230]

St. Thomas Aquinas, *Sent. II, 28, Q. 1, A. 4, ad 4*: "If a man born among barbarian nations, does what he can, God Himself will show him what is necessary for salvation, either by inspiration or sending a teacher to him."[231]

St. Thomas Aquinas, Sent. III, 25, Q. 2, A. 2, solute. 2: "If a man should have no one to instruct him, God will show him, unless he culpably wishes to remain where he is."[232]

In the *Summa Theologica*, St. Thomas further taught the truth that all men above reason are bound to know the principal mysteries of Christ for salvation with no exceptions for ignorance.

St. Thomas, *Summa Theologica*: "<u>After grace had been revealed</u>, **both the learned and simple folk are bound to <u>explicit faith in the mysteries of Christ</u>**, chiefly as regards those which are observed throughout the Church, and publicly proclaimed, **such as** the articles which refer to **the Incarnation**, of which we have spoken above."[233]

Saint Thomas, *Summa Theologica*: "And consequently, when once grace had been revealed, **all were bound to explicit faith in the mystery of the Trinity.**"[234]

Therefore, St. Thomas, like all of the fathers of the Church, rejected the modern heresy of "invincible ignorance" saving those who die as non-Catholics. His speculation and erroneous teaching on baptism of blood/desire <u>only regarded catechumens</u>. And this point really shows the dishonesty of modern heretics, who like to quote St. Thomas Aquinas on baptism of desire to somehow justify their heretical idea that members of false religions can be saved by "baptism of desire." But the heretical idea of invincible ignorance saving persons who've never heard of Christ or who belong to false religions was never really heard of until after the year 1800.

15. Pope St. Leo the Great ends the debate

We have seen how Tradition doesn't teach baptism of desire and how the infallible teaching of the Church on the Sacrament of Baptism and John 3:5 excludes it. And we have seen how this error was perpetuated in the middle ages through flawed passages in the fallible texts of Churchmen. I will now discuss perhaps the most interesting pronouncement on this issue, the dogmatic letter of Pope St. Leo the Great to Flavian, which excludes the exact concept of baptism of desire and baptism of blood.

> Pope St. Leo the Great, **dogmatic** letter to Flavian, *Council of Chalcedon*, 451:
>
> **"Let him heed what the blessed apostle Peter preaches, that <u>sanctification by the Spirit is effected by the sprinkling of Christ's blood</u>** (1 Pet. 1:2); and let him not skip over the same apostle's words, *knowing that you have been redeemed from the empty way of life you inherited from your fathers, not with corruptible gold and silver but by the precious blood of Jesus Christ, as of a lamb without stain or spot* (1 Pet. 1:18). Nor should he withstand the testimony of blessed John the apostle: *and <u>the blood of Jesus, the Son of God, purifies us from every sin</u>* (1 Jn. 1:7); and again, *This is the victory which conquers the world, our faith. Who is there who conquers the world save one who believes that Jesus is the Son of God? It is He, Jesus Christ, who has come through water and blood, not in water only, but in water and blood. And because the Spirit is truth, it is the Spirit who testifies.* **For there are three who give testimony – Spirit and water and blood. And the three are one.** (1 Jn. 5:4-8) <u>**IN OTHER WORDS, THE SPIRIT OF SANCTIFICATION AND THE BLOOD OF REDEMPTION AND THE WATER OF BAPTISM. THESE THREE ARE ONE AND REMAIN INDIVISIBLE. NONE OF THEM IS SEPARABLE FROM ITS LINK WITH THE OTHERS.**"**[235]

Before I get into the tremendous significance of this pronouncement, I will give a little background on this dogmatic letter. This is Pope St. Leo the Great's famous dogmatic letter to Flavian, originally written in 449, and later accepted by the Council of Chalcedon – the fourth general Council of the Church – in 451 (quoted in *Decrees of the Ecumenical Councils*, Georgetown Press, Vol. 1, pp. 77-82). It is one of the most important documents in the history of the Church. This is the famous letter which, when read aloud at the dogmatic *Council of Chalcedon*, caused all of the fathers of the Council (more than 600) to rise to their feet and proclaim: *"This is the faith of the Fathers, the faith of the apostles; **Peter has spoken through the mouth of Leo**."* The very letter in itself embodies the term *ex cathedra* (speaking from the Chair of Peter), as proven by the reaction of the fathers at Chalcedon. This dogmatic letter of Pope Leo was accepted by the *Council of*

Chalcedon in its definition of Faith, which was approved authoritatively by Pope Leo himself.

And if that were not sufficient to prove that Pope Leo's letter is without question infallible and dogmatic, consider the fact that it was also approved by Pope Vigilius at the *Second Council of Constantinople* (553)[236] and by Pope St. Agatho at the *Third Council of Constantinople* (680-681).[237] It was also confirmed infallibly by a number of other Popes, including: Pope St. Gelasius, 495,[238] Pope Pelagius II, 553,[239] and Pope Benedict XIV, *nuper ad nos*, 1743.[240]

Because of the tremendous significance of Pope Leo's letter to the topic at hand, I will quote an extract from Pope St. Gelasius which shows how no one can contradict, in the slightest way, this dogmatic epistle of Pope St. Leo to Flavian.

> Pope St. Gelasius, *Decretal*, 495: "**Also the epistle of blessed Leo the Pope to Flavian… if anyone argues concerning the text of this one even in regard to one iota,** and does not receive it in all respects reverently, **let him be anathema.**"[241]

Here we have Pope St. Gelasius speaking *ex cathedra* to condemn anyone who would depart, even in regard to one iota, from the text of Pope Leo's dogmatic epistle to Flavian.

Now, in the section of Pope Leo's dogmatic letter quoted above, he is dealing with Sanctification by the Spirit. "Sanctification by the Spirit" is the term for **Justification** from the state of sin. Justification is the state of grace. **No one can get to heaven without Sanctification by the Spirit [Justification]**, as everyone professing to be Catholic admits. **Pope St. Leo affirms, on the authority of the great apostles Sts. Peter and John, that this Sanctification by the Spirit is effected by the sprinkling of Christ's Blood.** It is only by receiving the Blood of Redemption, he proves, that one can be changed from the state of Adam (original sin) to the state of grace (justification/sanctification). It is only by this Blood that Sanctification by the Spirit works. This dogma was also defined by the Council of Trent.

> Pope Paul III, *Council of Trent*, Sess. 5, on original sin, *ex cathedra*: "**If anyone asserts that this sin of Adam… is taken away either by the forces of human nature, or by any remedy other than the merit of the one mediator**, our Lord Jesus Christ, **who has reconciled us to God <u>in his own blood</u>, 'made unto us justice, sanctification, and redemption' (1 Cor. 1:30); <u>or if he denies that the merit of Jesus Christ is applied to adults as well as to infants by the sacrament of baptism</u>… let him be anathema.**"[242]

Pope Paul III, *Council of Trent*, Sess. 6, Chap. 3, *ex cathedra*: "But although Christ died for all, yet not all receive the benefit of His death, **but those <u>only</u> to whom the merit of His Passion is communicated.**"[243]

It is a divinely revealed truth that no one can be freed from the state of sin and sanctified without the application of the Blood of Redemption to him. Of this no Catholic can doubt.

Baptism of desire/blood advocates – and this would also include the St. Benedict Center, since they also believe in justification by desire – argue that the Blood of Redemption, which effects the Sanctification by the Spirit, is applied to the soul by the desire for baptism or by his martyrdom, *without water baptism*. Remember that: **baptism of desire/blood advocates argue that <u>the Blood of Redemption</u>, which effects Sanctification by the Spirit, <u>is applied to the soul without water baptism</u>**. But this is *exactly* the opposite of what Pope Leo the Great defines dogmatically! I will quote the crucial portions of his statement again:

> Pope St. Leo the Great, dogmatic letter to Flavian, *Council of Chalcedon*, 451: "Let him heed what the blessed apostle Peter preaches, that sanctification by the Spirit is effected by the sprinkling of Christ's blood (1 Pet. 1:2)… It is He, Jesus Christ, who has come through water and blood, not in water only, but in water and blood. And because the Spirit is truth, it is the Spirit who testifies. For there are three who give testimony – Spirit and water and blood. And the three are one. (1 Jn. 5:4-8) **IN OTHER WORDS, <u>THE SPIRIT</u> OF SANCTIFICATION AND <u>THE BLOOD</u> OF REDEMPTION AND <u>THE WATER</u> OF BAPTISM. THESE THREE ARE ONE AND REMAIN INDIVISIBLE. NONE OF THEM IS SEPARABLE FROM ITS LINK WITH THE OTHERS.**"[244]

Pope St. Leo defines that in Sanctification, the Spirit of Sanctification and the Blood of Redemption *cannot* be separated from <u>the water of baptism</u>! Thus, there can be no Justification by the Spirit and the Blood without the Sacrament of Baptism.

This infallibly excludes the very concept of baptism of desire and baptism of blood, which is that sanctification by the Spirit and the Blood <u>without water</u> is possible.

In light of this dogmatic letter, as well as the other facts already brought forward, baptism of desire and baptism of blood cannot be held; for these theories separate the Spirit and the Blood from the water in sanctification.

And lest someone tries to find fault with this infallible definition by arguing that the Blessed Virgin Mary is an exception to it, it should be recognized that Pope St. Leo is defining on *sanctification/justification* from the state of sin.

> Pope St. Leo the Great, **dogmatic** letter to Flavian, *Council of Chalcedon*, 451: "Let him heed what the blessed apostle Peter preaches, that *sanctification* by the Spirit is effected by the sprinkling of Christ's blood (1 Pet. 1:2); and let him not skip over the same apostle's words, *knowing that **you have been redeemed from the empty way of life** you inherited from your fathers, not with corruptible gold and silver but by the precious blood of Jesus Christ, as of a lamb without stain or spot* (1 Pet. 1:18). Nor should he withstand the testimony of blessed John the apostle: *and the blood of Jesus, the Son of God, **purifies us from every sin*** (1 Jn. 1:7)…"

The Blessed Virgin Mary had no sin. She was conceived already in a state of perfect sanctification. Since Pope Leo is defining on sanctification/justification from sin, his definition does not apply in any way to her.

Therefore, there can be no Justification of a sinner without water baptism (*de fide*). There can be no application to a sinner of Christ's Redemptive Blood without water baptism (*de fide*). There can be no salvation without water baptism (*de fide*).

To further prove the point that this dogmatic pronouncement specifically <u>eliminates the entire theory of baptism of desire</u>, notice how St. Thomas Aquinas (in teaching baptism of desire) says exactly the opposite of what Pope St. Leo the Great defined.

> St. Thomas Aquinas, *Summa Theologica* III, Q. 68, Art. 2: "…a man can obtain salvation **without the sacrament of Baptism,** by means of the invisible **sanctification**…"

St. Thomas says that baptism of desire gives one <u>sanctification</u> without <u>the water</u> of Baptism. Pope St. Leo the Great says dogmatically and infallibly that one cannot have sanctification without the water of baptism! A Catholic must accept Pope St. Leo the Great's teaching.

> Pope St. Leo the Great, **dogmatic** letter to Flavian, *Council of Chalcedon*, 451: "IN OTHER WORDS, THE SPIRIT OF **SANCTIFICATION** AND THE BLOOD OF REDEMPTION AND **THE WATER OF BAPTISM.** THESE THREE **ARE ONE AND REMAIN INDIVISIBLE. <u>NONE OF THEM IS SEPARABLE</u> FROM ITS LINK WITH THE OTHERS.**"[245]

The significance of Pope St. Leo's pronouncement is extraordinary. It naturally crushes any idea of salvation for the supposedly "invincibly ignorant." These souls cannot be sanctified and cleansed by the Blood of Christ without receiving the saving waters of baptism, which God will bring to all of good will.

The dogma that the Blood of Christ is applied to a sinner in the Sacrament of Baptism was defined by the Council of Trent; however, the definition is not as specific as Pope Leo's. The difference is that, whereas Trent's definition on the Blood of Christ sets forth the principle that the Blood of Christ is applied to a sinner in the Sacrament of Baptism, Pope Leo's definition **confirms** that this means that the Blood of Christ can *only* be applied to a sinner by the Sacrament of Baptism.

> Pope Paul III, *Council of Trent*, Sess. 5, on original sin, *ex cathedra*: "If anyone asserts that this sin of Adam... is taken away either by the forces of human nature, or by any remedy other than the merit of the one mediator, our Lord Jesus Christ, who has reconciled us to God **in his own blood**, 'made unto us justice, sanctification, and redemption' (1 Cor. 1:30); **or if he denies that the merit of Jesus Christ is applied to adults as well as to infants by the sacrament of baptism**… let him be anathema."[246]

Pope St. Leo's pronouncement also radically confirms the Church's consistent understanding of the words of Jesus Christ in John 3:5 in their absolutely literal sense: Unless a man is born again of water and the Spirit, he cannot enter into the kingdom of God.

> Pope Eugene IV, *The Council of Florence*, "Exultate Deo," Nov. 22, 1439, *ex cathedra*: **"And since death entered the universe through the first man, 'unless we are born again of water and the Spirit, we cannot,' as the Truth says, 'enter into the kingdom of heaven' [John 3:5].** The matter of this sacrament is real and natural water."[247]

> Pope Paul III, *The Council of Trent*, On Original Sin, Session V: "By one man sin entered into the world, and by sin death... so that in them there may be washed away by regeneration, what they have contracted by generation, *'For unless a man be born again of water and the Holy Ghost, he cannot enter into the kingdom of God* [John 3:5]."[248]

Pope Paul III, *The Council of Trent*, canons on the Sacrament of Baptism, Session 7, canon 2, *ex cathedra*: "If anyone shall say that real and natural water is not necessary for baptism, and on that account those words of Our Lord Jesus Christ: '**Unless a man be born again of water and the Holy Spirit**' [John 3:5], are distorted into some sort of metaphor: let him be anathema."[249]

Pope Paul III, *The Council of Trent*, canons on the Sacrament of Baptism, canon 5, *ex cathedra*: "**If anyone says that baptism is optional, that is, not necessary for salvation (cf. Jn. 3:5): let him be anathema.**"[250]

One can see the harmony of Pope St. Leo the Great's dogmatic pronouncement with all of these others: there is no salvation without water and the Spirit because the Blood of Christ – without which no one is justified – is itself inseparable from the water and the Spirit.

Those who comprehend this pronouncement from Pope St. Leo must reject any belief in the theories of baptism of desire and blood. They must admit that the theologians who believed in baptism of desire and blood were mistaken. They must cease believing and teaching that Sanctification by the Spirit comes without the water of baptism. Those who *refuse* to do this are *obstinately* contradicting the teaching of the Church. To obstinately contradict the teaching of the Church is to fall into heresy. To fall into heresy without repentance is to lose one's salvation.

Some may wonder why some saints and theologians taught baptism of desire and blood even after the time of Pope Leo's pronouncement. The answer is simple: They were unaware of Pope Leo's definitive pronouncement in this regard; they were erring in good faith; they were fallible human beings; they were not aware that their position was contrary to this infallible teaching of the Catholic Church.

But once one recognizes that this position on baptism of desire and blood is contrary to the infallible teaching of the Catholic Church – as a careful consideration of Pope Leo's pronouncement proves – **one must change his position if he wants to remain Catholic and save his soul**. St. Peter has spoken through the mouth of Leo and confirmed for us that the Spirit of Sanctification and the Blood of redemption cannot be separated from their link with water baptism, so we must align our position with this or else we don't have the faith of Peter.

16. Major Objections

SESS. 6, CHAP. 4 OF THE COUNCIL OF TRENT

<u>OBJECTION</u>- In Session 6, Chapter 4 of its decree on Justification, the Council of Trent teaches that justification can take place by the water of baptism or the desire for it! So there!

<u>ANSWER</u>- [**Preliminary Note**: If Sess. 6, Chap. 4 of Trent were teaching what the baptism of desire advocates claim (<u>which it isn't</u>), then it would mean that every man must receive baptism <u>or at least have the actual desire/vow for baptism to be saved</u>. It would mean that it would be <u>**heresy**</u> to say that any unbaptized person could be saved if he doesn't have at least the desire/vow <u>for water baptism</u>. But 99% of the people who quote this passage in favor of baptism of desire don't even believe that one must desire baptism to be saved! They believe that Jews, Buddhists, Hindus, Muslims, etc. can be saved <u>who don't desire water baptism</u>. Thus, 99% of those who quote this passage **reject even what they claim it is teaching.** Frankly, this fact just shows the dishonesty and the bad will of most baptism of desire advocates in attempting to quote this passage as if they were devoted to its teaching when, in fact, they don't believe in it at all and are in heresy for teaching that non-Catholics can be saved who don't even desire water baptism.]

That being noted, this passage of the Council of Trent does <u>not</u> teach that Justification <u>can</u> take place by the water of baptism or the desire for it. It says that justification in the impious <u>**CANNOT TAKE PLACE WITHOUT**</u> the water of baptism or the desire for it. This is totally different from the idea that justification <u>can</u> take place by the water of baptism or the desire for it.

> Pope Paul III, *Council of Trent*, Sess. 6, Chap. 4: "In these words there is suggested a description of the justification of the impious, how there is a transition from that state in which a person is born as a child of the first Adam to the state of grace and of adoption as sons of God through the second Adam, Jesus Christ our savior; indeed, this transition, once the gospel has been promulgated, **CANNOT TAKE PLACE WITHOUT** the laver of regeneration or a desire for it, <u>**AS IT IS WRITTEN**</u>: *Unless a man is born again of water and the Holy Spirit, he cannot enter the kingdom of God* **(John 3:5)."**[251]

First off, the reader should note that this crucial passage from Trent has been horribly mistranslated in Denzinger, the Sources of Catholic Dogma. The critical phrase, *"this transition, once the gospel has been promulgated,* ***cannot take place <u>without</u>*** *the laver of regeneration or a desire for it"* has been mistranslated to read: *"this transition, once the gospel* *has been promulgated,* **cannot take place** <u>*except through*</u> *the laver of regeneration or a desire for it…"* This mistranslation of the Latin word *"sine"* (without) to "except through" completely alters the meaning of the passage to favor the error of baptism of desire. This is important to keep in mind because this mistranslation is still being used all the time by baptism of desire apologists (often deliberately), including in recent publications of the SSPX and CMRI. That being mentioned, I will proceed to discuss what the Council actually says here.

Looking at a correct translation, which is found in many books, the reader also should notice that, in this passage, the Council of Trent teaches that John 3:5 is to be taken *as it is written* **(Latin:** *sicut scriptum est***), which excludes any possibility of salvation without being born again of** <u>water</u> **in the Sacrament of Baptism.** There is no way that baptism of desire can be true if John 3:5 is to be taken as it is written, because John 3:5 says that every man must be born again of <u>water</u> and the Spirit to be saved, which is what the theory of baptism of desire denies. The theory of baptism of desire and an interpretation of John 3:5 as it is written are mutually exclusive (they cannot both be true at the same time) – and every baptism of desire proponent will admit this. That is why all of them must – and do – opt for a <u>non-literal</u> interpretation of John 3:5.

> Fr. Francois Laisney (Believer in Baptism of Desire), *Is Feeneyism Catholic*, p. 33: "Fr. Feeney's greatest argument was that Our Lord's words, *'Unless a man be born again of water and the Holy Ghost, he cannot enter into the kingdom of God'* (John 3:5) mean the absolute necessity of baptism of water with no exception whatsoever… The great question is, then, how did the Church explain these words of Our Lord?"

Fr. Laisney, a fierce baptism of desire advocate, is <u>admitting</u> here that John 3:5 cannot be understood *as it is written* if baptism of desire is true. He therefore holds that the true understanding of John 3:5 is that it does not apply literally to all men; that is, John 3:5 is not to be taken *as it is written*. But how does the Catholic Church understand these words? What does the passage in Trent that we just discussed say: It says infallibly, **"*<u>AS IT IS WRITTEN</u>, UNLESS A MAN IS BORN AGAIN OF WATER AND THE HOLY GHOST, HE CANNOT ENTER INTO THE KINGDOM OF GOD.*"**

But what about the claim of the baptism of desire people: that the use of the word "or" (Latin: *aut*) in the above passage means that justification *__can__* take place by the water of baptism or the desire for it. A careful look at the correct translation of this passage shows this claim to be false. Suppose I said, *"This shower cannot take place <u>without</u> water or the desire to take one."* Does this mean that a shower can take place by the desire to take a shower? No it doesn't. It means that both (water and desire) are necessary.

Or suppose I said, *"There cannot be a Wedding <u>without</u> a Bride or a Groom."* Does this mean that you can have a Wedding with a Groom and not a Bride? Of course not. It means that both are necessary for the Wedding. One could give hundreds of other examples. Likewise, the passage above in Trent says that Justification **CANNOT TAKE PLACE WITHOUT** water or desire; in other words, both are necessary. It does <u>not</u> say that Justification *does take place* by either water or desire!

AUT (OR) USED TO MEAN "AND" IN THE CONTEXT OF COUNCILS

In fact, the Latin word *aut* ("or") is used in a similar way in other passages in the Council of Trent and other Councils. In the famous Bull *Cantate Domino* from the Council of Florence, we find the Latin word *aut* ("or") used in a context which definitely renders it meaning "and."

> Pope Eugene IV, *Council of Florence*, "Cantate Domino," 1441, *ex cathedra*:
> "The Holy Roman Church firmly believes, professes and preaches that all those who are outside the Catholic Church, not only pagans but also Jews *[aut]* **or** heretics and schismatics, cannot share in eternal life and will go into the everlasting fire which was prepared for the devil and his angels, unless they are joined to the Church before the end of their lives; that the unity of this ecclesiastical body is of such importance that only those who abide in it do the Church's sacraments contribute to salvation and do fasts, almsgiving and other works of piety and practices of the Christian militia productive of eternal rewards; and that nobody can be saved, no matter how much he has given away in alms and even if he has shed blood in the name of Christ, unless he has persevered in the bosom and unity of the Catholic Church."[252]

Here we see the Council of Florence using the word "or" (*aut*) to have a meaning that is equivalent to "and." The Council declares that not only pagans, but also Jews <u>or</u> (aut) heretics and schismatics cannot be saved. Does this mean that either Jews or heretics will be saved? Of course not. It clearly means that none of the Jews and none of the heretics can be saved. Thus, this is an example of a context in which the Latin word *aut* (or) does have a meaning that is clearly "and."

Similarly, in the introduction to the decree on Justification, the Council of Trent strictly forbids anyone to **"believe, preach <u>or</u> teach"** (*credere, praedicare **aut** docere*) other than as it is defined and declared in the decree on Justification.

> Pope Paul III, *Council of Trent*, Sess. 6, Introduction: "… strictly forbidding that anyone henceforth may presume to **believe, preach <u>or</u> teach, otherwise than is defined and declared by this present decree.**"[253]

Does "or" (*aut*) in this passage mean that **one is only forbidden to preach contrary** to the Council's decree on Justification, but one is allowed to teach contrary to it? No, obviously "or" (*aut*) means that **both** preaching and teaching are forbidden, just like in chapter 4 above "*or*" means that justification cannot take place <u>without</u> both water and desire. Another example of the use of *aut* to mean "and" (or "both") in Trent is found in Sess. 21, Chap. 2, the decree on Communion under both species (Denz. 931).

Pope Pius IV, *Council of Trent,* Sess. 21, Chap. 2: "Therefore holy mother Church… has decreed that it be considered as a law, **which may not be repudiated <u>or</u> be changed** at will without the authority of the Church."[254]

Does *aut* in this declaration mean that the Council's decree may not be repudiated, but it may be changed? No, obviously it means that <u>both</u> a repudiation and a change are forbidden. This is another example of how the Latin word *aut* can be used in contexts which render its meaning "and" or "both." **And these examples, when we consider the wording of the passage, refute the claim of baptism of desire supporters: that the meaning of *aut* in Chapter 4, Session 6 is one which favors baptism of desire.**

But why does Trent define that the desire for Baptism, along with Baptism, is necessary for Justification? In the past we did not answer this question as well as we could have, because we thought that Sess. 6, Chap. 4 was distinguishing between adults and infants. But further study of the passage reveals that in this chapter Trent is defining what is necessary for the *iustificationis impii* – the justification of the impious (see quote above). The impii *("impious")* does not refer to infants – who are incapable of committing *actual* sins (Trent, Sess. V, Denz. 791). The word "impii" in Latin is actually a very strong word, according to a Latin scholar I consulted, and he agreed that it is too strong to describe an infant in original sin only. It is sometimes translated as "wicked" or "sinner." Therefore, in this chapter, Trent is dealing with those above the age of reason who have committed actual sins, and for such persons <u>the desire for baptism is necessary for Justification</u>. In fact, the next few chapters of Trent on Justification (Chaps. 5-7) are all about adult Justification, further demonstrating that the Justification of adult sinners is the context, especially when the word *impii* is considered. That is why the chapter defines that Justification cannot take place **without** the water of baptism *or* the desire for it (both are necessary).

> *Catechism of the Council of Trent*, On Baptism - Dispositions for Baptism, p. 180: "INTENTION - … **In the first place they must <u>desire</u> and intend to receive it…**"[255]

AN INTERESTING E-MAIL REGARDING THIS PASSAGE OF TRENT

Interestingly, I happened to e-mail a question about this passage from the Council of Trent and its use of the word "or" (*aut*) to a Latin Scholar from England, just to get the person's thoughts. I do not even know this person whom I e-mailed, and I don't think that she is even a Catholic. She is a Latin Scholar from Oxford Latin and I believe she answered honestly and impartially. Her response is very interesting and very important, especially for those people who are convinced that the Council of Trent taught "baptism of desire." I wrote to her as follows:

"The passage in Latin is this: '*quae quidem translatio ... sine lavacro regenerationis aut eius voto fieri non potest...*'

"It is translated: 'This transition... cannot take place without the laver of regeneration or a desire for it.'

"This literally says that the transition cannot happen without the laver of regeneration or a desire for it (meaning you must have both). It does not say that it can take place with either one, don't you agree? Is it not equivalent to my saying: This shower cannot take place without water or the desire to take one (meaning both are necessary); and is it not equivalent to saying: this article cannot be written without pen or pad (meaning both are necessary)? You can use *aut* in this way in Latin, can you not?

"Any thoughts you have I would be very interested in. Thank you."

And she responded on Dec. 1, 2003 as follows:

"This is not easy! **It is possible to make sense of it in both ways, <u>with aut as 'or' and as 'and'</u>.**
"*Aut* as 'or' is more common, **but here the interpretation depends on whether you think that the desire for baptism is enough on its own or whether the phrase signifies that you need the desire as well as the sacrament itself.**
I'll leave it to you to decide!
Best wishes,
Carolinne White
OXFORD LATIN"

While I disagree with Ms. White that the passage can be read in both ways, her testimony is nevertheless very interesting. (I disagree with that point because to say that something cannot take place <u>without</u> "x" or "x" is not necessarily to say that something can take place <u>with</u> either "x" alone or "x" alone. I don't believe that Ms. White is reading the passage literally enough. For example: to say a sacrament cannot take place <u>without</u> matter *or* form is not to say that a sacrament can take place <u>with</u> matter alone or form alone.) Nevertheless, Ms. White's statement is very important and very interesting in that it shows that in her professional opinion as a Latin Scholar, the passage using "or" (*aut*) **can definitely be read as "and," something many baptism of desire advocates absolutely reject as impossible! She further admits that the interpretation depends upon whether one believes that the desire for baptism is enough** – I believe a very honest statement in her regard! And she said this without my giving her the rest of the context; namely, where the Council of Trent declares, <u>immediately after</u> using the words "or the desire for it," that John 3:5 is to be understood *as it is written*.

> Pope Paul III, *Council of Trent*, Sess. 6, Chap. 4: "[Justification]… **cannot take place without** the laver of regeneration or a desire for it, **AS IT IS WRITTEN**: *Unless a man is born again of water and the Holy Spirit, he cannot enter the kingdom of God (John 3:5).*" [256]

The point is, therefore, that, <u>at the very least</u>, all baptism of desire advocates must admit that this passage can be read both ways, and therefore that **the understanding depends upon whether one believes that the desire for baptism is enough or not. But if a baptism of desire advocate admits (as he must in honesty) that this passage** *may* **not teach baptism of desire, then he is admitting that the understanding of it must be garnered not only from the immediate context (which affirms John 3:5** *as it is written* **and therefore excludes baptism of desire), but also from all of the other statements on Baptism and Justification in Trent.** And what do all of the other passages in Trent say on the necessity of Baptism? Do they teach an understanding open to baptism of desire, or do they exclude any salvation without water baptism? The answer is undeniable.

> Pope Paul III, *The Council of Trent*, canons on the <u>Sacrament</u> of Baptism, canon 5, *ex cathedra*: **"If anyone says that baptism [the sacrament] is optional, that is, not necessary for salvation (cf. Jn. 3:5): let him be anathema."**[257]

> Pope Paul III, *The Council of Trent*, On Original Sin, Session V, *ex cathedra*: "By one man sin entered into the world, and by sin death… so that in them there may be washed away by regeneration, what they have contracted by generation, *'For unless a man be born again of water and the Holy Ghost, he cannot enter into the kingdom of God* [John 3:5]."[258]

> Pope Paul III, *The Council of Trent*, canons on the Sacrament of Baptism, Session 7, canon 2, *ex cathedra*: **"If anyone shall say that real and natural water is not necessary for baptism, and on that account those words of Our Lord Jesus Christ: 'Unless a man be born again of water and the Holy Spirit' [John 3:5], are distorted into some sort of metaphor: let him be anathema."**[259]

The interpretation of "or" in Sess. 6., Chap. 4 as "and" is not only possible (as Ms. White admits), but it is <u>perfectly compatible with all of these infallible definitions</u>, while the interpretation of "*or*" as meaning baptism of desire is <u>incompatible</u> with all of these definitions, not to mention (most importantly) the words "*as it is written*, unless a man is born again of water and the Spirit he cannot enter into the kingdom of God," **which come immediately after** "or a desire for it" **and in the same sentence**.

The interpretation of "or" as meaning baptism of desire is also incompatible with the teaching of the Council of Florence on John 3:5, and there cannot exist disharmony between dogmatic councils.

> Pope Eugene IV, *The Council of Florence*, "Exultate Deo," Nov. 22, 1439, *ex cathedra*: "Holy baptism, which is the gateway to the spiritual life, holds the first place among all the sacraments; through it we are made members of Christ and of the body of the Church. **And since death entered the universe through the first man, 'unless we are born again of <u>water and the Spirit</u>, we cannot,' as the Truth says, 'enter into the kingdom of heaven' [John 3:5].** The matter of this sacrament is real and natural water."[260]

The interpretation of "or" as meaning baptism of desire is also incompatible with the Council of Trent's extensive definition just three chapters later on the causes of Justification. Just three chapters later, the Council lists four causes for Justification in the impious.

> Pope Paul III, Council of Trent, Sess. 6, Chap. 7, the Causes of Justification: "The causes of this Justification are: <u>the final cause</u> is the glory of God and of Christ… <u>the efficient cause</u> is truly a merciful God… <u>the meritorious</u> cause is His most beloved and only-begotten Son… **the instrumental cause is the sacrament of baptism, which is the sacrament of faith**, without faith no one is ever justified… **This faith**, in accordance with apostolic tradition, **catechumens beg of the Church before the sacrament of baptism**, when they ask for faith which bestows life eternal…"[261]

In listing all of the causes of Justification, why didn't the Council mention the possibility of "baptism of desire"? It had ample opportunity to do so, just as it clearly taught no less than 3 times that the graces of the Sacrament of Penance can be attained by the desire for that Sacrament (Sess. 14, Chap. 4; and twice in Sess. 6, Chap. 14). But "baptism of desire" is mentioned nowhere, simply because it is not true. And it is further interesting to consider that **the word "desire" shows up <u>not in Chapter 7 on the Causes</u> of Justification, but in Chapter 4 where the Council is talking about <u>what cannot be missing in the Justification of the impious</u>** (namely, neither water nor desire can be missing in the justification of the impious).

But some will say: "*I see your point and I cannot deny it, but why didn't the passage use the word 'and' instead of 'or'; it would have been clearer then?*" This question is best answered by considering a number of things:

First, it must be remembered that the passage describes what Justification **CANNOT TAKE PLACE WITHOUT** (i.e., what cannot be missing in Justification); it does not say that Justification *does take place* by either water or desire.

Second, the Council didn't have to use "and" because "or" can mean "and" in the context of words given in the passage, as shown already.

Third, those who ask this question should consider another, namely: *why in the world, if baptism of desire is true and was the teaching of Trent, didn't the Council say anywhere (when it had so many opportunities to do so) that one can be justified without the Sacrament or before the Sacrament is received* just as it clearly and repeatedly did in regard to the Sacrament of Penance? This amazing *omission* (obviously because the Holy Ghost didn't allow the Council to teach baptism of desire in its many statements on the absolute necessity of baptism) simply confirms the points that I've made above, because if the passage meant baptism of desire it would have said so.

Fourth, the above question is best answered by a parallel example: In 381 the Council of Constantinople defined that the Holy Ghost proceeds from the Father. The Council did not say that the Holy Ghost proceeds from the Father and the Son. The omission of the words "*and the Son*" (*filioque* in Latin) caused countless millions to erroneously conclude that the Holy Ghost does not proceed from the Son, a heresy that was later condemned by the Church. **If the Council of Constantinople had simply included that little statement, that the Holy Ghost also proceeds from the Son, it would have eliminated over a thousand years of controversy with the Eastern Schismatics** – a controversy which still continues to this day. That little phrase ("and the Son"), if it had been included in Constantinople, surely would have stopped millions of people from leaving the Catholic Church and embracing Eastern Orthodoxy, because the Eastern Orthodox thought and still think that the Catholic Church's teaching that the Holy Ghost proceeds from Father and the Son is contrary to the Council of Constantinople, which only said that the Holy Ghost proceeds from the Father.

So, did the Council of Constantinople err? Of course not. But could Constantinople have been more clear by adding that little phrase which would have eliminated a controversy? Absolutely. So why did God allow this controversy to occur, when He could have prevented it by simply inspiring the Council Fathers at Constantinople in 381 to include that tiny phrase? The answer is that there must be heresies.

1 Cor. 11:19: "For there must be also heresies: that they also, who are approved, may be manifest among you."

God allows heresies to arise in order to see who will believe the truth and who will not, to see who will look at the truth sincerely and who will pervert things to suit his own heretical desires. God never allows His Councils, such as Constantinople and Trent, to teach any error, but He can allow the truth to be stated in ways that give people the opportunity to twist and pervert the meaning of the words used if they so desire (no pun intended), as the Eastern Schismatics did in regard to Constantinople's omission of the phrase: *and the Son*.

In fact, <u>it doesn't even matter if some of the Council Fathers at Constantinople believed that the Holy Ghost does not proceed from the Son</u>; and there were probably some who didn't believe that the Holy Ghost proceeds from the Son. All that matters is what the Council of Constantinople actually declared, a declaration which says nothing *contrary* to the fact that the Holy Ghost does proceed from the Son. The <u>intentions</u> of the Council Fathers at Constantinople or any other Council have nothing to do with Papal Infallibility. **All that matters is what the actual dogma declares or finalizes in the Profession of Faith.**

> Pope Pius IX, *First Vatican Council*, Sess. 3, Chap. 2 on Revelation, 1870, *ex cathedra*: "Hence, also, that understanding of its sacred dogmas must be perpetually retained, which Holy Mother Church <u>has once declared</u>; and there must never be a recession from that meaning under the specious name of a deeper understanding."[262]

Interesting in this regard is the fact that numerous Popes point out that, in the 28th canon of the *Council of Chalcedon,* the fathers at Chalcedon drew up a canon that elevated the status of the Bishop of Constantinople. **The fathers of the *Council of Chalcedon*, therefore, *intended* to elevate the status of the See of Constantinople in drawing up Canon 28. But the canon was rejected by the Pope in his confirmation of the acts of Chalcedon, and therefore was considered worthless.**

Pope Leo XIII, *Satis Cognitum* (#15), June 29, 1896: "The 28th Canon of the Council of Chalcedon, by the very fact that it lacks the assent and approval of the Apostolic See, <u>is admitted by all to be worthless</u>."[263]

This shows that the intention or thoughts of the fathers at a General Council mean nothing – they are worthless. All that matters is what the Church actually declares. Therefore, the fact that some of the Council Fathers at Trent – and even eminent and sainted theologians after Trent – thought the aforementioned passage of Trent taught baptism of desire means nothing; for the fathers at *Chalcedon* also thought the Council was elevating the status of Constantinople, when it didn't; and some of the fathers at Constantinople probably thought that the Council was denying that the Holy Ghost proceeds from the Son, when it didn't. The bottom-line is that only those things that are actually declared by the Councils matter – nothing else. And the aforementioned passage of Trent does not teach baptism of desire; it does not teach that desire justifies without baptism; and it does not contain error.

The fact is that <u>God made sure that the words "as it is written" were included in that very sentence</u> to ensure that the Council was not teaching baptism of desire by its wording in that passage. The passage thus teaches – *as it is written* – *unless a man is born again of water and the Holy Ghost he cannot enter into the Kingdom of God*. And **if what baptism of desire proponents say were correct, we would actually have the Council teaching us in the first part of the sentence that** *John 3:5 is <u>not</u> to be taken as it is written* **(desire sometimes suffices), while simultaneously contradicting itself in the second part of the sentence by telling us to take John 3:5** *as it is written* **(***sicut scriptum est***)! But this is absurd, of course.** Those who obstinately insist that this passage teaches baptism of desire are simply wrong and are contradicting the very words given in the passage about John 3:5. **The inclusion of "***<u>AS IT IS WRITTEN</u>***,** *unless a man is born again of water and the Holy Spirit, he cannot enter the kingdom of God (John 3:5)"* **shows the perfect harmony of that passage in Trent with all of the other passages** in Trent and other Councils which affirm the absolute necessity of water baptism <u>with no exceptions</u>.

THE DOGMA, POPE PIUS IX AND INVINCIBLE IGNORANCE

<u>OBJECTION</u>- What about Invincible Ignorance?

<u>ANSWER</u>-

> 2 Corinthians 4:3: "***And if our gospel be hid, it is hid to them that are lost***, *in whom the god of this world [Satan] hath blinded the minds of unbelievers, that the light of the gospel of the glory of Christ, who is the image of God, should not shine unto them.*"

The dogma Outside the Catholic Church There is No Salvation has been solemnly defined at least seven times by Popes speaking from the Chair of St. Peter. Never once were any exceptions mentioned about "invincible ignorance." In fact, it is just the opposite: <u>all exceptions were always excluded</u>.

Pope Innocent III, *Fourth Lateran Council*, Constitution 1, 1215, *ex cathedra*: "There is indeed one universal Church of the faithful, outside of which <u>nobody at all is saved</u>, in which Jesus Christ is both priest and sacrifice."[264]

Pope Boniface VIII, *Unam Sanctam*, Nov. 18, 1302, *ex cathedra*:
"With Faith urging us we are forced to believe and to hold the one, holy, Catholic Church and that, apostolic, and we firmly believe and simply confess this Church outside of which there is <u>no salvation</u> nor remission of sin… Furthermore, we declare, say, define, and proclaim to <u>every human creature</u> that they by absolute necessity for salvation are entirely subject to the Roman Pontiff."[265]

Pope Clement V, *Council of Vienne*, Decree # 30, 1311-1312, *ex cathedra*:" Since however there is for both regulars and seculars, for superiors and subjects, for exempt and non-exempt, *one universal Church, outside of which there is <u>no salvation</u>*, for all of whom there is *one Lord, one faith, and one baptism…*"[266]

Pope Eugene IV, *Council of Florence*, Sess. 8, Nov. 22, 1439:
"<u>Whoever</u> *wishes* to be saved, needs above all to hold the Catholic faith; unless <u>each one</u> preserves this whole and inviolate, he will without a doubt perish in eternity."[267]

Pope Eugene IV, *Council of Florence*, "Cantate Domino," 1441, *ex cathedra*:
"The Holy Roman Church firmly believes, professes and preaches that <u>all those who are outside</u> the Catholic Church, not only <u>pagans</u> but also Jews or <u>heretics</u> and <u>schismatics</u>, cannot share in eternal life and will go into the everlasting fire which was prepared for the devil and his angels, unless they are joined to the Church before the end of their lives; that the unity of this ecclesiastical body is of such importance that <u>only those who abide in it</u> do the Church's sacraments contribute to salvation and do fasts, almsgiving and other works of piety and practices of the Christian militia productive of eternal rewards; and that <u>nobody</u> can be saved, no matter how much he has given away in alms and even if he has shed blood in the name of Christ, unless he has persevered in the bosom and unity of the Catholic Church."[268]

Pope Leo X, *Fifth Lateran Council*, Session 11, Dec. 19, 1516, *ex cathedra*: "For, regulars and seculars, prelates and subjects, exempt and non-exempt, belong to the one universal Church, outside of which <u>no one at all is saved</u>, and they all have *one Lord and one faith*."[269]

Pope Pius IV, Council of Trent, *Iniunctum nobis*, Nov. 13, 1565, *ex cathedra*: *"This true Catholic faith, outside of which <u>no one</u> can be saved*… I now profess and truly hold…"[270]

Pope Benedict XIV, *Nuper ad nos*, March 16, 1743, Profession of Faith: "This faith of the Catholic Church, without which <u>no one</u> can be saved, and which of my own accord I now profess and truly hold…"[271]

Pope Pius IX, *Vatican Council I*, Session 2, Profession of Faith, 1870, *ex cathedra*: "This true Catholic faith, outside of which <u>none</u> can be saved, which I now freely profess and truly hold…"[272]

The Catholic Church is infallible; Her dogmatic definitions are infallible; Popes speaking from the Chair of Peter are infallible. Thus, it is very simple: If it were true that so-called "invincibly ignorant" non-Catholics could be saved, then GOD WOULD NEVER HAVE ALLOWED THE CATHOLIC CHURCH TO DEFINE THE DOGMA THAT <u>NO ONE</u> AT ALL CAN BE SAVED OUTSIDE THE CATHOLIC CHURCH! But

God did allow His infallible Church to define this truth, WHICH SPECIFICALLY EXCLUDES FROM SALVATION <u>EVERYONE</u> WHO DOES NOT DIE A CATHOLIC.

Thus, the idea that a non-Catholic who is ignorant of the Faith can be saved is <u>heretical</u>; it is a direct denial of the dogma that *"no one,"* (Pope Pius IV; Benedict XIV; Pius IX) *"nobody at all,"* (Innocent III) *"nobody,* even if he shed his blood in the name of Christ" (Eugene IV) can be saved as a non-Catholic. It is a denial of the dogma that **"every human creature"** (Boniface VIII) must be a Catholic, and that *"only those"* (Eugene IV) inside the bosom and unity of the Church can achieve salvation.

> Pope Gregory XVI, *Summo Iugiter Studio* (# 2), May 27, 1832:
> "Finally some of **these misguided people attempt to persuade themselves and others that men are not saved only in the Catholic religion**, but that even heretics may attain eternal life."[273]

Those who insist that "invincible ignorance" can possibly save a person who dies as a non-Catholic simply depart from and deny the dogmatic teaching of the Catholic Church.

POPE PIUS IX AND INVINCIBLE IGNORANCE

What about Pope Pius IX? Isn't it true that he taught that the invincibly ignorant could be saved in two documents? What about *Singulari Quadem* and *Quanto Conficiamur Moerore?*

Confusion on this topic has increased as a result of a few misunderstood statements from Pope Pius IX. As we analyze these statements, **it is imperative to keep in mind that, even if Pope Pius IX had taught that the invincibly ignorant could be saved on these two occasions, it wouldn't mean that such a position is true, because they were <u>fallible</u> documents which could have contained error**. No Pope can change or contradict dogma. Pope Honorius, who reigned in the 7th century, was, in fact, later condemned for propagating heresy, though not in his solemn capacity teaching to the universal Church. Thus, no one, not even a Pope, can change the dogma that no one who dies outside the Catholic Church, ignorant or not, can be saved. Here are some more quotes on ignorance.

> Pope Benedict XV, *Humani Generis Redemptionem* (# 14), June 15, 1917:
> "…'Ignorance is the mother of all errors,' as the Fourth Lateran Council so truthfully observes."[274]

> *The Errors of Peter Abelard*, Condemned by Innocent II, July 16, 1140, #10: "That they have not sinned who being ignorant have crucified Christ, **and that**

whatever is done through ignorance must not be considered sin." - Condemned[275]

SINGULARI QUADEM, AN ALLOCUTION (A SPEECH TO THE CARDINALS)

The first of the documents from Pope Pius IX, frequently quoted by those who believe in salvation outside the Church, is *Singulari Quadem*, an Allocution (a speech to the Cardinals) given December 9, 1854:

"....those who are affected by ignorance of the true religion, if it is invincible ignorance, are not subject to any guilt in this matter before the eyes of the Lord."

First of all, this is a <u>speech</u> of Pope Pius IX to the Cardinals. It is not a dogmatic pronouncement, not even an encyclical, nor even an encyclical addressed to the entire Church. But is Pope Pius IX saying that the invincibly ignorant can be justified and saved in their condition? No. Rather, he is stating that the "invincibly ignorant" will not be held accountable for the sin of infidelity, but they will still go to Hell. Read carefully the last part of the sentence, "are not subject to any guilt <u>IN THIS MATTER</u>," that is, in the matter of infidelity. St. Thomas Aquinas explains that **unbelievers who have never heard of the Gospel are damned for their other sins**, which cannot be remitted without Faith, not because of the sin of infidelity (or disbelief in the Gospel).[276] These other sins of the unbelievers serve as the reason why God does not reveal the Gospel to them and which ultimately exclude them from salvation. If one among them, however, were truly sincere and of good will, and cooperating with the natural law, then God would send a preacher (even miraculously, if necessary) to bring the Catholic Faith and baptism to him. Pope Pius IX goes on to say in the same Allocution concerning a person of good will who is invincibly ignorant:

"the gifts of heavenly grace will assuredly not be denied to those who sincerely want and pray for refreshment by the divine light."

St. Thomas Aquinas, *De Veritate*, 14, A. 11, ad 1: Objection- **"It is possible that someone may be brought up in the forest, or among wolves; such a man cannot explicitly know anything about the faith.** St. Thomas replies- It is the characteristic of Divine Providence to provide every man with what is necessary for salvation... provided on his part there is no hindrance. In the case of a man who seeks good and shuns evil, by the leading of natural reason, **God would either reveal to him through internal inspiration what had to be believed, or would send some preacher of the faith to him...**"[277]

St. Thomas Aquinas, *Sent. II, 28, Q. 1, A. 4, ad 4*: "If a man born among barbarian nations, does what he can, God Himself will show him what is necessary for salvation, either by inspiration or sending a teacher to him."[278]

St. Thomas Aquinas, Sent. III, 25, Q. 2, A. 2, solute. 2: **"If a man should have no one to instruct him, God will show him,** unless he culpably wishes to remain where he is."[279]

Thus, Pope Pius IX was not teaching that people who are ignorant of the Catholic Faith can be saved; he was, rather, stating that such unbelievers are not damned for the matter of infidelity. The fact that <u>all</u> who die as ignorant non-Catholics are not saved is the affirmation of all of Catholic Tradition and all the Saints, besides being the dogmatic teaching of the Catholic Church.

St. Alphonsus Liguori, Sermons (c. +1760): **"How many are born among the pagans, among the Jews, among the Mohometans and heretics, <u>and all are lost</u>."**[280]

St. Alphonsus: "If you are ignorant of the truths of the faith, you are obliged to learn them. Every Christian is bound to learn the Creed, the Our Father, and the Hail Mary under pain of mortal sin. **Many have no idea of the Most Holy Trinity, the Incarnation, mortal sin, Judgment, Paradise, Hell, or Eternity; and this deplorable ignorance damns them.**"[281]

St. Alphonsus, Preparation For Death, (c. +1760): "How thankful we ought to be to Jesus Christ for the gift of faith! **What would have become of us if we had been born in Asia, Africa, America, or in the midst of heretics and schismatics? He who does not believe is lost**. This, then, was the first and greatest grace bestowed on us: our calling to the true faith. O Savior of the world, **what would become of us if Thou hadst not enlightened us? We would have been like our fathers of old, who adored animals and blocks of stone and wood: and thus we would have all perished**."[282]

Though *Singulari Quadem* of Pius IX did not teach the HERESY that one can be saved without the Catholic Faith by invincible ignorance, it is weakly worded. Pope Pius IX should not have concerned himself with trying to satisfy the heretical minds of liberals and apostates who refuse to accept Church dogma. He should have simply repeated the many times defined dogma that everyone who dies without the Catholic Faith is lost, and clearly explained that no one who is of good will will be left in ignorance of the true religion. But because of his weakly worded statement, and the following one we will examine, **a veritable disaster has resulted. Almost every single person who wants to advance his heretical belief that one can be saved outside the Catholic Church quotes this <u>fallible</u> statement from Pope Pius IX and the other one we will examine.**

What's interesting, however, and further confirms the point above, is that in *Singulari Quadem*, after explaining how the invincibly ignorant are not held guilty in <u>this matter</u>,

Pope Pius IX declares that a Catholic must hold one Lord, one Faith and one Baptism, and that it is unlawful to proceed further in inquiry! – probably in an attempt to stem the tide of belief that one could be saved outside the Church by "baptism of desire." The people who believe in salvation outside the Church almost never quote this part of the Allocution.

> **Pope Pius IX,** *Singulari Quadem*: "For, in truth, when released from these corporeal chains, 'we shall see God as He is' (1 John 3:2), we shall understand perfectly by how close and beautiful a bond divine mercy and justice are united; but, as long as we are on earth, weighed down by this mortal mass which blunts the soul, **let us hold most firmly that, in accordance with Catholic teaching, there is 'one God, <u>one faith, one baptism'</u> [Eph. 4:5]; <u>it is unlawful to proceed further in inquiry</u>.**"[283]

Therefore, even **Pope Pius IX,** in the very statement wrongly quoted by the liberals against the dogma Outside the Church There is No Salvation, **admonishes that such theorizing about salvation by** *other baptisms and other faiths* **is unlawful.**

QUANTO CONFICIAMUR MOERORE

Pope Pius IX proceeded to speak about the invincibly ignorant again seven years later in his encyclical *Quanto Conficiamur Moerore*, August 10, 1863. *Quanto Conficiamur Moerore* does not meet the requirements for infallibility; it is addressed only to the Cardinals and Bishops of Italy.[284]

> *"And here, beloved Sons and Venerable Brothers, **We should mention again and censure a very grave error in which some Catholics are unhappily engaged, who believe that men living in error, and separated from the true faith and from Catholic unity, can attain eternal life.** Indeed, this is certainly quite contrary to Catholic teaching. It is known to us and to you that they who labor in invincible ignorance of our most holy religion AND WHO ZEALOUSLY KEEPING THE NATURAL LAW AND ITS PRECEPTS ENGRAVED IN THE HEARTS OF ALL BY GOD, AND BEING READY TO OBEY GOD, LIVE AN HONEST AND UPRIGHT LIFE, can, by the OPERATING POWER OF DIVINE LIGHT AND GRACE, attain eternal life since God...will by no means suffer anyone to be punished with eternal torment who has not the guilt of deliberate sin."*[285]

<u>First</u>, notice that Pope Pius IX specifically condemns the idea that a man "living in error and separated from the true Faith" can be saved. What, may I ask, is the idea of salvation for the "invincibly ignorant"? Why, of course, it is the idea that a man living in

error and separated from the true Faith can be saved. So, the very concept of salvation for the "invincibly ignorant" is condemned as QUITE CONTRARY TO CATHOLIC TEACHING in this very document of Pope Pius IX.

Second, notice again that Pope Pius IX does not say anywhere that the invincibly ignorant can be saved where they are. Rather, he is reiterating that the ignorant, if they cooperate with God's grace, keep the natural law and respond to God's call, they can by God's *"operating power of divine light and grace" [being enlightened by the truth of the Gospel]* attain eternal life, since God will certainly bring all of his elect to the knowledge of the truth and into the Church by baptism. According to the specific definition of Sacred Scripture, *"divine light"* is the Gospel truth of Jesus Christ (the Catholic Faith) which removes the ignorant from darkness.

> Ephesians 5:8 "For **you were heretofore darkness, <u>but now light in the Lord</u>.** Walk then as children of the light."

> 1 Thess. 5:4-5 "But you, **brethren [believers]**, are not in darkness… For all **<u>you are the children of the light</u>**."

> Colossians 1:12-13: "Giving thanks to God the Father, **who hath made us worthy to be partakers** of the lot of the saints **<u>in light</u>: Who hath delivered us from the power of darkness,** and hath translated us **into the kingdom of the Son** of His love."

> 1 Peter 2:9: "But you are a chosen generation… a purchased people: that you may declare his virtues, who hath called you **out of darkness into <u>His marvelous light</u>**."

> 2 Corinthians 4:3-4: **"And if our gospel be hid, it is hid to them that are lost,** In whom the god of this world [Satan] hath blinded the minds of unbelievers, that **<u>the light of the gospel</u>** of the glory of Christ, who is the image of God, should not shine unto them."

> 2 Timothy 1:10: "But is now made manifest <u>by the illumination of **our Savior Jesus Christ**</u>, who hath destroyed death, and hath **<u>brought to light</u>** life and incorruption by the Gospel."

> Pope Pius IX, Vatican I (+1870): **"… no one can 'assent to the preaching of the Gospel,' <u>as he must to attain salvation</u>, without the <u>illumination</u> and inspiration of the Holy Spirit**, who gives to all a sweetness in consenting to and believing the truth."[286]

So, we must not interpret Pius IX's words in *Quanto Conficiamur Moerore* about the good-willed ignorant being saved by receiving "divine light and grace" contrary to their clear scriptural and Traditional meaning, which is that divine light and grace is received by hearing of the Gospel, believing it and being baptized. Thus, in *Quanto Conficiamur Moerore*, Pius IX is saying that the good-willed, sincere person who is ignorant of the Faith will be "illuminated" by receiving the "divine light" (hearing the Gospel) and will enter the Catholic Church so that he can be saved.

I realize that Pope Pius IX was not nearly as clear as he could have been in the second half of *Quanto Conficiamur Moerore*. The heretics have had a field day with it, because they think that they can exploit its wording to favor their heresy that there is salvation outside the Church. If Pope Pius IX had repeated in a strong way the previous definitions of the popes, without any ambiguous language, he would have avoided the danger of modernists *misinterpreting* his words. This is a shame because almost all of his statements on this topic do very clearly affirm Church dogma without any ambiguity that heretics can jump on.

> Pope Pius IX, *Nostis et Nobiscum* (# 10), Dec. 8, 1849: "In particular, **ensure that the faithful are deeply and thoroughly convinced of the truth of the doctrine that the Catholic faith is necessary for attaining salvation**. (This doctrine, received from Christ and emphasized by the Fathers and Councils, is also contained in the formulae of the profession of faith used by Latin, Greek and Oriental Catholics)."[287]

> Pope Pius IX, *Ubi primum* (# 10), June 17, 1847: "**For 'there is one universal Church outside of which <u>no one at all</u> is saved**; it contains regular and secular prelates along with those under their jurisdiction, **who all profess one Lord, one faith and one baptism.**"[288]

> Pope Pius IX- *Syllabus of Modern Errors*- Proposition 16, Dec. 8, 1854: "Man may, in the observance of any religion whatever, <u>find the way of eternal salvation</u>, and <u>arrive</u> at eternal salvation." [289] – **Condemned**

Notice again that the concept of salvation for the "invincibly ignorant" is condemned here. The concept of salvation for the "invincibly ignorant," as it is held by almost everyone who holds it today, is that some men – including those who observe non-Catholic religions – <u>can find and arrive at salvation in these religions</u> because they are "without fault of their own." But this is heretical and condemned by Pius IX's own Syllabus of Errors above.

Fr. Michael Muller, C.SS.R. was a Catholic priest who lived during the time of Pope Pius IX. He wrote a famous book entitled *The Catholic Dogma* in which he defended the

Church's teaching that a person who is "invincibly ignorant" of the Faith cannot be saved. He also defended the true meaning of Pope Pius IX's teaching on this topic.

> Fr. Michael Muller, C.SS.R., *The Catholic Dogma*, pp. 217-218, 1888: "**Inculpable or invincible ignorance has never been and will never be a means of salvation**. To be saved, it is necessary to be justified, or to be in the state of grace. In order to obtain sanctifying grace, it is necessary to have the proper dispositions for justification; that is, true divine faith **in at least the necessary truths of salvation**, confident hope in the divine Savior, sincere sorrow for sin, together with the firm purpose of doing all that God has commanded, etc. **Now, these supernatural acts of faith, hope, charity, contrition, etc., which prepare the soul for receiving sanctifying grace, <u>can never</u> be supplied by invincible ignorance; and if invincible ignorance cannot supply the preparation for receiving sanctifying grace, much less can it bestow sanctifying grace itself. 'Invincible ignorance,' says St. Thomas, 'is a punishment for sin.'** (De, Infid. Q. x., art. 1).
>
> "It is, then, a curse, but not a blessing or a means of salvation… **<u>Hence Pius IX said</u>** *'that, were a man to be invincibly ignorant of the true religion, such invincible ignorance would not be sinful before God; that, if such a person should observe the precepts of the Natural Law and do the will of God to the best of his knowledge,* **God, in his infinite mercy, may enlighten him so as to obtain eternal life**; *for, the Lord, who knows the heart and the thoughts of man will, in his infinite goodness, not suffer anyone to be lost forever without his own fault.'* Almighty God, **who is just condemns no one without his fault, puts, therefore, such souls as are in invincible ignorance of the truths of salvation, in the way of salvation, either by natural or supernatural means.**"[290]

In these well-written lines we see Catholic dogma affirmed. Invincible ignorance can never save a man; those who are invincibly ignorant, if they strive to do their best and are of good will, will be enlightened by God of the Catholic Faith "either by natural or supernatural means"; Fr. Muller confirms that **Pope Pius IX was not teaching the heresy that invincible ignorance justifies and saves**, but that a soul in such a state – who is of good will and follows the natural law – will be enlightened by God about the Catholic Faith so that he can be saved. In fact, Fr. Muller's rendering of Pius IX's words in *Quanto Conficiamur Moerore* show more clearly the Pope's actual meaning. This indicates that perhaps the copy from which Fr. Muller was working has been mistranslated in our day, giving later generations a much weaker and more ambiguous rendering of Pius IX's words.

Though it's clear that these documents of Pope Pius IX did not teach that "invincible ignorance" could save someone, as Fr. Muller confirms, this is not the main issue in regard to this extremely important topic of the necessity of the Catholic Church for salvation. The main issue concerns **what the Church has <u>infallibly</u> taught**, not what Pope Pius IX <u>fallibly</u> taught. Both of these documents were fallible, not dogmatic, and could have contained error! The heretics who believe in salvation outside the Church love to dump all of the dogmatic teaching of the Church on this issue and focus *ad nauseam* on what they think Pope Pius IX fallibly taught. They ignore **all of the dogmatic definitions** (quoted already in this document), while intent on trying to exploit two fallible documents from Pope Pius IX. They pit their own misinterpretation of a few lines in a speech of Pius IX to the Cardinals and in a letter to the Clergy of Italy against the dogmatic definitions of the Fourth Lateran Council, Pope Boniface VIII and the Council of Florence! This is absolutely absurd and totally dishonest. One priest expressed it well:

> **"Just imagine, my dear listeners, the whole secret of salvation being missed in the Gospels, in the teachings of the Apostles, in the protestations of the Saints, in the defined teachings of the Popes, in all the prayers and the liturgies of the Church – and imagine it suddenly coming clear in one or two carelessly worded sentences** in an encyclical of Pope Pius IX, on which the Liberals base their teaching that there is salvation outside the Church."[291]

The truth is that the Liberals recognize what is being said here; they realize that even if Pope Pius IX did teach what they claim (which he didn't), his statements were not infallible and would carry no weight when compared with the dogmatic definitions on the topic. But they don't care about that, because, as one priest who believes in salvation outside the Church told me: *"I like what Pius IX said."* Yes, he likes what he *thinks* Pius IX said, and he doesn't like what God has said via the Church's infallible statements.

That pretty much sums it up: those who obstinately insist on salvation for the "invincibly ignorant" while ignoring these facts, and obstinately quote Pius IX to attempt to prove it, simply reject dogma, in favor of their own contrived interpretations of fallible statements, an interpretation which leads them to conclusions <u>which were explicitly condemned by Pope Pius IX himself</u>. Thus, these people "choose" their heretical ideas over Catholic dogma – heresy, in the Greek, means "choose" – and in so doing they demonstrate bad will and actually mock God. Such persons are void of the true Faith; they don't possess the gift of acceptance of the supernatural revelation of God; they assert that Jesus Christ is not important enough that everyone above reason must know Him to be saved; and they want the truth their own way.

> St. John Chrysostom (+390): "So the Machabees are honored in that they preferred to die rather than betray the Law… **Then [in the Old Law] it sufficed to salvation to know God alone. Now it is no longer so; the knowledge of Christ is necessary to salvation**…"[292]

INVINCIBLE IGNORANCE BECOMES A DESTRUCTIVE HERESY, OBLITERATING THE NECESSITY OF THE CATHOLIC FAITH ALL OVER THE WORLD

One never really heard of the heresy that non-Catholics can be saved by "invincible ignorance" from anyone before the year 1800. But thanks to the growing modernism in the 1850's, combined with the liberals hijacking of Pope Pius IX's weak statements, the heretical theory of salvation for the invincibly ignorant exploded and became the belief of many priests in the latter half of the 19th century and the first half of the 20th century. This has culminated in our situation today, in which almost 100% of people who claim to be "Catholics" (and even "traditional Catholics") believe that Jews, Buddhists, Muslims, Hindus, Protestants, etc. can be saved. We can thank the heretical idea of salvation for the "invincibly ignorant" for this, but there will be much more on this later in the document. Heresy and modernism were so widespread even at the time of the *First Vatican Council* in 1870, that **St. Anthony Mary Claret, the only canonized saint at the Council, had a stroke because of the heresies that were being promoted**. None of these heresies, of course, did God permit to be included in the decrees of Vatican I.

The fact is that all cultures are demonic and under the dominion of the Devil until they are evangelized. This is the incontrovertible teaching of Tradition and Scripture. All the people who die in cultures which have never been penetrated by the Gospel go to hell for sins against the natural law and the other grave sins which they commit – which bad will and failure to cooperate with God's grace is the reason He does not reveal the Gospel to them. The First Vatican Council defined infallibly, based on Romans 1, that the one true God can be known with certitude by the things which have been made, and by the natural light of human reason.[293]

> St. Paul, *Romans 1:18-20*: "For the wrath of God is revealed from Heaven against all ungodliness and injustice of those men that detain the truth of God in injustice: Because that which is known of God is manifest in them. For God hath manifested it to them. **For the invisible things of him, from the creation of the world, are clearly seen, being understood by the things that are made; his external power also, and divinity:** <u>so that they are inexcusable</u>."

Everyone can know with certainty that there is a supreme spiritual being, Who is the One True God and the Creator of the world and all that it contains. Everyone knows that God is not something that they have carved out of wood or jade or stone. They know that God is not the tree that they worship or the river they worship or the rock or the snake or the sacred tree frog. They know that these things aren't the Creator of the universe. Every such person knows that he is worshipping a creature rather than the Creator. They are, as St. Paul says in verse 20, without excuse. St. Augustine explains this well in reference to persons who died ignorant of the Faith and without baptism.

St. Augustine (+428): "… **God foreknew that if they had lived and the gospel had been preached to them, they would have heard it without belief.**"[294]

And if somebody accepted the truth, if he were intellectually honest enough to say, "God, this piece of wood can't be You, reveal Yourself to me," then God would send an angel, if necessary, as He sent an angel to Cornelius in Acts chapter 10; and He would follow it up with a missionary who would bring the good news and the Sacrament of Baptism.

John 18:37: "For this was I born, and for this came I into the world, that I should give testimony to the truth: <u>every one who is of the truth, heareth my voice</u>."

Pope Pius XI *Quas Primas* (# 15), Dec. 11, 1925 : "Indeed this kingdom is presented in the Gospels as such, into which men prepare to enter by doing penance; <u>moreover, they cannot enter it except through</u> **faith and baptism,** which, although <u>an external rite</u>, yet signifies and effects an interior regeneration."[295]

St. Augustine (+426): "Consequently **both <u>those who have not heard the gospel</u> and those who, having heard it,** and having been changed for the better, **did not receive perseverance**… **<u>none of these are separated from that lump which is known to be damned</u>,** as all are going… into condemnation."[296]

St. Prosper of Aquitane (+450): "Certainly God's manifold and indescribable goodness, as we have abundantly proved, always provided and does yet provide for the totality of mankind, so that **none of those perishing can plead the excuse that he was excluded from the light of truth**…"[297]

Romans 8:29-30- "*<u>For whom He foreknew, he also predestinated to be made conformable to the image of his Son</u>: that he might be the first-born amongst many brethren. <u>And whom he predestinated, them he also called</u>:* and whom he called, them he also justified: and whom he justified, them he also glorified."

As Catholics, of course, we don't believe as the heretic John Calvin, who held a predestination according to which no matter what one does he is either predestined for heaven or hell. That is <u>a wicked heresy</u>. Rather, as Catholics we believe in the true understanding of predestination, which is expressed by Romans 8 and the Fathers and Saints quoted already. This true understanding of predestination simply means that God's foreknowledge from all eternity makes sure that those who are of good will and are sincere will be brought to the Catholic faith and come to know what they must – and that all those who are not brought to the Catholic faith and don't know what they must simply were not among the elect.

OTHER POPES AND SAINTS AGAINST INVINCIBLE IGNORANCE

Defenders of salvation for the "invincibly ignorant" might be disquieted to hear that **two other Popes, Pope Benedict XIV and Pope St. Pius X, explicitly reiterated the Church's dogma that <u>there are certain mysteries of faith about which no one who wishes to be saved can be ignorant</u>**. These mysteries are the mysteries of the Trinity and the Incarnation, as it was defined by the Athanasian Creed.

> Pope Benedict XIV, *Cum Religiosi* (# 4), June 26, 1754:
> "See to it that every minister performs carefully the measures laid down by the holy Council of Trent… that confessors should perform this part of their duty whenever anyone stands at their tribunal who does not know **what he must by *necessity of means* know to be saved…**"[298]

> Pope St. Pius X, *Acerbo Nimis* (# 2), April 15, 1905:
> "And so Our Predecessor, Benedict XIV, had just cause to write: '**We declare that <u>a great number of those who are condemned to eternal punishment suffer that everlasting calamity because of ignorance</u> of those mysteries of faith <u>which must be known and believed in order to be numbered among the elect</u>.'**"[299]

Every person above the age of reason must have a positive knowledge of these mysteries of Faith to be saved. There are no exceptions. And this truth of the Catholic Faith is why scores of Popes and Saints have taught that every single member of that mass of humanity who lives in ignorance of Christ is under the devil's dominion and will not be saved, unless he is incorporated into Christ's marvelous light by faith and baptism.

> Pope Gregory XVI, *Probe Nostis* (#6), Sept. 18, 1840: **"We are thankful for the success of apostolic missions in America, the Indies, and other faithless lands…They search out those <u>who sit in darkness and the shadow of death</u>** to summon them to the light and life of the Catholic religion… **At length they snatch them from the devil's rule**, by the bath of regeneration and promote them to the freedom of God's adopted sons."[300]

That great "Apostle of the Rocky Mountains," Fr. Pierre De Smet, who was the extraordinary missionary to the American Indians in the 19th century, was also convinced – with all the great Catholic missionaries before him – <u>that all the Indians whom he did not reach would be eternally lost</u>. (See also the section later on St. Isaac Jogues and St. Francis Xavier)

Fr. De Smet, S.J., Jan. 26, 1838: "New priests are to be added to the Potawatomi Mission, and my Superior, Father Verhaegen gives me hope that I will be sent. **How happy I would be could I spend myself for the salvation of so many souls, <u>who are lost because they have never known truth</u>!**"[301]

Fr. De Smet, S.J., Dec. 8, 1841: "My heart aches at the thought of so many souls left to perish for lack of priests to instruct them."[302]

Fr. De Smet, S.J., Oct. 9, 1844: "**What emotion at the sight of this vast country, where, for lack of missionaries, thousands of men are born, grow to manhood, <u>and die in the darkness of infidelity</u>!** But now through our efforts, the greater number, if not all, shall know the truth."[303]

This truth on salvation is why St. Louis De Montfort says the following in his masterpiece *True Devotion to Mary* (which we strongly recommend for everyone):

St. Louis De Montfort, *True Devotion to Mary* # 61: "There has been no name given under heaven, except the name of Jesus, by which we can be saved.... Every one of the faithful who is not united to Him as a branch to the stock of the vine, shall fall, shall wither and shall be fit only to be cast into the fire. **Outside of Him there exists nothing but error, falsehood, iniquity, futility, death and damnation.**"[304]

This truth on salvation is why St. Francis De Sales stated the following in *The Catholic Controversy*:

St. Francis De Sales, *The Catholic Controversy* (+1672): "Yes, truly; for outside the Church there is no salvation, **out of this Ark every one is lost.**"[305]

St. Francis De Sales, *The Catholic Controversy* (+1672): "…[that] men can be saved outside the true Church, **which is impossible.**"[306]

St. Francis De Sales, *The Catholic Controversy* (+1672): "Who should ever detract from the glory of **so many religious of all orders**, and of so many secular priests, who leaving their country, **have exposed themselves to the mercy of wind and tide, to get to the nations of the New World, in order to lead them to the true faith, and to enlighten them with the light of the Gospel**… amongst the Cannibals, Canarians… Brazilians, Malays, Japanese, and other foreign nations, and made themselves prisoners there, banishing themselves from their own early country **in order that these poor people might not be banished from the heavenly paradise.**"[307]

This truth on salvation is why Pope Leo XIII says that Christopher Columbus' discovery of America led to the salvation of hundreds of thousands of mortals who would otherwise have been lost for dying in a state of ignorance of the true faith.

> Pope Leo XIII, *Quarto Abeunte Saeculo* #1 (+1902): "**By his (Christopher Columbus') toil another world emerged from the unsearched bosom of the ocean: hundreds of thousands of mortals have**, from a state of blindness been raised to the common level of the human race, reclaimed from savagery to gentleness and humanity; **and, greatest of all, by the acquisition of those blessings of which Jesus Christ is the author, they have been recalled from destruction to eternal life.**"[308]

This truth on salvation is why Pope Pelagius I, representing the mind and Tradition of the entire early Catholic Church, declared that those who "did not know the way of the Lord" were lost.

> Pope Pelagius I, *Fide Pelagii* to Childebert, April, 557: "For I confess that all men from Adam… will then rise again and stand before the judgment seat of Christ, that every one may receive the proper things of the body, according as he has done, whether it be good or bad [Rom. 14:10; 2 Cor. 5:10]… **the wicked, however, remaining by choice of their own with vessels of wrath fit for destruction [Rom. 9:22], who either did not know the way of the Lord**, or knowing it left it when seized by various transgressions, **He will give over by a very just judgment to the punishment of eternal and inextinguishable fire**, that they may burn without end."[309]

SACRED SCRIPTURE AGAINST INVINCIBLE IGNORANCE

The fact remains that God has revealed that all who wish to be saved must believe in the Catholic Faith (the Trinity and the Incarnation being "the Catholic Faith" in its simplest mysteries – see the Athanasian Creed). The fact that God will make sure that souls of good will hear His voice and receive the Catholic Faith **should not be hard for a Catholic to accept. After all, in the Apostles' Creed alone, Catholics are required to profess belief in numerous supernatural events: the Virgin Birth, the Resurrection and the Ascension. A Catholic is also required to believe in Sacred Scripture, which is filled with miracles and supernatural phenomena. Transubstantiation (the Real Presence of Christ in the Eucharist) is also an everyday miracle which Traditional Catholics believe.** So why is it hard to believe that God removes ignorance from souls of good will no matter where they are, even miraculously, if necessary? The name of Jesus is the only name under all of heaven (Acts. 4:12) by which one can be saved; and those who enter in not by Jesus are thieves and robbers (John 10).

John 10:1,9: "[Jesus saith] Amen, Amen, I say to you: he that entereth not by the door into the sheepfold, but climbeth up another way, <u>the same is a thief and a robber</u>… I am the door."

In a famous case, **Ven. Mary of Agreda** is said to have bilocated from her convent in Spain to the wilds of Texas in order to instruct Indians in the true Faith. "There is a large mural over the main entrance to the Cathedral of Ft. Worth depicting this lengthy visitation, as well as its huge original that hangs in the Church of St. Anne in Beaumont, Texas."[310] Her miraculous bilocations to America are said to have occurred for 11 years (from 1620-1631), from Texas to New Mexico to Arizona, spanning over a thousand miles.

It is also taught in numerous places in the New Testament that the Gospel was, even in the time of the Apostles, preached throughout the entire world.

Acts 1:8: "[Jesus saith]… you shall receive the power of the Holy Ghost coming upon you, and **you shall be witnesses unto me in Jerusalem, and in all Judea, and Samaria, <u>and even to the uttermost part of the earth</u>**."

Colossians 1:13- "If so ye continue in the faith, grounded and settled, and immoveable from the hope of **the gospel which you have heard, <u>which is preached in all the creation that is under heaven</u>**, whereof I Paul am made minister."

Colossians 1:4-6: "Hearing your faith in Christ Jesus… **the truth of the gospel: Which is come to you, <u>as also it is in the whole world</u>**…"

1 Thessalonians 1:9- "For from you was spread abroad the word of the Lord, not only in Macedonia and in Achaia, **<u>but also in every place</u>** …"

Romans 10:13-18: "For whosoever shall call upon the name of the Lord shall be saved. How then shall they call on him, in whom they have not believed? Or how shall they believe him, of whom they have not heard? And how shall they hear, without a preacher… Faith then cometh by hearing: and by hearing the word of Christ. But I say: Have they not heard? **Yes, verily, their sound went forth over all the earth, and their words unto the ends of the whole earth**."

The New Testament is clear that the Gospel reached "the uttermost part of the earth" (Acts 1), "all the creation which is under heaven" (Colossians 1) and "unto the ends of the whole earth" (Romans 10). It is quite possible that the Apostles were transported to the "uttermost part of the earth" to preach the Gospel and baptize in the same vessel by which the prophet Elias was miraculously taken from the earth – a fiery chariot.

2 Kings 2:11- "And as they went on, walking and talking together, **behold a fiery chariot, and fiery horses parted them both asunder: and Elias went up by a whirlwind into heaven**."

In fact, we know that St. Philip the Apostle was transported in a manner similar to Elias, after Philip baptized the Eunuch of Candace.

Acts 8:38-39: "And Philip commanded the chariot to stand still; and they went down into the water, both Philip and the eunuch: and he baptized him. **And when they were come up out of the water, the Spirit of the Lord took away Philip; and the eunuch saw him no more**. And he went on his way rejoicing."

We also know that the Holy Ghost specifically forbade the Apostles to preach the Gospel in certain places, most probably because of the bad will that they would encounter.

Acts 16:6- "And when they had passed through Phrygia, and the country of Galatia, **they were forbidden by the Holy Ghost to preach the word in Asia**."

Acts 16:7- "And when they were come into Mysia, **they attempted to go into Bithynia, and the Spirit of Jesus suffered them not**."

On the other hand, we know that the Holy Ghost specifically directed the Apostles – by way of supernatural inspiration – to preach the Gospel in places where there were sincere souls in need of it, such as in Macedonia.

Acts 16:9-10: "**And a vision was shewed to Paul in the night**, which was a man of Macedonia standing and beseeching him, and saying: Pass over into Macedonia, and help us. **And as soon as he had seen the vision, immediately we sought to go into Macedonia, being assured that God had called us to preach the gospel to them**."

Acts 8:26- "Now an angel of the Lord spoke to Philip, saying: Arise, go towards the south … **And the Spirit said to Philip: Go near, and join thyself to his chariot**."

None of this is to suggest, of course, that one should not preach the Gospel to a person without supernatural inspiration. It is merely to illustrate that God is fully aware of the souls of good will and the souls of bad will; He is fully aware of who is truly desirous of the truth of the Gospel and who is not, and there is nothing stopping Him from getting His truth to those who are sincere.

St. Paul further says that men (i.e., men above reason who wish to be saved) cannot have the faith in Christ which is necessary for salvation <u>if they have not heard of him</u>. *"Or how shall they believe in him, of whom they have not heard?"* (Romans 10). Since all above the age of reason must hear the word of Christ to have the Faith (Romans 10), they must hear the word of Christ to have salvation, because no one is justified without Faith – the one true Catholic Faith.

> Pope Pius IX, *Vatican I*, Sess. 3, Chap. 3, 1870, on Faith: "But, since 'without **faith** it is impossible to please God' [Heb. 11:6] and to attain to the fellowship of His sons, hence, **no one is justified** without it…"[311]

> Pope Pius IV, Council of Trent, *Iniunctum nobis*, Nov. 13, 1565, *ex cathedra*: *"This true Catholic faith, outside of which no one can be saved*… I now profess and truly hold…"[312]

The fact that no one can be saved without the Catholic Faith is surely why there is evidence of Christianity's arrival in the New World long before Christopher Columbus ever discovered it. St. Brendan the Navigator (484-577 A.D.) is reported to have made travels across the Atlantic long before Christopher Columbus,[313] and there is archeological evidence that has been unearthed to support this claim. The words of the New Testament about the Gospel being preached in all creation under heaven, and Our Lord's words that the Apostles would witness to Him in "the uttermost part of the earth" in His very last discourse before His Ascension, suggest that perhaps some of the apostles themselves were miraculously transported to areas in the world where souls of good will were to be found. But regardless of what one takes from the scriptural passages above, the fact is that the Gospel is preached where good willed souls are to be found, and where it is not preached there is <u>no</u> salvation.

> St. Louis De Montfort, *The Secret of the Rosary*, c. +1710: "… **no one can possibly be saved without the knowledge of Jesus Christ**."[314]

Luke 24:47: "And that penance and remission of sins should be preached in his name, unto all nations, beginning at Jerusalem."

SALVATION FOR THE "INVINCIBLY IGNORANT" REDUCED TO ITS ABSURD PRINCIPLE

The theory that "invincible ignorance" saves can also be refuted by reducing it to its absurd principle, which is this: If being ignorant of the Savior could render one worthy of salvation, then Catholics are actually doing non-Christians a disservice in preaching Jesus Christ to them. St. Paul, St. Vincent Ferrer, St. Francis Xavier, Fr. Pierre De Smet, the North American Martyrs and the other countless heroic missionaries in Church history, who suffered mind-boggling hardships to preach the Gospel to the ignorant pagans, *were simply making these people more culpable and more guilty before God*, according to the modern heresy of salvation for the "invincibly ignorant." If the missionaries had just stayed home, according to the invincible ignorance heresy, the sincere pagans could have been saved for never having heard of Christ through *no fault of their own*. But by making the effort to preach Christ to them, as the missionaries did, they were – according to the invincible ignorance heresy – rendering these persons *without excuse* if they failed to live up to the obligations of the Gospel or rejected it altogether. Thus, preaching the Gospel to the non-Christians, according to the heretical "invincible ignorance" theory, puts the pagans in a situation in which it is more likely that they are going to be damned. Thus, the modern heresy of salvation by being "invincibly ignorant" actually makes preaching to the pagans *counterproductive* for the salvation of souls. But such a notion is absurd, of course, and proves the illogical and false nature of the invincible ignorance heresy.

But, in fact, the heresy has gotten so bad today in the time of the Great Apostasy in which we live (See Section 34) that most "Catholics" today readily profess that pagans, Jews, Buddhists, etc. who know of the Gospel *and reject it* can also be saved by "invincible ignorance." But this is only the necessary result of the invincible ignorance heresy; for if pagans who've never heard of Christ can be saved "in good faith," then pagans who reject Christ could also be in good faith too, for how much does one have to hear to lose his "invincible ignorance"? Once one strays from the principle – that is to say, once one rejects the divinely revealed truth – that *all* who die as pagans are definitely lost without exception (Pope Eugene IV, *de fide*), **the clear cut lines of demarcation are rejected**, and a gray area necessarily takes over, a gray area according to which *one cannot possibly know or set limits on who is possibly in good faith and who is not.*

I was recently talking to a scholar who considers himself a "traditional Catholic." This person holds the invincible ignorance heresy. We were discussing his belief that Jews and other non-Catholics can be saved. In the discussion, he admitted that he held that Jews who hate Christ can possibly be saved. Before he admitted that, however, he said: *"it depends on how much he [the Jew] has heard of Christ. If he has just seen a Crucifix..."* His point was that if the Jew had just seen a Crucifix, but had not heard of Jesus Christ in any substantial way, the Jew might be able to be saved in good faith; whereas if Our Lord Jesus Christ had been fully preached to the Jew, he probably wouldn't be in good faith. (As I've said, the scholar eventually admitted that even the latter case – the Jew who totally rejects and/or hates Christ – could also be in good faith, but I bring up the argumentation he employed before admitting that point to illustrate my following point). The "scholar" is actually showing the absurdity of the invincible ignorance heresy by his argumentation; **he is admitting that the Jew who has seen the Crucifix but not heard of Christ may be in good faith, but if the Jew makes the effort to investigate the one hanging on the Crucifix – or has a friend preach to him the one hanging on the Crucifix – he probably wouldn't be in good faith! Thus, preaching Christ crucified**, according to this "scholar" who had fully imbibed the "invincible ignorance" heresy, **would not save, but possibly damn the Jew.** But this is obviously false and heretical.

> 1 Corinthians 15:1-2: "Now I make known unto you, brethren, **the gospel which I preached to you**, which also you have received, and wherein you stand. _By which also you are saved_…"

The other heretical consequence of the invincible ignorance heresy is that it would mean that infants could also be saved without baptism, because infants are the most "invincibly ignorant" persons on earth. Hence, the argument would go, if "invincible ignorance" saves non-Catholics, then it can save the "invincibly ignorant" infants also. But such an idea has been repeatedly condemned by the Catholic Church; it is a divinely revealed truth that not one infant can enter heaven without water baptism (See "Infants Cannot Be Saved Without Baptism Section").

JESUS CHRIST AGAINST INVINCIBLE IGNORANCE

Perhaps nothing in the New Testament is as clear as the fact that Our Lord Jesus Christ is the Son of God, and that you must believe in Him to have eternal life.

> John 3:16: "For God so loved the world, as to give His only begotten Son: _that whosoever believeth in Him_, **may not perish**, but may have life everlasting."

> John 3:36: "**He that believeth in the Son hath life everlasting**: but he that believeth not the Son, shall not see life, but the wrath of God abideth on him."

> John 17:3: "Now **this is life everlasting, that they may know thee, the only true God, and Jesus Christ**, whom thou hast sent."

> John 8:23-24: "And he said to them [the Jews]: You are from beneath, I am from above. You are of this world, I am not of this world. Therefore, I said to you, that you shall die in your sins: **for if you believe not that I am he, you shall die in your sin**."

> John 14:6: "Jesus saith to them: I am the way, and the truth, and the life. **No man cometh to the Father, but by me**."

And Our Lord is clear that those who don't know Him are not saved.

John 10:14: "I am the good shepherd, and _I know mine, and mine know me_."

I don't think that there is any passage in the New Testament that is as destructive to the modern heresy of "invincible ignorance" as John 10:14. Our Lord clearly and definitively tells us that He knows His sheep and that His sheep "**know Him**." And if Our Lord's words weren't clear enough, He goes on to say, as recorded just two verses later in St. John's Gospel:

John 10:16: "And other sheep I have, that are not of this fold: **them also I must bring**, **and they shall hear my voice**, and there shall be one fold and one shepherd."

Could anything be more clear? Almost all theologians understand Our Lord's words here about the "other sheep" to be referring to the Gentiles. Our Lord is telling the Jews that He has sheep among the Gentiles, who are of the truth, and that He will bring them into the Church and they shall hear His Voice.

John 18:37: "For this was I born, and for this came I into the world, that I should give testimony to the truth: **every one who is of the truth, heareth my voice**."

THE "PRIVATE INTERPRETATION" OBJECTION

OBJECTION- You are acting just like a Protestant. The Protestant privately interprets Sacred Scripture, while you privately interpret dogmatic statements.

ANSWER- This objection has already been refuted in Section 2 of this document, *"Believe Dogma As It Was Once Declared."*

> Pope Pius IX, *First Vatican Council*, Sess. 3, Chap. 2 on Revelation, 1870, *ex cathedra*: "**Hence, also, that understanding of its sacred dogmas must be perpetually retained, which Holy Mother Church has once declared**; and there must never be a recession from that meaning under the specious name of a deeper understanding."[315]

But there are a few additional points in refuting and breaking down the utter nonsense and heretical mentality that lies at the heart of this objection. If a Catholic who is going exactly by what the Chair of Peter (the dogmatic text) has declared is not finding the truth, but is engaging in "private interpretation," as they claim, then what does he go by? Who interprets the dogmatic statement? And who interprets the interpretation of the dogmatic statement? And who interprets the interpretation of the interpretation of the dogmatic statement? And who interprets the interpretation of the interpretation of the interpretation of the dogmatic statement? The answer is that <u>it would never end,</u> and no one could ever arrive at the truth on anything. In that system, the deposit of faith – and the dogmatic teachings of the Church – would then be nothing more than private opinions, which is SHEER PROTESTANTISM.

St. Francis De Sales explained it well against the Protestants.

> St. Francis De Sales (Doctor of the Church), *The Catholic Controversy*, c. 1602, p. 228: **"The Councils… decide and define some article**. If after all this *another test* has to be tried before their [the Council's] determination is received, will not *another* also be wanted? Who will not want to apply his test, and <u>whenever will the matter be settled</u>?... And why not a third to know if the second is faithful? – and then a fourth, to test the third? Everything must be done over again, and posterity will never trust antiquity but will go ever turning upside down the holiest articles of faith in the wheel of <u>their understandings</u>… **what we say is that when a Council has applied this test, *our brains have not now to revise but to believe.***"[316]

The "interpretation" ends with the words of the dogma itself! If it doesn't, then <u>it never ends</u>, as we saw above – you just have *fallible interpretation after fallible interpretation after fallible interpretation after fallible interpretation*. If the buck doesn't stop with the infallible definition (the Chair of Peter), then it never stops. I pointed this fact out to a somewhat well-known "apologist" for the Vatican II sect in a telephone conversation. He was arguing that our usage of Catholic dogmatic teaching (the teaching of the Chair of Peter) is like Protestant "private interpretation." He was saying this in an attempt to defend some of his heretical beliefs which contradict dogma, such as his belief that non-Catholics can be saved. I said to him, "then who interprets the dogma? And who interprets the interpretation of the dogma?" After I said "who interprets the interpretation of the dogma… and who interprets the interpretation of the interpretation… and who interprets the interpretation of the interpretation of the interpretation…" he remained deadly silent for the first time in the conversation. He obviously had no response to the factual point that was made, simply because there is no response. In the heretical view of dogmatic teaching that he espoused, the Catholic Faith is nothing more than Protestantism – fallible, private, human interpretation with no Chair of Peter to give one the final word. The following quotation also illustrates this point very well.

"Why did Athanasius know he was right? Because he clung to the infallible definition, no matter what everyone else said. **Not all the learning in the world, nor all the rank of office, can substitute for the truth of one infallibly defined Catholic**

teaching. Even the simplest member of the faithful, clinging to an infallible definition, will know more than the most 'learned' theologian who denies or undermines the definition. _That_ is the whole purpose of the Church's infallibly defined teaching – to make us independent of the mere opinions of men, however learned, however high their rank."[317]

That is why in adhering to exactly what the dogma "has once declared" (Vatican I) one is not engaging in Protestant "private interpretation," but is rather being most faithful to the infallible truth of Christ and the directly infallible way of knowing it (the dogmatic definitions of the Church). Those who depart from the actual declaration of the dogma, and the actual meaning of its words, are Protestant heretics who engage in condemned, sinful, fallible and private interpretation, against the direct words of the dogma (against the infallible definitions) and thus destroy all faith and render Papal Infallibility pointless. If one can't go by what the dogmatic statement says, then Christ would have just told us to _always follow those with learning or authority_; He would never have instituted an infallible Magisterium exercised by the Popes, which can clarify issues once and for all times with no possibility of error and regardless of who agrees or disagrees with the definition.

BUT CAN'T MEN MISUNDERSTAND A DOGMATIC DEFINITION?

Of course they can. Men can misunderstand anything. If Jesus Christ (the Truth Himself) were here speaking to us, many people would without doubt misunderstand what He said, just as many did when He came the first time. Likewise, just because some can and do misunderstand what the Chair of Peter is declaring, it does not mean that those who faithfully adhere to its definition are engaging in Protestant "private interpretation." That is utterly blasphemous against the entire institution of the Papacy and the whole point of dogmatic definitions and the Chair of St. Peter. **The dogmatic statements of the Catholic Church constitute the truth of heaven being declared to us directly** by the Popes.

Pope Pius X, _Lamentabile_, The Errors of the Modernists, July 3, 1907, #22:
"The dogmas which the Church professes as revealed are not truths fallen from heaven, but they are a kind of interpretation of religious facts, which the human mind by a laborious effort prepared for itself."- **Condemned**[318]

Pope Pius X, _Lamentabile_, The Errors of the Modernists, July 3, 1907, #54:
"The dogmas, the sacraments, the hierarchy, **as far as pertains both to the notion and to the reality, are nothing but interpretations** and the evolution of

Christian intelligence, which have increased and perfected the little germ latent in the Gospel."- **Condemned**[319]

Pope Gregory XVI, *Mirari Vos* (#7), Aug. 15, 1832: "… nothing of the things appointed ought to be diminished; nothing changed; nothing added; **but they must be preserved both as regards expression and meaning**."[320]

17. Some Other Objections

There are a number of other objections that are raised against the true meaning of the dogma Outside the Church There is No Salvation and the necessity of receiving the Sacrament of Baptism for salvation. In this section, I will respond to them. These objections, of course, are all proven to be wrong by the infallible teaching of the Church examined thus far; but, once again, for the sake of completeness, each one will be addressed individually.

What the modern proponents of the false doctrine of baptism of desire try to do is to throw together a combination of things which appear to favor their position, but which actually don't. They throw together a combination of fallible statements (which don't prove their point), misinterpreted texts and/or mistranslated texts (which don't say what they claim), as well as some other things which don't prove their point. The average layperson, however, not having the facts at his or her disposal or not willing to make the effort to see through all of the fallacious arguments, misrepresented points and invalid reasoning, comes away with the impression that "baptism of desire" must be a teaching of the Church. But when each of the things that the baptism of desire advocates claim is examined individually, one can see that not one of them proves the false doctrine of baptism of desire in any way; they all crumble when scrutinized. And while these people misunderstand and misrepresent the teaching of the Church, they dishonestly don't even attempt to address the many arguments from the highest teaching authority of the Catholic Church (the Chair of Peter) which show that there is no such thing as "baptism of desire" or salvation for those who die as non-Catholics (see Section 33). They don't address these arguments simply because they can't answer them.

Since some of the following sections are more involved and technical, those who are not necessarily looking for or interested in the answers to these objections may as well skip over this section to Section 18.

THE CATECHISM OF THE COUNCIL OF TRENT

OBJECTION- The Catechism of the Council of Trent taught that one's determination to receive baptism could avail him to grace and righteousness if it is impossible for him to receive baptism.

Catechism of the Council of Trent, *Ordinarily They Are Not Baptized At Once*, p. 179: "On adults, however, the Church has not been accustomed to confer the Sacrament of Baptism at once, but has ordained that it be deferred for a certain time. The delay is not attended with the same danger as in the case of infants, which we have already mentioned; should any unforeseen accident make it impossible for adults to be washed in the salutary waters, their intention and determination to receive Baptism and their repentance for past sins, will avail them to grace and righteousness."[321]

ANSWER- The Catechism of the Council of Trent is not infallible. Fathers John A. McHugh, O.P. and Charles J. Callan, O.P. wrote the introduction for a common English translation of the Catechism of the Council of Trent. Here is what they had to say about its authority.

Catechism of the Council of Trent- Fifteenth printing, TAN Books, Introduction XXXVI: "Official documents have occasionally been issued by Popes to explain certain points of Catholic teaching to individuals, or to local Christian communities; whereas the Roman Catechism comprises practically the whole body of Christian doctrine, and is addressed to the whole Church. **Its teaching is not infallible**; *but it holds a place between approved catechisms and what is de fide."*[322]

The fact that the Catechism of Trent is not infallible is proven by the fact that small errors can be detected within its text. For example:

Catechism of the Council of Trent, Tan Books, p. 243: "For the Eucharist is the end of all the Sacraments, and the symbol of unity and brotherhood in **the Church, outside of which none can attain grace.**"[323]

Here the Catechism teaches that outside the Church none can attain grace. **This is not true**. Predisposing or prevenient graces are given to those outside the Church so that they can turn to God, change their lives and enter the Church. Without these graces no one would ever convert. Pope Clement XI in the dogmatic constitution *Unigenitus* (Sept. 8, 1713) condemned the proposition that, *"Outside the Church, no grace is granted."*[324] Thus, what we have here is an *error* in the Catechism of Trent. The Catechism probably intended to teach that outside the Church no sinner can attain *sanctifying* grace, which is true, since outside the Catholic Church there is no remission of sins (Pope Boniface VIII, *Unam Sanctam*, 1302, *ex cathedra*).[325] Nevertheless, **God**

allowed the Catechism to err in this manner because it is not infallible in everything it teaches.

Furthermore, in the entire Catechism of the Council of Trent there is no mention at all of the so-called "three baptisms," nor is there any mention of "baptism of desire" or "baptism of blood," nor is there any clear statement that one can be saved without the Sacrament of Baptism. What we find, rather, is one ambiguous paragraph which seems to teach that one can achieve grace and righteousness without baptism. But even in this paragraph we find errors. For instance, the passage says that *"should any unforeseen accident make it impossible for an adult to receive baptism, his intention and determination to receive baptism will avail him to grace and righteousness."*

There is no such thing as an "unforeseen accident" which could make it "impossible" to receive baptism. This is clearly erroneous.

> Pope Pius IX, *Vatican Council I*, Sess. 3, Chap. 1, On God the creator of all things: "EVERYTHING THAT GOD HAS BROUGHT INTO BEING HE PROTECTS AND GOVERNS BY HIS PROVIDENCE, *which reaches from one end of the earth to the other and orders all things well. All things are open and laid bare before His eyes, even those which will be brought about by the free activity of creatures.*"[326]

God has commanded all men to receive baptism, and He does not command impossibilities.

> Pope Paul III, *Council of Trent*, Session 6, Chap. 11 on Justification, *ex cathedra*: "... no one should make use of **that rash statement forbidden under anathema by the Fathers, that the commandments of God are impossible to observe for a man who is justified. 'FOR GOD DOES NOT COMMAND IMPOSSIBILITIES**, but by commanding admonishes you both to do what you can do, and to pray for what you cannot do…"[327]

Therefore, **the reference to the unforeseen and impossible to avoid accident in the Catechism demonstrates, once again, that not everything it says is infallible**. An infallible document could not assert that accidents are unforeseen or impossible to avoid.

Even though the Catechism of Trent is not infallible in every sentence, as just proven, taken as a whole it is an excellent Catechism which expresses the Catholic Faith accurately and effectively. But most importantly, **the Catechism of Trent makes statement after statement clearly and unambiguously teaching that the Sacrament of Baptism is absolutely necessary for all for salvation with no exceptions,** thereby repeatedly exluding any idea of salvation without water baptism.

Catechism of the Council of Trent, *Comparisons among the Sacraments*, p. 154: "Though all the Sacraments possess a divine and admirable efficacy, it is well worthy of special remark that all are not of equal necessity or of equal dignity, nor is the signification of all the same.

"Among them three are said to be necessary beyond the rest, although in all three this necessity is not of the same kind. **The universal and absolute necessity of Baptism our Savior has declared in these words: *Unless a man be born again of water and the Holy Ghost, he cannot enter into the kingdom of God* (Jn. 3:5)."**[328]

This means that the Sacrament of Baptism is absolutely and universally necessary for salvation with no exceptions! It excludes any idea of salvation without water baptism. It also means that John 3:5 is understood literally.

Catechism of the Council of Trent, *On Baptism – Necessity of Baptism*, pp. 176-177: "If the knowledge of what has been hitherto explained be, as it is, of highest importance to the faithful, **it is no less important to them to learn that THE LAW OF BAPTISM, AS ESTABLISHED BY OUR LORD, EXTENDS TO ALL, so that unless they are regenerated to God through the grace of Baptism, be their parents Christians or infidels, they are born to eternal misery and destruction.** Pastors, therefore, should often explain these words of the Gospel: *Unless a man be born again of water and the Holy Ghost, he cannot enter into the kingdom of God (Jn. 3:5).***"[329]

This clearly means that no one can be saved without the Sacrament of Baptism and that John 3:5 is literal with no exceptions!

Catechism of the Council of Trent, *Definition of Baptism*, p. 163: **"*Unless, says our Lord, a man be born again of water and the Holy Ghost, he cannot enter into the kingdom of God (Jn. 3:5);* and, speaking of the Church, the Apostle says, *cleansing it by the laver of water in the word of life*

(Eph. 5:26). Thus it follows that Baptism may be rightly and accurately defined: *The Sacrament of regeneration by water in the word.*"[330]

The Catechism of Trent also teaches that if there is danger of death for an adult, Baptism must not be deferred.

> Catechism of the Council of Trent, *In Case of Necessity Adults May Be Baptized At Once,* p. 180: "**Sometimes, however, when there exists a just and necessary cause, as in the case of imminent danger of death, Baptism is not to be deferred,** particularly if the person to be baptized is well instructed in the mysteries of faith."[331]

The customary delay in baptizing adults that we see in history was for the instruction and the testing of the catechumens. This delay was not because it was believed that adults could be saved without baptism, as proven already in the section on Pope St. Siricius.

> Catechism of the Council of Trent, *Baptism made obligatory after Christ's Resurrection,* p. 171: "<u>**Holy writers are unanimous in saying**</u> that after the Resurrection of our Lord, when He gave His Apostles the command to go and teach all nations: *baptizing them in the name of the Father, and of the Son, and of the Holy Ghost,* <u>**the law of Baptism became obligatory on all who were to be saved.**</u>"[332]

> Catechism of the Council of Trent, *Matter of Baptism - Fitness,* p. 165: "Upon this subject pastors can teach in the first place that <u>**water, which is always at hand and within the reach of all,**</u> was the fittest matter of <u>**a Sacrament which is necessary to all for salvation.**</u>"[333]

Notice that the Catechism teaches that water is "within the reach of all," a phrase which excludes the very notion of baptism of desire – that water is not within the reach of all. Also notice that the Catechism declares that <u>the Sacrament</u> is necessary <u>for all</u> for salvation! This excludes any notion of salvation without the Sacrament of Baptism. Thus, the Catechism of Trent teaches repeatedly and unambiguously that it is the teaching of Jesus Christ and the Catholic Church that the Sacrament of Baptism is necessary for all for salvation. All of this is clearly contrary to the theories of baptism of desire and baptism of blood.

Moreover, the Catechism also teaches that Christians are distinguished from non-Christians by the Sacrament of Baptism.

> Catechism of the Council of Trent, *On Baptism – Second Effect*: *Sacramental Character*, p. 159: "In the character impressed by **Baptism**, both effects are exemplified. **By it we are qualified to receive the other Sacraments, and <u>the Christian is distinguished from those who do not profess the faith</u>.**"[334]

Those who assert that <u>the Sacrament</u> of Baptism is not necessary for all for salvation (e.g., all those who believe in "baptism of desire") contradict the very teaching of the Catechism of Trent.

> Catechism of the Council of Trent, *Matter of Baptism - Fitness*, p. 165: "Upon this subject pastors can teach in the first place that **water, which is always at hand and within the reach of all, was the fittest matter of <u>a Sacrament which is necessary to all for salvation</u>.**"[335]

SESS. 7, CAN. 4 ON THE SACRAMENTS

OBJECTION- In Sess. 7, Can. 4 on the *Sacraments in General*, the Council of Trent teaches that people can obtain justification by the sacraments or the desire for them.

ANSWER- Session 7, Can. 4 on the *Sacraments in General* says nothing of the sort. An awkward translation of this canon, as well as the mistaken notion that Trent teaches baptism of desire in another place in Trent (which has already been refuted), has led to this erroneous assertion. Let's take a look at the canon.

> Pope Paul III, *Council of Trent*, Session 7, Can. 4, On the Sacraments: "If anyone says that the sacraments of the new law are not necessary for salvation but are superfluous, **and that people obtain the grace of justification from God without them or a desire for them, by faith alone,** though all are not necessary for each individual: let him be anathema."[336]

When one carefully examines this canon, he sees that it is <u>not</u> declaring that either the sacraments or the desire for them is sufficient for justification; but rather it is condemning those who would say that neither the sacraments nor the desire for them is necessary for justification. I repeat, it is not *declaring* that *either is sufficient*; it is _condemning_ those who would say _neither is necessary_. Precisely, it is condemning those who would say that _neither is necessary_ and that _faith alone_ suffices.

Consider the following canon that I have made up: "_If anyone says that the Virgin Mary possesses the Queenship of Heaven without God's permission or her being worthy of it, but assumes this Queenship by usurpation alone, let him be anathema._"

The sentence construction of this imaginary canon is similar to the canon we are discussing. Consider it carefully. After considering it, I ask: does this canon mean that the Blessed Mother possesses her Queenship solely by "_her being worthy of it_"? No, she must also have God's permission. The canon does not say that either "her being worthy of it" or "God's permission" **is sufficient** for Mary to possess the Queenship. Rather, it **condemns** those who would say that **neither** "God's permission" nor "_her being worthy of it_" is necessary. In other words, the canon is condemning those who would say that both God's permission and Mary's worthiness are useless, since she assumes the Queenship by usurping it.

Likewise, canon 4 above **does not say** that either the sacraments or the desire for them is sufficient for justification; it condemns those who would say that both the sacraments and the desire are unnecessary in obtaining justification, since faith alone is all one needs. Canon 4 does not in any way teach the possibility of baptism of desire.

POPE INNOCENT II

OBJECTION- Pope Innocent II taught that a priest could be saved without the Sacrament of Baptism by his desire for it and his confession of the true faith (Denzinger 388):

> "To your inquiry we respond thus: We assert without hesitation (on the authority of the holy fathers Augustine and Ambrose) that the priest whom you indicated (in your letter) had died without the water of baptism, because he persevered in the faith of holy mother Church and in the confession of the name of Christ, was freed from original sin and attained the joy of the heavenly fatherland. Read (brother) in the eighth book of Augustine's City of God where, among other things it is written, 'Baptism is ministered invisibly to one whom not contempt of religion but death excludes.' Read again in the book of the blessed Ambrose concerning the death of Valentinian where he says the same thing. Therefore, to questions concerning the dead, you should hold the opinions of the learned Fathers, and in your church you should join in prayers and you should have sacrifices offered to God for the priest mentioned (Apostolicam Sedem)."[337]

ANSWER- First of all, there is no such thing as a *priest* who has not been baptized. The Church teaches that one who has not been baptized cannot receive the priesthood validly. This problem alone demonstrates that the above statement is not infallible. **Secondly, the date of this document is unknown, the author is unknown – it is by no means clear that it was Innocent II – and the person to whom it is addressed is unknown! Could such a document ever prove anything? No.** It remains a mystery why a document of such doubtful authenticity found its way into Denzinger, a handbook of dogmatic statements. This is probably because Denzinger was edited by Karl Rahner, a notorious heretic, whose heretical bias caused him to present this clearly non-magisterial statement as Magisterial, for he is a believer in baptism of desire.

To illustrate the lack of magisterial authority of the previous letter *allegedly* from Pope Innocent II, I will quote from Thomas Hutchinson's book, *Desire and Deception (pp. 31-32)*:

> "We speak of the letter Apostolicam Sedem, **written at the behest of Pope Innocent II (1130-1143), at an unknown date to an unnamed bishop of Cremona.** The latter had written an inquiry to the Pope regarding the case of a priest who apparently had died without being baptized. Of course, it has been defined that, in such a case, he was no priest, since the sacrament of orders may only be conferred validly upon the baptized.

> ---- Text of letter omitted because it has been listed already ----

> "Now, there are more than a few problems connected with this letter. Firstly, it depends entirely on the witness of Saints Ambrose and Augustine for its conclusion. Its premises are false, as the Fathers in question did not actually hold the opinions herein imputed to them. (author: as noted a mere sentimental speculative utterance does not prove they hold to this as official teaching)…
> "**Lastly, there is even a question of who wrote this letter.** Many authorities ascribe it to Innocent III (1198-1216). This question is mentioned in Denzinger. The letter is certainly not in keeping with the totality of his declarations either. In any case, a gap of 55 years separated the two pontificates. **So a private letter of uncertain date, authorship, and destination, based upon false premises and contradicting innumerable indisputably valid and solemn documents, is pretended to carry the weight of the Magisterium on its shoulders. Were any other doctrine concerned, this missive (letter) would not even be given any consideration.** As we shall see, however, mystification and deception are part and parcel of the history of this topic of Salvation. Perhaps this letter was attributed to Innocent III because of his statement that the words of consecration at Mass do not actually have to be said by the priest, but only thought internally -- a sort of Eucharist by Desire. Later Saint Thomas Aquinas took him to task on this point.

"But Innocent III is indeed the key to understanding the original teaching of the Church on this topic. It was in his time (as always until the Second Plenary Council of Baltimore) forbidden to bury the unbaptized (whether catechumens or even children of Catholic parents) in consecrated ground. He explained the rationale for this law, writing: 'It has been decreed by the sacred canons that we are to have no communion with those who are dead, if we have not communicated with them while alive' (Decr. III, XXVIII, xii)." - end of transcript from *Desire and Deception*.

These considerations dismiss any argument in favor of baptism of desire from this letter. The letter, while certainly not infallible, may indeed be a forgery.

POPE INNOCENT III

OBJECTION- Pope Innocent III taught that a person who baptized himself could be saved by the desire for the Sacrament of Baptism.

> Pope Innocent III, to the Bishop of Metz, Aug. 28, 1206: "We respond that, since there should be a distinction between the one baptizing and the one baptized, as is clearly gathered from the words of the Lord, when he says to the Apostles: 'Go, baptize all nations in the name etc.," the Jew mentioned must be baptized again by another, that it may be shown that he who is baptized is one person, and he who baptizes another...If, however, such a one had died immediately, he would have rushed to his heavenly home without delay because of the faith of the sacrament, although not because of the sacrament of faith."[338]

This proves the theory of baptism of desire.

ANSWER- It is true that Pope Innocent III apparently said that a person who baptized himself could be saved by his desire for the Sacrament, but it is false to say that this proves the theory of baptism of desire. Baptism of desire is disproved by the infallible teaching of Pope St. Leo the Great, the Council of Florence and the Council of Trent on the necessity of the Sacrament of Baptism for salvation. But the first thing that should be said about this letter from Innocent III is that a letter to the Bishop of Metz does not meet the requirements for an infallible pronouncement. This is a fact hardly anyone would dispute.

To prove this point consider the following: In the letter *Ex parte tua*, Jan. 12, 1206, the same Innocent III teaches that *original sin was remitted by the mystery of circumcision*.

> Pope Innocent III, *Ex Parte tua*, to Andrew, the Archbishop of Lyons, Jan. 12, 1206: "**Although original sin was remitted by the mystery of circumcision**, and

the danger of damnation was avoided, nevertheless there was no arrival at the kingdom of heaven, which up to the death of Christ was barred to all."[339]

This is definitely wrong, since the Council of Trent defined as a dogma (Session VI, Chap. 1 on Justification) that *"not even the Jews by the very letter of the law of Moses were able to be liberated or to rise"* from original sin.[340]

Pope Paul III, *Council of Trent*, Session 6, Chap. 1 on Justification: "… whereas all men (*except the Blessed Virgin - as Trent says in Sess. V*) had lost their innocence in the prevarication of Adam, 'having become unclean', and (as the Apostle says), 'by nature children of wrath… **but not even the Jews by the very letter of the law of Moses were able to be liberated or to rise therefrom**…"[341]

In other words, not even the observance of Circumcision and the rest of the Mosaic Law enabled Jews to be freed from original sin (*de fide*), contrary to what Innocent III taught in his letter *Ex parte tua*. **So we have Innocent III teaching blatant error** in the letter *Ex parte tua* to Andrew, the Archbishop of Lyons. Since *Ex parte tua* is at least as authoritative as the other two statements allegedly from Innocent II and Innocent III, which are often quoted by baptism of desire supporters, it proves that they are likewise fallible and non-Magisterial. And this, in summary, is the complete extent of the evidence which baptism of desire supporters try to bring forth from the Papal Magisterium: a dubious letter alleged to be from Innocent II – with no date or addressee – and a letter from Innocent III to an Archbishop, which ranks on the same level as *Ex Parte Tua* which contains things contrary to Catholic dogma. Thus, the evidence in favor of baptism of desire from the Papal Magisterium is **zero**.

In fact, as mentioned already, it was during Innocent III's time forbidden to bury the unbaptized (whether catechumens or even children of Catholic parents) in consecrated ground. And it is the <u>infallible</u> teaching of the same Pope at the Fourth Lateran Council which affirms the absolute necessity of water baptism for salvation.

Pope Innocent III, *Fourth Lateran Council*, Constitution 1, 1215, *ex cathedra*: **"There is indeed one universal Church of <u>the faithful</u>, outside of which nobody at all is saved**, in which Jesus Christ is both priest and sacrifice."[342]

"The faithful" only includes those baptized with water, as section 6 of this document proves.

Pope Innocent III, *Fourth Lateran Council*, Constitution 1, 1215, *ex cathedra*: **"But the sacrament of baptism is consecrated in water at the invocation of the undivided Trinity – namely, Father, Son and Holy Ghost – and brings salvation to both children and adults** when it is correctly carried out by anyone in the form laid down by the Church."[343]

And here is another statement from the same Pope which, though not infallible, insists on the absolute necessity of rebirth in water.

> Pope Innocent III, letter to Thorias, Archbishop of Nidaros: "You have asked whether children ought to be regarded as Christians whom, when in danger of death, on account of scarcity of water and absence of a priest, the simplicity of some has anointed on the head and the breast, and between the shoulders with a sprinkling of saliva for baptism. **We answer that since in baptism two things always, that is, 'the word and the element,' are required by necessity**, according to which Truth says concerning the word: 'Going into the world etc.' [Luke 16:15; Matt. 28:19], and the same concerning the element says: 'Unless anyone etc.' [John 3:5] you ought not to doubt that those do not have true baptism in which not only both of the above mentioned (requirements) but one of them is missing."[344]

Perhaps Pope Innocent III's blunders in his fallible capacity as Pope are the reason we read the following vision about him barely avoiding Hell and being allegedly condemned to suffer in Purgatory until the end of the world.

> "In *The Mourning of the Dove,* St. Robert Bellarmine (+ c. 1600) tells us about a person appearing to St. Lutgarde all clothed in flame and in much pain. **When St. Lutgarde asked him who he was, he answered her: 'I am [Pope] Innocent III, who should have been condemned to eternal Hell-fire for several grievous sins, had not the Mother of God interceded for me in my agony and obtained for me the grace of repentance. Now I am destined to suffer in Purgatory till the End of the World**, unless you help me. Once again the Mother of Mercy has allowed me to come to ask you for your prayers."[345]

ST. ALPHONSUS LIGUORI

OBJECTION- St. Alphonsus taught that baptism of desire is "de fide" (of the faith). This means that baptism of desire is dogma!

> St. Alphonsus: "Baptism by fire, however, is the perfect conversion to God through contrition, or the love of God above all things, with the explicit desire, or implicit desire, for the true river of baptism. As the Council of Trent says (Sess. 14, Chap. 4), it takes the place of the latter with regard to the remission of the guilt, but does not imprint a character nor take away all the debt of punishment. It is called fire because it is made under the impulse of the Holy Spirit, who is given this name… Thus it is of faith (de fide) that men are saved even by the baptism of fire, according to c. Apostolicam, de pres. non bapt. and the Council

of Trent, Sess. 6, Chap. 4, where it is said that no one can be saved without the laver of regeneration or the desire for it."

ANSWER- First, St. Alphonsus was not infallible. It is simply a fact that St. Alphonsus made some theological mistakes, as the following discussion will show. To advance St. Alphonsus' opinion about some aspect of the faith as if it were a dogma is not Catholic.

Second, St. Augustine held that it was *de fide* that unbaptized infants suffer the fires of hell and St. Cyprian held that it was *de fide* that heretics cannot validly baptize. Both were dead wrong.

> *The Catholic Encyclopedia*, Vol. 9, 1910, "Limbo," p. 258: **"...St. Thomas and the Schoolmen generally were in conflict with what St. Augustine and other Fathers considered to be** *de fide* [*on unbaptized infants suffering the fires of hell*]..."[346]

> St. Cyprian, 254 A.D.: "We... *judging and holding it as certain* that no one beyond the pale [*that is, outside the Church*] is able to be baptized..."[347]

Third, the root of St. Alphonsus' error on baptism of desire was that he misunderstood Sess. 6, Chap. 4 of Trent (his opinion on this passage simply does not hold up under scrutiny – see the discussion of that passage). And this mistake led to his false conclusion that baptism of desire is a teaching of the Catholic Church. The passage which St. Alphonsus thought taught baptism of desire does not teach baptism of desire, but affirms: *as it is written, unless a man is born again of water and the Holy Ghost he cannot enter into the Kingdom of God.*

Fourth, in teaching baptism of desire, St. Alphonsus was teaching that one can be sanctified by the Spirit and the Blood of Christ without the water of baptism and **this is contrary to that which Pope St. Leo the Great infallibly defined**. When a clash occurs between dogmatic definitions and the opinions of Saints, the Catholic, of course, goes with the dogmatic definitions, no matter how great or learned the Saint may be.

Finally, most theologians after St. Alphonsus who believed in "baptism of desire" didn't even hold his opinion that baptism of desire is *de fide*. Most of them said that baptism of desire is *close to the faith*, not defined of the faith. Hardly any of them said that it is defined of the faith. This fact proves that it is __NOT__ of the faith, because such a discrepancy would not exist among the theologians who claim to favor it if it could be demonstrated that baptism of desire is of the faith. Here is an admission by a defender of baptism of desire:

Fr. Jean-Marc Rulleau, *Baptism of Desire*, p. 43: "The existence of baptism of desire is, then, a truth which, *although it has not been defined as a dogma by the Church*, **is at least proximate to the faith**."[348]

If the Council of Trent taught baptism of desire, then baptism of desire is a defined article of the Faith. But the Council of Trent did not teach baptism of desire, which is why Fr. Rulleau is forced to admit that it is not defined of the faith, but only (in his view) "proximate to the faith." "Proximate to the faith" and "of the faith" are not the same. Fr. Rulleau (a fierce advocate of the theory) would not be caught softening his own position if he could prove that it is of the faith, but he cannot. Thus, St. Alphonsus' statement is wrong for several reasons: 1) it is contrary to defined dogma (Pope St. Leo the Great and the understanding of Trent on John 3:5 *as it is written*); 2) his statement cannot be proven – no definition can be cited; 3) it is not shared by even the theologians who believe in baptism of desire; 4) there are errors in the very paragraph in which it is stated.

Let's examine # 4) *there are errors in the very paragraph in which it is stated*. To substantiate his position on baptism of desire, St. Alphonsus first makes reference to Sess. 14, Chap. 4 of the Council of Trent. He says:

> "**As the Council of Trent says (Sess. 14, Chap. 4),** it takes the place of the latter with regard to the remission of the guilt, but does not imprint a character nor take away all the debt of punishment."

This is completely wrong. Sess. 14, Chap. 4 of the Council of Trent does not say that baptism of desire "*takes the place of the latter (i.e., baptism) with regard to the remission of the guilt,*" as St. Alphonsus claims. Let's look at the passage:

> Pope Paul III, *Council of Trent*, Sess. 14, Chap. 4, on the Sacrament of Penance: **"The Council teaches, furthermore, that though it sometimes happens that this contrition is perfect because of charity and reconciles man to God, before this sacrament is actually received**, this reconciliation must not be ascribed to the contrition itself without the desire of the sacrament which is included in it."[349]

The Council here defines that perfect contrition with the desire for the Sacrament of *Penance* can restore a man to the grace of God before the Sacrament is received. It says nothing of *baptism*! St. Alphonsus' very premise – that *baptism* of desire is taught in Sess. 14, Chap. 4 – is erroneous. Trent says nothing of the sort. If the very premises upon which he argued baptism of desire were flawed and erroneous, how can one be bound to the conclusions that flow from such false premises? In fact, the incredibly dishonest author of the Society of St. Pius X on baptism of desire, Fr. Francois Laisney, does not include St. Alphonsus' erroneous reference to Sess. 14, Chap. 4 of Trent when Laisney quotes the passage from St. Alphonsus on baptism of desire![350] This is incredibly dishonest, of course, but Fr. Laisney of the SSPX omits it because he knows that St. Alphonsus was <u>wrong</u> in referencing Trent in that way; and, therefore, he knows that it pokes a big hole in his argument in favor of baptism of desire based on the obviously <u>fallible</u> St. Alphonsus.

And this shows again what I have been demonstrating throughout this document: that basically all the saints and theologians who expressed belief in baptism of desire contradicted themselves in explaining it while making other errors in the same document.

It should also be noted that, although St. Alphonsus mentioned that he believed that an adult could be saved by the explicit desire or implicit desire for the Sacrament of Baptism, he uses the word *implicit* not to mean "not known," but rather "not expressed in words" – in other words, an adult who <u>knows</u> of Baptism and desires it, but does not express this desire in words. St. Alphonsus, even though wrong about baptism of desire, did not hold to the modern day heresy of *invincible ignorance* – the idea that an adult can be saved by baptism of desire who does not believe in Christ or the Church and does not know of Baptism. St. Alphonsus would rightly condemn such an idea as heretical.

1. St. Alphonsus: "See also the special love which God has shown you in bringing you into life in a Christian country, and in the bosom of the Catholic or true Church. **How many are born among the pagans, among the Jews, among the Mohometans and heretics, <u>and all are lost</u>.**"[351]

It's interesting to consider that when the people who quote St. Alphonsus in favor of baptism of desire – and treat him as if he were infallible – are asked if they agree with his teaching here (that all who die as heretics, Jews, Muslims and pagans go to Hell), almost all of them avoid the question like the plague. They avoid the question because, in this case, they do not share St. Alphonsus' position. Rather, they believe that heretics, Jews, Muslims and pagans can be saved as heretics, Jews, Muslims and pagans and therefore they are in heresy for that reason alone.

2. St. Alphonsus: "We must believe that the Roman Catholic Church is the only true Church; hence, they who are out of our Church, or if they are separated from it, cannot be saved."[352]

3. St. Alphonsus: "If you are ignorant of the truths of the faith, you are obliged to learn them. Every Christian is bound to learn the Creed, the Our Father, and the Hail Mary under pain of mortal sin. **Many have no idea of the Most Holy Trinity, the Incarnation, mortal sin, Judgment, Paradise, Hell, or Eternity; and this deplorable ignorance damns them.**"[353]

4. St. Alphonsus: "How thankful we ought to be to Jesus Christ for the gift of faith! What would have become of us if we had been born in Asia, Africa, America, or in the midst of heretics and schismatics? **He who does not believe is lost**. This, then, was the first and greatest grace bestowed on us: our calling to the true faith. O Savior of the world, **what would become of us if Thou hadst not enlightened us? We would have been like our fathers of old, who adored animals and blocks of stone and wood: and thus we would have all perished**."[354]

One can see that, although St. Alphonsus was incorrect in his belief that baptism of desire could be efficacious in an adult who died before receiving the sacrament, he condemned the modern day heresy which asserts that one can attain salvation in another religion or without faith in Christ and the Catholic Mysteries of Faith.

Another point that is useful in refuting the objection from St. Alphonsus' teaching on baptism of desire is what St. Alphonsus taught concerning the so-called baptism of blood.

> St. Alphonsus, Moral Theology, Bk. 6, nn. 95-97: "**Baptism of blood** is the shedding of one's blood, i.e. death, suffered for the faith or for some other Christian virtue. Now this Baptism is comparable to true baptism because, like true Baptism, it remits both guilt and punishment as it were ex opere operato… **Hence martyrdom avails also for infants** seeing that the Church venerates the Holy Innocents as true martyrs. That is why Suarez rightly teaches that the opposing view is at least temerarious."

What St. Alphonsus teaches here is completely wrong. He teaches that infants can be saved without the Sacrament of Baptism by martyrdom. This is directly contrary to the *ex cathedra* teaching of Pope Eugene IV at the Council of Florence.

> Pope Eugene IV, *Council of Florence*, Session 11, Feb. 4, 1442, *ex cathedra*: "**Regarding children**, indeed, because of danger of death, which can often take place, <u>when no help can be brought to them by another remedy than through the sacrament of baptism</u>, through which they are snatched from the domination of the Devil and adopted among the sons of God, it advises that holy baptism ought not be deferred for forty or eighty days, or any time according to the observance of certain people…"[355]

Pope Eugene IV here defines *from the Chair of Peter* that there is no other remedy for infants to be snatched away from the dominion of the devil other than the Sacrament of Baptism. **St. Alphonsus teaches that there is another remedy in martyrdom**. St. Alphonsus' opinion on this matter cannot be held, since it contradicts the Council of Florence. Now, we know that St. Alphonsus is a Saint in heaven because the Church has told us this – in fact, he is my favorite spiritual writer; but here St. Alphonsus was contradicting the solemn teaching of the Magisterium: that the Sacrament of Baptism is the only remedy for infants. We must conclude, therefore, that St. Alphonsus was not obstinate in his teaching on baptism of blood for infants; that is, he was not aware that his opinion contradicted the teaching of the Church, especially the teaching of the Council of Florence. However, if he or anyone else were to hold such an opinion obstinately (i.e., after being shown that it contradicted Florence), then such a one would be a heretic and outside the Catholic Church. This proves that it is possible for brilliant saints, who are even doctors of the Church, to err in a very significant way on certain matters of the faith. Other saints have as well, as I have shown in the section on the Fathers.

Another error we find in the paragraph from St. Alphonsus is his reference to the Holy Innocents as an example of baptism of blood. This is erroneous because the Holy Innocents' deaths occurred before the Resurrection of Christ – before the law of baptism was instituted.

> Catechism of the Council of Trent, *Baptism made obligatory after Christ's Resurrection*, p. 171: "Holy writers are unanimous in saying that after the Resurrection of our Lord, when He gave His Apostles the command to go and teach all nations: *baptizing them in the name of the Father, and of the Son, and of the Holy Ghost,* **the law of Baptism became obligatory on all who were to be saved.**"[356]

Further, notice how St. Alphonsus says above that the opinion that baptism of blood is not efficacious in infants is temerarious (reckless). In other words, he is teaching with Suarez that it is "reckless" to believe that infants who die without sacramental baptism will not be saved. In teaching this he was actually proposing the very error of John Wyclif solemnly anathematized at the Council of Constance.

> Pope Martin V, *Council of Constance*, Session 15, July 6, 1415 - Condemning the articles of John Wyclif - Proposition 6: "**Those who claim that the children of the faithful dying without sacramental baptism will not be saved, are stupid and presumptuous in saying this**."[357] - Condemned

This is a fascinating proposition from *The Council of Constance*. The arch-heretic John Wyclif was proposing that those (such as ourselves) are stupid for teaching that infants who die without *water* (*i.e., sacramental*) baptism cannot possibly be saved. And he was anathematized for this proposition, among many others. I have already quoted what *The Council of Constance* had to say about John Wyclif's anathematized propositions, such as #6 above, but I will quote it again here.

Pope Martin V, *Council of Constance*, Session 15, July 6, 1415: "The books and pamphlets of John Wyclif, <u>of cursed memory</u>, were carefully examined by the doctors and masters of Oxford University… **This holy synod, therefore, in the name of our Lord Jesus Christ, repudiates and condemns, by this perpetual decree, the aforesaid articles and each of them in particular; and it forbids each and every Catholic henceforth, under pain of anathema, to preach, teach, or hold the said articles or any one of them."**[358]

St. Alphonsus is actually the best-selling author of all time, **having written more than 111 books, not including his letters**.[359] It is not at all surprising that he, being a fallible human being, made some mistakes in matters of faith. But his error on baptism of desire stemmed from the fact that he erroneously thought that it was taught in Sess. 6, Chap. 4 of Trent. That is the main reason he believed in it: he thought it was taught by Trent and from that mistake he erroneously interpreted the Canons on Baptism in Trent (including the all exclusive Canon 5) as somehow to be understood in light of baptism of desire.

Pope Paul III, *The Council of Trent*, canons on the <u>Sacrament </u>of Baptism, canon 5, *ex cathedra*: **"If anyone says that baptism is optional, that is, not necessary for salvation (cf. Jn. 3:5): let him be anathema."**[360]

If St. Alphonsus had more literally examined Sess. 6, Chap. 4 of Trent, he would have seen that it does not teach baptism of desire (as discussed in the section on that passage), but affirms John 3:5 *as it is written*.

<u>It is also important to note that</u> while the principle of Papal infallibility was always believed in the Church (expressed from the earliest times by such phrases as *in the apostolic see the Catholic religion has always been preserved untainted and holy doctrine celebrated),* there is no doubt that after the definition of Papal infallibility at the *First Vatican Council* in 1870 **there is much more clarity about which documents are infallible and which are not. St. Alphonsus and others who lived before 1870 did not necessarily have this degree of clarity, which caused many of them to lessen the distinction, in certain cases, between the infallible decrees of Popes and the fallible teaching of theologians**. <u>It also caused them to not look quite as literally at what the dogma actually says, but rather at what the dogma might mean in light of the opinion of popular theologians of the time.</u>

For instance, in arguing that baptism of desire is *de fide*, St. Alphonsus referenced the statement from Innocent III or Innocent II (they don't even know which one) on the "priest" who was unbaptized, which I have discussed. But obviously that letter of Innocent (?) or whoever it was to an Archbishop did not meet the requirements for Papal Infallibility, and contains a clear error (referring to an unbaptized person as a "priest"). The fallibility of this document is not something that St. Alphonsus seems to have given much consideration. And this proves what I said above, that St. Alphonsus' conclusions are fallible and that one cannot unfailingly rely upon them.

When Our Lord spoke to Peter about Satan's desire to sift the apostles (Lk. 22:31-32), He told him that He prayed for "*thee (singular), that thy (Peter's) faith fail not…*" He did not say, "*but I have prayed for all of you, that your faith fail not.*" Only St. Peter and his successors have been promised an unfailing faith, and this when speaking from the Chair of St. Peter (cf. Vatican I, Sess. 4, Chap. 4, Denz. 1837). The Popes when speaking with this unfailing faith, such as Pope St. Leo the Great in his dogmatic tome to Flavian, the Council of Florence on John 3:5, and the Council of Trent on the Sacrament of Baptism (Sess. 7, Can. 5), exclude any possibility of salvation without water baptism and affirm infallibly that unless a man is born again of water and the Spirit he cannot enter into the Kingdom of God. That is what a Catholic must adhere to and believe.

TRENT'S TEACHING ON THE NECESSITY OF PENANCE VS. ITS TEACHING ON THE NECESSITY OF BAPTISM

OBJECTION- I know that the Council of Trent defines in Canon 5 on the Sacrament of Baptism that the Sacrament of Baptism is necessary for salvation. But the Council of Trent says the same thing about the Sacrament of Penance.

> Pope Paul III, *The Council of Trent*, canons on the <u>Sacrament</u> of Baptism, canon 5, *ex cathedra*: **"If anyone says that baptism [the Sacrament] is optional, that is, not necessary for salvation (cf. Jn. 3:5): let him be anathema."**[361]

> Pope Paul III, *Council of Trent*, Sess. 14, Can. 6 on the Sacrament of Penance: "If anyone denies that sacramental confession was instituted by divine law <u>or is necessary to salvation</u>… let him be anathema."[362]

ANSWER- This argument falters primarily because this translation of Sess. 14, Can. 6 on the Sacrament of Penance is not precise. The Latin for this canon reads:

> Pope Paul III, *Council of Trent*, Sess. 14, Can. 6 on the Sacrament of Penance: "6. *Si quis negaverit, confessionem sacramentalem vel institutam vel ad salutem necessariam esse iure divino… a.s.*"[363]

This is more properly translated as it is found in *Decrees of the Ecumenical Councils* by Fr. Norman Tanner:

> "If anyone denies that the institution of sacramental confession <u>*or its necessity for salvation*</u> are from divine law… let him be anathema."

This translation is accurate. And one can see that this translation has a different meaning than the former. This one condemns anyone who would deny that "*its* (*i.e., the Sacrament of Penance's) necessity*" for salvation are from divine law, not anyone who would deny that "it is necessary for salvation." "Its" necessity is not the same as baptism; "its" necessity is for those who have fallen into mortal sin and do not possess the requisite dispositions for perfect contrition. Therefore, in sum, this canon (Sess. 14. Can. 6) does not define that the Sacrament of Penance is necessary for salvation; it says something slightly – but significantly – different from that.

But baptism of desire advocates will also quote Sess. 14, Chap. 2 of Trent to try to prove the point.

> Pope Julius III, Council of Trent, Sess. 14, Chap. 2, <u>On Penance</u>: **"This sacrament of Penance, moreover, is necessary for the salvation of those who have fallen after baptism, as baptism itself is necessary for those not yet regenerated."**[364]

They argue that people who have fallen into mortal sin can be justified and saved without the Sacrament of Penance by perfect contrition, and therefore people can be saved without the Sacrament of Baptism, since Trent says that the necessity of the Sacrament of Penance for those in mortal sin is the same as the necessity of Baptism. But this argument also falters because <u>just two Chapters later</u> the Council of Trent explicitly states that one can be justified <u>without the Sacrament of Penance</u> by perfect contrition plus the desire for it. One cannot take one chapter of Trent out of context.

> Pope Julius III, Council of Trent, Sess. 14, Chap. 4, <u>On Penance</u>: **"The Council teaches, <u>furthermore</u>, that though it sometimes happens that this contrition is perfect because of charity and reconciles man to God, <u>before this sacrament is actually received</u>**, this reconciliation must not be ascribed to the contrition itself without the desire of the sacrament which is included in it."[365]

The Council of Trent clearly teaches <u>three times</u> that the grace of <u>the Sacrament of Penance</u> can be attained by the desire for the Sacrament of Penance (twice in Sess. 6, Chap. 14; and once in Sess. 14, Chap. 4), while it nowhere teaches the false doctrine of baptism of desire.

> Pope Paul III, Council of Trent, Sess. 6, Chap. 14 on Justification: "Hence it must be taught that the repentance of a Christian after his fall is very different from that at his baptism, and that it includes not only a cessation from sins… **but also the sacramental confession of the same, at least in desire** and to be made in its season, and sacerdotal absolution, as well as satisfaction by fasting, almsgiving, prayers, and other devout exercises of the spiritual life, not indeed for the eternal punishment, **which is remitted together with the guilt either by the sacrament or the desire of the sacrament**, but for the temporal punishment…"[366]

The fact that Trent clearly teaches at least three times that the desire for the Sacrament of Penance is efficacious for Justification, while it nowhere teaches baptism of desire, should tell baptism of desire advocates something; namely, that baptism of desire is not true.

And this is why the statement by Trent in Sess. 14, Chap. 2 on the necessity of the Sacrament of Penance does not equate to Trent's statements on the necessity of the Sacrament of Baptism for salvation, because the Council clearly clarifies its meaning on the necessity of the Sacrament of Penance just two Chapters later by defining that perfect contrition restores such a man to Justification without the Sacrament of Penance. While dogmatic canons stand alone, chapters must be taken in their complete context.

A few baptism of desire advocates will also cite Sess. 6, Can. 29 from the Council of Trent.

> Council of Trent, Sess. 6, Canon 29 on Justification: "If anyone says that he who has fallen after baptism cannot by the grace of God rise again; **or that he can indeed recover lost justice, but by <u>faith alone</u> without the sacrament of Penance, contrary to what the holy Roman and universal Church**, taught by Christ the Lord and His apostles, has hitherto professed, observed, and taught: let him be anathema."[367]

They argue as follows: 1) this Canon condemns anyone who says that Justification can be restored without the Sacrament of Penance; and 2) we know that Justification can be restored *by the desire for the Sacrament of Penance*; therefore 3) the statement in Trent on the absolute necessity of the Sacrament of Baptism (Sess. 7, Can. 5 on the Sacrament) does not mean that desire for it cannot grant Justification. But, as is the case with the statements above, this Canon (Sess. 6, Can. 29) does not state what they claim. It does not condemn anyone who says that Justification can be restored without the Sacrament of Penance. It condemns anyone who says that Justification can be restored by "<u>faith alone</u>" without the Sacrament of Penance. Thus, the argument of baptism of desire advocates – and their attempted analogy with Trent's teaching on the absolute necessity of the Sacrament of Baptism – fails. The fact remains that Trent defines that the Sacrament of Baptism is necessary for salvation without qualification; and Trent nowhere makes the same unqualified definition about the Sacrament of Penance.

> Pope Paul III, *The Council of Trent*, Can. 5 on <u>the Sacrament of Baptism</u>, *ex cathedra*: **"If anyone says that baptism [the Sacrament] is optional, that is, not necessary for salvation (cf. Jn. 3:5): <u>let him be anathema</u>."**[368]

THE ARGUMENT FROM SILENCE

OBJECTION- If it is true that there is no such thing as baptism of desire or baptism of blood, then why didn't any Pope come out and condemn these theories as they were appearing in so many Catechisms in the late 1800's and following?

ANSWER- Baptism of desire and Baptism of blood are shown in various ways to be excluded by the infallible teaching of the Catholic Church. The fact that no Pope came out and explicitly condemned the theories by name doesn't change that fact. The fact that no Pope since the late 1800's removed these theories from inclusion in Catechisms doesn't prove anything either. It was being taught in Catechisms at the same time that one can be saved in a non-Catholic religion. To my knowledge, the heresy that souls can be saved in non-Catholic religions was not removed by express order of any Pope. Does this mean that these Popes believed in the heresy that one can be saved in a non-Catholic religion? Does this mean that it's okay to believe the heresy that one can be saved in a non-Catholic religion? Absolutely not.

Popes are very busy people – with tons of responsibilities – so they can be unaware of what is being taught catechetically at the diocesan level. They rely on their bishops to preserve the faith in their respective dioceses, which unfortunately did not happen in the last 100 years. One example that is very interesting to consider in this regard is the fact that **no Pope ever ordered St. Thomas Aquinas' opinion on the Immaculate Conception to be removed from the** *Summa Theologica*, even though many of them were consistently recommending it!

> St. Thomas Aquinas, *Summa Theologica*, Pt. III, Q. 14, A. 3, Reply to Obj. 1:
> "**The flesh of the Virgin was conceived in original sin**, and therefore contracted these defects. But from the Virgin, Christ's flesh assumed the nature without sin…"[369]

St. Thomas taught that Mary was not conceived immaculately more than once in the *Summa Theologica*. Obviously, he taught this before the definition of Mary's immaculate conception by Pope Pius IX in 1854, but to hold St. Thomas' position after that time would be heretical. Yet, the Popes from 1854 on consistently recommended the *Summa Theologica* to seminarians and priests without ordering that St. Thomas' (now heretical) opinion be removed! This proves that the theory of baptism of desire can be contrary to defined dogma – and even heretical – and yet no Pope ever ordered it to be removed from the Catechisms, for whatever reason.

But I believe that the main reason why the false doctrine of baptism of desire was never explicitly condemned by name is the fact that God allows heresies to arise – to see who will believe the truth and who won't – and the denial of the necessity of Baptism and the necessity of the Catholic Church is the key heresy to the Great Apostasy.

1 Cor. 11:19: **"For there must be also heresies: that they also, who are approved, may be manifest among you**."

THE 1917 CODE OF CANON LAW

OBJECTION- The 1917 Code of Canon Law gives Christian Burial to unbaptized catechumens.

ANSWER- As we've pointed out before, the 1917 Code of Canon Law is <u>not</u> infallible. In fact, the 1917 Code contradicts the entire Tradition of the Catholic Church for 1900 years on whether unbaptized persons can be given Christian burial.

> Canon 1239, 1917 Code: "1. Those who die without baptism are not to be accorded ecclesiastical burial. 2. **Catechumens who through no fault of their own die without baptism are to be reckoned as baptized**."

Since the time of Jesus Christ and throughout all of history, the Catholic Church universally refused ecclesiastical burial to catechumens who died without the Sacrament of Baptism, as *The Catholic Encyclopedia* admits:

> *The Catholic Encyclopedia*, "Baptism," Volume 2, 1907: "A certain statement in the funeral oration of St. Ambrose over the Emperor Valentinian II has been brought forward as a proof that the Church offered sacrifices and prayers for catechumens who died before baptism. **There is not a vestige of such a custom to be found anywhere**… The practice of the Church is more correctly shown in the canon (xvii) of the Second Council of Braga (572 AD): '**Neither the commemoration of Sacrifice** [*oblationis*] **nor the service of chanting** [*psallendi*] **is to be employed for catechumens who have died without baptism**.'"[370]

This is the law of the Catholic Church since the beginning and throughout all of history. So, since this issue is tied to the Faith and not merely disciplinary, either the Catholic Church was wrong since the time of Christ for *refusing ecclesiastical burial for catechumens who died without baptism* or the 1917 Code is wrong for granting it to them. It is either one or the other, because the 1917 Code <u>directly contradicts</u> the Traditional and constant law of the Catholic Church for nineteen centuries on this point which is tied to the Faith. The answer is, obviously, that the 1917 Code is <u>wrong</u> and not infallible, and the Catholic Church's law for all of history refusing ecclesiastical burial to catechumens is right. In fact, it is interesting to note that the Latin version of the 1917 Code contains many footnotes to traditional Popes, councils, etc. to show from where certain canons were derived. **Canon 1239.2 on giving ecclesiastical burial to unbaptized catechumens has no footnote, not to any Pope, previous law or Council, simply because there is nothing in Tradition which supports it!**

The Catholic Encyclopedia (1907) quotes an interesting decree from Pope Innocent III wherein he commented on *the traditional, universal and constant law of the Catholic Church from the beginning* which refused ecclesiastical burial to all who died without the Sacrament of Baptism.

> *The Catholic Encyclopedia*, "Baptism," Volume 2, 1907: "The reason of this regulation [forbidding ecclesiastical burial to all unbaptized persons] is given by **Pope Innocent III (Decr., III, XXVIII, xii): 'It has been decreed by the sacred canons that we are to have no communion with those who are dead, <u>if we have not communicated with them while alive</u>.'"**[371]

The 1917 Code was definitely not an *ex cathedra* pronouncement because it does not bind the whole Church, but only the Roman Rite, as stipulated in Canon 1 of the 1917 Code. The 1917 Code is not infallible Church discipline either, as proven by the fact that it contains a law which directly contradicts the infallible discipline of the Church since the beginning on a point tied to the Faith. The actual Bull promulgating the 1917 Code, *Proventissima Mater Ecclesia*, was not signed by Benedict XV, but by Cardinal Gasparri and Cardinal De Azevedo. Cardinal Gasparri, the Secretary of State, was the main author and compiler of the canons. Some theologians would also argue that only disciplines which bind the whole Church – unlike the 1917 Code – are protected by the infallibility of the governing authority of the Church, an argument which may be supported in the following teaching of Pope Pius XII.

> Pope Pius XII, *Mystici Corporis Christi* (# 66), June 29, 1943:
> "**Certainly the loving Mother is spotless** in the Sacraments, by which she gives birth to and nourishes her children; in the faith which she has always preserved inviolate; **in her sacred laws <u>imposed upon all</u>**; in the evangelical counsels which she recommends; in those heavenly gifts and extraordinary graces through which, with inexhaustible fecundity, she generates hosts of martyrs, virgins, and confessors."[372]

Regardless, the 1917 Code doesn't enjoy infallibility. This is further proven by the following canons.

1) The 1917 Code teaches that <u>heretics can be in good faith</u>.

Canon 731.2, 1917 Code: "It is forbidden that the Sacraments of the Church be ministered to **heretics and schismatics, even if they ask for them and are in good faith**, unless beforehand, rejecting their errors, they are reconciled with the Church."

A heretic, **by infallible definition, is of bad faith** and brings down upon his head eternal punishment.

> Pope St. Celestine I, *Council of Ephesus*, 431:
> "... **all heretics** corrupt the true expressions of the Holy Spirit **with their own evil minds** and they **draw down on their own heads an inextinguishable flame**."[373]

> Pope Eugene IV, *Council of Florence*, "Cantate Domino," 1441, *ex cathedra*: "The Holy Roman Church firmly believes, professes and preaches that **all those** who are outside the Catholic Church, not only pagans but also Jews or **heretics** and schismatics, cannot share in eternal life and **will go into the everlasting fire** which was prepared for the devil and his angels, unless they are joined to the Church before the end of their lives…"[374]

> Pope Gregory XVI, *Summo Iugiter Studio* (# 2), May 27, 1832: "Finally some of these **misguided people attempt to persuade themselves** and others that men are not saved only in the Catholic religion, but **that even heretics may attain eternal life**."[375]

A person in *good faith* who is erring innocently about a dogma (loosely and improperly called a "material heretic" in theological discussions) is not a heretic, but a Catholic erring in good faith. So the statement in the 1917 Code about heretics and schismatics in good faith is definitely theologically erroneous and it proves that it was not protected by infallibility.

2) The 1917 Code teaches that Catholics may be present at non-Catholic forms of worship, including non-Catholic weddings and non-Catholic funerals!

> Canon 1258, 1917 Code: "1. It is not licit for the faithful by any manner to assist actively or to have a part in **the sacred [rites] of non-Catholics**. 2. **Passive or merely material presence can be tolerated for the sake of honor or civil office, for grave reason approved by the Bishop in case of doubt, at the funerals, weddings, and similar solemnities of non-Catholics**, provided danger of scandal is absent."

Note: this canon is not talking about Catholic Masses or Catholic worship presided over by a heretic, *but non-Catholic or non-Christian (false) worship and rites*. This is outrageous! This Canon allows one to travel to and attend <u>a Jewish Synagogue or a Buddhist Temple</u> or a Lutheran Service, etc., etc., etc. for the wedding or funeral of infidels or heretics – *just as long as one doesn't actively participate*! This is ridiculous, for to go out of one's way to be <u>present</u> at such non-Catholic services where false worship is conducted (for the sake of honoring or pleasing the person involved in it) is a scandal in itself. It is honoring a person who is sinning against the First Commandment. To go to the funeral of a non-Catholic is to imply that there was some hope for him for salvation outside the Church; and to attend the Wedding of a non-Catholic is to imply that God condones his or her marriage outside the Church. A Catholic can neither take part *actively* in false worship nor go out of one's way to travel to the false worship or the non-Catholic ceremony to honor it with his "passive" presence. Hence, this canon also proves that this Code is not infallible.

    3) The 1917 Code condemns any written or spoken criticism of Cardinals or Ordinary Bishops of the Church!

> Canon 2344, 1917 Code: "**Whoever gives injury to the Roman Pontiff, a Cardinal of the Holy Roman Church, a Legate of the Roman Pontiff, to Sacred Roman Congregations, Tribunals of the Apostolic See, and their major Officials, and their own Ordinary <u>by public journals, sermons, or pamphlets</u>, whether directly or indirectly, <u>or who excites animosity or odium against their acts, decrees, decisions, or sentences</u>** shall be punished by an Ordinary not only at the request of the party but even by office with censures and, in order to accomplish satisfaction, other appropriate penalties and penances for the gravity of the fault and the repair of the scandal."

All of Catholic Tradition teaches us that Catholic priests and laypeople not only have the right, but, when occasion arises, the duty to correct or even rebuke a wayward prelate, if God's honor or the Faith requires it. But this canon says that any opposition to (or criticism of) the abuses or bad actions of an Ordinary or a Cardinal or a Pope is forbidden, *whether in a sermon by a priest or in written form*! It would mean that every act, decree, decision or sentence by a bishop is infallible, which is clearly false. Need one say more to prove that this and the thousands of other laws and propositions in the 1917 Code are not protected by infallibility? No; this has been thoroughly proven. The 1917 Code contradicts the immemorial Tradition of the Church on ecclesiastical burial and it holds no weight for a moment against the infallible declaration of the Chair of St. Peter (binding the entire Church) that no one can enter heaven without the Sacrament of Baptism.

> Pope Paul III, *The Council of Trent*, Can. 5 on <u>the Sacrament</u> of Baptism, *ex cathedra*: "**If anyone says that baptism [the sacrament] is optional, that is, <u>not necessary for salvation</u> (cf. Jn. 3:5): <u>let him be anathema</u>.**"[376]

THE ARGUMENT THAT BAPTISM IS IMPOSSIBLE FOR SOME TO RECEIVE

OBJECTION- Baptism of desire supporters assert that **for some people the command to be baptized is simply impossible to fulfill**.

ANSWER- God does not command impossibilities (*de fide*). Thus, it is not impossible for any man to get baptized.

> Catechism of the Council of Trent, On Baptism, Tan Books, p. 171:
> "Holy writers are unanimous in saying that after the Resurrection of our Lord, **WHEN HE GAVE HIS APOSTLES THE COMMAND** to go and teach all nations: baptizing them in the name of the Father, and of the Son, and of the Holy Ghost, **THE LAW OF BAPTISM became obligatory on all who were to be saved**."

> Pope Paul III, *Council of Trent*, Session 6, Chap. 11 on Justification, *ex cathedra*: "... no one should make use of that rash statement forbidden under anathema by the Fathers, that the commandments of God are impossible to observe for a man who is justified. '**FOR GOD DOES NOT COMMAND IMPOSSIBILITIES**, but by commanding admonishes you both to do what you can do, and to pray for what you cannot do...'"[377]

THE ERRORS OF MICHAEL DU BAY

OBJECTION- Wasn't the idea that catechumens cannot have the remission of sins condemned in the Errors of Michael Du Bay?

ANSWER- No! And the fact that certain baptism of desire advocates obstinately attempt to quote the Errors of Michael Du Bay in favor of baptism of desire simply shows: 1) their dishonesty; and 2) their lack of evidence for "baptism of desire."

> Errors of Michael Du Bay, Condemned by St. Pius V in "Ex omnibus afflictionibus," Oct. 1, 1567: "31. **Perfect and sincere charity**, which is from a 'pure heart and good conscience and a faith not feigned' [1 Tim. 1:5], **can be in catechumens as well as in penitents without the remissions of sins**."[378] - Condemned

> Errors of Michael Du Bay, Condemned by St. Pius V in "Ex omnibus afflictionibus," Oct. 1, 1567: "33. **A catechumen lives justly and rightly and holily, and observes the commandments of God, and fulfills the law through**

charity, which is only received in the laver of baptism, <u>before the remission of sins has been obtained</u>."[379] - Condemned

Michael Du Bay's propositions above are condemned because they assert that perfect charity can be in catechumens and penitents <u>without the remission of sins</u>. (Note: this says nothing one way or the other about whether or not perfect charity can be in catechumens *with the remission of sins*.) Du Bay's propositions above are false because one cannot have perfect charity without the remission of sins.

> Pope Paul III, *Council of Trent*, Session 6, Chap. 7 on Justification, *ex cathedra*: **"Justification** … is not merely remission of sins, but also the sanctification and renewal of the interior man… Hence **man** through Jesus Christ, into whom he is ingrafted, <u>*receives in the said justification together with the remission of sins all these gifts infused at the same time: faith, hope and charity*</u>."[380]

Faith, hope, charity and the remission of sins are inseparable in a Justified person. Thus, Michael Du Bay was <u>rightly condemned</u> for his <u>false</u> statement that catechumens and penitents can have perfect charity *without the remission of sins*. His assertion contradicts Catholic teaching. And when a Pope condemns propositions like the false propositions of Michael Du Bay, he condemns *the entire proposition as such*. In condemning such an error, **no assertion is made positively or negatively about either part of the statement**, *nor is any assertion made, positively or negatively, about whether catechumens can have remission of sins <u>with perfect charity</u>*, which is <u>not</u> the topic of Michael Du Bay's statement. But we know from other teachings that unbaptized catechumens cannot have the remission of sins at all since they are outside the Church.

> Pope Boniface VIII, *Unam Sanctam*, Nov. 18, 1302, *ex cathedra*: "With Faith urging us we are forced to believe and to hold the one, holy, Catholic Church and that, apostolic, and we firmly believe and simply confess **this Church outside of which there is no salvation <u>NOR REMISSION OF SIN</u>**…"[381]

A good example which further serves to show how the baptism of desire advocates are completely wrong in using Michael Du Bay as an argument for "baptism of desire" is found Denz. 646, an error of John Hus, condemned by the Council of Constance:

> Errors of John Hus: "#20. **If the Pope is wicked** and especially if he is foreknown (as a reprobate), then as Judas, the Apostle, he is of the devil, a thief, and a son of perdition, **and he is not the head of the holy militant Church, since he is not a member of it.**"[382] - Condemned

Based on this passage, some people have erroneously concluded that the argument of Sedevacantists (that *a Pope who becomes a heretic loses his office and ceases to be head of the Church since he is not a member of it*) is condemned here. But the Council of Constance is not condemning that at all; it is not asserting anything one way or the other in that regard. Rather, it is condemning *the entire proposition* as such, which asserts that because a Pope is <u>wicked</u> (or immoral) he is not the head of the Church since he is not a member of it. And this is false: just because a Pope is <u>wicked</u> does not mean that he is not a member of the Church and therefore he is not the head of the Church. The Sedevacantists, on the other hand, correctly point out that a **heretical** pope (not merely a wicked one) *is not a member of the Church and therefore cannot be the head* of the Church (and thus he loses his office automatically when he becomes a heretic). This is actually the teaching of the Church.

Pope Innocent III, *Eius exemplo*, Dec. 18, 1208:
"By the heart we believe and by the mouth we confess **the one Church, not of heretics**, but the Holy Roman, Catholic, and Apostolic Church outside of which we believe that no one is saved."[383]

Therefore….

St. Francis De Sales (17th century), Doctor of the Church: "Thus we do not say that the Pope cannot err in his private opinions, as did John XXII; or be altogether a heretic, as perhaps Honorius was. **Now when he [the Pope] is explicitly a heretic, he falls ipso facto from his dignity and out of the Church**..."[384]

St. Antoninus (1459): "In the case in which the pope would become a heretic, he would find himself, by that fact alone and without any other sentence, separated from the Church. A head separated from a body cannot, as long as it remains separated, be head of the same body from which it was cut off. A pope who would be separated from the Church by heresy, therefore, would by that very fact itself cease to be head of the Church. **He could not be a heretic and remain pope, because, since he is outside of the Church, he cannot possess the keys of the Church.**" (*Summa Theologica*, cited in *Actes de Vatican I*. V. Frond pub.)

St. Robert Bellarmine, *De Romano Pontifice*, II, 30:
"**A pope who is a manifest heretic automatically (*per se*) ceases to be pope and head**, just as he ceases automatically to be a Christian and a member of the Church. Wherefore, he can be judged and punished by the Church. *This is the teaching of all the ancient Fathers* who teach that manifest heretics immediately lose all jurisdiction."

St. Robert Bellarmine, *De Romano Pontifice*, II, 30:
"For, in the first place, **it is proven with arguments from authority and from reason that the manifest heretic is 'ipso facto' deposed**. The argument from authority is based on St. Paul (Titus 3:10), who orders that the heretic be avoided after two warnings, that is, after showing himself to be manifestly obstinate - **which means before any excommunication or judicial sentence**. And this is what St. Jerome writes, adding that the other sinners are excluded from the Church by sentence of excommunication, but the heretics exile themselves and separate themselves by their own act from the body of Christ."

St. Robert Bellarmine, *De Romano Pontifice*, II, 30:
"**This principle is most certain. The non-Christian cannot in any way be Pope, as Cajetan himself admits (ib. c. 26). The reason for this is that he cannot be head of what he is not a member;** now he who is not a Christian is not a member of the Church, **and a manifest heretic is not a Christian, as is clearly taught by St. Cyprian (lib. 4, epist. 2), St. Athanasius (Scr. 2 cont. Arian.), St.**

Augustine (lib. De great. Christ. Cap. 20), St. Jerome (contra Lucifer.) and others; <u>therefore the manifest heretic cannot be Pope</u>."

Pope Leo XIII, *Satis Cognitum* (#15), June 29, 1896:
"**No one, therefore, unless in communion with Peter can share in his authority, since IT IS <u>ABSURD TO IMAGINE</u> THAT HE WHO IS OUTSIDE CAN COMMAND IN THE CHURCH.**"[385]

Thus, as we can see, <u>the second half</u> of John Hus' condemned statement, "*[a Pope] is not the head of the holy militant Church, since he is not a member of it,*" is true. But Hus' proposition is condemned *as it is* because *in the beginning* it asserted that this cessation of membership (and therefore headship) *comes about from simply being a wicked Pope*, which is <u>false</u>. Thus, taken as a whole, Hus' proposition, like Du Bay's, is false and therefore it was condemned.

So, the error of John Hus is a valuable example in demonstrating that the baptism of desire advocates <u>are completely wrong</u> again in citing the errors of Michael Du Bay as an argument. In condemning such a proposition from Michael Du Bay, the Pope makes no statement positively or negatively about *whether catechumens can have remission of sins with perfect charity*, because that was not what Du Bay asserted. The fact is that catechumens cannot have remission of sins at all because they are outside the Church.

But the baptism of desire advocates know that the Errors of Michael Du Bay don't prove their point or they could figure that out if they tried, so why do some of them keep using this non-argument as an argument? It's simply dishonesty! It is actually an outrage that they obstinately try to play upon the laypeople's ignorance by using these errors of Michael Du Bay as an argument in favor of baptism of desire. The dishonest CMRI out of Spokane, Washington, for example, recently published a pamphlet and an article on baptism of desire. The pamphlet and the article not only totally <u>misquoted</u> the Council of Trent's teaching in Sess. 6, Chap. 4 (*using "except through" instead of "without"*), but quite dishonestly used the above errors of Michael Du Bay as a "proof" for baptism of desire. In using these tactics in their pamphlet and article, the CMRI deceived their readers who don't care enough about the Faith to examine the issue carefully and weigh the merits of their argument – those readers who simply believed what the CMRI concluded because it seemed documented, which is probably a great number. This is how heretics kill souls and lead them astray.

CORNELIUS THE CENTURION

OBJECTION- Acts 10:47 says that Cornelius and his companions received the Holy Ghost. This means that they were justified without Baptism.

ANSWER- Acts 10:47 does not say that Cornelius and his companions were justified without Baptism. Nothing there says that their sins were remitted or that they were "saved," a phrase frequently used to describe those who have been justified by Baptism. The context of Acts 10 is dealing with *receiving the Holy Ghost by receiving the gift of speaking in tongues*, not having one's sins remitted. Acts 10:47, therefore, is merely speaking of Cornelius and his companions having received the gift of tongues. The description "receiving the Holy Ghost" or "being filled with the Holy Ghost" is actually used frequently in scripture to describe a person making a godly prophesy or receiving some spiritual gift. It does not necessarily mean that one has received the remission of sins. The following two passages are examples of the phrase "filled with the Holy Ghost" being used to describe a spiritual gift (prophesy, etc.), not the remission of sins.

> Luke 1:41-42 "And it came to pass, that when Elizabeth heard the salutation of Mary, the infant leaped in her womb: **and Elizabeth was filled with the Holy Ghost: <u>And she cried out</u>** with a loud voice…"

> Luke 1:67 "And Zachary, his father, **was filled with the Holy Ghost, <u>and he prophesied</u>**, saying…"

THE GOOD THIEF AND THE HOLY INNOCENTS

<u>OBJECTION-</u> What about the Good Thief and the Holy Innocents?

<u>ANSWER-</u> This was addressed already in the section on St. Augustine, but it will be repeated here for those who may be looking for it in this section of "Other Objections." The Good Thief cannot be used as an example of baptism of blood primarily because the Good Thief died under the Old Law, not the New Law; he died before the Law of Baptism was instituted by Jesus Christ after the Resurrection. For that reason, the Good Thief, <u>like the Holy Innocents</u>, constitutes no argument against the necessity of receiving the Sacrament of Baptism for salvation.

> Catechism of the Council of Trent, *Baptism made obligatory after Christ's Resurrection*, p. 171: "<u>Holy writers are unanimous in saying that after the Resurrection of our Lord</u>, when He gave His Apostles the command to go and teach all nations: *baptizing them in the name of the Father, and of the Son, and of the Holy Ghost*, **the law of Baptism became obligatory on all who were to be saved.**"[386]

In fact, when Our Lord said to the Good Thief, *"This day you will be with Me in paradise,"* Jesus was not referring to heaven, but actually to hell. As Catholics know, no one entered heaven until after Our Lord did, after His Resurrection. On the day of the Crucifixion, Christ descended into hell, as the Apostles' Creed says. He did not descend to the hell of the damned, but to the place in hell called the *Limbo of the Fathers*, the waiting place of the Just of the Old Testament, who could not enter heaven until after the Savior came.

2 Peter 3:18-19 "Christ also died once for our sins… **In which also coming he preached to those spirits that were in prison**…"

To further prove the point that the Good Thief did not go to heaven on the Day of the Crucifixion, there is the fact that on Easter Sunday, when Mary Magdalene met the Risen Lord, He told her, *"Do not touch Me, for I have not yet ascended to My Father."*

John 20:17- "**[On the Day of the Resurrection]** Jesus saith to her; Mary. She turning, saith to him; Rabboni, (that is to say, Master). Jesus saith to her; Do not touch me, **for I have not yet ascended to my Father**…"

Our Lord hadn't even yet ascended to Heaven on the Sunday of the Resurrection. It is therefore a fact that Our Lord and the Good Thief were not in heaven together on Good Friday; they were in the Limbo of the Fathers, the prison described in 2 Peter 3:18-19. Jesus called this place Paradise because He would be there with the just of the Old Testament.

THE "YOU CAN'T JUDGE" HERESY

OBJECTION- You can't judge if all non-Catholics go to hell. You are not God. You must leave such judgments to Him.

ANSWER- God has already revealed His judgment to us. To say that one cannot be sure or "cannot judge" if all who die as non-Catholics go to hell **is simply to reject God's judgment as *possibly untrue* – which is heresy and blasphemy** and pride of the worst kind. It is **to sinfully judge as possibly worthy of heaven those whom God has explicitly revealed He will not save**. To put it simply: to say that one cannot judge that all who die as non-Catholics go to hell (when God has revealed this) is to judge in the most gravely sinful way – in a way directly contrary to God's revealed truth and revealed judgment.

Pope Eugene IV, Council of Florence, "Cantate Domino," 1441, ex cathedra:
"The Holy Roman Church firmly believes, professes and preaches that all those who are outside the Catholic Church, not only pagans but also Jews or heretics and schismatics, cannot share in eternal life and will go into the everlasting fire which was prepared for the devil and his angels, unless they are joined to the Church before the end of their lives…"[387]

And the "You Can't Judge" heresy is incredibly widespread today. On Dec. 15, 2003 I had a conversation with a "traditionalist monk" named Fr. Giardina of Christ the King Monastery in Alabama. I asked him if he believes that all who die as non-Catholics cannot be saved. He said that he didn't know and couldn't judge. I then asked him if he believes that it's possible that Rabbis who reject Christ can be saved, and he told me that it's possible because he can't judge. By refusing to assent to what God has revealed under the pretext of the "You Can't Judge" heresy, this person fell into a rejection of the Gospel and of the necessity of Christ Himself. On the contrary, the great St. Francis Xavier shows how a Catholic must affirm that all those who die outside the Church are definitely lost, as he does in regard to a pagan privateer who died on a ship on which he was traveling.

> St. Francis Xavier, Nov. 5, 1549: "The corsair who commanded our vessel died here at Cagoxima. He did his work for us, on the whole, as we wished… **He himself chose to die in his own superstitions; he did not even leave us the power of rewarding him by that kindness which we can after death do to other friends who die in the profession of the Christian faith, in commending their souls to God, since the poor fellow <u>by his own hand cast his soul into hell</u>,** where there is no redemption."[388]

THE OBJECTIVE-SUBJECTIVE HERESY

<u>**OBJECTION-**</u> Objectively speaking, there is absolutely no salvation outside the Catholic Church. But *subjectively* speaking, we just don't know.

<u>**ANSWER-**</u> This is similar to the "You Can't Judge" heresy. Those who advance this heresy deny dogmatic truth; for the Objective-Subjective Heresy means that the dogma Outside the Church There is No Salvation is only true "objectively," which necessarily means that non-Catholics can be saved "subjectively," **which means that the end result is a denial of the defined dogma.**

The Objective-Subjective Heresy is just a clever way of saying that the dogma Outside the Church There is No Salvation might not mean what it says. It is diabolical double-talk. It is equivalent to asserting:

> "Jesus Christ is *objectively* the Son of God."

Could a Catholic hold that? No, he could not, because Jesus Christ is not just *objectively* the Son of God; He is the Son of God – period! But this is exactly what those who hold the Objective-Subjective heresy are saying! For to say that one dogma (Outside the Church There is No Salvation) is only true *objectively* is to say that any other dogma (e.g., Jesus Christ is the Son of God) is only true objectively. There is no way around this. The Objective-Subjective Heresy **asserts the heresy that <u>dogmas are not really divinely revealed truths</u>, but** only presumptions or policies that we go by, and **this is condemned Modernism.**

Pope Pius X, *Lamentabile*, The Errors of the Modernists, July 3, 1907, #22: "**<u>The dogmas which the Church professes as revealed are not truths fallen from heaven</u>, but they are a kind of interpretation** of religious facts, which the human mind by a laborious effort prepared for itself."- **Condemned**[389]

Pope Pius X, *Lamentabile*, The Errors of the Modernists, July 3, 1907, #26: "**The dogmas of faith are to be held only according to a practical sense**, that is, as preceptive norms for action, <u>but not as norms for believing</u>."- Condemned[390]

The idea that we can preach that there is <u>no</u> salvation outside the Church while we believe in our hearts that there is salvation outside the Church or <u>may</u> be salvation outside the Church is heretical. That only Catholics can be saved is a truth revealed from heaven which every Catholic must **believe first,** and profess second.

Pope Eugene IV, Council of Florence, "Cantate Domino," 1441, *ex cathedra*: "The Holy Roman Church **firmly believes**, professes and preaches that all those who are outside the Catholic Church, not only pagans but also Jews or heretics and schismatics, cannot share in eternal life and will go into the everlasting fire which was prepared for the devil and his angels, unless they are joined to the Church before the end of their lives..."[391]

Since dogmas are truths fallen from heaven, **to say that any dogma (e.g., the dogma that all who die as non-Catholics are lost) <u>may have a "subjective" reality that is *different* from the revealed truth</u> is heresy** – it is a denial of that truth. Therefore, the idea that *subjectively* non-Catholics can be saved is blatant heresy; it is a denial of the revealed truth that all who die as non-Catholics are necessarily lost.

The same Objective-Subjective heresy is taught in the book *The Devil's Final Battle*, which is promoted by a number of "traditionalist" organizations.

The Devil's Final Battle, compiled and edited by "Fr." Paul Kramer, p. 69: "**This teaching must not be understood to preclude the possibility of salvation for those who do not become formal members of the Church** if, through no fault of their own, they do not know of their *objective* obligation to do so... **only God knows whom He will save** (in some extraordinary manner) from among the great mass of humanity which has not exteriorly professed the Catholic religion."[392]

This is completely heretical. It is particularly pernicious, in fact, because this book pretends to uphold the dogma Outside the Catholic Church There is No Salvation and it will be read in "traditional circles" – all the while rejecting the dogma. The above statement is a denial of Papal Infallibility and a repudiation of the <u>divinely revealed truth</u> that God will only save Catholics and those who become Catholics. The heretical statement above literally means that *we just don't know if what God has revealed is true or not*. And it shows again how prevalent and virulent the Objective-Subjective heresy is, finagling its way into all kinds of places. The truth remains, however, that the Catholic Church teaches that Church membership is necessary for salvation. It nowhere teaches what the modern heretics love to say: that *Church membership is <u>objectively</u> necessary for salvation*.

BAYSIDE, MEDJUGORJE AND OTHER FALSE APPARITIONS

<u>OBJECTION-</u> Our Lady herself revealed at Bayside and Medjugorje that non-Catholics can be saved, so you are wrong.

> "Our Lady" of Bayside, August 14, 1979: "Do not judge your brothers and sisters who have not been converted. For My Father's House, **My Son has repeated over and over, remember always – that in My Father's House, there are many rooms in the Mansion, <u>signifying faiths and creeds</u>**."[393]

<u>ANSWER-</u> Our Lady does not contradict infallible dogma and the Chair of St. Peter. To say otherwise is blasphemous heresy. The statement above allegedly from "Our Lady of Bayside," that in the Father's House *there are many mansions representing many faiths and creeds,* is one of the most heretical statements I've ever seen. It totally rejects Catholic dogma, which is the teaching of Jesus Christ. This heresy in Bayside totally gives away the Bayside Message as a false apparition of the devil.

> Pope Leo XII, *Ubi Primum* (# 14), May 5, 1824:
> "**It is impossible for the most true God**, who is Truth itself, the best, the wisest Provider, and the Rewarder of good men, **to approve all sects who profess false teachings** which are often inconsistent with one another and contradictory, **and to confer eternal rewards on their members**… **by divine faith we hold one Lord, one faith**, one baptism… **This is why we profess that there is <u>no</u> salvation outside the Church**."[394]

The Bayside Message contradicts what Catholics must hold by divine faith, that there is only one faith that leads to heaven, the Catholic Faith, outside of which there is no salvation. The *many mansions* in the Father's house that Our Lord refers to in the Gospel represent different rewards for Catholics who die in the state of grace. Those who continue to believe in Bayside and dismiss these facts are following the deception of the devil; they are rejecting the Catholic Faith and leaving the Catholic Church. They are choosing to follow the "Message" of Bayside over the teaching of the Catholic Church. Those who are aware of this heresy and continue to believe in Bayside are not Catholics and not followers of Our Lady, but rather are followers of the deception the devil has set up for them.

And it is sad to say, but for many followers of false apparitions such as Bayside, the false messages become their "dogma" and replace the real dogma defined by the Popes.

What Does Medjugorje Say?

"The Madonna always stresses that there is but one God and that people have enforced unnatural separation. **One cannot truly believe, be a true Christian, if he does not respect other religions as well.**"[395] – "Seer" Ivanka Ivankovic

"The Madonna said that religions are separated in the earth, **but the people of all religions are accepted by her Son.**"[396] – "Seer" Ivanka Ivankovic

Question: "Is the Blessed Mother calling all people to be Catholic?" Answer: "No. The Blessed Mother says <u>all religions are dear to her and her Son</u>."[397] – "Seer" Vicka Ivankovic

This is total apostasy. It is a total rejection of Catholic dogma; it is a total rejection of the dogma Outside the Catholic Church There is No Salvation; and it is a total rejection of the clear teaching of the Gospel on the necessity of believing in Jesus Christ, the Son of God, for salvation. This proves that Medjugorje, like the rest of the false modern apparitions, is a deception of the devil. Those who are aware of these facts and refuse to reject it as a false apparition are rejecting the Catholic Faith.

THE BROWN SCAPULAR

<u>OBJECTION-</u> Our Lady said that whoever dies wearing the Brown Scapular will not go to hell. This means that you are wrong: non-Catholics and the unbaptized can be saved who die wearing the Scapular.

<u>ANSWER-</u> Everyone should wear the Brown Scapular; it is a sign of devotion to Our Lady and a powerful sacramental. And we too originally believed that whoever dies wearing the Brown Scapular could not go to hell. We were convinced that God would make sure that only baptized Catholics in the state of grace died with it on. But in researching the history behind the Brown Scapular promise, one will discover <u>that the Catholic Church has never stated that Our Lady promised that whoever dies wearing the Brown Scapular will not suffer eternal fire</u>. I refer the reader to the articles in *The Catholic Encyclopedia* (Volume 13) on "Scapular" and the "Sabbatine Privilege." *The*

Catholic Encyclopedia points out that the promise that has been declared by the Church relating to the Brown Scapular is the Sabbatine Privilege, which has various requirements attached, <u>one of which is to be a baptized Catholic who dies in the state of grace</u>. The authors of *The Catholic Encyclopedia* note that nowhere has a Pope authoritatively stated that *whoever* dies with the Scapular will be saved.

In *The Glories of Mary*, St. Alphonsus tells us about the Scapular.

> St. Alphonsus, *The Glories of Mary*, p. 272: "… the sacred scapular of Carmel… It was also confirmed by Alexander V, Clement VII, Pius V, Gregory XIII, and Paul V, who, in 1612, in a bull said: 'That Christians may piously believe that the blessed Virgin will aid by her continual intercession, by her merits and special protection, after death, and principally on Saturday, which is a day consecrated by the Church to the blessed Virgin, the souls of the members of the confraternity of holy Mary of Mount Carmel, <u>who shall have departed this life in the state of grace</u>, worn the scapular, observing chastity, according to their state of life, recited the office of the Virgin, and if they have not been able to recite it, shall have observed the fasts of the Church, abstaining from flesh-meat on Wednesdays, except on Christmas day.'"

St. Alphonsus here lists the promises of the Sabbatine Privilege; he mentions nothing about the alleged promise that "whoever dies wearing this scapular shall not suffer eternal fire." He points out that <u>one must be in the state of grace</u> (which presupposes the Catholic Faith and Baptism); one must be a member of the confraternity, etc. So it is possible for a person to die with the Brown Scapular on and still go to Hell, if the person is a non-Catholic or a Catholic in the state of mortal sin. This is the teaching of the Catholic Church. Those who say otherwise are simply mistaken.

18. The Soul of the Church Heresy

<u>OBJECTION</u>- It's possible to belong to the "Soul" of the Church without belonging to her Body. In this way those who die as members of non-Catholic religions can be joined to the Church and saved, as the Baltimore Catechism (1921) explains:
Q. 512 How are such persons said to belong to the Church?

A. Such persons are said to belong to the "Soul of the Church"; that is, they are really members of the Church without knowing it. Those who share in its Sacraments are said to belong to the body or visible part of the Church.

<u>ANSWER</u>- Modern men are desperate to find ways to deny *extra ecclesiam nulla salus (outside the Church there is no salvation)*. Hence comes the "Soul" of the Church heresy. The Soul of the Church heresy is that which teaches that one can be saved in another

religion or without the Catholic Faith <u>by being united to the Soul of the Church, but not the Body</u>. (This heresy is rampant and is held by multitudes of "traditionalists" and "traditional" priests.) The purveyors of this heresy are forced to admit that belonging to the Body of the Church only comes with the Sacrament of Baptism.

The "Soul of the Church Heresy" will now be soundly refuted by a study of various magisterial pronouncements.

<u>First</u>, this heresy stems from a misunderstanding of the true meaning of the term "Soul of the Church." The Soul of the Church is the Holy Ghost. **It is <u>not</u> an invisible extension of the mystical body which includes the unbaptized**.

> Pope Pius XII, *Mystici Corporis*, June 29, 1943: "… Leo XIII, of immortal memory in the Encyclical, "Divinum illud," [expressed it] in these words: '**Let it suffice to state this, that, as Christ is the Head of the Church, the Holy Spirit is her soul.**'"[398]

<u>Second</u>, the Church is essentially (i.e., in its essence) a Mystical <u>Body</u>.

> Pope Leo X, *Fifth Lateran Council*, Session 11, Dec. 19, 1516: "… **the mystical body, the Church** (*corpore mystico*)…"[399]

> Pope St. Pius X, *Editae saepe* (# 8), May 26, 1910: "… **the Church, the Mystical Body of Christ**…"[400]

> Pope Leo XII, *Quod Hoc Ineunte* (# 1), May 24, 1824: "… **His mystical Body**."[401]

Therefore, to teach that one can be saved without belonging to the Body is to teach that one can be saved without belonging to the Church, since <u>the Church is a Body</u>. And this is without question HERETICAL.

A man can be either inside the Church or outside the Church. He can be either inside or outside **the Body**. There isn't a third realm in which the Church exists – an invisible Soul of the Church. Those who say that one can be saved by belonging to the Soul of the Church, while not belonging to her Body, deny the undivided unity of the Church's Body and Soul, which is parallel to denying the undivided unity of Christ's Divine and Human natures.

> Pope Leo XIII, *Satis Cognitum* (# 3), June 29, 1896: "For this reason the Church is so often called in Holy Writ a body, and even the body of Christ… From this it follows that <u>those who</u> arbitrarily <u>conjure up and picture to themselves a hidden and invisible Church are in grievous and pernicious error</u>… **It is assuredly impossible that the Church of Jesus Christ can be the one or the other, as that**

man should be a body alone or a soul alone. <u>The connection and union of both elements is as absolutely necessary</u> to the true Church <u>as the intimate union of the soul and body is to human nature</u>. <u>The Church is</u> not something dead: it is <u>the body of Christ</u> endowed with supernatural life."[402]

The denial of the union of the Church's Body and Soul leads to the heresy that the Church is invisible, which was condemned by Popes Leo XIII (above), Pius XI[403] and Pius XII.[404]

<u>Third</u>, the most powerful proof against the "Soul of the Church" heresy logically follows from the first two already discussed. The third proof is that **the infallible magisterium of the Catholic Church has defined that belonging to the <u>Body</u> of the Church is necessary for salvation**!

Pope Eugene IV, in his famous Bull *Cantate Domino,* defined that the unity of the **ecclesiastical <u>body</u> (*ecclesiastici corporis*)** is so strong that no one can be saved outside of it, even if he sheds his blood in the name of Christ. This <u>destroys</u> the idea that one can be saved by belonging to the Soul of the Church without belonging to its Body.

> Pope Eugene IV, *Council of Florence*, "Cantate Domino," 1441, *ex cathedra*: "The Holy Roman Church firmly believes, professes, and proclaims that none of those existing outside the Catholic Church, not only pagans, but also Jews, heretics and schismatics can become participants in eternal life, but they will depart 'into everlasting fire which was prepared for the devil and his angels' [Matt. 25:41], unless before the end of life they have been added to the flock; **and that the unity of *this* ecclesiastical body (*ecclesiastici corporis*)** is so strong **that only for those who abide in it are the sacraments of the Church of benefit for salvation**, and do fasts, almsgiving, and other functions of piety and exercises of a Christian soldier productive of eternal reward. No one, whatever almsgiving he has practiced, even if he has shed blood for the name of Christ, can be saved, unless he has persevered within the bosom and unity of the Catholic Church."[405]

This definition of Pope Eugene IV demolishes the "Soul of the Church Heresy." Pope Pius XI destroys it as well.

Pope Pius XI, *Mortalium Animos* (# 10), Jan. 6, 1928: "For since the mystical body of Christ, in the same manner as His physical body, is one, compacted and fitly joined together, it were foolish and out of place to say that <u>the mystical body</u> is made up of members which are disunited and scattered abroad: **<u>whosoever therefore is not united with the body is no member of it</u>, neither is he in communion with Christ its head**."[406]

So much for the "Soul of the Church Heresy."

Pope Leo X, *Fifth Lateran Council*, Session 11, Dec. 19, 1516, *ex cathedra*: "For, regulars and seculars, prelates and subjects, exempt and non-exempt, belong to **the one universal Church, outside of which no one at all is saved**, and they all have *one Lord and one faith*. That is why it is fitting that, **<u>belonging to the one same body</u>**, they also have the one same will…"[407]

Pope Clement XIV, *Cum Summi* (# 3), Dec. 12, 1769: "**One is the body of the Church**, whose head is Christ, **and all cohere in it**."[408]

19. Baptism of Desire vs. The Universal and Constant teaching of Theologians

Recently, an article was published by Fr. Anthony Cekada called *Baptism of Desire and Theological Principles*. Fr. Cekada is a "traditionalist" priest who rightly rejects Vatican II but yet holds the heresy common to almost all today: that those who die as non-Catholics can be saved. Fr. Cekada is, therefore, a person who rejects the Catholic dogma that the Catholic Faith is necessary for salvation. Not surprisingly, Fr. Cekada is also a fierce advocate of baptism of desire (although, as I just said, Fr. Cekada holds that members of false religions *who don't even desire baptism* can be saved). When I asked him via e-mail whether he agreed with the common teaching of heretical, 20th century pre-Vatican II theologians (see the "Heresy before Vatican II Section") that souls can be saved "outside the Church" by "invincible ignorance," he conveniently chose not to respond. That is simply because he <u>does</u> believe that those who die in non-Catholic religions can be saved and he rejects the defined dogma which declares that they cannot.

In his article, *Baptism of Desire and Theological Principles*, Fr. Cekada attempts to prove that Catholics are bound by the "common" teaching of theologians, according to Pope

Pius IX in *Tuas Libenter*. He further argues that baptism of desire was the "common" teaching of theologians before Vatican II; and he concludes that Catholics are, therefore, bound to believe in baptism of desire under pain of mortal sin. Since his article has had some influence on traditional Catholics, and the subject matter ties in directly to a central point under discussion in this document (namely, the universal and constant teaching on *the necessity of rebirth of water and the Spirit based on John 3:5*), I feel it necessary to show how Fr. Cekada has completely perverted the very principles he applies, has misled his readership and is contradicted by the authorities he quotes.

TUAS LIBENTER AND THE SO-CALLED "COMMON" CONSENT OF THEOLOGIANS

In his <u>letter</u> to the Archbishop of Munich (*Tuas Libenter*), upon which Fr. Cekada bases his argument, Pope Pius IX says that Catholic writers are bound by those matters which, though not taught by express decree of the Roman See, are nevertheless taught by the ordinary and universal Magisterium as divinely revealed and held by theologians in *universal and common agreement*.

> Pope Pius IX, *Tuas Libenter*, Letter to the Archbishop of Munich, Dec. 21, 1863: "For, even if it were a matter concerning that subjection which is to be manifested by an act of divine faith, nevertheless, it would not have to be limited to those matters which have been defined by express decrees of ecumenical Councils, or of the Roman Pontiffs and of this See, but would have to be extended also to those matters which are handed down as divinely revealed by the ordinary teaching power of the whole Church spread throughout the world, and therefore, by <u>universal and common</u> consent are held by Catholic theologians to belong to faith."[409]

As referenced at the beginning of this document, it was defined as a dogma by the *First Vatican Council* that the ordinary and universal Magisterium is infallible. In his letter to the Archbishop of Munich, Pope Pius IX teaches that Catholic writers are bound by those matters which "**are handed down as divinely revealed by the ordinary teaching power of the whole Church** spread throughout the world, **and therefore**, by universal and common consent are held by Catholic theologians to belong to faith." **Notice, the obligation to the opinion of the theologians** *only arises from the fact that these matters were already taught* **as divinely revealed by the ordinary teaching power of the Church and therefore also held by** <u>universal</u> **and common agreement.** In his application of this teaching in his article, **Fr. Cekada conveniently skips over the "universal" requirement, focusing only on the word "common."**

> Fr. Anthony Cekada, *Baptism of Desire and Theological Principles*, 1. General Principle: "All Catholics are obliged to adhere to a teaching if Catholic

theologians hold it by <u>common consent</u>, or hold it as *de fide*, or Catholic doctrine, or theologically certain."

Notice how Fr. Cekada conveniently ignores the requirement stipulated by Pope Pius IX that the theologians must be in "<u>universal</u> and common agreement"! If he had faithfully applied the "universal" part of it throughout his article, the attentive and sincere reader would easily have picked up the flaw in his feeble argumentation. And is baptism of desire something that has been held by <u>*universal*</u> and *common* agreement? Most certainly not; in fact, it is just the opposite.

Fr. William Jurgens: **"If there were not <u>a constant tradition</u> in the Fathers that the Gospel message of '*Unless a man be born again of water and the Holy Ghost he cannot enter into the kingdom of God*' is to be taken absolutely**, it would be easy to say that Our Savior simply did not see fit to mention the obvious exceptions of invincible ignorance and physical impossibility. **But the tradition in fact is there; and it is likely enough to be found so constant as to constitute revelation**."[410]

As we can see, exactly the opposite of baptism of desire is what is taught in universal and constant agreement! **It is the universal and constant teaching of Catholic Fathers and theologians since the beginning that absolutely no one can be saved without water baptism.** Thus, the very principle that Fr. Cekada attempts to apply in favor of baptism of desire is used against it.

Fr. Anthony Cekada, *Baptism of Desire and Theological Principles*, 2. Particular Fact: "But, Catholic theologians *do* hold the teaching on baptism of desire and baptism of blood by <u>common consent</u>, or hold it as *de fide*, or Catholic doctrine, or theologically certain. 3. Conclusion (1 + 2): Therefore, all Catholics are obliged to adhere to the teaching on baptism of desire and baptism of blood."

The fact that baptism of desire did become a common and almost unanimous error among 20th century "theologians" means nothing, which is why Pope Pius IX included that important word "universal" in *Tuas Libenter*, which Fr. Cekada conveniently ignores.

The Catholic Encyclopedia, Vol. 9, "Limbo," p. 257: "**After enjoying several centuries of undisputed supremacy,** St. Augustine's teaching on original sin was first successfully challenged by St. Anselm, who maintained that it was not concupiscence, but the privation of original justice, that constituted the essence of inherited sin. **On the special question, however, of the punishment of original** sin after death, <u>St. Anselm was at one with St. Augustine in holding that unbaptized infants share in the positive sufferings of the damned; and Abelard was the first to rebel against the severity of the Augustinian tradition on this point</u>."[411]

The Catholic Encyclopedia is saying here that basically from the time of Augustine (4th century) to Abelard (12th century) it was the <u>common</u> and almost unanimous teaching of theologians that unbaptized infants suffer the fires of hell after death, a position that was later condemned by Pope Pius VI. This proves that the "common" error of one period (or even for hundreds of years) is <u>not</u> the *universal and constant* teaching of the Church from the beginning. <u>This point alone totally blows Fr. Cekada's thesis away.</u>

Furthermore, the heresy that one can be saved "outside" the Church by "invincible ignorance" was also the <u>common</u> and almost unanimous teaching at the beginning of the 20th Century, thus proving again that **the common teaching (or common error) at any particular time does not replace the *universal and* constant teaching of all Catholic theologians <u>throughout history</u> on the absolute necessity of water baptism for salvation.**

Catechism of the Council of Trent, *Baptism made obligatory after Christ's Resurrection*, p. 171: "**Holy writers are unanimous in saying** that after the Resurrection of our Lord, when He gave His Apostles the command to go and teach all nations: *baptizing them in the name of the Father, and of the Son, and of the Holy Ghost,* **the law of Baptism became obligatory on all who were to be saved**."[412]

Notice here that the *Catechism of Trent* is inculcating that the absolute necessity of water baptism for salvation is the <u>unanimous</u> teaching of theologians. But that is the very position which Fr. Cekada's article – in the name of the "common" consent of theologians – says is a mortal sin to hold! <u>One can easily see from these facts that Fr. Cekada has erred in a major way and is actually completely wrong: the *universal and constant* teaching of theologians, as Fr. Jurgens and the Catechism of Trent say, is the very position he is condemning!</u> And his error stems from his false conclusion that the "common" errors of one time (a time of widespread heresy and modernism and apostasy leading up to Vatican II: the period between approx. 1880 and 1960) constitute the universal and constant teaching of Catholic theologians of all times, which is clearly false. In fact, it is ridiculous. **And this is why in his discussion of this issue he conveniently dropped the word "universal" from the requirement**, which would have made his invalid reasoning all the more easy to detect.

Archbishop Patrick Kenrick (19ᵗʰ Century), *Treatise on Baptism*: **"Hence, <u>all</u> the illustrious writers of antiquity proclaimed in unqualified terms its (Baptism's) absolute necessity."**[413]

In fact, if the "common" error of theologians at a particular time constituted a teaching of the Church that one is bound to follow, then all Catholics would be bound by the heresy of religious liberty (besides all the others) taught at Vatican II, since this has been accepted by "common" consent of the so-called "Catholic theologians" since Vatican II. And this is why Fr. Cekada offers the following pitiful response to that very objection to his quite obviously false thesis.

> Fr. Anthony Cekada, *Baptism of Desire and Theological Principles*, Answering **the Objection about Vatican II – D. Theologians and Vatican II**: "The group of <u>European modernist theologians</u> primarily responsible for the Vatican II errors were <u>enemies of traditional scholastic theology</u> and had been censured or silenced by church authority: Murray, Schillebeeckx, Congar, de Lubac, Teilhard, etc. When the strictures were removed under John XXIII, they were able to spread their errors freely. If anything, the fact that they had been previously silenced demonstrates the Church's vigilance against error in the writings of her theologians."

Oh, I see, because Fr. Cekada deems that the "theologians" who were "primarily responsible" for Vatican II were "European Modernists" and "enemies of traditional scholastic theology," he is free to dump his entire thesis that a Catholic is bound to follow the "common" consent of theologians under pain of mortal sin. How convenient! The reader should easily see that by such a statement Fr. Cekada is arguing hypocritically and completely refuting himself. Fr. Cekada must be quite dedicated to his heresy to argue in such a contradictory fashion. Furthermore, his claim that because a few of the more radical of the Vatican II theologians were silenced, he is therefore free to reject the common consent of "theologians" after Vatican II, is a hopeless argument; **for the fact remains that the "common" consent of purported "Catholic" theologians since Vatican II was to endorse Vatican II's heretical documents**, even if a few of the more radical ones were timidly "silenced" before Vatican II.

Hence, as anyone with eyes to see can see, if one is free to reject the "common" consent of Vatican II theologians because one deems them "enemies of traditional scholastic theology," then one can just as well dump the fallible, <u>contradictory</u> teaching of the pre-Vatican II theologians on baptism of desire, since it is patently contrary to "traditional dogmatic theology" (viz., *the defined dogma* on *the necessity of rebirth of water and the Spirit*), not to mention the universal Tradition of the Church from the beginning on John 3:5.

Furthermore, if a Catholic were bound to follow the "common" teaching of theologians at a particular time, and had lived during the Arian period in the 4th century, then one would have been bound by the Arian heresy (the denial of the Divinity of Jesus Christ), since this was not only the "common" teaching of alleged "Catholic" theologians and Bishops at the time, but almost the unanimous teaching.

> Fr. William Jurgens: "At one point in the Church's history, only a few years before Gregory's [Nazianz] present preaching (+380 A.D.), perhaps the number of Catholic bishops in possession of sees, as opposed to Arian bishops in possession of sees, was no greater than something between 1% and 3% of the total. Had doctrine been determined by popularity, today we should all be deniers of Christ and opponents of the Spirit."[414]

> Fr. William Jurgens: "In the time of the Emperor Valens (4th century), Basil was virtually the only orthodox Bishop in all the East who succeeded in retaining charge of his see… If it has no other importance for modern man, a knowledge of the history of Arianism should demonstrate at least that the Catholic Church takes no account of popularity and numbers in shaping and maintaining doctrine: else, we should long since have had to abandon Basil and Hilary and Athanasius and Liberius and Ossius and call ourselves after Arius."[415]

Fr. Cekada's argument, in fact, would rule out the possibility of a great apostasy, and would render Our Lord's words in Luke 18:8 (*When the Son of Man returns do you think He will find faith on earth?*) impossible, since all Catholics would always be bound to follow what the majority of "Catholic" theologians say, no matter how heretical it is. Needless to say, Fr. Cekada's argument is completely absurd, as is obvious to the sincere Catholic with common sense.

> Fr. Anthony Cekada, *Baptism of Desire and Theological Principles*, B. Proof of the Thesis. "1. *Major Premise.* The consent of theologians in matters of faith and morals is so intimately connected with the teaching Church that an error in the consensus of theologians would necessarily lead the whole Church into error. 2. *Minor Premise.* But the whole Church cannot err in faith and morals. (The Church is infallible) 3. *Conclusion.* **The consensus of theologians in matters of faith and morals is a certain criteria of divine Tradition.**"

We have seen how this claim of Fr. Cekada, in his attempt to apply it to "baptism of desire," is false, illogical, historically ridiculous and easily refuted. I will quote Pope Pius XII again, who himself contradicts the above assertion.

> Pope Pius XII, *Humani generis* (# 21), Aug. 12, 1950: "**This deposit of faith our Divine Redeemer has given for authentic interpretation not to each of the faithful, <u>not even to theologians</u>,** but only to the Teaching Authority of the Church.'"[416]

And what is ironic and very important is that the fallible theologians Fr. Cekada references in his article not only disagree among themselves about whether this so-called "baptism of desire" is of the Faith or merely close to the faith, **but the "theologians" he cites actually prove the position of those who reject the false doctrine of baptism of desire.**

THE VERY "THEOLOGIANS" HE BRINGS FORWARD ALSO DISPROVE HIS POSITION

One of the 25 pre-Vatican II theologians that Fr. Cekada references in his article on *Baptism of Desire and Theological Principles* is the German theologian Dr. Ludwig Ott, whose book *Fundamentals of Catholic Dogma* is somewhat popular in traditional Catholic circles. Dr. Ott was a modernist heretic who believed in baptism of desire and salvation "outside" the Church, as is stated <u>clearly</u> in his book (See the "Heresy Before Vatican II Section"). But despite this, in his quarter-million-word compendium (*Fundamentals of Catholic Dogma*), Dr. Ott is forced to admit the following based on the overwhelming testimony of Catholic Tradition and defined dogma.

> Dr. Ludwig Ott, *Fundamentals of Catholic Dogma*, The Necessity of Baptism, p. 354: "1. Necessity of Baptism for Salvation- **Baptism by water (Baptismus Fluminis) is, since the promulgation of the Gospel, <u>necessary for all</u> men <u>without exception</u>, for salvation. (*de fide*.)**"[417]

Excuse me, but this *de fide* (i.e., of the Faith) teaching of the Catholic Church on the absolute necessity of water baptism <u>for all without exception</u> for salvation is precisely why Catholics must reject the false doctrine of "baptism of desire"! Baptism of desire is directly contrary to the above *de fide* teaching of the Church: baptism of desire is the idea that *baptism of water is not necessary for all men without exception for salvation*!

But Fr. Cekada, the illogical heretic, would have us believe that based on the testimony of Ludwig Ott (and others) we are supposed *to accept baptism of desire* under pain of mortal sin, when Dr. Ludwig Ott himself is affirming that the absolute necessity of water baptism for all without exception is *de fide* – the very truth which compels one to reject baptism of desire! Thus, Fr. Cekada is simply refuted and condemned by the testimony of the very authorities he brings forward.

The fact that Dr. Ludwig Ott immediately proceeds to contradict the above statement on the absolute necessity of water baptism *without exception* in his book, and proceeds to teach baptism of desire and blood <u>on the very same page</u> – which ideas he interestingly does not term *de fide* (of the faith) but close to the faith – simply shows that the common error of baptism of desire, that became almost unanimous among "theologians" such as Ott in the late 19th and early 20th century, is simply not in harmony with the universal, constant (and *de fide*) teaching of the Church on the absolute necessity of water baptism without exception for salvation.

Another example would be the famous book, ***The Catechism Explained*, by Fr. Spirago and Fr. Clarke**. Like Dr. Ott's book, *The Catechism Explained* taught baptism of desire and that there is salvation "outside" the Church. Yet despite this fact, these "theologians" (Frs. Spirago and Clarke) were compelled to admit the following truth, which is confessed universally by all purported Catholic theologians.

> Fr. Francis Spirago and Fr. Richard Clarke, *The Catechism Explained*, 1899, Baptism: "3. **BAPTISM IS <u>INDISPENSABLY NECESSARY TO SALVATION</u>**. Hence children who die unbaptized cannot enter heaven. Our Lord says: '*Unless a man be born again of water and of the Holy Ghost, he cannot enter into the kingdom of heaven*' (John 3:5). **He makes <u>no exception</u>, not even in the case of infants… Baptism is no less indispensable in the spiritual order than water in the natural order**…"[418]

This shows, again, how the universal teaching of theologians is that baptism of water is absolutely necessary for salvation, and that Our Lord's words in John 3:5 have no exceptions. The fact that Frs. Spirago and Clarke proceed to contradict this statement and teach baptism of desire (and the heresy of salvation "outside" the Church) just shows their own inconsistency – and the inconsistency of all who favor baptism of desire.

> Fr. Francis Spirago and Fr. Richard Clarke, *The Catechism Explained*, 1899, Baptism: "… for adults the simple desire is sufficient, if actual baptism is impossible."[419]

How can water baptism be indispensably necessary for salvation (as they just told us), if the simple desire for it is sufficient in its place? That is a direct contradiction. And anyone who says that it is not simply denies the law of non-contradiction. One cannot say that:

- Water Baptism is indispensably necessary for salvation

And at the same time….

- Water Baptism is not indispensably necessary for salvation (desire can replace it)

These two statements are contradictory, but this is exactly what people were being taught all over the world in Catechisms since the late 1800's. They were being taught the truth (1st proposition), while simultaneously they were taught the opposite of that truth (2nd proposition). This shows how – even in the time of growing apostasy, heresy and modernism that was the period from approximately 1850 to 1950 – all theologians and catechisms still affirmed the universally taught truth on the absolute necessity of water baptism for salvation, even though they did not remain consistent with it.

THEOLOGIANS ARE ALSO UNANIMOUS THAT ONLY THE WATER BAPTIZED ARE PART OF THE CATHOLIC CHURCH!

Additionally devastating to Fr. Cekada's article is the fact that even the theologians that he references *in favor of baptism of desire* affirm that **it is of the Faith that only the water baptized are part of the Catholic Church**, outside of which there is no salvation. I quote Dr. Ludwig Ott again, in his *Fundamentals of Catholic Dogma*.

> Dr. Ludwig Ott, *Fundamentals of Catholic Dogma*, Membership in the Church, p. 309: "3. **Among the members of the Church are not to be counted: a) The unbaptized**… The so-called blood Baptism and the Baptism of desire, it is true, replace Baptism by water (sic) in so far as the communication of grace is concerned, **but do not effect incorporation into the Church… Catechumens are not to be counted among the members of the Church**… The Church claims no jurisdiction over them (D 895). The Fathers draw a sharp line of separation between Catechumens and 'the faithful.'"[420]

Here we see Dr. Ludwig Ott, one of the "theologians" cited by Fr. Cekada to "prove" baptism of desire, clearly affirming the universal Catholic teaching that only water baptized persons are inside the Church. Dr. Ott has no problem admitting this since he believes in salvation "outside" the Church (see "Heresy Before Vatican II Section").

But there are three very important admissions here by Dr. Ott, each relating, ironically, to the three most famous dogmatic definitions on *Outside the Church There is No Salvation*.

1) The most expansive definition on Outside the Church There is No Salvation was from Pope Eugene IV at the Council of Florence. In this definition, Pope Eugene IV defined infallibly that it is necessary to be inside the unity of the ecclesiastical body, which

means that it is necessary to be incorporated into **the ecclesiastical body (*ecclesiastici corporis*).**

> Pope Eugene IV, *Council of Florence*, "Cantate Domino," 1441, *ex cathedra*: "The Holy Roman Church firmly believes, professes, and proclaims that none of those existing outside the Catholic Church, not only pagans, but also Jews, heretics and schismatics can become participants in eternal life, but they will depart 'into everlasting fire which was prepared for the devil and his angels' [Matt. 25:41], unless before the end of life they have been added to the flock; **and that the unity of** *this ecclesiastical body (ecclesiastici corporis)* is so strong **that only for those who abide in it are the sacraments of the Church of benefit for salvation**, and do fasts, almsgiving, and other functions of piety and exercises of a Christian soldier productive of eternal reward. No one, whatever almsgiving he has practiced, even if he has shed blood for the name of Christ, can be saved, unless he has persevered within the bosom and unity of the Catholic Church."[421]

Please focus on the necessity of **incorporation** into the *ecclesiastici corporis* (the ecclesiastical body). Then notice that in the quotation above from Dr. Ott, he admits that "baptism of desire" and "baptism of blood" <u>do not effect incorporation</u> – that is to say, they do not bring one into the *Mystici Corporis* (the Mystical Body)!

> Dr. Ludwig Ott, *Fundamentals of Catholic Dogma*, Membership in the Church, p. 309: "3. The so-called blood Baptism and the Baptism of desire, it is true, replace Baptism by water (sic) in so far as the communication of grace is concerned, **but do not effect <u>incorporation</u> into the Church…**'"[422]

By this statement, Dr. Ott is admitting that "baptism of desire" and "baptism of blood" are not compatible with Pope Eugene IV's infallible definition on the absolute necessity of <u>incorporation</u> into the ecclesiastical Body (*ecclesiastici corporis*) for salvation. Thus, Dr. Ott proves that baptism of desire/blood cannot be true and is actually contrary to dogma.

2) The second infallible definition on Outside the Church There is No Salvation was from Pope Boniface VIII in the Bull *Unam Sanctam*. In this definition, Pope Boniface VIII defined infallibly that it is necessary for every human creature to be entirely **subject** to the Roman Pontiff (and therefore the Catholic Church) for salvation.

> Pope Boniface VIII, *Unam Sanctam*, Nov. 18, 1302, *ex cathedra*:
> **"Furthermore, we declare, say, define, and proclaim to <u>every human creature</u> that they by absolute necessity for salvation <u>are entirely subject</u> to the Roman Pontiff."**[423]

I pointed out the fact that without water baptism <u>no one is a subject of the Church or the Roman Pontiff</u>. I quoted the Council of Trent to prove the point.

Pope Julius III, *Council of Trent*, On the Sacraments of Baptism and Penance, Sess. 14, Chap. 2, *ex cathedra*: "… **the Church exercises judgment on no one who has not previously entered it by the gate of baptism.** *For what have I to do with those who are without* (1 Cor. 5:12), says the Apostle. It is otherwise with those of the household of the faith, whom Christ the Lord by the laver of baptism has once made 'members of his own body' (1 Cor. 12:13)."[424] (Denz. 895)

Now, notice how Dr. Ott admits that "baptism of desire" and "baptism of blood" neither make one a subject nor place one under the jurisdiction of the Church!

Dr. Ludwig Ott, *Fundamentals of Catholic Dogma*, Membership in the Church, p. 309: "3. Among the members of the Church are not to be counted: a) The unbaptized… **Catechumens are not to be counted among the members of the Church**… **The Church claims no jurisdiction over them** (D 895).'"[425]

By this statement, Dr. Ott is admitting that "baptism of desire" and "baptism of blood" are not compatible with Pope Boniface VIII's infallible definition on the absolute necessity of subjection to the Church and the Roman Pontiff for salvation! Dr. Ott is showing us that baptism of desire/blood cannot be true (and that it is, in fact, contrary to dogma), and he is even referencing the very decree that I referenced (D. 895 from Trent) to prove the point!

3) The first infallible definition on Outside the Church There is No Salvation was from Pope Innocent III at the *Fourth Lateran Council*. In this definition, Pope Innocent III defined infallibly that the Catholic Church is a Church of "the faithful" and that outside of this "faithful" no one at all is saved.

Pope Innocent III, *Fourth Lateran Council*, Constitution 1, 1215, *ex cathedra*: **"There is indeed one universal Church of the faithful, outside of which nobody at all is saved…"**[426]

I pointed out how Catholic Tradition, Catholic Liturgy and all of the fathers teach that only the water baptized are part of the faithful. Now, notice how in the quotation cited above from Dr. Ott, he admits that "baptism of desire" and "baptism of blood" do not make one part of the faithful! I quote it again:

Dr. Ludwig Ott, *Fundamentals of Catholic Dogma*, Membership in the Church, p. 309: "3. Catechumens are not to be counted among the members of the Church… The Church claims no jurisdiction over them (D 895). **The Fathers draw a sharp line of separation between Catechumens and 'the faithful.'"**[427]

By this statement, Dr. Ott is admitting that "baptism of desire" and "baptism of blood" are not compatible with Pope Innocent III's infallible definition on the absolute necessity of belonging to "the faithful" for salvation!

Therefore, in just one paragraph, Dr. Ott makes at least three admissions, based on defined Catholic dogma, which show that baptism of desire and baptism of blood are not compatible with Catholic teaching; and **he makes these admissions on points that are central to the three *most famous infallible definitions* on Outside the Church There is No Salvation!**

And this rather crucial series of admissions by Dr. Ott – quite devastating to the theory of baptism of desire – brings me to my next point: **the theologians, based on the testimony of Tradition and Catholic teaching, all define the Catholic Church the same way** – a union of faith and <u>sacraments</u>.

THEOLOGIANS UNANIMOUSLY DEFINE THE CATHOLIC CHURCH AS A UNION OF SACRAMENTS – THE TESTIMONY OF ST. ROBERT BELLARMINE, ST. FRANCIS DE SALES, THE CATECHISM OF TRENT AND ALL THEOLOGIANS

Saint Robert Bellarmine, Doctor of the Church, has given a famous definition of the Catholic Church. St. Robert Bellarmine's formula is recognized by many as the most precise scholastic definition of the Church to this day.

> St. Robert Bellarmine (16th century):"**The Church is one**, not twofold, and this one true [Catholic] Church is **the assembly of men united <u>in the profession of the same Christian faith and in the communion of the same sacraments</u>**, under the rule of legitimate pastors, and in particular, that of the one Vicar of Christ on earth, the Roman Pontiff. The first part excludes all infidels, those who were never in the Church such as Jews, Turks, and pagans, or those who once were in it and later fell away, like the heretics and apostates. **<u>The second part excludes the catechumens</u>** and excommunicated, **since the former are not admitted to the sacraments** and the latter are excluded from them…"[428]

Here we see the definition of the Church <u>which is accepted by all theologians</u>: a union of faith *and sacraments*. According to this definition of the Church, **there can be no baptism of desire because those who have not received any of the sacraments (the unbaptized, including unbaptized catechumens) don't share in the unity of the sacraments and therefore are not part of the Catholic Church.** Could anything be more simple and clear?

But it is a fact, which may surprise some, that St. Robert Bellarmine did not remain consistent with his definition of the Church above. He actually adopted the false idea of baptism of desire, which became somewhat widespread among theologians in the late middle ages, as I discussed in the section on the history of baptism of desire. But in adopting the false idea of baptism of desire, St. Robert simply failed to remain consistent with his own definition of the Church above, as well as the unanimous definition of theologians on the Church.

But this was not the only issue on which St. Robert did not remain entirely consistent; he failed to remain consistent in his struggle with the true teaching on Limbo, as *The Catholic Encyclopedia* points out.

> *The Catholic Encyclopedia*, Vol. 9, 1910, "Limbo," p. 258: **"It is clear that Bellarmine found the situation [on Limbo] embarrassing, being unwilling, as he was**, to admit that St. Thomas and the Schoolmen generally <u>were in conflict with what St. Augustine and other Fathers considered to be *de fide* [on Limbo]</u>, and what the Council of Florence seemed to have taught definitively."[429]

Here we see again that the fathers, Doctors and Saints, including Robert Bellarmine, actually contradicted themselves on Limbo, even what some of them held to be *de fide*. This again shows us why Catholics don't form definite doctrinal conclusions from the teaching of Saints, including St. Robert Bellarmine. Catholics form definite doctrinal conclusions from Catholic dogma, and the teaching of saints <u>only when it is in line with dogma</u>. And St. Robert Bellarmine's definition of the Church above, which excludes all unbaptized persons from the Catholic Church, <u>is consistent with dogma</u>; his statements on baptism of desire are not.

> Pope Boniface VIII, *Unam Sanctam*, Nov. 18, 1302, *ex cathedra*: "… <u>the one mystical body</u> … And in this, 'one Lord, one faith, **one baptism**' (Eph. 4:5). **Certainly Noe had one ark at the time of the flood, prefiguring one Church… outside which we read that all living things on the earth were destroyed**… which body he called the 'Only one' namely, the Church, **because of <u>the unity</u> of the spouse, the faith, <u>the sacraments</u>**, and the charity of the Church. "[430]

Here we see that Pope Boniface VIII defined as a dogma that the Church is a union of Sacraments. The Catholic Church is infallibly defined as a union of sacraments also by Pope Eugene IV.

> Pope Eugene IV, *Council of Florence*, "Cantate Domino," 1441, *ex cathedra*: "The Holy Roman Church firmly believes, professes, and proclaims… **that <u>the unity of *this ecclesiastical body* (*ecclesiastici corporis*) is so strong that only for those who abide in it are the sacraments</u>**

of the Church of benefit for salvation, and do fasts, almsgiving, and other functions of piety and exercises of a Christian soldier productive of eternal reward. No one, whatever almsgiving he has practiced, even if he has shed blood for the name of Christ, can be saved, unless he has persevered within the bosom and unity of the Catholic Church."[431]

The obvious meaning and sense of this dogmatic text is that the Catholic Church is an ecclesiastical Body and a union of <u>sacraments</u>, a union "so strong." This is the truth confessed by all theologians. St. Francis De Sales teaches the exact same truth.

St. Francis De Sales, Doctor of the Church: "**The Church is a holy university or general company of men united and collected together** in the profession of one same Christian faith; <u>**in the participation of the same sacraments**</u>…"[432]

Here we see that St. Francis De Sales repeats the same truth and defines the Church the same way. This is how *everybody* defines the Church! The *Catechism of Trent* affirms the same teaching:

Catechism of the Council of Trent, *The Members of the Church Militant*, pp. 99-100: "**The Church militant is composed** of two classes of persons, the good and the bad, **both professing the same faith and <u>partaking of the same sacraments</u>**…"[433]

Is any teaching more consistent? The Catechism of Trent concludes:

Catechism of the Council of Trent, p. 159: "In the character impressed by **Baptism**, both effects are exemplified. **By it we are qualified to receive the other Sacraments, and <u>the Christian is distinguished from those who do not profess the faith</u>.**"[434]

So again, we see how baptism of desire advocates, such as Fr. Cekada, are <u>completely wrong</u> and actually pervert the truth when they assert that the teaching of theologians binds one to "baptism of desire." It is exactly the opposite. The unanimous teaching of theologians <u>contradicts the false doctrine of baptism of desire</u>, by defining the Church as only those who have received the sacraments, which definition is also a dogma (*Eugene IV; Boniface VIII, de fide*). Catholics are <u>not</u> bound, and in fact must reject, the fallible statements and speculations of men, however great, such as St. Robert Bellarmine, when they are not in harmony with Catholic dogma, not to mention when they contradict the very principles they elsewhere affirm.

And this is precisely why St. Robert Bellarmine <u>was at a complete loss</u> to cogently explain the idea of "baptism of desire" when he had already defined the Catholic

Church as a body excluding all the unbaptized. He failed miserably in attempting to explain how catechumens can be saved when only baptized persons are part of the Catholic Church.

> St. Robert Bellarmine, *De Ecclesia Militante*: "**Concerning catechumens there is a greater difficulty**, because they are faithful [have the faith] and can be saved if they die in this state, <u>and yet outside the Church no one is saved</u>… the <u>catechumens are in the Church</u>, **though not in actual fact**, *yet at least in resolution*, therefore they can be saved…"[435]

Notice the difficulty St. Robert encounters in trying to explain baptism of desire; he immediately has to compromise and contradict his own definition of the Church.

> St. Robert Bellarmine (16th century): "**The Church is one**, not twofold, and this one true [Catholic] Church is **the assembly of men united in <u>the profession of the same Christian faith and in the communion of the same sacraments</u>**, under the rule of legitimate pastors, and in particular, that of the one Vicar of Christ on earth, the Roman Pontiff. First part excludes all infidels, those who were never in the Church such as Jews, Turks, and pagans, or those who once were in it and later fell away, like the heretics and apostates. **<u>The second part excludes the catechumens</u>** and excommunicated, **since the former are not admitted to the sacraments** and the latter are excluded from them…"[436]

<u>First</u>, St. Robert's "difficulty" in attempting to explain his (fallible) position that catechumens can be saved, when catechumens are excluded from the Church by his own definition, is simply because the idea that an unbaptized person can be part of the Church is found nowhere in any Council or statement from the Papal Magisterium. The Catholic Church has exclusively held and taught that *only those who have received the Sacrament of Baptism are part of the Church* and no dogmatic decree has ever taught anything else.

And this is why St. Robert is constrained to admit that catechumens <u>are not actually inside the Church</u>, but he argues that they can be saved by being in it in resolution, but not in fact. (Note: St. Robert was only applying this idea to catechumens, not pagans, heretics and schismatics, as our Modernists today love to assert). But contrary to St. Robert's fallible and false assertion that catechumens can be saved by being in the Church *"not in actual fact, yet at least in resolution,"* it is defined that one must be in actual fact part of the Church. It is defined that one must be "in the bosom and unity" (Eugene IV); that one must be incorporated into the "ecclesiastical body" (Eugene IV); that one must be "entirely subject to the Roman Pontiff" (Boniface VIII); that one must be in the union of "sacraments" and "the faithful" (Eugene VI; Boniface VIII; Innocent III). And these things only come with water baptism, as attested to by St. Robert's own definition of the Church. But in trying to explain the unexplainable (how baptism of desire is compatible with Catholic dogma), and in trying to defend the indefensible (how unbaptized catechumens can be in a Church which is defined by a union of sacraments), St. Robert contradicted these principles and made a mistake.

Second, in attempting to substantiate his erroneous belief in baptism of desire, St. Robert says that catechumens are "faithful." This is contrary to the fathers and the teaching of Traditional Catholic Liturgy since apostolic times, which excluded catechumens from "the faithful" (as discussed in the Section on "The One Church of the Faithful"). It is also contrary to the ready admissions of baptism of desire advocates such as Ludwig Ott, which I've already quoted.

> Dr. Ludwig Ott, *Fundamentals of Catholic Dogma*, Membership in the Church, p. 309: "3. Catechumens are not to be counted among the members of the Church... The Church claims no jurisdiction over them (D 895). **The Fathers draw a sharp line of separation between Catechumens and 'the faithful.'**"[437]

By now the reader should again be discovering the theme which I've been showing throughout this extensive examination of the history of the baptism of desire issue: that baptism of desire is a fallible, erroneous tradition of man, which has never been taught by the Papal Magisterium, which has gained momentum based on the fallible and flawed passages of some nevertheless great men, who contradicted themselves and violated their own principles in trying to explain it, while almost always making other errors in the same documents.

In fact, St. Robert's statement that catechumens are "faithful" also contradicts the Catechism of the Council of Trent.

> Catechism of the Council of Trent, *Communion of Sacraments*, p. 110: "**The fruit of all the sacraments is common to all the faithful,** and these sacraments, **particularly baptism**, the door, as it were, by which we are admitted into the Church, are so many sacred bonds which bind them and unite them to Christ."[438]

This means that those who haven't received the sacraments are not part of the "faithful," again contrary to what Bellarmine asserted in his admittedly "difficult" attempt to reconcile the false idea of baptism of desire with his own definition of the Catholic Church, which excluded all the unbaptized. When Saints enter into "difficult" attempts to explain speculative things that are not clearly taught by the Church they are bound to make mistakes. And so Catholics must not follow St. Robert in this "difficult" (or rather, impossible) attempt to explain baptism of desire, but rather they should follow St. Gregory Nazianz (Doctor of the Church), who stated regarding the idea that one can *reckon as baptized him who desired baptism but did not receive it*, "I cannot see it."[439]

St. Robert indeed erred on the subject of baptism of desire, just as he did on Limbo; but what is most important to remember, as stated already, is this: while the principle of Papal infallibility was always believed in the Church (expressed from the earliest times by such phrases as *in the apostolic see the Catholic religion has always been preserved untainted and holy doctrine celebrated),* there is no doubt that after the definition of Papal infallibility at the *First Vatican Council* in 1870 there is much more clarity about which documents are infallible and which are not. St. Robert Bellarmine and others who lived before 1870 did not necessarily have this degree of clarity, which caused many of them to lessen the distinction, in certain cases, between the infallible decrees of Popes and the fallible teaching of theologians. <u>It also caused them to not look quite as literally at what the dogma actually declares, but rather at what they thought the dogma might mean in light of the opinion of popular theologians of the time</u>.

Catholics who live today can say that they understand more about Papal Infallibility than the theologians and doctors in the middle ages all the way down to 1870, and that they possess an advantage in evaluating this issue not only because they live after the definition of Papal Infallibility, but also because they can review the entire history of Papal pronouncements of the Church on this issue **and see the harmony among them on the absolute necessity of water baptism.**

UNIVERSAL TRADITION ON BAPTISM AFFIRMED EVEN BY HERETICAL MODERN CATECHISMS

To further illustrate the point that the absolute necessity of water baptism for salvation <u>is the universal and constant teaching of all theologians</u> even during the time of the apostasy and even by those same persons who proceeded to deny this truth, let's take, for example, a recent edition of the Baltimore Catechism and the Catechism attributed to Pope St. Pius X.

> *The New St. Joseph Baltimore Catechism*, No. 2, Q. 320- "Why is Baptism necessary for the salvation of all men? A. **Baptism is necessary for the salvation of all men because Christ has said: *'Unless a man be born again of water and the Spirit, he cannot enter into the kingdom of God.'***"[440]

Notice how this edition of the Baltimore Catechism, which taught the error of baptism of desire to multitudes (as we will see), **reiterates the universal and constant teaching of the Catholic Church, <u>based on the words of Jesus Christ in John 3:5</u>, that Baptism of water is necessary for the salvation of all men.** The Baltimore Catechism, therefore, teaches the exact same truth of Faith that has been a constant echo in Catholic Tradition since the beginning.

> Hermas, 140 A.D., quoting Jesus in John 3:5: "They had need to come up through <u>the water</u>, so that they might be made alive; **for they could not otherwise enter into the kingdom of God.**"[441]

St. Justin the Martyr, 155 A.D.: "… they are led by us to a place where there is water; and there they are reborn in the same kind of rebirth in which we ourselves were reborn… in the name of God… they receive the washing of water. For Christ said, '*Unless you be reborn, you shall not enter into the kingdom of heaven.*' **The reason for doing this we have learned from the apostles.**"[442]

So, contrary to popular belief, those who reject "baptism of desire" <u>actually follow the teaching of the Baltimore Catechism</u> on the absolute necessity of water baptism. They don't, however, follow the teaching of the *fallible* Baltimore Catechism when it proceeds to contradict this truth on the absolute necessity of water baptism for salvation and teach baptism of desire.

> *The New St. Joseph Baltimore Catechism*, No. 2, Q. 321- "How can those be saved who through no fault of their own have not received the Sacrament of Baptism. A. **Those who through no fault of their own have not received the sacrament of Baptism can be saved** through what is called baptism of blood or baptism of desire."[443]

This statement blatantly contradicts the truth taught in Q. 320, *that baptism of water is absolutely necessary for all men to be saved.* In the Baltimore Catechism the people have been taught two directly contradictory notions one after the other:

- *Baptism of water is absolutely necessary for the salvation of all;*
  and…
- *Baptism of water is not absolutely necessary for the salvation of all.*

Can both be true at the same time? No, they cannot. As a Catholic, one must follow the first statement, which is in accord with defined dogma and the universal Tradition since the beginning of the Church, and is based on the declaration of Christ Himself.

Furthermore, <u>the edition of the Baltimore Catechism from which I'm quoting also makes the same devastating admissions which Dr. Ott was compelled to make</u> in his discussion of what the so-called "baptism of desire" is not.

> *The New St. Joseph Baltimore Catechism*, No. 2, Q. 321- "However, **only baptism of water actually makes a person a member of the Church.** It (baptism of blood/desire) might be compared to a ladder up which one climbs into the Bark of Peter, as the Church is often called. **Baptism of blood or desire** makes a person a member of the Church in desire. **These are the two lifelines trailing from the sides of the Church <u>to save those who are outside the Church</u> through no fault of their own.**"[444]

Here we see this edition of the Baltimore Catechism teaching that: 1) Baptism of desire doesn't make one a member of the Church; 2) Baptism of desire does make one a member of the Church in desire; 3) there is salvation <u>outside the Church</u> by baptism of desire and blood.

The first two statements contradict each other, while the third is <u>direct heresy</u> against the dogma that *Outside the Church no one at all is saved* (Pope Innocent III, *de fide*). Thus, this edition of the Baltimore Catechism's explanation of "baptism of desire" is not only fallible, but directly heretical.

> Pope Innocent III, *Fourth Lateran Council*, Constitution 1, 1215, *ex cathedra*: **"There is indeed one universal Church of the faithful, <u>outside of which nobody at all is saved</u>, in which Jesus Christ is both priest and sacrifice."**[445]

But having taught that baptism of desire "saves" people "outside" the Church, this version of the Baltimore Catechism proves the point again that baptism of desire is incompatible with defined dogma – not to mention its own teaching on the absolute necessity of water baptism for salvation.

THE CATECHISM ATTRIBUTED TO ST. PIUS X

The Catechism attributed to Pope St. Pius X repeats for us the same *de fide* teaching of the Catholic Church on the absolute necessity of water baptism for salvation.

> The Catechism of Pope St. Pius X, *The Sacraments*, "Baptism," Q. 16: "Q. Is Baptism necessary to salvation? A. **Baptism is absolutely necessary to salvation**, for Our Lord has expressly said: *'Unless a man be born again of water and the Holy Ghost, he cannot enter into the Kingdom of God.'*"[446]

So, contrary to popular belief, those who reject "baptism of desire" <u>actually follow the teaching of the Catechism attributed to Pope St. Pius X</u> on the absolute necessity of water baptism. They don't follow, however, the teaching of this *fallible* Catechism when it proceeds to contradict this truth on the absolute necessity of water baptism for salvation.

> The Catechism of Pope St. Pius X, *The Sacraments*, "Baptism," Q. 17: "Q. Can the absence of Baptism be supplied in any other way? A. **The absence of Baptism can be supplied** by martyrdom, which is called Baptism of Blood, or by an act of perfect love of God, or of contrition, along with the desire, at least implicit, of Baptism, and this is called Baptism of Desire."[447]

This again is a total contradiction to what is stated in Question 16. It should be noted that this Catechism, while attributed to Pope St. Pius X, <u>did not come from his pen and was not solemnly promulgated by him</u>. There is no Papal Bull from him promulgating the Catechism, so it is just a fallible Catechism that went out during his reign and was given his name. But, even if St. Pius X had himself authored the above words (which he didn't), it wouldn't make a bit of difference to the points I've made. This is because a Pope is only infallible when speaking Magisterially. This Catechism is not infallible because it wasn't promulgated solemnly from the Chair of Peter or even specifically by the Pope. Further, this Catechism is proven not to be infallible by the fact that it teaches the abominable heresy that there is salvation "outside" the Church (as I will show)!

But I will first quote where the Catechism affirms the dogma.

> The Catechism of Pope St. Pius X, *The Apostles' Creed*, "The Church in Particular," Q. 27: "Q. Can one be saved outside the Catholic, Apostolic and Roman Church? A. **No, <u>no one can be saved outside the Catholic, Apostolic Roman Church</u>, just as no one could be saved from the flood outside the Ark of Noah, which was a figure of the Church**."[448]

Here the Catechism attributed to Pope St. Pius X reaffirms the defined dogma. But it proceeds to deny this dogma just two questions later!

> The Catechism of Pope St. Pius X, *The Apostles' Creed*, "The Church in Particular," Q. 29: "Q. But if a man through no fault of his own is **outside** the Church, can he be saved? A. **If he is <u>outside the Church</u> through no fault of his, that is, if he is in good faith,** and if he has received Baptism, or at least has the implicit desire of Baptism; and if, moreover, he sincerely seeks the truth and does God's will as best as he can, <u>such a man is indeed separated from the body of the Church</u>, but is united to the soul of the Church and consequently is on the way of salvation."[449]

Here we see this fallible Catechism <u>word for word</u> denying the dogma Outside the Church There is No Salvation! It teaches that there can be salvation "outside" the Church, which directly denies the truth it taught to the people in question 27. This statement is so heretical, in fact, **that it would be repudiated even by most of the crafty heretics of our day, who know that they cannot say that people are saved "outside," so they argue that non-Catholics are not "outside" but are "inside" somehow**. So even those crafty heretics who reject the true meaning of Outside the Church There is No Salvation would have to admit that the above statement is heretical!

Further, notice that the Catechism attributed to St. Pius X teaches the heresy that persons can be united to the "Soul" of the Church, <u>but not the Body</u>. As proven already, the Catholic Church is a Mystical <u>Body</u>. Those who are not part of the Body are no part at all.

> Pope Pius XI, *Mortalium Animos* (# 10), Jan. 6, 1928: "For since the mystical body of Christ, in the same manner as His physical body, is one, compacted and fitly joined together, it were foolish and out of place to say that <u>the mystical body</u> is made up of members which are disunited and scattered abroad: **<u>whosoever therefore is not united with the body is no member of it</u>, neither is he in communion with Christ its head.**"[450]

This discussion on the Catechisms should demonstrate to the reader how the rampant denial of Outside the Church There is No Salvation and the necessity of Water Baptism has been perpetuated through <u>fallible texts with imprimaturs</u> and why it has been imbibed today by almost all who profess to be Catholic. It has been perpetuated by fallible documents and texts which contradict themselves, which contradict defined dogma, and which teach heresy, and which – all the while – elsewhere affirm the immutable truths of the absolute necessity of the Catholic Church and water baptism for salvation. And this is why Catholics are bound to adhere to <u>infallibly defined dogma</u>, not fallible Catechisms or theologians.

> **Pope Pius IX**, *Singulari Quadem*: "For, in truth, when released from these corporeal chains, 'we shall see God as He is' (1 John 3:2), we shall understand perfectly by how close and beautiful a bond divine mercy and justice are united; but, as long as we are on earth, weighed down by this mortal mass which blunts the soul, **let us hold most firmly that, in accordance with Catholic teaching, there is 'one God, one faith, <u>one baptism</u>' [Eph. 4:5]; <u>it is unlawful to proceed further in inquiry</u>.**"[451]

> Pope Paul III, *The Council of Trent*, Can. 5 on the **<u>Sacrament</u>** of Baptism, *ex cathedra*: **"If anyone says that baptism [the sacrament] is optional, that is, not necessary for salvation (cf. Jn. 3:5): <u>let him be anathema</u>.**"[452]

20. *Exultate Deo* also ends the debate

I have discussed the teaching of the Council of Florence on Baptism in earlier sections; but, due to the fact that the teaching of *Exultate Deo* from the Council of Florence excludes the possibility of baptism of desire and baptism of blood, I want to show clearly that **it is infallible and cannot be contradicted**.

> Pope Eugene IV, *The Council of Florence*, "Exultate Deo," Nov. 22, 1439, *ex cathedra*: "Holy baptism, which is the gateway to the spiritual life, holds the first place among all the sacraments; through it we are made members of Christ and of the body of the Church. **And since death entered the universe through the first man, 'unless we are born again of water and the Spirit, we cannot,' as the Truth says, 'enter into the kingdom of heaven' [John 3:5].** The matter of this sacrament is real and natural water."[453]

It is important to point out that not everything in the Bull *Exultate Deo* (the Decree for the Armenians) deals with faith and morals to be believed by the universal Church. Those areas are not taught *ex cathedra* (from the Chair of Peter). But this quotation above most certainly does deal with faith and morals to be believed by the universal Church and is therefore taught *ex cathedra*. Some people point out the fact that *Exultate Deo* does not have the same solemn language as *Cantate Domino* from the Council of Florence, which everyone agrees is infallible. Some conclude, therefore, that it's possible that *Exultate Deo* might not be infallible in faith and morals. But this argument is easily refuted. Not only was the Bull *Exultate Deo* approved by Pope Eugene IV and included in the decrees of the Council, but it was required for the Armenians as a profession of faith, as the true doctrine of the Catholic religion. This proves that it is infallible.

> Pope Leo XIII, *Paterna caritas* (# 2), July 25, 1888: "**Then the Constitution of the Council, _Exultate Deo_, was published by the pope, in which he taught them all that he considered to be necessary for the right knowledge of Catholic truth**; and upon this, the Legates, in the name of their Patriarch, and of the whole Armenian race, declared that **they received the Constitution in entire submission and readiness to obey,**

'promising in the same name, as true sons of obedience, loyally to obey the behests and commands of the Apostolic See."[454]

Furthermore, *Exultate Deo* (the Decree for the Armenians) was solemnly confirmed by a number of other infallible Bulls in the same Council, including *Cantate Domino*.

Pope Eugene IV, *Council of Florence*, "Cantate Domino," Sess. 11, Feb. 4, 1442, *ex cathedra*: "**The Holy Roman Church embraces, approves and accepts** all other universal synods which were legitimately summoned, celebrated and confirmed by the authority of a Roman Pontiff, and **especially this holy synod of Florence,** in which, among other things, most holy unions with the Greeks and the Armenians have been achieved and **many most salutary definitions in respect of each of these unions have been issued, as is contained in full in the decrees previously promulgated,** which are as follows: Letentur coeli; <u>Exultate Deo</u>…"[455]

In Sess. 13 of the Council of Florence, Pope Eugene IV issued another Bull – this one on union with the Syrians – in which he again infallibly approves of the doctrine contained in *Exultate Deo* (the Decree for the Armenians). The Bull ends with Pope Eugene IV invoking the wrath of God upon anyone who would contradict it. Here is the pertinent portion of the text.

Pope Eugene IV, *Council of Florence*, Bull of Union with the Syrians, Sess. 13, Nov. 30, 1444: "**Eugenius, bishop, servant of the servants of God, for an everlasting record… we ordain and decree** that he (the archbishop Abdala) ought to receive and embrace, in the name of the above persons, **whatever has been defined and established at various times by the holy Roman Church, especially the decrees on the Greeks and <u>the Armenians (*Exultate Deo*)</u>** and the Jacobites, which were issued in the sacred ecumenical council of Florence…"[456]

In addition, *Exultate Deo* itself begins its section on the Sacraments – in which the quote on the necessity of the Sacrament of Baptism is contained – with authoritative language which proves that it is the infallible teaching of the Catholic Church.

Pope Eugene IV, *The Council of Florence*, "Exultate Deo," Nov. 22, 1439: "Eugenius, bishop, servant of the servants of God, for an everlasting record… for the easier instruction of the Armenians today and in the future **we reduce <u>the truth</u> about the sacraments of the Church to the following brief scheme**."[457]

Therefore, there is no doubt that the teaching contained in *Exultate Deo*, concerning points of faith and morals to be believed by the universal Church, is infallible and dogmatic. It cannot contain error. Thus, when *Exultate Deo* defines that *unless we are born again of water and the Holy Ghost, we cannot, as the Truth says, enter into the kingdom of God*, this excludes any possibility of salvation without water baptism. What's interesting about this definition in particular is that it is not merely a quotation of John 3:5 incorporated into the Council's definition. Rather, it is the Council of Florence teaching the same thing as John 3:5, *while presenting it in its own words*. That is to say, the Council of Florence is *defining the doctrine found in John 3:5*, not simply quoting the scripture.

> Pope Eugene IV, *The Council of Florence*, **"Exultate Deo,"** Nov. 22, 1439, *ex cathedra*: "Holy baptism, which is the gateway to the spiritual life, holds the first place among all the sacraments; through it we are made members of Christ and of the body of the Church. **And since death entered the universe through the first man, 'unless we are born of water and the Spirit, we cannot,' as the Truth says, 'enter into the kingdom of heaven' [John 3:5].** The matter of this sacrament is real and natural water."[458]

To hold that one can enter into the kingdom of heaven without being born again of water and the Spirit is to contradict this infallible definition.

21. The New Testament is clear that the Sacrament of Baptism is Indispensable for Salvation

I have already discussed John 3:5, so I will now look at some of the other New Testament passages which affirm the absolute necessity of the Sacrament of Baptism for salvation.

THE GREAT COMMISSION – MATTHEW 28 AND MARK 16

> Matthew 28:19-20- "And Jesus coming, spoke to them, saying: All power is given to me in heaven and in earth. Going, therefore, **teach ye all nations: <u>baptizing them in the name of the Father, and of the Son, and of the Holy Ghost;</u>** Teaching them to observe all things whatsoever I have commanded you..."

In the very last scene recorded in St. Matthew's Gospel, known as the Great Commission – THE VERY LAST INSTRUCTION THAT JESUS CHRIST GIVES THE APOSTLES BEFORE LEAVING THIS WORLD – Jesus Christ gives His apostles two commands: to teach all nations and to baptize. Since this is Christ's very last command to His Apostles, these words carry a special significance. This should tell everyone something about the importance of baptism. The Sacrament of Baptism is inextricably bound up, by Our Lord Jesus Christ Himself, with the very command to teach all nations the Christian faith. St. Mark's Gospel reveals the same truth in his version of the Ascension scene, the last scene in his Gospel.

Mark 16:15-16- "And he (Jesus) said to them: Go ye into the whole world, and **preach the Gospel** to every creature. **He that believeth <u>and is baptized</u> shall be saved**: but he that believeth not shall be condemned."

Here we see Our Lord Jesus Christ Himself saying that those *who are baptized* will be saved, **clearly indicating that those who are not baptized will <u>not</u> be saved**. But some ask, why didn't Our Lord say, *"he that believeth not and is not baptized shall be condemned,"* after saying he that believeth <u>and is baptized</u> shall be saved. The answer is that those who don't believe are <u>not going to get baptized</u>, so it is not necessary to mention baptism again. Besides, Our Lord says that very thing (that those who are not baptized will not be saved) in John 3:5.

So we see that, **in the very last command of Our Lord to the Apostles, the notion of belief and receiving baptism are wrapped up; they are one and the same formula which is necessary for salvation**. To believe and to receive the Sacrament of Baptism are one and the same saving event.

St. Francis Xavier, Dec. 31, 1543: "After all this he [one of the heathen] asked me in my turn to explain the principal mysteries of the Christian religion, promising to keep them a secret. I replied, that I would not tell him a word about them unless he promised beforehand to publish them abroad [to tell everyone] what I should tell him of the religion of Jesus Christ. He made the promise, and then I carefully explained to him **those words of Jesus Christ in which our religion is summed up: 'He who believes <u>and is baptized</u> shall be saved'** (Mark 16:16)."[459]

ROMANS 5 AND 6

In Romans Chapters 5 and 6 we find St. Paul explaining how men are born in the state of original sin, because the sin of the first man, Adam, has caused his descendants to be born bankrupt of the state of grace. St. Paul further explains that Christ reconciles us to God, removes our Original Sin and makes us members of the family of God. In Romans 6:2, St. Paul says that Christians are now dead to sin. **And in Romans 6:3, St. Paul explains how this dying to sin has been accomplished.**

Romans 6:3-4 "**Know you not that all we, who are baptized in Christ Jesus, <u>are baptized in his death</u>? For <u>we are buried together with him by baptism</u> unto death**."

In this <u>very strong language</u>, St. Paul and the infallible word of God identify the Sacrament of Baptism as the means by which one has died to sin. They also identify the Sacrament of Baptism as the means by which one is incorporated into Christ Jesus.

THE COUNCIL OF TRENT CONFIRMS ROMANS 6:4

In accordance with the infallible declaration of St. Paul in Sacred Scripture, the Catholic Church has defined that there is no condemnation in those who are buried together with Christ <u>by the Sacrament of Baptism unto death</u>.

> Pope Paul III, *The Council of Trent*, On Original Sin, Session V, *ex cathedra*: **"For unless a man be born again of water and the Holy Ghost, he cannot enter into the kingdom of God [John 3:5]…** For in those who are born again, God hates nothing, **because 'there is no condemnation, to those who are truly <u>buried together with Christ by baptism unto death</u>' (Rom. 6:4)…"**[460]

And here is another regional Council which, though not dogmatic, teaches the same truth as the dogmatic statement above: namely, that only by being *buried by the Sacrament of Baptism* unto death, can one hope to have remission of sin, incorporation with Christ and salvation.

> St. Remigius, Bishop of Lyons, *Council of Valence III*, 855, Can. 5: "Likewise we believe that we must hold most firmly that *all the multitude of the faithful*, <u>regenerated</u> 'from water and the Holy Spirit' (John 3:5), and through this truly <u>incorporated</u> into the Church, **and according to the apostolic doctrine *baptized in the death of Christ* (Rom. 6:3),** in His blood has been absolved from its sins…"[461]

1 CORINTHIANS 12:13

1 Corinthians 12:13- "**For in one Spirit <u>were we all baptized into one body</u>, whether Jews or Gentiles, whether bond or free; and in one Spirit we have all been made to drink**."

Here we see St. Paul and the word of God forcefully teaching that one comes into contact with the Body of Christ and the Holy Spirit *through the Sacrament of Baptism*.

THE COUNCIL OF TRENT CONFIRMS 1 COR. 12:13 – NO WATER BAPTISM, NO BODY MEMBERSHIP

Based on this very text ["For in one Spirit <u>were we all baptized into one body</u>"], the Catholic Church infallibly teaches that only through the Sacrament of Baptism is one incorporated into the Body of the Church.

> Pope Julius III, *Council of Trent*, on <u>the Sacraments of Baptism</u> and Penance, Sess. 14, Chap. 2, *ex cathedra*: "… <u>the Church exercises judgment on no one who has not previously entered it by the gate of baptism</u>. *For what have I to do with those who are without* (1 Cor. 5:12), says the Apostle. **It is otherwise with those of the household of the faith, <u>whom Christ the Lord by the laver of baptism has once made 'members of his own body' (1 Cor. 12:13)</u>."**[462]

It is a dogma, based on 1 Corinthians, that those who have not received the laver of baptism are *"without"* the Church; they are not *"members of His body"*; they are not *"of the household of the faith"*; and the Church exercises no *"judgment"* over them. I have already discussed the profound significance of this dogmatic statement in section 7 on "Subjection to the Roman Pontiff," but I will very briefly repeat that here for the reader's sake. It is *de fide* that every human creature must be subject to the Church to be saved, because every human creature must be subject to the Roman Pontiff to be saved.

> Pope Boniface VIII, *Unam Sanctam*, Nov. 18, 1302, *ex cathedra*:
> **"Furthermore, we declare, say, define, and proclaim to <u>every human creature</u> that they by absolute necessity for salvation are entirely <u>subject</u> to the Roman Pontiff."**[463]

And if the definition of Trent above on 1 Cor. 12:13 proves that no one can be subject to the Church without water baptism (as it does), <u>this means that no one can be saved without water baptism</u>. All persons are made subject to the Church (and therefore the Roman Pontiff) only by receiving the Sacrament of Baptism.

> Pope Leo XIII, *Nobilissima* (# 3), Feb. 8, 1884:
> "The Church … is consequently bound to watch keenly over the teaching and upbringing of **<u>the children placed under its authority by baptism</u>**…"[464]

GALATIANS 3 – FAITH IS BAPTISM

In Galatians 3 we find one of the most famous parts of Saint Paul's teaching on faith.

In Galatians 3:23 he says: "But before the **faith** came…"
In verse 24 he says: "that we may be justified <u>by faith</u>…"
In verse 25 he says: "But after <u>the faith</u> is come…"
In verse 26 he says: "For you are all the children of God **by faith**, in Christ Jesus."

But what does St. Paul mean here by this extensive discussion on "faith"? What does he mean when he says, *"For you are all the children of God <u>by faith, in Christ Jesus</u>"*? Most people probably believe that St. Paul is speaking here of believing that Jesus is the Son of God. This, of course, is indispensable, but it is not even mentioned by St. Paul! Rather, St. Paul explains exactly what he means by "faith in Christ Jesus" – quite naturally in the flow of his epistle – in the very next verse (verse 27).

Galatians 3:27: "**<u>For as many of you as have been baptized in Christ, have put on Christ</u>**. There is neither Jew nor Greek: there is neither bond nor free: there is neither male nor female. For you are all one in Christ Jesus."

This very interesting chapter of Scripture should give a message to Protestants and Catholics alike. St. Paul and the word of God are clearly teaching what the Catholic Church has held for 2000 years: that it is <u>by means of the Sacrament of Baptism that one receives faith</u>. That is why the Sacrament of Baptism has been called since apostolic times, "the Sacrament of Faith," as touched upon already in the section on "The One Church of the Faithful." And that is why only the water baptized are called *the faithful*.

St. Ambrose, (4th Century) Bishop and Doctor of the Church:
"… **for in the Christian what comes first is faith.** *And at Rome for this reason those who have been baptized are called the faithful* (fideles)… <u>it was because you believed that you received Baptism</u>."[465]

St. Augustine (+405): "That is why [at Baptism] response is made that the little one believes, though he has as yet no awareness of faith. **Answer is made that <u>he has faith because of the Sacrament of faith</u>** (Baptism)."[466]

St. Augustine (+405): "Although the little one has not yet that faith which resides in the will of believers, **the Sacrament of that same faith already makes him one of the faithful**. For since response is made that they believe, **they are called faithful not by any assent of the mind to the thing itself but by their receiving the sacrament of the thing itself.**"[467]

Thus, St. Paul was teaching in Galatians 3 that the Sacrament of Baptism is full assurance of faith in Christ Jesus, for without it you do not have the faith and are not among the faithful.

THE COUNCIL OF TRENT CONFIRMS GAL. 3, THAT FAITH = BAPTISM

Pope Paul III, *Council of Trent*, Session 6, Chap. 7 on Justification, *ex cathedra*: "… **the instrumental cause [of Justification] is the Sacrament of Baptism, which is the 'Sacrament of Faith,'** without faith no one is ever justified… This Faith, in accordance with Apostolic Tradition, catechumens beg of the Church before the Sacrament of Baptism, when they ask for 'faith which bestows life eternal,' (Rit. Rom., Ordo Baptismi)."[468]

TITUS 3:5 – BAPTISM SAVES US

In Titus 3:5 we find one of the strongest of all the passages in Sacred Scripture on the necessity of the Sacrament of Baptism.

Titus 3:5- *"Not by the works of justice, which we have done*, but according to his mercy, **he saved us, by the laver of regeneration, and renovation of the Holy Ghost**…"

Here, St. Paul and the infallible word of God tell us that the laver of regeneration (the Sacrament of Baptism) saves us! This means that the water (the laver) and the Spirit (renovation of the Holy Ghost) in the Sacrament of Baptism is *the* means by which we are justified and saved.

What is very interesting about this passage is that the word of God tells us that it is not "by the works of justice which _we_ have done" that we are saved. In other words, it is not by *our* desire or *our* blood or *our* contrition that we are saved, but by the Sacrament itself that Christ instituted (the laver of regeneration and renovation of the Holy Ghost).

THE FOURTH LATERAN COUNCIL DEFINES THE TRUTH OF TITUS 3:5

Pope Innocent III, *Fourth Lateran Council, ex cathedra*: **"But the sacrament of baptism is consecrated in water at the invocation of the undivided Trinity – namely, Father, Son and Holy Ghost – and brings salvation to both children and adults** when it is correctly carried out by anyone in the form laid down by the Church."[469]

St. Augustine (+412): **"It is an excellent thing that the Punic Christians call Baptism itself nothing else but salvation**… Whence does this derive, except from an ancient and, as I suppose, apostolic tradition..."[470]

St. Fulgence (+512): **"For he is saved by the Sacrament of Baptism**…"[471]

EPHESIANS 4:5 – One Spirit – One Body – One Faith – One Lord – *One Baptism*.

Ephesians 4:4-6: "Careful to keep the unity of the Spirit in the bond of peace. One body and one Spirit; as you are called in the hope of your calling. **One <u>Lord</u>, one <u>faith</u>, one <u>baptism</u>. One <u>God</u> and <u>Father</u>** of all…"

Here St. Paul (in the infallible word of God) is describing the unity in the Church of Jesus Christ. And look at the list that he gives: *One Lord, One Faith, One God, One Father.* And right up there with "Lord" and "Faith" and "God" and "Father" is *Baptism.* This tells us that St. Paul sees Baptism as <u>loaded</u> with importance; in fact, as having an importance in terms of the unity of the Body of Christ equivalent to things which nobody can dispute: one Lord, one Faith, one God. This is because it is through this Baptism that we are united to God and the Body of the Church. To deny that the members of Christ's Body have this one Baptism is equivalent to denying that they have one Lord and one Faith.

St. Jerome (+386): **"The Lord is one** and **God is one**… Moreover **the faith is said to be one**… **And there is one baptism, <u>for it is in one and the same way that we are baptized</u>** in the Father and in the Son and in the Holy Spirit."[472]

What's interesting about this quotation from St. Jerome is that he is pointing out that the "one baptism" shared by all in the Church (according to Ephesians 4:5) is not simply one in terms of the number of baptisms, but it is "one" in regard to the <u>manner</u> in which all have been baptized: all have been baptized in the name of the Father and of the Son and of the Holy Ghost in the Sacrament.

And so essential and inextricably bound up with the Christian Faith is the necessity of the Sacrament of Baptism that St. Aphraates, the oldest of the Syrian Fathers, wrote in 336:

"This, then, is faith: that a man believe in <u>God</u> … <u>His Spirit</u> …<u>His Christ</u>… Also, that a man believe in the resurrection of the dead; **and moreover, that <u>he believe in the Sacrament of Baptism</u>. This is the belief of the Church of God.**"[473]

THE COUNCIL OF VIENNE CONFIRMS THE TRUTH OF EPH. 4:5

Pope Clement V, *Council of Vienne*, Decree # 30, 1311-1312, *ex cathedra*: "… *one universal Church, outside of which there is no salvation*, **for all of whom there is** *one Lord, one faith, and <u>one baptism</u>*…"[474]

Pope Clement V, *Council of Vienne*, 1311-1312, *ex cathedra*: "Besides, **one baptism** which regenerates all who are baptized in Christ **must be faithfully confessed by all** just as 'one God and one faith' [Eph. 4:5], **<u>which celebrated in water</u>** in the name of the Father and of the Son and of the Holy Spirit we believe **to be commonly the perfect remedy for salvation for adults as for children.**"[475]

We see that all who are part of the Catholic Church have the one Baptism of water.

ACTS 2 AND THE FIRST PAPAL SERMON

In Acts Chapter 2 we find the Pentecost scene, the birthday of the New Testament Church. And there we find many extraordinary events recorded, including the first sermon in the New Testament Church by the first Pope, St. Peter.

Acts 2:37-38- "Now when they had heard these things they had compunction in their heart, and said to Peter, and to the rest of the apostles: What shall we do, men and brethren? But Peter said to them: Do penance, **and <u>be baptized every one of you in the name of Jesus Christ, for the remission of your sins</u>: and you shall receive the gift of the Holy Ghost.**"

Here we see the word of God and the first Pope teaching the necessity of the Sacrament of Baptism for the remission of sins, as proclaimed in the very first sermon in the Catholic Church.

THE NICENE-CONSTANTINOPLE CREED CONFIRMS ACTS 2

In accordance with this infallible declaration of the word of God, that one must receive the Sacrament of Baptism for the remission of sins, the Catholic Church has defined that there is one baptism given for the remission of sins.

> The Nicene-Constantinople Creed, *ex cathedra*: "We confess **one baptism for the remission of sins**."[476]

1 PETER 3:20-21 – WATER BAPTISM AND THE ARK

> 1 Peter 3:20-21: "… **when they waited for the patience of God in the days of Noe, when the ark was a building: wherein a few, that is, eight souls were saved by water. Whereunto baptism being of the like form, now saveth you also**…"

This is also one of the strongest passages in all of Sacred Scripture on the necessity of the Sacrament of Baptism. Notice the force of St. Peter's assertion here. *__Baptism now saves you__*. And he is talking about Water Baptism (the Sacrament), of course, because he draws an analogy between the Baptismal waters and the Flood waters! St. Peter compares receiving the Sacrament of Water Baptism to being on the ark of Noe. As no one escaped physical death outside the ark of Noe during the time of the flood (only eight souls survived the flood by being firmly planted on the ark), likewise now no one avoids spiritual death or is saved from original sin without the Sacrament of Baptism!

POPE BONIFACE VIII CONFIRMS THE ARK – WATER BAPTISM – FLOOD – CHURCH CONNECTION OF 1 PET. 3

As St. Peter says in 1 Peter 3:20-21, that in the days of Noe eight souls were saved from the water by getting into the ark, and now the Sacrament of Baptism being *of the like form* (*that is, of water*) now saves us also, so too has the Catholic Church defined as a dogma that entering the Church is as necessary for salvation as being on the ark was necessary in being saved from death. And the only way to enter the Church is through the one baptism of water.

Pope Boniface VIII, *Unam Sanctam*, Nov. 18, 1302, *ex cathedra*: "… <u>the one mystical body</u> … And in this, 'one Lord, one faith, **one baptism**' (Eph. 4:5). **Certainly Noe had one ark at the time of the flood, <u>prefiguring one Church… outside which we read that all living things on the earth were destroyed</u>…** which body he called the 'Only one' namely, the Church, because of <u>the unity</u> of the spouse, the faith, **the sacraments**, and the charity of the Church."[477]

Notice how Pope Boniface VIII defines the unity of the Church as the unity of "the sacraments," which means that no one can be inside the Church without having received at least the first of the sacraments: Baptism.

St. Maximus the Confessor (+ c. 620): "**The flood of those days was, as I say, a Figure of baptism. For that was then prefigured which is now fulfilled;** that is, just as when the fountains of water overflowed, iniquity was imperiled, and justness alone reigned: sin was swept into the abyss, and holiness upraised to heaven. Then, as I said, that was prefigured which now is fulfilled in Christ's Church. **For as Noe was saved in the Ark, while the iniquity of men was drowned in the Flood, so by the waters of baptism the Church is carried close to heaven**…"[478]

22. Other Scriptural Considerations

Besides the infallible teaching of the Catholic Magisterium, there are a few other things from Sacred Scripture that are interesting to consider in regard to the topic at hand.

THE BAPTISM OF GOD

At the end of Mass in the Roman Rite is recited the Last Gospel. These profound words found in the first chapter of the Gospel of St. John are very powerful, striking the reader by the depths of their wisdom and meaning. It is in these very words that we find a provocative argument against baptism of desire:

John 1:12-13-*"But as many as received Him, to them He gave power to become the sons of God: to them that believe in His name:* **WHO ARE <u>BORN</u>, <u>NOT OF BLOOD</u>, <u>NOR OF THE WILL OF THE FLESH</u>, <u>NOR OF THE WILL OF MAN</u>, BUT OF GOD."**

The context of the passage is dealing with "becoming the sons of God," that which St. Paul called "adoption of sons" (Rom. 8:15). This is the theological and scriptural term for Justification, the state of sanctifying grace (*Trent*, Sess. 6, Chap. 4).[479] The term signifies the transition from being a child of Adam (the state of original sin) to becoming an adopted son of God (the state of sanctifying grace). Pope St. Leo the Great, in fact, confirms that this passage of St. John's Gospel is talking about becoming a son of God by the Sacrament of Baptism.

Pope St. Leo the Great, *Sermon 63: On the Passion* (+ c. 460 A.D.): **"… from the birth of <u>baptism</u> an unending multitude are born to God, <u>of whom it is said</u>:** *<u>Who are born, not of blood, nor of the will of the flesh, nor of the will of man, but of God</u>* (Jn. 1:15)."[480]

So as God, through St. John, is describing man's being "born again" to the state of grace in Baptism, He speaks of those who are born, "**<u>NOT OF BLOOD</u>, <u>NOR OF THE WILL OF THE FLESH</u>, <u>NOR OF THE WILL OF MAN</u>, BUT OF GOD**"! The "will of the flesh" is desire. The "will of man" is desire. "Blood" is blood. In my opinion, what God is saying here in this very verse is that in order to become a son of God – in order to be justified – it does not suffice to be born again of blood or desire (i.e., baptism of blood or desire). One must be born again of God. The only way to be born again of God is to be baptized with water in the name of God: in the name of the Father, and of the Son, and of the Holy Ghost (Mt. 28:19).

JOHN 3:5 VS. JOHN 6:54

Some writers have tried to refute a literal interpretation of John 3:5 by appealing to the words of Our Lord in John 6:54: *"Amen, amen I say to you: Except you eat the flesh of the Son of man, and drink his blood, you shall not have life in you."* They argue that the language in this verse is the same as in John 3:5, and yet the Church doesn't take Jn. 6:54 literally – for infants don't need to receive the Eucharist to be saved. But the argument falters because the proponents of this argument have missed a crucial difference in the wording of these two verses.

John 6:54- "Amen, amen I say to you: <u>EXCEPT YOU</u> eat the flesh of the Son of man, and drink his blood, you shall not have life in you."

John 3:5- "Amen, amen I say to thee, <u>UNLESS A MAN</u> be born again of water and the Holy Ghost, he cannot enter into the kingdom of God."

Our Lord Jesus Christ, when speaking on the necessity of receiving the Eucharist in John 6:54, does not say: "unless *a man* eat the flesh of the Son of man…" **He says: "Except you…"** His words, therefore, are clearly intended for the people to whom He was speaking, not every man. Since the people to whom He was speaking could eventually receive the Eucharist, they had to in order to be saved. This applies to all who can receive the Eucharist, that is, all who hear that command and can fulfill it, which is what the Church teaches. But in John 3:5, Our Lord unequivocally speaks of every man. **This is why the Catholic Church's magisterial teaching**, in every single instance it has dealt with John 3:5, has taken it *as it is written*.

The difference in the wording of these two verses actually shows the supernatural inspiration of the Bible and the absolute necessity of water baptism for every man.

23. All True Justice and the Causes of Justification

ALL TRUE JUSTICE MEETS UP WITH THE SACRAMENTS (*de fide*)

In the Foreword to Sess. 7 of the Council of Trent's Decree on the Sacraments there is a very important statement.

Pope Paul III, *Council of Trent*, Sess. 7, Foreword, *ex cathedra*: "For the completion of the salutary doctrine of Justification… it has seemed fitting to treat of **the most holy sacraments of the Church, through which all true justice either begins, or being begun is increased or being lost is restored**."[481]

The Council of Trent here defines that all true justice (sanctifying grace) either begins or is increased or is restored at the sacraments. I repeat, all true justice either begins or is increased or is restored at the sacraments. **This means that all true justice must be <u>at least one of the three</u>: begun at the sacraments, increased at the sacraments or restored at the sacraments.** But the baptism of desire theory is that some persons can have a true justice (sanctifying grace) that is none of the above three! They argue that some persons can have true justice that is: 1) not begun at the sacraments, but before; and also 2) not increased at the sacraments (since the person dies before getting to the sacraments); and 3) not restored at the sacraments (for the same reason as # 2). Thus, the "baptism of desire" theory posits a true justice which is neither begun nor increased nor restored at the sacraments. But such an idea is contrary to the above teaching of Trent, and therefore such a "true justice" which they posit cannot be true justice. This shows again that baptism of desire is not a true teaching, but a false teaching littered with contradictions against infallible truths such as that above.

> St. Ambrose (+ 390): "… when the Lord Jesus Christ was about to give us the form of baptism, He came to John, and John said to Him: *I ought to be baptized by thee, and comest thou to me? And Jesus answering said: Suffer it to be so for now. For so it becometh us to fulfill all justice* (Mt. 3:14-15). **See how all justice rests on baptism**."[482]

THE INSTRUMENTAL AND EFFICIENT CAUSES OF JUSTIFICATION

We have seen how the Council of Trent defines that the Sacrament of Baptism is necessary for salvation. We have seen how, in every single instance (that is, four), the Council of Trent infallibly declares that John 3:5 applies literally and to every man. We have seen how even the passage that baptism of desire advocates mistakenly think favors their position (Sess. 6, Chap. 4), actually excludes baptism of desire by declaring that John 3:5 is to be understood *as it is written*. I will now briefly discuss two other points in this venerable Council.

In Sess. 6, Chap. 7, the Council of Trent defines what the causes of Justification are in the impious. Justification is the term for the state of sanctifying grace. If desire or blood were a cause for Justification, as the baptism of desire advocates argue, then you would think that they would be mentioned in the chapter on the Causes of Justification, wouldn't you? Why isn't either mentioned in Chapter 7 on the causes of Justification? What we *do* find mentioned is that the Sacrament of Baptism is the instrumental cause of Justification.

> Pope Paul III, *Council of Trent*, Session 6, Chap. 7, *ex cathedra*:"… **the instrumental cause [of Justification] is the Sacrament of Baptism**, which is 'the Sacrament of Faith,' without faith no one is ever justified…"[483]

In this Chapter, the Council of Trent listed in all 5 causes of Justification, four of which are God or the attributes of God, and one of which (the instrument of that Justice) is the Sacrament of Baptism.

If there were exceptions to the truth that the Sacrament of Baptism is the cause of Justification in the impious, as the baptism of desire advocates claim, then the exceptions would have been included by the Council, <u>just like the Council specifically declared in its decree on Original Sin that Mary was not included in its definition on Original Sin</u>.

> Council of Trent, Sess. 5, #6: "This holy Synod declares nevertheless **that it is not its intention to include in this decree, where original sin is treated of, the blessed and immaculate Virgin Mary…**"[484]

The Virgin Mary is also excluded in Sess. 6 of Trent by the context, because the entire decree in Sess. 6 deals with the Justification of the <u>impious</u>/sinner. The context of the "impious," therefore, does not include Mary since she was never impious – she was always in a state of perfect sanctification. But the point is that the Council <u>needed to specify that</u> Mary was <u>not</u> included in its definition on Original Sin in Sess. 5 and <u>it did so</u>, **thus demonstrating that if there are any exceptions to a dogmatic statement they will always be mentioned in the decree; for an infallible statement cannot declare that which is false.**

Furthermore, look at what the Council of Trent says about the efficient cause of Justification in the impious.

> Pope Paul III, *Council of Trent*, Session 6, Chap. 7, *ex cathedra*: "… **the efficient cause [of Justification] is a truly merciful God who gratuitously 'washes and sanctifies', '<u>signing</u> and anointing with the Holy Spirit…**"[485]

This is very interesting. Trent defines here that the efficient cause of Justification in the impious is God who washes and sanctifies, **signing** and anointing. Notice the term *signing*. This term (*signing*) is a clear reference to the character or mark of the Sacrament of Baptism; for the "sign" of Baptism only comes with the Sacrament of Baptism, as everyone admits. I quote Fr. Laisney of the SSPX again.

> Fr. Francois Laisney, *Is Feeneyism Catholic*, p. 9: "Baptism of Desire is not a sacrament… it does not produce the sacramental character."

Therefore, if Trent defines that the efficient cause of Justification is God who <u>signs</u>, this means that the efficient cause of Justification is God who signs us in the Sacrament of Baptism. And one cannot have the effect (<u>Justification</u>) without the cause (<u>God signing in the Sacrament of Baptism</u>).

24. Catholics Must Believe and Profess that the Sacramental System as a whole is Necessary for Salvation (*de fide*)

Another very important aspect to this issue is the Dogmatic Profession of Faith issued by the Council of Trent and by Vatican Council I. Both Councils infallibly declared that the Sacramental System as a whole is necessary for salvation, and this truth must be professed and believed by all Catholics and by converts.

> Pope Pius IV, "Iniunctum nobis," Nov. 13, 1565, *ex cathedra*: "I also profess that **there are truly and properly seven <u>sacraments of the New Law instituted by Jesus Christ our Lord, <u>and necessary for the salvation of mankind</u>, although all are not necessary for each individual</u>…"**[486]

Notice that Pope Pius IV in "Iniunctum nobis," the Profession of Faith of the Council of Trent, declares that "the sacraments" as such (i.e., *the sacramental system as a whole*) are necessary for man's salvation, but it adds that <u>all</u> are not necessary for each individual. This is very interesting and it proves two points:

1) It proves that every man must receive *at least one sacrament* to be saved; otherwise, "the sacraments" as such (i.e. the sacramental system) couldn't be said to be necessary for salvation. Hence, this definition (besides the others) **shows that each man must at least receive the Sacrament of Baptism in order to be saved.**

2) Notice that the Council of Trent (and Vatican I below) made it *a special point* when defining this truth to emphasize that each person does not need to receive <u>all</u> of the sacraments to be saved! This proves that where exceptions or clarifications are necessary in defining truths the Councils will include them! Thus, if some men could be saved without "the sacraments" by "baptism of desire" then the Council could have and would have simply said that.

But nothing about salvation being possible without the sacraments was taught in these dogmatic professions of Faith. Rather, the truth that <u>the sacraments are necessary for salvation</u> was defined, with the necessary and correct qualification that <u>all</u> 7 of the sacraments are not necessary for each person.

The First Vatican Council repeated the same Profession of Faith, which is a dogma. It made this Profession in the very first statement on Faith at Vatican I.

Pope Pius IX, *Vatican Council I*, Sess. 2, Profession of Faith, *ex cathedra*: "I profess also that **there are seven sacraments of the new law, truly and properly so called, instituted by our Lord Jesus Christ and necessary for salvation**, though each person need not receive them <u>all</u>."[487]

No matter how hard one tries to avoid it, "baptism of desire" is incompatible with this truth, a truth which must be professed and believed by Catholics and by converts from heresy. In fact, this dogma blows away the theory of baptism of desire.

> Fr. Francois Laisney (Believer in Baptism of Desire), *Is Feeneyism Catholic*, p. 9: "Baptism of Desire is not a sacrament... it does not produce the sacramental character."

25. St. Isaac Jogues and St. Francis Xavier Against Invincible Ignorance and on the Necessity of Baptism

In this work on Outside the Catholic Church There is No Salvation and the Necessity of the Sacrament of Baptism, I could not leave out a section on the incredible lives of two of the most illustrious missionaries in Church history, St. Isaac Jogues (17th century missionary to the North American Savages) and St. Francis Xavier (16th century missionary to the Far East). The trials of St. Isaac Jogues in bringing the Gospel to the North American heathen, and the incredible success of St. Francis Xavier in bringing the Gospel to India, Japan and the areas thereabout, are simply amazing. But what is most obvious about both of their lives is that **the exact same sentiments and belief animated them in regard to the heathen to whom they journeyed**. They were both absolutely convinced that <u>all the heathen men and women without exception</u> who died without knowledge of Jesus Christ would not be saved and would be lost forever. It is, in fact, impossible for a sincere person to read the lives of these missionaries and still believe in the idea of salvation for the "invincibly ignorant," simply because their lives illustrate most profoundly the undeniable teaching of <u>the whole of Catholic Tradition</u> that all the souls who die ignorant of the Gospel and the principal mysteries of the Catholic Faith (the Trinity and the Incarnation) are lost. Any idea that these souls could be saved ignorant of Christ was a foreign world to them, a perverted and corrupted view of the supernatural world. If they had believed in "invincible ignorance" they never would have done what they did.

In their lives we also find remarkable occurrences relating to people receiving the Sacrament of Baptism, occurrences which demonstrate again the truth of the dogma received from Jesus Christ Himself: *Unless a man is born again of water and the Holy Ghost, he cannot enter into the Kingdom of God* (John 3:5). We will now look at some different occurrences and quotes from their lives.

ST. ISAAC JOGUES AGAINST INVINCIBLE IGNORANCE

St. Isaac Jogues and his companions were preaching the Gospel to the most savage of the North American heathen in the areas of Canada and New York. In trying to bring the Gospel (the Catholic Faith) to this kind of heathen, Isaac Jogues and his companions braved incredible hardships and risked capture and mind-boggling tortures at the hands of the savages. And this is exactly what happened when St. Isaac Jogues, St. Rene Goupil and companions were captured by the Iroquois savages on a missionary journey in 1642:

> *The Life of St. Isaac Jogues, pp. 219,221:* "The executioners chose Rene Goupil as the next victim. **They sawed off the thumb of his right hand with an oyster shell. So much blood spurted out that they feared he would die** [they wanted to torture him more or trade him]… Then they turned to Couture… **They pricked him with awls and pointed stakes, carved off shreds of his flesh, burned him with firebrands and glowing irons, until he fell lifeless under their cruelties**… One of them discovered [later] that two of Couture's fingers had been left intact… Towering with rage… **he began to saw off the index finger of his right hand with the ragged edge of a shell.** He pressed down with all his might on the flesh and tore it, but he could not sever the tendons… **Frenzied, he gripped the finger and twisted it until he tore it out, dragging with it a tendon as long as the palm.**"[488]

But why did St. Isaac Jogues and his companions feel compelled to subject themselves to the possibility of falling into the hands of these savages? What was the point? The answer is that they knew that there was no such thing as "salvation for the invincibly ignorant." They knew that if these savages didn't come to know Jesus Christ and the Trinity (the Catholic Faith) and get baptized they would be eternally lost without any doubt.

> *The Life of St. Isaac Jogues, p. 197:* "**They tore Ondessonk [St. Isaac Jogues] away and beat him with insane fury, with clubs and muskets, about the head and shoulders, until he sank to the earth.** They kicked him and jumped on him till he was insensible. The four Iroquois passed on, but others took up the bloody revenge. Two younger men, especially, grasped his arms and clenched the nails of his forefingers in their teeth. **They tugged and yanked till they drew the fingernails from their sockets. They took each of his forefingers in their**

mouths and ground and crushed them with their teeth until the fingers were a jelly of blood and flesh and splinters of bone."[489]

St. Isaac Jogues and his companions were subjected to many other things, including mind-boggling cold:

> St. Isaac Jogues: "**Indeed, under the influence of that terrific hate of the savages, I suffered beyond telling from the cold,** from the contempt of the basest of them, from the furious ill temper of the women… Great hunger, also, I had to endure. **Since nearly all the venison, and on the hunt they eat scarcely anything else, was offered in sacrifice to the demons, I spent many days without eating**… I suffered greatly from the cold, in the midst of the deep snows, **with nothing to wear but a short and threadbare cloak…Though they had plenty of deerskins, many of which they were not using, they would give me none. Sometimes, on an extremely bitter night, shivering from the cold, I would take one of the skins secretly; as soon as they discovered it, they would rise up and take it away from me.** That shows how terribly much they hated me… My skin was split open with the cold, all over my body, and caused me intense pain."[490]

Yet, after all this, St. Isaac Jogues <u>still refused to escape from these savages when at first he had the opportunity</u>! He wanted to stay and baptize infants who were dying, and instruct and baptize the heathen adults who would listen. Why? If he had left the people, surely those who were sincere would have been saved for being ignorant *"through no fault of their own,"* right? After all, it wouldn't have been their fault if Isaac Jogues said that he couldn't endure this any longer. No! St. Isaac knew that there was no salvation for them without the presence of the baptizing Church and knowledge of the Catholic Faith. The following quote is one of the most interesting that one will ever see against the heretical idea of salvation for the "invincibly ignorant."

> St. Isaac Jogues: "Although, in all probability, I could escape [from the Iroquois] either through the Europeans or through the other savages living around us, if I should wish it, I decided to live on this cross on which Our Lord had fixed me in company with Himself, and to die with His grace helping me… **Who could instruct the prisoners who were being constantly brought in? Who could baptize them when they were dying, and strengthen them in their torments? Who could pour the sacred waters on the heads of the children? Who could look after the salvation of the adults who were dying, and after the instruction of those in good health?** Indeed, I believe that it happened not without a singular providence of the Divine Goodness, that I should have fallen into the hands of these very savages… **These savages, I must confess, unwillingly and reluctantly have thus far spared me, by the will of God, <u>so that thus through**</u>

me, although unworthy, they might be instructed, they might believe, and be baptized, as many of them as are preordained for eternal life."[491]

Could any statement from a Saint refute the heresy of salvation for the "invincibly ignorant" better? St. Isaac knew that those heathen who did not come to know the Catholic Faith and get baptized simply were not preordained for eternal life.

Romans 8:29-30- "*For whom He foreknew, he also predestinated to be made conformable to the image of his Son*: that he might be the first-born amongst many brethren. *And whom he predestinated, them he also called*: and whom he called, them he also justified: and whom he justified, them he also glorified."

As Catholics, of course, we don't believe as the heretic John Calvin, who held a predestination according to which no matter what one does he is either predestined for heaven or hell. That is a wicked heresy. Rather, as Catholics we believe in the true understanding of predestination, which is expressed by St. Isaac Jogues and Romans 8 above. This true understanding of predestination simply means that God's foreknowledge from all eternity makes sure that those who are of good will and are sincere will be brought to the Catholic faith and come to know what they must – and that those who are not brought to the Catholic faith and don't know what they must were not among the elect.

There is another interesting story in Jogues' life which confirms this. After having much success in converting people in various places, he and his companions began to be shut out from all the villages in a certain section of the heathen savages. The devil had convinced the heathen savages in this area – and the idea was spreading – that the presence of the missionaries was the reason why there were famine and disease among them. So, being totally exhausted and shut out from every hut in the area, and freezing from the cold and dying for a place to rest and warm themselves, we pick up the story:

The Life of St. Isaac Jogues, pp. 145-146: "…wandering about from place to place, and everywhere meeting with blows and threats and hatred, Jogues and Garnier came to a little cluster of cabins in the heart of the hills. **They were both exhausted by the terrible exposure to the cold and by the lack of food. They forced themselves upon one of the cabins and were grudgingly received.** Jogues felt feverish and sick through all his body. **He could not move from his mat.** Then came a messenger from one of the villages in which they had been welcomed on their entry into the Petun land. The runner told them that some of the people who were sick were begging them to return.

"It was a call from God. They could not but heed it. **In order to complete the journey of thirty-five miles by daylight,** they started out about three o'clock in the morning. All the country was pale with snow in the dawn, and the mountain air was painfully cold. Jogues was still gripped by the fever and unsteady on his legs. They slid their snowshoes laboriously over the crackling crust of the icy snow. Frequently, they stopped for breath in deadly exhaustion.

"But they had to shorten their rests, for fear lest they die of the cold. **Their only food, a lump of corn bread about the size of the fist, was hard as ice.** They arrived at the village late at night, covered with sweat and yet half-frozen, they said. **The sick persons were still alive. They were baptized. 'Some souls gone astray here and there, <u>who are placed on the road to heaven when they are just about to be swallowed up in hell</u>,'** was their comment, 'deserve a thousand times more than these labors, since these souls have cost the Savior of the world much more than that.'"[492]

As St. Isaac Jogues says, he knew that if he did not reach these people, instruct them and baptize them they would be "swallowed up in hell." That is why he forced himself at the very moment he had just found a bit of rest and warmth to make the thirty-five mile trip, though he was starving, freezing and exhausted – a trip which almost killed him. There is another interesting story which illustrates the same truth.

"When dawn trickled through the firs, they [Jogues and Garnier] struck out along the trail, now blanketed with snow. Some distance on, beyond a clear field, they noticed a few cabins. The families, they found, were just abandoning their huts and were going to the nearest Petun village, for they had neither corn nor any other food… **They [Jogues and Garnier] attached themselves to the band and traveled all the day**… **'We had no special plan to go to this village** [which we named] St. Thomas rather than to any other,' **they remarked** 'but since we had accepted what company the savages offered, and since we followed them there, <u>there is no doubt but that we arrived where God was leading us for the salvation of a predestined soul which awaited nothing but our arrival in order to die</u> to its earthly miseries.' They had finished their supper and were conversing with their hosts, when a young man entered and asked the Blackrobes to visit his mother who was sick. 'We go there,' they exclaim, 'and find the poor woman in her last extremities. **She was instructed, and happily received, with the Faith, the grace of Baptism. Shortly after that, she [died and] beheld herself in the glory of heaven. In that whole village <u>there was only that one who had need of our help</u>.**"[493]

ST. FRANCIS XAVIER AGAINST INVINCIBLE IGNORANCE

St. Francis Xavier was arguably the greatest missionary in Church history after the Apostle Paul. He was responsible for the baptism of millions in the Far East. Like St. Isaac Jogues, he was firmly convinced of the Catholic truth that there is no such thing as "salvation for the invincibly ignorant."

St. Francis Xavier, Dec. 31, 1543: "**There is now in these parts [of India]** *a very large number of persons who have only one reason for not becoming Christians, and that is that there is no one to make them Christians.* **It often comes into my mind to go round all the Universities of Europe, and especially that of Paris, crying out everywhere like a madman, and saying to all the learned men there whose learning is so much greater than their charity, '**Ah! *What a multitude of souls is through your fault shut out of heaven and falling into hell!***'**… They labor night and day in acquiring knowledge… but if they would spend as much time in that which is the fruit of all solid learning, and be as diligent in teaching the ignorant the things necessary to salvation, they would be far better prepared to give an account of themselves to our Lord when He shall say to them: 'Give an account of thy stewardship.'"[494]

Here we see that St. Francis Xavier is saying that these ignorant heathen in India would easily become Christians if there were someone to instruct them, and yet they are still going to go to hell if they don't hear about the Faith! This totally eliminates the idea of salvation for the "invincibly ignorant" or salvation by "implicit baptism of desire."

St. Francis Xavier, Jan. 20, 1545: "Since your Highness [King John III of Portugal] well understands that God will require of you an account of the salvation of **so many nations,** *who are ready to follow the better path if any one will show them it,* **but meanwhile, for want of a teacher, lie in blind darkness,** and the filth of the most grievous sins, offending their Creator, **and casting their own souls headlong into the misery of eternal death.**"[495]

Here again we see St. Francis Xavier eliminating any idea of salvation for "the invincibly ignorant," excluding from salvation even those ignorant souls whom he thought would embrace the Faith if they were taught it!

St. Francis Xavier, May, 1546: "In this island of Amboyna the heathen are far more numerous than the Mussulmans [Muslims], and there is a bitter hatred between the two… **If there were people here to teach them the true religion, they would join the fold of Christ without much difficulty,** for they have less objection to the name of Christ than that of Mahomet… I write all this to you at so much length that you may share my solicitude, and conceive, as is only right, **an immense sorrow at the miserable loss of so many souls who are perishing daily, utterly destitute of aid.**"[496]

St. Francis Xavier, Jan. 28, 1549: "I intend to write what I have found, not only to India, but to the Universities of Portugal, of Italy, and above all of Paris, and admonish them, while they are devoting themselves heart and soul to learned studies, not to think themselves so free and disengaged from responsibility **as to** take no trouble at all about <u>the ignorance of the heathen and the loss of their immortal souls</u>."[497]

St. Francis Xavier, Jan. 29, 1552: "**Nothing leads me to suppose that there are any Christians there [in China]**…if the Chinese accept the Christian faith, the Japanese would give up the doctrines which the Chinese have taught them… **I am beginning to have great hopes that God will soon provide free entrance to China,** not only to our Society, but to religious of all Orders, that a large field may be laid open to pious and holy men of all sorts, **in which there may be great room for devotion and zeal, in recalling <u>men who are now lost</u> to the way of truth and salvation.**"[498]

In all of these quotes we again see that St. Francis Xavier, like St. Isaac Jogues and all of the Saints, <u>totally rejected</u> the heretical idea that souls who are ignorant of the Gospel can be saved.

ST. ISAAC JOGUES ON THE NECESSITY OF WATER BAPTISM

In the life of these extraordinary missionaries, we also find many quotes and instances which confirm the absolute necessity of water baptism for salvation. As in the life of the great missionary Fr. De Smet, **both men saw the remarkable occurrence that many of the people that they would reach to baptize would die almost immediately after.** They clearly saw this as a sign that God had preserved the lives of these persons until they were able to receive that most necessary Sacrament.

The Life of St. Isaac Jogues, p. 92: "Then, most of all [the heathens concluded], the Blackrobes caused people to die by pouring water on their heads; **practically everyone they baptized died soon after.**"[499]

The Life of St. Isaac Jogues, p. 136: "Fr. Lalemant [one of Jogues companions and superiors] confesses: '**It happened very often, <u>and has been remarked more than a hundred times</u>, that <u>in those places where we were most welcome, where we baptized most people, there it was, in fact, where they died most</u>**. On the contrary, in the cabins to which we were denied entrance, although they were sick to the extremity, at the end of a few days one saw every person prosperously cured.'"[500]

The Life of St. Isaac Jogues, pp. 97-98: "[St. John] De Brebeuf and Jogues waited for the hysteria to pass. They had the consolation of **baptizing a few souls and sending them to God. One was a squaw [an Indian woman] who had resisted all their attempts to talk to her until just before her end,** when she begged to be baptized. Another was a young brave who eagerly wished for baptism, but whose relatives guarded him against the approach of Echon [De Brebeuf] and

Ondessonk [Jogues]. De Brebeuf waited until the relatives were absent from the cabin and then poured the saving waters on his head a moment before his mother-in-law returned to prevent him."[501]

The Life of St. Isaac Jogues, p. 142: "There is hardly any corn in this village of Ehwae, and nevertheless, almost every day some Attiwandarons arrive, bands of men, women, and children, all pale and disfigured… Fleeing from the famine, they here find death; rather, here they find a blessed life, for we see to it that not one dies without baptism. **Among these people was a little child about one year old, which looked more like a monster than a human being. It was happily baptized. God preserved its life only by a miracle, it would seem, so that it might be washed in the blood of Jesus Christ and might bless His mercies forever."**[502]

The Life of St. Isaac Jogues, p. 279: "… in February he walked the six miles to the nearer town, where the Mohawks were holding their winter festival and games… **he wandered through the cabins, searching for the sick and for those affably inclined. In one lodge he discovered five babies, all dangerously ill. He baptized them,** without attracting notice, and three days later, says Fr. Lalemant, 'he heard that these little innocents were no longer in the land of the dying [they were dead]. **What an admirable stroke of predestination for those little angels.**"[503]

The Life of St. Isaac Jogues, p. 199: **"Rene called Father Jogues' attention to one of the old men [an Indian who was captured with them]… The man had not yet been baptized,** and it might possibly happen that he would be the victim chosen by the Iroquois as a blood sacrifice before they left the camp. Ondessonk [Fr. Jogues] persuaded the old man to accept baptism… The Mohawks finished their council and the division of the booty… The old man whom Fr. Jogues had just before baptized refused to stir from where he was sitting… **Scarcely had he [the old man] finished speaking [refusing to move] when one of the braves smashed his skull and scalped him.** Father Jogues rejoiced in the sorrow, **for the waters of baptism had scarce dried on his head."**[504]

The Life of St. Isaac Jogues, pp. 122-123: "At Teanaustayae, Jogues witnessed a torture and a conversion that surpassed anything human. A chief belonging to the Oneida nation of the Iroquois Confederacy, together with eleven warriors, was to be executed. The chief listened to the Blackrobes Ondessonk [Jogues] and Echon, declared he wished to be baptized, and urged his followers to follow his lead. **After the ordinary cruelties had been inflicted, just prior to the killings, the chief was baptized Peter.** One by one, his companions, also baptized, succumbed to the fire and knives. Peter remained alone on the platform. He was scalped, mutilated, and scorched over his entire body. Suddenly, as if inspired, he attacked his Huron persecutors…The Hurons threw him into a huge bonfire. He rose out of the flames, with flaring torches in his hands, and rushed on his enemies. They retreated as he ran toward the palisades to set the village on fire. They felled him with a club and cut off his feet and hands. Then, they held him over nine different fires… Finally they crushed him under an overturned tree trunk, all on fire. Extricating himself, he crawled elbows and knees, pulling himself a space of ten steps towards his persecutors. They fled before him as before a fiend. One, finally, struck him down and slashed off his head."[505]

The missionaries were convinced that it was only because Peter had received the Sacrament of Baptism that he had the miraculous strength to undergo all of these incredible tortures, survive and still move against his persecutors.

The Life of St. Isaac Jogues, pp. 298-299: "Once, when he had entered a cabin in one of the villages to inquire about the sick, **Jogues heard his name called from the darkness of a corner.** Going over, he found a young man desperately ill.
'Ondessonk,' the sick young man exclaimed, 'do you not know me?'
'I do not remember ever having seen you before,' Fr. Jogues replied.
'Do you not remember well the favor I did you at your entrance into the country of the Iroquois?' the man questioned.
'But what favor did you do me?' asked Jogues, puzzled.
'Don't you remember the man who cut your bonds, in the third village of the Agnieronon Iroquois, when you were at the end of your strength?' he continued.
'Of course I remember that very well. That man put me in his debt very, very much. I have never been able to thank him. I beg you, give me some news of him, if you are acquainted with him.'
'It was I, myself, who did it. I who took pity on you and loosed you.'…
Father Jogues told the dying man about God, of the happiness in the next life with God for those who believed, of what it was necessary to believe in order to be baptized and be made happy forever after death. The man listened with attention. With deep sincerity, he begged for baptism and for the happiness Ondessonk promised him. **Father Jogues poured on his head the water of salvation. While he prayed beside the mat, a few hours later, the man died peacefully.**"[506]

AMAZING BAPTISMS

Especially in the life of St. Isaac Jogues, we find incredible stories about his baptizing people under amazing and/or miraculous circumstances. These stories also show the truth of the dogma, *Unless a man is born again of water and the Holy Ghost he cannot enter into the kingdom of God* (John 3:5).

The Life of St. Isaac Jogues [while captive among the Iroquois Mohawks], p. 272: "The camps at night were in the open, in a hollow of the snow. **He had no furs, like the others, to protect him, and he could not move the hearts of any of the party to lend him any covering,** though they carried several skins back as their spoils of the chase…

"**Along the way, <u>they had to cross a gorge of a swift mountain stream</u>. The bridge was a tree trunk stretched a few feet above the swirling, deep waters**. It was unsteady with slippery moss. One of the party was a pregnant woman, who also carried a baby in the basket on her back and was otherwise burdened with the camp utensils. The strap of the cradle was across her forehead, and the bundles were fastened to her shoulders. **The squaw [Indian woman] started to climb across the tree, while Father Jogues waited to follow her. She lost her balance and toppled over into the tumbling rapids.** The baggage strapped to her shoulders weighed her to the bottom, the thong that held the cradle slipped from her forehead to her neck and was strangling her.

"**In an instant, Father Jogues leaped into the gorge and the icy current**. Wading and swimming, he fought his way to the woman, unstrapped the bundles and the cradle, and dragged her and the baby back to the bank. **He took good care to baptize the baby before he lifted it out of the water.** The Mohawks made a roaring fire and revived the woman, who was numbed almost to death. They allowed Ondessonk [Fr. Jogues] to warm himself and even commended him, for they realized that the woman would have been drowned except for his aid. **She recovered, but the newly baptized child died within a few days.**"[507]

This fascinating story shows us how the Almighty can and does get any soul that He wants to baptism. If the woman hadn't fallen into the icy waters, St. Isaac wouldn't have had the opportunity to baptize her baby. It's quite obvious that God arranged it so that this little child received the Sacrament just before He took it from the earth.

The Life of St. Isaac Jogues, p. 225: "**Two of the Hurons, Jogues learned, were to be burned to death that night at Tionontoguen. He stayed with them on the platform and concentrated his appeals on them. Finally they consented. <u>About that moment</u>,** the Mohawks threw the prisoners some raw corn that had been freshly plucked. The sheaths [of the corn] <u>were wet</u> from the recent rains. **Father Jogues carefully gathered the precious drops of water on a leaf and poured them over the heads of the two neophytes [new converts],** baptizing them in the name of the Father and of the Son and of the Holy Spirit. The Mohawks understood that his [Jogues'] act meant to bring happiness to these hated victims. They raged at his audacity and beat him down, threatening to slaughter him with the Hurons… That night the two Hurons [whom he had baptized] were burned over the fire."[508]

If the sheaths of corn had not been thrown at that very moment, Jogues wouldn't have had the water with which to baptize the two Indians. And, as noted in his life, St. Isaac Jogues always instructed the heathen in the essentials they had to know for baptism (e.g., the Trinity and the Incarnation).

> John 3:5,7 – "[Jesus saith] Amen, amen I say to thee, *unless a man be born again of water and the Holy Ghost*, he cannot enter into the kingdom of God… ***wonder not, that I said to thee, you must be born again***."

OTHER QUOTES FROM JOGUES AND XAVIER ON BAPTISM

In the life of St. Isaac Jogues, there is a fascinating account of his party's capture by the Iroquois savages. In it we find the description of Jogues' focus on baptizing an unbaptized Huron Indian who was accompanying them. Here is the account of when their party was suddenly and unexpectedly attacked by the Iroquois savages, who wanted to capture and torture them:

> *The Life of St. Isaac Jogues*, p. 205: "The most devoted of all was Atieronhonk, **whom Jogues had baptized at the first volley. The man could not get over his astonishment.** [Atieronhonk said]: 'It must be admitted that these people who come to instruct us have no doubt whatever of the truths they teach us. It must be that God alone is their reward. There is Ondessonk [Isaac Jogues]. He forgot himself at the moment of danger. He thought only of me, and spoke to me of becoming a Christian. **The musket balls whisked past our ears, death was before our very eyes. He thought only of baptizing me, and not of saving himself.** He did not fear death. <u>But he [Jogues] did think that I would be lost forever if I died without baptism</u>."[509]

Below is another interesting account of an Indian named Ahatsistari, who was converted by St. Isaac Jogues and his companions. Ahatsistari addressed St. Isaac Jogues and St. John De Brebeuf as follows:

> *The Life of St. Isaac Jogues*, p. 168: "I have the faith deep down in my heart, and my actions during the past winter have proved it sufficiently. In two days I am departing on the warpath. If I am killed in battle, tell me: where will my soul go if you refuse me baptism? If you saw into my heart as clearly as the great Master of our lives, I would already be numbered among the Christians; and the fear of the flames of hell would not accompany me, now that I am about to face death. I cannot baptize myself. **All that I can do is to declare with utmost honesty the desire that I have for it. After I do that, if my soul be burned in hell, you will bear the guilt of it.** Whatever you may decide to do, however, I will always pray to God, since I know Him. Perhaps He will have mercy on me, for you say that He is wiser than you are."[510]

It is obvious that Ahatsistari hadn't been taught "baptism of desire." He understood that he would go to hell if he died without the Sacrament of Baptism. Shortly after this speech, Ahatsistari was solemnly baptized.

> St. Francis Xavier, May, 1546: "Here there are altogether seven towns of Christians, all of which I went through and baptized all the newborn infants and the children not yet baptized. **A great many of them died soon after their baptism, <u>so that it was clear enough that their life had only been preserved by God until the entrance to eternal life should be opened to them</u>**."[511]

> St. Francis Xavier, Feb, 1548: "The thing which I wish to commend to you above everything else is that you should employ special diligence and watchfulness in the baptism of little children, so as not to leave any lately born child not regenerated in the saving laver of Christ in any of the villages… **Make search and inquiry for yourselves, and baptize with your own hands all those whom you find in want of <u>that most necessary Sacrament</u>**."[512]

> *The Life of St. Isaac Jogues*, p. 94: "**On one occasion, Father Jogues found a savage named Sonoresk** favorably disposed and sufficiently instructed, who was grasping his last breath. All through the night the man kept repeating 'Rihouiosta' (I believe). **Ondessonk [St. Isaac Jogues] baptized him, and the man suddenly recovered. He announced that baptism cured him:** the water that had been poured on his head by Ondessonk [Jogues] had flowed down through his throat, so that he felt no more pains. **His rejoicing in this life was not for long, however, for he died the next day.**"[513]

26. The Case of Father Feeney

Heretics and modernists resist the truth, just as they resist Him who is the Truth (Jn. 14:6). And because they resist the truth they resist facts, because facts report truth without any admixture of error. One of the facts that the modernists and heretics resist most of all, is the fact that the Catholic Church has infallibly taught that Outside the Catholic Church There is No Salvation and that John 3:5 is to be taken as it is written and that the Sacrament of Baptism is necessary for salvation (Trent, Sess. 7, Can. 5 on the Sacrament).

So what do these people do with these facts staring them in the face? They resort to attacking the reporter of these facts (*argumentum ad hominem*), which enables them to ignore the facts themselves. The episode of Father Leonard Feeney, S.J. is a case in point.

The dogma Outside the Catholic Church There is No Salvation really has nothing to do with Father Leonard Feeney. (In fact, I had never heard of Fr. Feeney when I came to the same conclusion – based upon Catholic dogma – that the Sacrament of Baptism is absolutely necessary for salvation and that all those who die as non-Catholics are lost.) It has to do with the teaching of the Chair of St. Peter, as I have shown, which is the authentic and infallible teaching of Christ. To reject this Catholic dogma is to reject Christ Himself.

> Pope Leo XIII, *Satis Cognitum* (# 5), June 29, 1896: "But he who dissents even in one point from divinely revealed truth absolutely rejects all faith, **since he thereby refuses to honor God as the supreme truth and the formal motive of faith.**"[514]

Father Feeney became famous for his public stand for the dogma Outside the Catholic Church There is No Salvation in the 1940's and 1950's. Most people fail to realize that, at that time, the world's bishops were by no means staunch traditionalists. Most of the world's bishops had already embraced the heresy of indifferentism, which explains why almost all of them signed the heretical Vatican II documents just a short time later. They had embraced the heretical idea that "invincible ignorance" saves those who die as non-Catholics, as I've discussed in certain previous sections. This is why one can easily detect heresy against the dogma in <u>most</u> theology manuals and texts beginning as early as the late 19th century. In fact, during his time, Father Feeney wrote to all of the bishops of the world about the dogma Outside the Church There is No Salvation and received only three positive responses. In other words, only three of the world's bishops at that time manifested a positive belief in the dogma Outside the Catholic Church There is No salvation *as it had been defined*. It is no wonder that Vatican II went through with virtually no resistance from the Episcopacy.

Father Feeney *believed* and preached the dogma – as it had been defined – publicly in Boston. He believed and preached that unless a man embraces the Catholic Faith – whether he be a Jew, Muslim, Protestant or agnostic – he will perish forever in Hell. Many converted, and many were angry. He had not a few enemies, especially among the increasingly modernist, politically correct and compromised clergy.

One of his main enemies was the Archbishop of Boston, Richard Cushing, a B'nai Brith (Jewish Freemasons) man of the year, and someone who called the dogma Outside the Catholic Church There is No Salvation "nonsense." In April of 1949, Cushing silenced Fr. Feeney and interdicted St. Benedict Center (the apostolate affiliated with Fr. Feeney). The reason given by Cushing was "disobedience," but the real reason was Father Feeney's public stand for the dogma Outside the Catholic Church There is No Salvation. It was not due to Father Feeney's stand against the theory of baptism of desire either, since this wasn't first published until 1952. Cushing's dissatisfaction with

Fr. Feeney was strictly based on Father Feeney's stand for the defined dogma that only Catholics – and those who become Catholics – can be saved.

Cushing had allies with other heretical clergymen in Boston, the area where the controversy erupted. Father John Ryan, S.J., head of the Adult Education Institute of Boston College, stated in the fall of 1947: "I do not agree with Father Feeney's doctrine on salvation outside the Church."[515] Father Stephen A. Mulcahy, S.J., Dean of the College of Arts and Sciences of Boston College, termed it: "Father Feeney's doctrine that there is no salvation outside the Church."[516] And Father J.J. McEleney, S.J., Provincial of the New England Province of the Society of Jesus, told Father Feeney in a personal meeting, that he was being ordered to transfer to Holy Cross College because of "Your doctrine."[517] Father Feeney quickly responded, "My doctrine on what?" To which Fr. McEleney replied, "I'm sorry, we can't go into that."

Right from the start, these fallen clergymen fused the issue with Father Feeney rather than the real source from which it came. This enabled them to focus on Father Feeney, **and ignore Jesus Christ, whose doctrine this was**.

> Pope Pius IX, *Nostis et Nobiscum* (# 10), Dec. 8, 1849: "In particular, **ensure that the faithful are deeply and thoroughly convinced of <u>the truth of the doctrine that the Catholic faith is necessary for attaining salvation</u>. (<u>This doctrine, received from Christ</u>** and emphasized by the Fathers and Councils, is also contained in the formulae of the profession of faith used by Latin, Greek and Oriental Catholics)."[518]

These heretics failed to realize that to belittle a defined dogma to something of Father Feeney's invention is blasphemous and severely dishonest. But God is not mocked. We see the same thing today, especially rampant among so-called traditionalists. But I will return to this point.

On December 2, 1948, the President of Boston College, Father William L. Keleher, S.J., held an interview with Dr. Maluf, who was an ally of Father Feeney in the stand for the dogma. Fr. Keleher stated:

> "*Father Feeney came to me at the beginning of this situation and I would have liked to do something except that I could not agree with <u>his doctrine</u> on salvation… He (Fr. Feeney) kept repeating such phrases as 'There is no salvation outside the Catholic Church.'*"[519]

When Maluf (a member of the Boston College faculty) responded that this "phrase" is a defined dogma, Fr. Keleher said:

> "*the theologians at St. John's Seminary and Weston College disagree with Father Feeney's doctrine on the salvation of non-Catholics.*"[520]

So there you have the case of Father Feeney in a nutshell. Father Feeney held, as it had been defined, that there is no salvation for those who die as non-Catholics. Those against him, including Fr. Keleher (President of Boston College), the Archbishop of Boston, the priests at Boston College, and the "theologians" at St. John's Seminary, held a different doctrine "on the salvation of non-Catholics." **This was the battle**. This was the dividing-line. One was either on one side or the other. One believed that there is <u>no</u> salvation for those who die as non-Catholics or one believed that there <u>is</u> salvation for those who die as non-Catholics. Let me quickly remind the reader on which side he will find the Catholic Church.

> Pope Gregory XVI, *Summo Iugiter Studio* (# 2), May 27, 1832:
> **"Finally some of these <u>misguided people attempt to persuade themselves and others that men are not saved only in the Catholic religion,</u> but that even heretics may attain eternal life."**[521]

A Jesuit priest of the new Vatican II religion skillfully describes what the scene was like when "the Boston Heresy Case" (i.e., whether only those who die as Catholics can be saved) erupted into public view during Holy Week 1949.

> Mark S. Massa, "S.J.", *Catholics and American Culture*, p. 31: **"The Boston Heresy Case erupted into public view during Holy Week 1949. The firings of Feeney's disciples from Boston College made front-page news all over the Northeast:** the *New York Times* began a series on Feeney and his group, and *Newsweek, Life,* and *Time* magazines all featured stories on the Boston 'troubles.' On perhaps the most solemn holy day of the Catholic calendar, Good Friday, Feeneyites (sic) stood outside Boston parishes carrying placards warning of the impending subversion of true doctrine by Church leaders themselves and selling the latest issue of From the Housetops. **As one student of the event has observed, the question of salvation replaced the Red Sox as the topic of conversation in Boston bars, and anyone spied in a Roman collar became a potential 'lead' in the story. The only analogue [comparable thing] church historians could think of was Constantinople in the fourth century, where rioting crowds had battled in the streets over the definition of the divinity of Jesus,** and Greek theological phrases became the mottos of chariot teams."[522]

On April 13, 1949, Fr. Keleher (the President of Boston College) fired Dr. Maluf, James R. Walsh and Charles Ewaskio from the faculty at Boston College for accusing the school of heresy against the dogma Outside the Church There is No Salvation. In his April 14 statement to the press explaining the reason behind their dismissal, Fr. Keleher stated:

"They continued to speak in class and out of class on matters contrary to the traditional teaching of the Catholic Church, ideas leading to bigotry and intolerance. Their doctrine is erroneous and as such could not be tolerated at Boston College. They were informed that they must cease such teaching or leave the faculty."[523]

One cannot help but notice Fr. Keleher's double-tongue: these men were dismissed for ideas leading to intolerance, which could not be tolerated. If intolerance is the false doctrine here, as Fr. Keleher indicates, then he is condemned by his own mouth. Furthermore, one cannot pass over Fr. Keleher's brazen assertion that "Their doctrine (i.e., the solemnly defined dogma that those who die as non-Catholics cannot be saved) is erroneous." By this statement Keleher is asserting that the Church's doctrine (on no salvation outside the Church) is erroneous and in no way his own. This was the type of heretical, anti-Catholic character in league with Archbishop Richard Cushing in the quest to crush Fr. Feeney's preaching of the dogma.

This was the beginning of the end, so to speak, as will be seen when we look at what has resulted in Boston as a result of their selling out of the dogma Outside the Church There is No Salvation.

27. Protocol 122/49

About four months after the silencing of Fr. Feeney in April by Richard Cushing, the apostate Archbishop of Boston, the Holy Office issued a document on August 8, 1949. Actually, the document was a letter addressed to Bishop Cushing, and signed by Cardinal Marchetti-Selvaggiani, known to most as Protocol No. 122/49. It is also called *Suprema haec Sacra* and the Marchetti-Selvaggiani letter. It is arguably – and, in my opinion, by far – the most crucial document in regard to the modern apostasy from the faith. Protocol 122/49 was not published in the Acts of the Apostolic See (*Acta Apostolicae Sedis*) but in *The Pilot*, the news organ for the Archdiocese of Boston. Keep in mind that this letter was published in Boston, as the significance of this will become more clear in the Section: "The Verdict is in: Boston leads the Way in a Massive Priestly Scandal that Rocks the Nation."

The absence of Protocol 122/49 from the Acts of the Apostolic See proves that it has no binding character; that is to say, Protocol 122/49 is not an infallible or binding teaching of the Catholic Church. Protocol 122/49 was not signed by Pope Pius XII either, and has the authority of a correspondence of two Cardinals (Marchetti-Selvaggiani who wrote the letter, and Cardinal Ottaviani who also signed it) to one archbishop – which is none. The letter, in fact, and to put it simply, is fraught with heresy, deceit, ambiguity and betrayal. Immediately after the publication of Protocol 122/49, *The Worcester Telegram* ran a typical headline:

VATICAN RULES AGAINST HUB DISSIDENTS – [Vatican] Holds No Salvation Outside Church Doctrine To Be False[524]

This was the impression given to almost the entire Catholic world by Protocol 122/49 – the Marchetti-Selvaggiani letter. Protocol 122/49, as the above headline bluntly said, held the "No Salvation Outside the Church Doctrine" to be false. By this fateful letter, the enemies of the dogma and the Church appeared to have been vindicated and the defenders of the dogma seemed to have been vanquished. The problem for the apparent victors, however, was that this document was nothing more than a letter from two heretical Cardinals of the Holy Office, who had already embraced the heresy later adopted by Vatican II, to one apostate Archbishop in Boston. Some may be surprised that I describe Cardinal Ottaviani as heretical, since he is considered by many to have been orthodox. If his signature on the Protocol isn't enough proof for his heresy, consider that he signed all of the Vatican II documents and aligned himself with the post-Vatican II revolution. I rest my case.

Since almost the entire public was (and is) given the impression that Protocol 122/49 represented the official teaching of the Catholic Church, it constituted the selling out of Jesus Christ, His doctrine and His Church to the world, a selling out that had to take place before the wholesale apostasy of Vatican II. By Protocol 122/49 and the persecution of Fr. Feeney, **the public was given the impression that the Catholic Church had now overturned a 20 centuries' old dogma of the faith: that the Catholic Faith is definitely necessary for salvation.** And even to this day, if one were to ask almost every so-called Catholic priest in the world about the dogma Outside the Catholic Church There is No Salvation, he would be answered with a reference to the Father Feeney controversy and Protocol 122/49, even if the priest is unable to identify or recall the specific names and dates. Try it, I know from experience. Basically all of the Novus Ordo priests who know anything about the issue will use Protocol 122/49 and the "condemnation" of Fr. Feeney to justify their heretical, Anti-Catholic, Anti-Christ, Anti-Magisterial belief that men can be saved in non-Catholic religions and without the Catholic Faith. These are the fruits of the infamous Protocol 122/49. *And by their fruits you shall know them* (Mt. 7:16).

Now let's take a look at a few excerpts from the Protocol:

Protocol 122/49, Aug. 8, 1949: "Now, among those things which the Church has always preached and will never cease to preach is contained also <u>that infallible statement by which we are taught that there is no salvation outside the Church.</u>

"However, this dogma must be understood in that sense in which the Church herself understands it."[525]

Let's stop it right there. Already it's clear that the author of the Protocol is preparing the reader's mind to accept something different than simply "that infallible statement by which we are taught that there is no salvation outside the Church." The author is clearly easing into an explanation of the phrase "Outside the Church There is No Salvation" other than what the words themselves state and declare. If the author were not preparing the reader to accept an understanding other than what the words of the dogma themselves state and declare, then he would have simply written: "This dogma must be understood as the Church has defined it, exactly as the words state and declare."

Compare the Protocol's attempt to explain the dogma away with Pope Gregory XVI's treatment of the same issue in his encyclical *Summo Iugiter Studio*.

> Pope Gregory XVI, *Summo Iugiter Studio*, May 27, 1832, on no salvation outside the Church: **"Finally some of these misguided people attempt to persuade themselves and others that men are not saved only in the Catholic religion, *but that even heretics may attain eternal life*…** You know how zealously Our predecessors taught that article of faith which these dare to deny, namely the necessity of the Catholic faith and of unity for salvation… Omitting other appropriate passages *which are almost numberless in the writings of the Fathers*, We shall praise St. Gregory the Great who expressly testifies that THIS IS INDEED THE TEACHING OF THE CATHOLIC CHURCH. He says: '*The holy universal Church teaches that it is not possible to worship God truly except in her and asserts that all who are outside of her will not be saved*.' **Official acts of the Church proclaim the same dogma. Thus, in the decree on faith which Innocent III published with the synod of Lateran IV, these things are written:** '*There is one universal Church of all the faithful outside of which no one is saved.*' Finally the same dogma is also expressly mentioned in the profession of faith proposed by the Apostolic See, not only that which all Latin churches use, but also that which… other Eastern Catholics use. **We did not mention these selected testimonies because We thought you were ignorant of that article of faith and in need of Our instruction. Far be it from Us to have such an absurd and insulting suspicion about you. But We are so concerned about this serious and well known dogma, which has been attacked with such remarkable audacity, that We could not restrain Our pen from reinforcing this truth with many testimonies."**[526]

Pope Gregory XVI does not say, "*However, this dogma must be understood in that sense in which the Church herself understands it*," as does the heretical Protocol 122/49. No, he unequivocally affirms that THIS IS INDEED THE TEACHING OF THE CATHOLIC

CHURCH. Throughout the whole encyclical, Gregory XVI does not fail to repeatedly affirm the true and literal meaning of the phrase Outside the Church There is No Salvation, without qualification or exception, as it had been defined. Father Feeney and his allies in defense of the dogma were reiterating exactly what Gregory XVI officially taught above. It doesn't take a rocket scientist to figure out that if Protocol 122/49 was written to "correct" the understanding of Father Feeney on Outside the Church There is No Salvation (which it was), then Protocol 122/49 was also "correcting" the understanding of Pope Gregory XVI and all of the infallible statements on the topic for 20 centuries.

Also, notice that Pope Gregory XVI **makes reference to the dogmatic definition** of the *Fourth Lateran Council* to substantiate his position and literal understanding of the formula Outside the Church There is No Salvation. Throughout the whole document, **Protocol 122/49 makes <u>no</u> reference to <u>any</u> of the dogmatic definitions** on this topic. This is because Pope Gregory XVI, being a Catholic, knew that the only understanding of a dogma that exists is that which Holy Mother Church has once declared; while the authors of the Protocol, being heretics, did not believe that a dogma is to be understood exactly as it was once declared. That explains why Pope Gregory cited exactly what Holy Mother Church has once declared and the authors of the Protocol did not.

> Pope Pius IX, *First Vatican Council*, Sess. 3, Chap. 4, On Faith and Reason: "Hence, also, **that understanding of its sacred dogmas must be perpetually retained, <u>which Holy Mother Church has once declared</u>; and there must never be a recession from that meaning under the specious name of a deeper understanding.**"[527]

If the understanding of the dogma Outside the Church There is No Salvation was not clear from the teaching of the Chair of Peter (the infallible definitions on the topic), then a 1949 letter of Cardinal Marchetti-Selvaggiani is certainly not going to give it to us! And if no exceptions or qualifications to this dogma were understood at the time of the definitions – nor at the time of Pope Gregory XVI – then it is impossible for exceptions to come into understanding after that point (e.g., in 1949), because the dogma had already been defined and taught long before. <u>Discovery</u> of a new understanding of the dogma in 1949 is a <u>denial</u> of the understanding of the dogma as it had been defined. But define new dogma is indeed what the Protocol tried to do. I continue with the Protocol.

> Protocol 122/49, Aug. 8, 1949: "Now, among the commandments of Christ, that one holds not the least place by which we are commanded to be incorporated by Baptism into the Mystical Body of Christ, which is the Church, and to remain united to Christ and to His Vicar... **Therefore, no one will be saved who, *knowing the Church to have been divinely established by Christ*, nevertheless refuses to submit to the Church or withholds obedience from the Roman Pontiff, the Vicar of Christ on earth.**"[528]

Here the Protocol begins to enter into its <u>new</u> explanation of the dogma Outside the Catholic Church There is No Salvation, but in a diabolically clever manner. The ambiguity lies in the fact that this statement is true: *no one who, <u>knowing</u> the Church to have been divinely established, nevertheless refuses to submit to Her and the Roman Pontiff will be saved.* But everyone reading this document is also given the clear impression by this language that some people, who have <u>unknowingly</u> failed to submit to the Church and the Roman Pontiff, can be saved. This is heretical and would actually make it counterproductive to convince people that the Catholic Church is divinely established!

Compare the dogmatic definition of the Catholic Church with the addition to the dogma by Protocol 122/49.

The Dogma:

> Pope Boniface VIII, *Unam Sanctam*, Nov. 18, 1302, *ex cathedra*:
> "Furthermore, we declare, say, define, <u>and proclaim to **every human creature**</u> that they by absolute necessity for salvation are entirely subject to the Roman Pontiff."[529]

The Addition by Protocol 122/49:

> Protocol 122/49, Aug. 8, 1949: "Therefore, no one will be saved <u>who, **knowing** the Church to have been divinely established</u> by Christ, nevertheless refuses to submit to the Church or withholds obedience from the Roman Pontiff, the Vicar of Christ on earth."[530]

The reader can easily see that the intended meaning of Protocol 122/49 **is a departure from the understanding of the dogma which Holy Mother Church has once declared.** No one can deny this. The dogma of the necessity of submission to the Roman Pontiff for salvation has gone from application to *every human creature* (Boniface VIII) to *"those knowing the Church to have been divinely established"* (Protocol 122/49), again making it foolish to convince people that the Church is divinely established. I continue with the Protocol:

> Protocol 122/49, Aug. 8, 1949: "In his infinite mercy God has willed that the effects, necessary for one to be saved, of those helps to salvation which are directed toward man's final end, not by intrinsic necessity, but only by divine institution, can also be obtained in certain circumstances when those helps are used only in desire and longing...
> "The same in its own degree must be asserted of the Church, in as far as she is the general help to salvation. Therefore, **that one may obtain eternal salvation, <u>it is not always required that he be incorporated</u> into the Church actually as a**

member, but it is necessary that at least he be united to her by desire and longing."[531]

Here one detects another denial of the dogma as it was defined, and a departure from the understanding of the dogma that Holy Mother Church has once declared. Compare the following dogmatic definition of Pope Eugene IV with these paragraphs from Protocol 122/49, especially the underlined portions.

The Dogma:

> Pope Eugene IV, *Council of Florence*, "Cantate Domino," 1441, *ex cathedra*: "The Holy Roman Church firmly believes, professes, and proclaims that none of those existing outside the Catholic Church, not only pagans, but also Jews, heretics and schismatics can become participants in eternal life, but they will depart 'into everlasting fire which was prepared for the devil and his angels' [Matt. 25:41], unless before the end of life they have been added to the flock; **and that the unity of** *this ecclesiastical body* **(***ecclesiastici corporis***)** is so strong **that only for those who abide in it are the sacraments of the Church of benefit for salvation**, and do fasts, almsgiving, and other functions of piety and exercises of a Christian soldier productive of eternal reward. No one, whatever almsgiving he has practiced, even if he has shed blood for the name of Christ, can be saved, unless he has persevered within the bosom and unity of the Catholic Church."[532]

We see that Protocol 122/49 (quoted above) is denying the necessity of *incorporation* into the *ecclesiastici corporis*, which is heresy!

It *was* necessary to be in the Church's "bosom and unity" (Eugene IV), *but now* it is "*not always required to be incorporated into the Church actually as a member*" (Protocol 122/49). The defined dogma of INCORPORATION and actually abiding in the ecclesiastical body (*ecclesiastici corporis*) has been denied. This is heresy!

There is no way on earth that the teaching of Protocol 122/49 is compatible with the teaching of Pope Eugene IV and Pope Boniface VIII. To accept, believe or promote the Protocol is to act contrary to these definitions.

I continue with the Protocol:

> Protocol 122/49, Aug. 8, 1949: "However, this desire need not always be explicit, as it is in catechumens; but when a person is involved in invincible ignorance, God accepts also an *implicit desire*, so called because it is included in that good disposition of soul whereby a person wishes his will to be conformed to the will of God."[533]

Here the heresy comes out quite bluntly. People who don't hold the Catholic Faith – who are "involved in invincible ignorance" – can also be united by "implicit" desire, as long as "a person wishes his will to be conformed to the will of God." **And I remind the reader that Protocol 122/49 was written in specific contradistinction to Fr. Feeney's statement that all who die as non-Catholics are lost.** That it to say, the Protocol was written to specifically distinguish its own teaching from Fr. Feeney's affirmation that all who die as non-Catholics are lost, which shows that the Protocol was teaching that people who die as non-Catholics and in false religions can be saved. Thus, the Protocol's statement above is quite obviously, and nothing other than, the heresy that one can be saved in any religion or in no religion, as long as morality is maintained.

> Fr. Michael Muller, C.SS.R., *The Catholic Dogma*, pp. 217-218: "**Inculpable or invincible ignorance has never been and will never be a means of salvation**. To be saved, it is necessary to be justified, or to be in the state of grace. In order to obtain sanctifying grace, it is necessary to have the proper dispositions for justification; that is, true divine faith in at least the necessary truths of salvation, confident hope in the divine Savior, sincere sorrow for sin, together with the firm purpose of doing all that God has commanded, etc. **Now, these supernatural acts of faith, hope, charity, contrition, etc., which prepare the soul for receiving sanctifying grace, <u>can never</u> be supplied by invincible ignorance; and if invincible ignorance cannot supply the preparation for receiving sanctifying grace, much less can it bestow sanctifying grace itself. 'Invincible ignorance,' says St. Thomas, 'is a punishment for sin.'** (De, Infid. Q. x., art. 1)."[534]

Compare the above passage from the Protocol with the following dogmatic definitions.

The Dogma:

> Pope Eugene IV, *Council of Florence*, Session 8, Nov. 22, 1439, "The Athanasian Creed", *ex cathedra*: "**<u>Whoever</u> wishes to be saved, before all things <u>it is necessary that he holds the Catholic faith</u>.** *Unless a person keeps this faith whole and undefiled, without a doubt he shall perish eternally.*"[535]

> Pope Pius IV, *Council of Trent*, "Iniunctum nobis," Nov. 13, 1565, *ex cathedra*: "***<u>This true Catholic faith</u>, outside of which <u>no one</u> can be saved*** … I now profess and truly hold…"[536]

> Pope Benedict XIV, *Nuper ad nos*, March 16, 1743, Profession of Faith: "**<u>This faith of the Catholic Church</u>, without which <u>no one</u> can be saved**, and which of my own accord I now profess and truly hold…"[537]

Pope Pius IX, *Vatican Council I*, Session 2, Profession of Faith: "**This true Catholic faith, outside of which none can be saved**, which I now freely profess and truly hold…"[538]

Less than three months after the Marchetti-Selvaggianni letter was published in part in *The Pilot*, Father Feeney was expelled from the Jesuit Order on October 28, 1949. Father Feeney stood strong against the heretics' attempts to beat him down and get him to submit to the heresy that non-Catholics can be saved. Referring to the August 8th letter of Marchetti-Selvaggiani (Protocol 122/49), Father Feeney rightly stated: "it can be considered as having established a two-sided policy in order to propagate error."

The reality was that Father Feeney's expulsion from the Jesuit Order had no validity. The men who expelled him and the clerics who were against him were automatically expelled from the Catholic Church for adhering to the heresy that those who die as non-Catholics can be saved. This is similar to the situation in the 5th century, when the Patriarch of Constantinople, Nestorius, began to preach the heresy that Mary was not the Mother of God. The faithful reacted, accused Nestorius of heresy and denounced him as a heretic who was outside the Catholic Church. And Nestorius was later condemned at the Council of Ephesus in 431. Here is what Pope St. Celestine I stated about those who had been excommunicated by Nestorius after he began to preach heresy.

Pope St. Celestine I, 5th Century:
"**The authority of Our Apostolic See has determined** that the bishop, cleric, or simple Christian who had been deposed or excommunicated by Nestorius or his followers, **after the latter began to preach heresy** *shall not be considered deposed or excommunicated.* **For he who had defected from the faith with such preachings, cannot depose or remove anyone whatsoever**."[539]

Pope St. Celestine authoritatively confirms the principle that a public heretic is a person with no authority to depose, excommunicate or expel. The quote is found in *De Romano Pontifice*, the work of St. Robert Bellarmine. This explains why all of the persecution against Father Feeney (expulsion, interdiction, etc.) had no validity, because he was right and those who were against him were wrong. He defended the dogma that there is no salvation outside the Church, while his opponents defended the heresy that there is salvation outside the Church.

St. Robert Bellarmine (1610), Doctor of the Church, *De Romano Pontifice*: "A pope who is a manifest heretic automatically (*per se*) ceases to be pope and head, just as he ceases automatically to be a Christian and a member of the Church. Wherefore, he can be judged and punished by the Church. **This is the teaching of all the ancient Fathers** who teach that **manifest heretics immediately lose all jurisdiction.**"

Things between Father Feeney and the heretics in Boston remained unchanged until September 14, 1952. At this point, Richard Cushing, the "Archbishop" of Boston, demanded that Father Feeney retract his "interpretation" of the dogma – which means retract the dogma – and make an explicit profession of submission to the Marchetti-Selvaggiani letter (Protocol 122/49). With four witnesses, Father Feeney presented himself before Cushing. He told him that his only option was to declare the letter of Marchetti-Selvaggiani **"absolutely scandalous because it was frankly heretical."** This is exactly what Pope Gregory XVI would have said about the horrible Protocol letter, as well as any Catholic.

During their meeting, Fr. Feeney asked "Archbishop" Cushing if he was in agreement with the Aug. 8, 1949 letter of Marchetti-Selvaggiani. Cushing responded, "I am not a theologian. All that I know is what I am told." This evasive and non-committal answer shows the true colors of Cushing, this heretic, false pastor and enemy of Jesus Christ. If Cushing believed that one was bound to the letter, then he should have responded without hesitation that he agreed with it. But because he didn't want to defend the letter in any of its details, especially its denials of dogma, he responded by evading the question. This evasion prohibited Fr. Feeney from putting him on the spot and convicting him with the dogma that was being denied. Father Feeney accused Cushing of failing in his duty and left.

28. Heresy before Vatican II

To fully appreciate the Father Feeney controversy one must understand that the denial of the faith that Father Feeney was combating was well in place in the years before Vatican II. Most people considering themselves to be "traditional Catholics" have the false impression that, *"if we could only go back to what people believed in the 1950's, everything would be fine."* No, it wouldn't. Most of the priests and bishops in the 1940's and 1950's had already lost the faith and had completely rejected the solemnly defined dogma that there is no salvation outside the Catholic Church. It is simply a fact that heresy against the dogma Outside the Church There is No Salvation was being taught in most seminaries in the 1940's and 50's. In fact, the breakdown of the faith began much earlier than the 1940's or 50's.

> Our Lady of La Salette, France, Sept. 19, 1846: **"In the year 1864, Lucifer together with a large number of demons will be unloosed from hell; they will put an end to faith little by little**, even in those dedicated to God. They will blind them in such a way, that, unless they are blessed with a special grace, these people will take on the spirit of these angels of hell;

**several religious institutions will lose all faith and will lose
many souls… Rome will lose the faith and become the seat of
the Antichrist… The Church will be in eclipse…"**

As I said earlier in this document, St. Anthony Mary Claret, the only canonized saint at the First Vatican Council, had a stroke because of the false doctrines that were being proposed even then, which never made their way into the Council. The step-by-step dismantling of the Catholic Faith by Lucifer began, not in 1964, but in 1864, long before Vatican II. Let's take a look at some examples of blatant heresy in pre-Vatican II books with Imprimaturs (i.e., the approval of a Bishop).

1.   The Catholic Encyclopedia, Vol. 3, "Church," 1908, G. H. Joyce: "The doctrine is summed up in the phrase, *Extra Ecclesiam nulla salus (Outside the Church there is no salvation)*… **It certainly does not mean that none can be saved except those who are in visible communion with the Catholic Church**. The Catholic Church has ever taught that nothing else is needed to obtain justification than an act of perfect charity and of contrition… Many are kept from the Church by ignorance. **Such may be the case of numbers among those who have been brought up in heresy**… Thus, **even in the case in which <u>God saves men apart from the Church</u>**, He does so through the Church's actual graces… In the expression of theologians, **they belong to the soul of the Church**, though not to its body."[540]

What we have here, in *The Catholic Encyclopedia*, in the year 1908, in a book with the Imprimatur of John Farley, the Archbishop of New York, is blatant heresy. The author, G.H. Joyce, completely rejects the dogma as it has been defined. He even employs the "Soul of the Church Heresy" which is completely heretical (as I showed in "The Soul of the Church Heresy" section). The defined dogma which declared that only those in the Catholic Church can be saved, has given way to the heresy that God saves men *"apart from the Church."*

Pope Leo XIII, *Tametsi futura prospicientibus* (# 7), Nov. 1, 1900: "Hence **<u>all who would find salvation apart from the Church, are led astray and strive in vain.</u>**"[541]

But to these heretics, no longer does this dogma mean that outside the Church there is no salvation, but rather that non-Catholics are saved in their false religions but *by* the Catholic Church. The necessity of Catholic faith and unity for salvation has been utterly repudiated.

Pope Gregory XVI, *Summo Iugiter Studio*, May 27, 1832:
"Finally some of these misguided people attempt to persuade themselves and others that men are not saved only in the Catholic religion, *but that even heretics may attain eternal life…* **You know how zealously Our predecessors taught <u>that article of faith which these dare to deny</u>, namely <u>the necessity of the Catholic faith and of unity</u> for salvation.**"[542]

And this proves that the dogma that those who die as non-Catholics cannot be saved was being denied publicly even as early as 1908.

2. *My Catholic Faith*, a Catechism by Bishop Louis LaRavoire, 1949: "Holy Mass may be offered for the living of whatever creed. It may be offered for departed Catholics. **<u>The priest may not offer Mass publicly for departed non-Catholics, but the persons hearing the Mass may do so.</u>**"[543]

Here we find more clear heresy in a Catechism written by the Bishop of Krishnager, Louis LaRavoire. This Catechism is still promoted today by many so-called "traditional Catholics." By permitting prayer for departed non-Catholics, Louis LaRavoire denies the dogma that all who depart life as non-Catholics are lost.

Pope Clement VI, *Super quibusdam*, Sept. 20, 1351:
"In the second place, we ask whether you and the Armenians obedient to you believe that **no man** of the wayfarers **outside the faith of this Church**, and outside the obedience to the Pope of Rome, **can finally be saved.**"[544]

3. Baltimore Catechism No. 3, 1921, Imprimatur Archbishop Hayes of New York: "Q. 510. Is it ever possible for one to be saved who does not know the Catholic Church to be the true Church? A. **It is possible for one to be saved who does not know the Catholic Church to be the true Church, provided that person (1) has been validly baptized; (2) firmly believes the religion he professes and practices to be the true religion, and (3) dies without the guilt of mortal sin on his soul.**"

Here we find blatant heresy in the Baltimore Catechism, imprimatured and published in 1921. The authors of this heretical Catechism are bold enough to assert that salvation for a non-Catholic is not only possible, but dependent upon whether the non-Catholic "<u>firmly believes</u> the religion he professes and practices to be the true religion." So if you're <u>firmly convinced</u> that Mormonism is the true religion, then you've got a good shot at salvation, according to the Baltimore Catechism; but if you're not firmly convinced of this then your chances are less. This makes an absolute mockery of the dogma: one Lord, one faith and one baptism (Eph. 4:5).

Pope Gregory XVI, *Mirari Vos* (# 13), Aug. 15, 1832: "With the admonition of the apostle that 'there is one God, one faith, one baptism' (Eph. 4:5) **may those fear who contrive the notion that the safe harbor of salvation is open to persons of any religion whatever.** They should consider the testimony of Christ Himself that 'those who are not with Christ are against Him,' (Lk. 11:23) <u>and that they disperse unhappily who do not gather with Him.</u> **Therefore, 'without a doubt, they will perish forever, unless they hold the Catholic faith whole and inviolate" (Athanasian Creed).**[545]

The words of Gregory XVI in *Mirari Vos* could have been written specifically to the authors of the Baltimore Catechism; and indeed they were addressed to other heretics in his day who proposed the same thing. **Notice how far the Baltimore Catechism has come from the dogmatic Athanasian Creed**, which Gregory XVI affirmed, which states that whoever wishes to be saved must hold the Catholic Faith. The authors of the Baltimore Catechism could not have, in their wildest imagination, pretended to believe in that dogmatic profession of faith.

The reader should also note that Pope Gregory XVI teaches that <u>those who have never been Catholic are lost,</u> as well as Catholics who leave the Church.

The Baltimore Catechism rejects the words of Jesus Christ, who declared that "*he that believeth not shall be condemned*" (Mk. 16:16). The revised edition of the Scriptures by the authors of the Baltimore Catechism would have to read: "*he that believeth firmly in false religions shall not be condemned.*"

4. *Fundamentals of Catholic Dogma*, by Ludwig Ott, Imprimatur 1954, p. 310: "The necessity for belonging to the Church is not merely a necessity of precept, but also of means, as the comparison with the Ark, the means of salvation from the biblical flood, plainly shows… In special circumstances, namely, in the case of invincible ignorance or of incapability, actual membership of the Church can be replaced by the desire for the same… **In this manner also those who are in point of fact outside the Catholic Church can achieve salvation.**"[546]

It's a pity that the Catholic Church was stupid enough to define more than seven times that outside the Catholic Church no one at all is saved, because (as the "great" Ludwig Ott reveals) "*those who are in point of fact <u>outside</u> the Catholic Church can achieve salvation.*" It's a shame that the Church didn't possess this profound enlightenment, that it didn't know that what it had been teaching "infallibly" for all of these years was actually just the opposite of the truth.

In truth, what Ludwig Ott says above is equivalent to declaring that the Blessed Virgin Mary was conceived in Original Sin. There is no difference whatsoever. If the

Church defines that outside the Church no one at all is saved (Pope Innocent III, etc.), and I assert that "those who <u>are in point of fact outside the Catholic Church</u> can achieve salvation," then I am doing the exact same thing as if I were to declare that the Virgin Mary was conceived in some sin, when the Church said she had no sin. I would be stating exactly the opposite of what the Church had infallibly defined, and this is precisely what Ludwig Ott does.

But shortly after explicitly denying the dogma that no one can be saved outside the Church, notice what Ludwig Ott says:

> Ludwig Ott, *Fundamentals of Catholic Dogma*, p. 311: "**It is the unanimous conviction of the Fathers that salvation <u>cannot be achieved outside</u> the Church.**"[547]

"*But let your speech be yea, yea: no, no: and that which is over and above these, is of evil*" (Mt. 5:37). From one page to the next, Ludwig Ott contradicts himself on whether those who are outside the Catholic Church can achieve salvation! He even uses the exact same verb – "achieve" – in both sentences, but with the opposite meaning from one to the next: 1) those "**outside the Church *can achieve* salvation**"; 2) "**salvation *cannot be achieved* outside** the Church." His speech is not of God, but of the devil. Black is white and white is black; good is evil and evil is good; truth is error and error is truth; salvation can be achieved outside the Church and salvation cannot be achieved outside the Church.

For the pre-Vatican II heretics who condemned Father Feeney and despised the dogma Outside the Catholic Church There is No Salvation, it is no problem believing that there is salvation outside the Catholic Church, while simultaneously believing that there is no salvation outside the Catholic Church. It is no problem for these people because they are of evil (Mt. 5:37).

> Pope Clement V, *Council of Vienne*, Decree # 30, 1311-1312, *ex cathedra*: "… *one universal Church, outside of which there is <u>no</u> salvation*, for all of whom there is one Lord, one faith, and one baptism…"[548]

Those who obstinately accept the heresy that is contained in these pre-Vatican II books – such as Ludwig Ott's *Fundamentals of Catholic Dogma* – should rightly fear, as Pope Gregory XVI says, because they will without a doubt inherit a place in Hell if they do not repent and convert.

> 5. *The Catechism Explained*, Rev. Spirago and Rev. Clark, 1898: "**If, however, a man, through no fault of his own, remains outside the Church, he may be saved** if he lead a God-fearing life; for such a one is to all intents and purposes a member of the Catholic Church."[549]

According to this, it's not only possible to be saved outside the Church (which is a direct denial of the dogma), but it's actually possible to be, "for all intents and purposes," a member of the Catholic Church while still outside of Her! This is so heretical and contradictory that it's not worthy of further comment, except to say that what *The Catechism Explained* proposes here – that a man can be saved outside the Church as long as he leads "a God-fearing life" – is exactly what Pope Gregory XVI condemned in *Mirari Vos*: that a man may be saved in any religion whatsoever, so long as morality is maintained.

> Pope Gregory XVI, *Mirari Vos* (# 13), Aug. 15, 1832: "**This perverse opinion is spread on all sides by the fraud of the wicked who claim that it is possible to obtain the eternal salvation of the soul by the profession of any kind of religion, as long as morality is maintained**… without a doubt, they will perish forever, unless they hold the Catholic faith whole and inviolate (Athanasian Creed)."[550]

I could continue with examples of pre-Vatican II imprimatured texts which contain heresy, but the point should be obvious: the denial of the dogma Outside the Catholic Church There is No Salvation was well in place in the minds of most priests and bishops before Vatican II, so the opposition Father Feeney experienced in defending this truth in the late 1940's and 1950's comes as no surprise. The Great Apostasy was well in place in the 1940's and 50's, having actually begun in the mid to late 1800's, and Father Feeney was attempting to stifle this tide of apostasy by cutting away at its root cause: the denial of the necessity of the Catholic Church for salvation.

29. Mystici Corporis

Some have the false impression that the horrific pre-Vatican II heresy, which was catalogued above, was also taught by Pope Pius XII in his encyclical *Mystici Corporis*. This is not true. The passage that the heretics love to quote from *Mystici Corporis* is weak, but not heretical. It is accurately translated as follows:

> Pope Pius XII, *Mystici Corporis*, June 29, 1943, Speaking of non-Catholics: "We wish that they, each and every one of them… may be zealous and eager to tear themselves out of that state in which it is not possible for them to be without fear regarding their eternal salvation. For, even though they may be ordained toward the mystic Body of the Redeemer, by a certain unknowing desire and resolution, they still remain deprived of so many helps from heaven, which one can enjoy only in the Catholic Church. Let them, therefore, come back to Catholic unity, and united with us in the organic oneness of the Body of Jesus Christ may they hasten to the one Head in the society of glorious love….We wait for them with

open arms to return, not to a stranger's house, but to their own, their Father's house."

First of all, this passage from *Mystici Corporis* has been incorrectly translated by many to further weaken and to pervert the actual words of Pius XII. The phrase (*ab eo statu se eripere studeant, in quo de sempiterna cuiusque propria salute securi esse non possunt*) which is correctly translated as "… *zealous and eager to tear themselves out of that state in which it is not possible for them to be without fear regarding their eternal salvation,*" has been mistranslated as "look to withdrawing from that state in **which they cannot be sure of their salvation.**"[551] This mistranslation gives the clear impression that non-Catholics have an outside chance at gaining salvation where they are. Secondly, the mistranslation gives the impression that Catholics can be sure of their salvation, which is a heresy condemned by the Council of Trent (Trent, Sess. 6, Chap. 9).[552]

The other part of this passage which has been abused by the heretics is the phrase, in Latin: *quandoquidem, etiamsi inscio quodam desiderio ac voto ad mysticum Redemptoris Corpus* **ordinentur.** This has been mistranslated by many to read: "*For even though unsuspectingly they are related in desire and resolution to the Mystical Body of the Redeemer…*" This is a deliberate mistranslation which alters the meaning of Pius XII's words. I will quote Bro. Robert Mary in *Father Feeney and the Truth About Salvation* to explain why this is an incorrect translation.

> "The abused word is **ordinentur**. The book, A Latin-English Dictionary of St. Thomas Aquinas, by Roy J. Deferrari, gives us the following meanings for the Latin verb ordino: 'Ordino, are, avi, atum – (1) to order, to set in order, to arrange, to adjust, to dispose, (2) to ordain…'"
>
> "Since the Pope uses the subjunctive mood to express a contingency of uncertainty, not a fact, the translation should read:
>
> 'For, even though they may be disposed toward (or ordained toward) the mystic Body of the Redeemer, by a certain unknowing desire and resolution…'
>
> "**In other words, the only thing this 'certain unknowing desire and resolution' (inscio quodam desiderio ac voto) may be doing for these non-Catholics is setting them in order for entrance into, or return to, the Church. In no way does the Pope say, as fact, that they are 'related' to the Mystical Body of the Redeemer, much less 'united to it.'**"[553]

Bro. Robert Mary has astutely pointed out how it is false to say that Pius XII taught that some non-Catholics are "related" to the Church by unknowing desire; and that Pius XII certainly did not teach that some non-Catholics are "united" to the Church. But this is how one finds *Mystici Corporis* translated in many papers, especially those written by priests who deny the dogma Outside the Church There is No Salvation.

While the important observation above shows how wrong the modern heretics' treatment of *Mystici Corporis* is, there is no doubt that Pius XII's statement in the above passage – even correctly translated – is still <u>pathetically</u> weak, and opens the door for liberal heretics to claim that he endorsed the heresy that non-Catholics can be saved *by their unknowing desire for the Catholic faith*. Its weakness displays the mindset of a man who allowed heresy against the dogma Outside the Church There is No Salvation to run rampant in the seminaries, theology texts and Catechisms during his reign, even if not explicitly taught by him. Pius XII had no business talking about the supposed unknowing desire and resolution of non-Catholics, even if he didn't assert that such could be saved. Everyone knows that even the mention of such a thing causes modernists to salivate like dogs over a tasty meal. Pius XII should have addressed non-Catholics in the manner of Pope Leo XII, and he should have reaffirmed that non-Catholics will surely perish if they don't hold the Catholic faith in the manner of Gregory XVI.

Pope Leo XII, *Quod hoc ineunte* (# 8), May 24, 1824: "**We address all of you who are still removed from the true Church and the road to salvation**. In this universal rejoicing, one thing is lacking: that having been called by the inspiration of the Heavenly Spirit and having broken every decisive snare, you might sincerely agree with **the mother Church, outside of whose teachings there is no salvation.**"[554]

Pope Gregory XVI, *Mirari Vos* (# 13), Aug. 15, 1832: "**Therefore, 'without a doubt, they will perish forever, unless they hold the Catholic faith whole and inviolate" (Athanasian Creed).**[555]

A strong reaffirmation of Catholic teaching such as this by Pius XII would have eliminated all of the heretics' claims against the dogma by referencing his encyclical. Nevertheless, here are a few other statements from Pope Pius XII which are worthy of note.

Pope Pius XII, *Mystici Corporis* (# 22), June 29, 1943: "**Actually only those are to be numbered among the members of the Church who have received the laver of regeneration and profess the true faith.**"[556]

Pope Pius XII, *Mediator Dei* (# 43), Nov. 20, 1947: "In the same way, actually that **baptism is the distinctive mark of all Christians, and serves to differentiate them from those who have not been cleansed in this purifying stream and**

consequently are not members of Christ, the sacrament of holy orders sets the priest apart from the rest of the faithful who have not received this consecration."[557]

These two statements exclude the idea that one can be saved by even an explicit desire for baptism, since they affirm that those who have not received the Sacrament of Baptism are not Christians or members of the Church or members of Christ. (*Those who are not Christians or members of the Church or members of Christ cannot be saved*.)

> John 15:6- "**If anyone abide not in me**, he shall be cast forth as a branch, and shall wither, and **they shall gather him up, and cast him into the fire**, and he burneth."

Actually, if one admits that the above quote from *Mediator Dei* is magisterial (and therefore infallible), **it alone eliminates any theory of baptism of desire,** because it asserts that the differentiation between those who have received the mark of baptism (and are members of Christ) and those who have not received the mark of baptism (and consequently are not members of Christ) is as pronounced as those who have been made priests by ordination and those who have not. **In other words, according to the pronouncement of Pope Pius XII in *Mediator Dei*, to assert that one could be a Christian or a member of Christ without the mark of baptism (which is what the theory of baptism of desire asserts) is akin to asserting that one can be a priest without ordination.**

Furthermore, in *Humani Generis* in 1950, Pope Pius XII actually put his finger directly on the heresy at work against Outside the Church There is No Salvation.

Pope Pius XII, *Humani Generis* (#27), 1950: "Some say they are not bound by the doctrine, explained in Our Encyclical Letter of a few years ago, and based on the sources of revelation, which teaches that the Mystical Body of Christ and the Roman Catholic Church are one and the same. **Some reduce to a meaningless formula the necessity of belonging to the true Church in order to gain eternal salvation.**"[558]

Pope Pius XII is here condemning the <u>exact</u> heresy common to all the modern day heretics who deny this dogma. They reduce the dogma Outside the Church There is No Salvation to a <u>meaningless formula</u> by saying that it doesn't mean what it says!

It should also be noted that even though Pope Pius XII <u>did not</u> teach that non-Catholics could be united to the Church and saved by a "certain unknowing desire and resolution," *if he had,* he would have been teaching **heresy** – a heresy refuted by his own statements above. As St. Paul tells us, *"But though we, or an angel from heaven, preach a gospel to you besides that which we have preached to you, let him be anathema"* (Gal. 1:8). The problem with Pope Pius XII, however, was not primarily what he *said* regarding this dogma, but what he *didn't say*, and more specifically, what he allowed by silence, neglect (and perhaps by direct support) to happen to the dogma Outside the Church There is No Salvation and Father Leonard Feeney, S.J. What he allowed to happen was a crime so momentous that it cannot be measured. What he allowed to happen would turn out to be an incalculable scandal to the faithful and an impediment to the salvation of millions of souls in his day, and for a generation to come.

30. Pope Pius XII, Father Feeney and the dogma

One of the reasons that the heretical and deadly Protocol 122/49 gained such momentum in the minds of so many bishops and priests, and was literally able to wipe out belief in the dogma (that those who die as non-Catholics are lost) in almost the entire Catholic world, was because they thought that it had at least the tacit approval of Pope Pius XII. Indeed the document claims that he did approve of it. The bottom-line is that he didn't sign it, nor did he promulgate it in any manner that would have affected infallibility. It wasn't even published officially. And obviously no Pope could have signed this document, because the Protocol is quite heretical, as I have shown.

If Pope Pius XII agreed with the Protocol and the persecution of Father Feeney for preaching the dogma, then he was just simply a mortal sinner against the Faith. If he had come out in favor of the Protocol and against Fr. Feeney then he would have been a heretic. This is just a fact. If Pope Pius XII denied the dogma – as did the priests at Boston College, for example – and assented to the stifling of Father Feeney's apostolic preaching of it, then Pius XII became a heretic and an enemy of the faith.

If Pope Pius XII thought that Father Feeney was preaching *his own* doctrine for asserting exactly what Pope Gregory XVI asserted in *Summo Iugiter Studio* and what the Chair of Peter has dogmatically defined (that all those who die as non-Catholics are lost), then he didn't understand the first thing about the Catholic Faith – and indeed he did not possess it.

As Pope Honorius I (625-638) was condemned for promoting heresy by the *III Council of Constantinople* and other ecumenical Councils[559] for favoring the monothelite heresy (the belief that Christ had only one will) in two letters to the Patriarch Sergius, so too would Pope Pius XII have fallen into heresy if he held that non-Catholics could be saved and supported the persecution of Father Feeney for affirming that they could not.

Remember, Pius XII was by no means a staunch traditionalist. His reforms, omissions and failures paved the way for Vatican II. Just a few things that Pius XII did and did not do are:

- He failed to consecrate Russia to the immaculate heart of Mary. This is an inexplicable omission. The very fact that Pope Pius XII failed to consecrate Russia in the manner requested by Our Lady demonstrates that there was something seriously wrong with him.
- He promoted Annibale Bugnini, the author of the New Mass, and began the liturgical reform with his allowance of reforms in the Holy Week Rites. A good number of liturgical scholars think that the reforms of Holy Week were terrible. One example is the allowance of distribution of Holy Communion on Good Friday. The decree of the Holy Office under Pope Pius X On Frequent Communion cites Pope Innocent XI who condemned such a practice.
- He promoted men like Giovanni Montini (later Paul VI) and Angelo Roncalli (later John XXIII), without which promotions these men could never have had the influence or caused the immeasurable destruction that they did.
- He said that theistic evolution could be taught in Catholic schools (*Humani Generis*, 1950), which is nothing short of ludicrous – and arguably heretical.
- He taught that birth control could be used by couples by means of the rhythm method (or Natural Family Planning), which is a frustration and a subordination of the primary *purpose* of the marriage act – conception.
- He allowed the persecution and subsequent excommunication of Father Leonard Feeney, whether through willful complicity or neglect, for doing what every Catholic priest should do – preach the Gospel, defend the faith and adhere to defined dogma.

This last offense was the most serious. With the persecution of Father Feeney, the "authorities" in Boston and Rome not only did not aid Father Feeney in his quest to convert non-Catholics, but actually stopped him! Think about that: The men who were supposed to foster the salvation of souls and conversion to the true faith actually made it as difficult as possible for Father Feeney to do so. They made his task of delivering Christ's saving message – that salvation only comes from membership in the Church He established – as hard as they could, while giving millions of non-Catholics the false impression that they were okay in the state of damnation in which they existed. Richard Cushing, the apostate Archbishop of Boston, who first silenced Father Feeney – not over baptism of desire, but over *extra ecclesiam nulla salus* (outside the Church there is no salvation) – **boasted before his death that he had not made a convert in his whole life**.[560]

It was on September 24, 1952 that Father Feeney addressed a long, detailed letter to Pius XII. The letter went unanswered. But one month later (in a letter dated Oct. 25, 1952) Cardinal Pizzardo of the Holy Office summoned him to Rome. On October 30, 1952, Father Feeney sent a reply to Pizzardo, requesting a statement of the charges against him – as required by Canon Law. On Nov. 22, 1952, Pizzardo replied:

"Your letter of 30th October clearly shows that you are evading the issue… You are to come to Rome immediately where you will be informed of the charges lodged against you… If you do not present yourself… before the 31st December this act of disobedience will be made public with the canonical penalties… The Apostolic Delegate has been authorized to provide for the expenses of your journey."[561]

On Dec. 2, 1952, Father Feeney responded:

"Your Eminence seems to have misconstrued my motives in replying to your letter of October 25, 1952. I had presumed that your first letter was to serve as a canonical citation to appear before Your Sacred Tribunal. As a citation, however, it is fatally defective under the norms of Canon 1715 especially in that it did not inform me of the charges against me. **This canon requires that the citation contain at least a general statement of the charges**. Under the norms of Canon 1723 any proceedings based on a citation so substantially defective are subject to a complaint of nullity."[562]

This exchange of letters between Father Feeney and Pizzardo is very interesting and valuable for our discussion. First of all, it shows that Father Feeney's desire was to operate within the confines of law, whereas Pizzardo and those at the Vatican showed a blatant disregard for law, even in the manner of summoning him to Rome. Canon Law stipulates that a man summoned to Rome must be informed at least in general of the charges lodged against him, and Father Feeney cited the relevant canons. Pizzardo and his cohorts consistently ignored these laws.

On Jan. 9, 1953, Pizzardo responded to the Dec. 2, 1952 letter of Fr. Feeney:

(Jan. 9, 1953) "In reply to your letter of the 2nd Dec. 1952 asking for further explanations… the Holy Office communicates to you herewith the orders received from His Holiness, that you are to present yourself to this Congregation before the 31st January 1953, under pain of excommunication incurred automatically (ipso facto) in case of failure to present yourself on the date indicated. This decision of His Holiness has been made after the arrival of the latest documents from St. Benedict Center."[563]

Once again, the canonical laws requiring a reason for the summons were completely ignored. But this was just par for the course in the case of Father Feeney: Justice, dogma and Christ's mandate to preach the Gospel and baptize were ignored and trampled upon. One cannot help but notice the annoyed tone of the Cardinal's letter. There is almost no doubt that Pizzardo also believed that non-Catholics could be saved as non-Catholics, and thus was not at all concerned that the case of Father Feeney was not handled in a just fashion.

Without having been given a reason for his summons to Rome as was required, Father Feeney justifiably stayed in the United States, knowing that his refusal to report to Rome by Jan. 31st might bring bogus canonical penalties down upon his head. But prior to that, on Jan. 13, 1953, Fr. Feeney "sent a long and strong letter to the Cardinal protesting the following:

    a) **Violation of the 'secrecy of the Holy Office' in leaking their correspondence to the public press.**
    b) **The Cardinal's repeated threats of imposing penalties without either accusations or proceedings, as required by the Canons.**
    c) The dissemination of Protocol 122/49 as a doctrinal pronouncement of the Holy See, knowing that it was never published in the *Acta Apostolicae Sedis* (Acts of the Apostolic See).[564]

Father Feeney ended this last communication to Cardinal Pizzardo with a statement of righteous indignation:

"I very seriously question both the good faith and the validity of any attempt to excommunicate me because I dared to call the substance of this decree to your attention, and because I dared to insist on my rights under it in both my letters of October 30 and December 2, 1952."[565]

On February 13, 1953, the Holy Office issued a decree declaring Father Feeney "excommunicated." It read as follows:

"Since the priest Leonard Feeney, a resident of Boston (Saint Benedict Center), who for a long time has been suspended from his priestly duties on account of grave disobedience of Church Authority, being unmoved by repeated warnings and threats of incurring excommunication ipso facto, has not submitted, the Most Eminent and Reverent Fathers, charged with safeguarding matters of faith and morals, in a Plenary Session held on Wednesday, 4 February 1953, declared him excommunicated with all the effects of the law.

"On Thursday, 12 February 1953, Our Most Holy Lord Pius XII, by Divine Providence Pope, approved and confirmed the decree of the Most Eminent Fathers, and ordered that it be made a matter of public law.

"Given at Rome, at the Headquarters of the Holy Office, 13 February 1953."

Marius Crovini, Notary
AAS (February 16, 1953) Vol. XXXXV, Page 100

In light of the above facts, this excommunication is an outrage and is worthless. Father Feeney was guilty of nothing: He denied no doctrine, and he operated strictly in accordance with the law. It was those who persecuted Father Feeney for teaching that all who die as non-Catholics cannot be saved who were excommunicated *ipso facto*.

One should also keep in mind that, although the "excommunication" originated from heretical clergymen opposing Fr. Feeney's preaching of the dogma, **the "excommunication" itself mentions nothing of doctrine**. It only mentions "grave disobedience of Church Authority." This is an important point, because we hear many today, who are ignorant of the facts of the case, erroneously assert that Father Feeney was excommunicated for teaching that non-Catholics cannot be saved. Such persons don't know what they are talking about. There is no doubt that the dogma that those who die as non-Catholics cannot be saved was the reason why the Father Feeney controversy erupted – which culminated in his "excommunication" – but the excommunication itself mentions nothing of doctrine. Therefore, even if one believed that this "excommunication" was valid (which is absurd), it would constitute no argument against the teaching that those who die as non-Catholics can't be saved because: 1) doctrine is not mentioned at all in the excommunication, and 2) this teaching is a defined dogma. So let those who are going to discuss this issue get the facts straight.

But the teaching that no one can be saved outside the Catholic Church was definitely *excommunicated from the mind of the public* as a result of the 1953 "excommunication" of Father Leonard Feeney, S.J. With this, Jesus Christ was publicly sold out to the world by giving the entire world the impression that it was not necessary to belong to the one Church He established – and indeed it was punishable to promote the contrary!

I recently called about 15 Vatican II/Novus Ordo churches and asked them whether they accepted the Catholic dogma Outside the Church There is No Salvation. All of them flatly rejected it or hung up the telephone. The few priests who gave a coherent response to my question about the dogma immediately stated "that's heresy" or words to that effect (meaning Outside the Church There is No Salvation is heresy); and they all referred to the "excommunication" of Fr. Leonard Feeney, S.J. to "substantiate" their point. I could have called 200 of these Vatican II churches and I would have received the same responses. This is simply because <u>it is a fact</u> that basically every Vatican II/Novus

Ordo priest today, as well as almost every "traditionalist" priest today, believes that souls can be saved in any religion, including Jews who reject Christ.

There is no doubt that the role Pope Pius XII played in the case of Father Feeney was crucial: crucial to the very core of the Catholic Faith, crucial to what would shortly thereafter transpire at Vatican II, and crucial to the salvation of millions of souls. **It was crucial because if Pope Pius XII had come to the defense of Father Feeney in the early 1950's, and reasserted that all who die as non-Catholics are lost (and therefore must be converted), there would never have been a Vatican II.** That's right. There is no doubt that the apostate Second Vatican Council could never have come about without the condemnation of Outside the Church There is No Salvation (*via the condemnation of Fr. Feeney*) shortly before. **Those who reject this fact have no concept of reality**. More than 90% of the Vatican II and post-Vatican II heresies deal directly or indirectly with the denial of the necessity of the Catholic Church and the denial of the evil of non-Catholic religions. If there had been a solemn, public affirmation of the dogma in the 1950's by Pope Pius XII – as Father Feeney exhibited – so that it was clear to everyone that Father Feeney was right in saying that non-Catholics cannot be saved as non-Catholics, then the heretics at Vatican II could never have been able to get away with the decree on ecumenism (*Unitatis Redintegratio*), the decree on non-Christian religions (*Nostra Aetate*) or the decree on religious liberty (*Dignitatis Humanae*), among others, which all give praise and esteem for false religions or assert that members of other religions can be saved.

Without the clear indication that it is wrong to hold that *all who die as non-Catholics are lost* (which is Catholic dogma), Vatican II, the liturgical reform and all the other horrors that we now see would not have been possible.

Unfortunately, Pius XII was the man who performed this task. Pius XII was the man during whose reign the world began to believe that it was wrong to believe that only Catholics can be saved. He served, whether knowingly or not, as the Judas who sold out Christ to the Jews so that they could crucify Him. The dogma was sold out to the world so that the Devil could crucify the entire framework of the faith at Vatican II.

So when people look at barren churches; empty confession lines; almost zero Mass attendance; homo-priests in the Novus Ordo church; less than 25% belief in the Eucharist; rampant sex-scandals; clown masses, kiddie masses, balloon masses; 50% of "Catholics" voting pro-abortion; consistent interreligious syncretism in the Vatican; topless girls at "Papal Masses"; voodoo high-priests preaching in the Church of St. Francis; Buddha on top of "Catholic altars"; almost universal ignorance about the teaching of the Church; almost universal immorality and perversion; sex-education in "Catholic" schools; "Catholic" universities denying the inerrancy of Scripture; "Catholic" universities promoting pro-aborts; the greatest widespread apostasy from the teaching of Christ of all-time; and an almost universal paganism, **they can thank the**

condemnation of Father Feeney, which was a necessary component in bringing it all about.

The "condemnation" of Fr. Feeney – combined with Protocol 122/49 – assured that not one seminary in the world after 1953 taught the dogma that only Catholics can be saved. And with the idea that those who die as non-Catholics can be saved deep-seated and universal, it was only a short time before the world started to figure out that believing the Catholic religion and practicing Catholic morality are pretty much worthless, since members of other religions have salvation, too. The precious gift of the true faith was broken down, and the Catholic Church's claim that it is the only true religion was killed in the minds of the public, since people could be saved in other religions. It was only logical that a short time after the "excommunication" of Father Feeney, Catholic teaching gave way to a universal apostasy among Catholics – with Vatican II being the vehicle to perpetuate it.

Those who deplore some, most or all of the things mentioned above, yet who condemn, despise or hate Father Feeney, are blind. They complain about the flames and the smoke, but do not realize that their very attitude is what started the fire. They cannot understand the simple effects of the breakdown of the Faith, and the denial of that most crucial dogma that only Catholics can be saved. And this issue does not merely involve the many practical consequences of denying the dogma that only Catholics can be saved. **It primarily involves the consequences for the faith, because the dogma Outside the Catholic Church There is No Salvation is not just something Catholics must live by, but something that they must primarily believe**. Pope St. Pius X <u>condemned</u> the following Modernist proposition on July 3, 1907 in "Lamentabili Sane":

> "The dogmas of faith are to be held only according to a practical sense, that is, as preceptive norms for action, but not as norms for believing."- Condemned[566]

The idea that we can preach that there is no salvation outside the Church, while we believe in our hearts that there is salvation outside the Church, is heretical. That only Catholics can be saved is a truth revealed from heaven which every Catholic must **believe first,** and <u>profess second</u>.

> Pope Eugene IV, *Council of Florence*, "Cantate Domino," 1441, *ex cathedra:"* ***<u>The Holy Roman Church firmly believes</u>, professes and preaches*** *that all those who are outside the Catholic Church, not only pagans but also Jews or heretics and schismatics, cannot share in eternal life and will go into the everlasting fire which was prepared for the devil and his angels, unless they are joined to the Church before the end of their lives; that the unity of this ecclesiastical body is of such importance that only those who abide in it do the Church's sacraments contribute to salvation and do fasts, almsgiving and other works of piety and practices of the Christian militia productive of eternal rewards;*

and that nobody can be saved, no matter how much he has given away in alms and even if he has shed blood in the name of Christ, unless he has persevered in the bosom and unity of the Catholic Church."[567]

This truth was ripped from the hearts and minds of almost the entire Catholic world with the condemnation of Father Feeney, who was its most public proponent. And it was allowed to happen by the negligence and weakness of Pius XII.

31. The Verdict is in: <u>Boston</u> Leads the Way in a Massive Priestly Scandal that Rocks the Nation

Novus Ordo Priest Fr. Mark S. Massa, "S.J.", *Catholics and American Culture*, p. 31, DESCRIBING WHEN THE CONTROVERSY ERUPTED IN BOSTON OVER THE DOGMA, *OUTSIDE THE CHURCH THERE IS NO SALVATION*: **"The Boston Heresy Case erupted into public view during Holy Week 1949. The firings of Feeney's disciples from Boston College made front-page news all over the Northeast:** the *New York Times* began a series on Feeney and his group, and *Newsweek, Life,* and *Time* magazines all featured stories on the Boston 'troubles.'… **As one student of the event has observed, the question of salvation replaced the Red Sox as the topic of conversation in Boston bars… The only analogue [comparable thing] church historians could think of was Constantinople in the fourth century, where rioting crowds had battled in the streets over the definition of the divinity of Jesus,** and Greek theological phrases became the mottos of chariot teams."[568]

As I have documented in the foregoing sections, it was in <u>Boston</u> where Fr. Leonard Feeney, S.J. was persecuted – the one priest in the 1950's who had publicly pinpointed and opposed the denial of the dogma, Outside the Church There is No Salvation. It was in the Archdiocese of <u>Boston</u> where the heretical Protocol 122/49 was published. It was in <u>Boston</u> where Fr. Feeney was silenced and interdicted which eventually led to his bogus "excommunication" from heretical clergymen in Rome. **And it is now <u>in Boston</u> that they are feeling the effects of God's wrath.**

> **BOSTON CONSIDERS BANKRUPTCY – The Archdiocese of Boston is reportedly considering filing a claim in U.S. Bankruptcy Court** unless prospects for a mediated settlement improve, the Boston Globe reported Dec. 1… A spokeswoman said the archdiocese has to consider all its options but said there is no timetable for deciding whether to file for bankruptcy. (National Catholic Register, Dec. 8-14, 2002, p. 1.)

BOSTON ARCHDIOCESE SELLS OR MORTGAGES ONCE UNTOUCHABLE PROPERTY TO PAY SEX SCANDAL SETTLEMENT

The Associated Press

BOSTON (AP) – THE SEX SCANDAL IN THE BOSTON ARCHDIOCESE HAS SHAKEN THE CHURCH ALMOST LITERALLY TO ITS FOUNDATIONS. To help pay the $85 million settlement reached with more than 500 victims of child-molesting priests, the archdiocese has mortgaged its very seat of power -- the Cathedral of the Holy Cross -- and is putting up for sale the archbishop's residence, an Italian Renaissance-style mansion that was a symbol of the church's grandeur and authority. Dozens of churches are also expected to be closed in a move at least accelerated by the scandal. (Dec. 18, 2003)

"And I will accomplish in my fury, and will cause my indignation to rest upon them, and I will be comforted: and they shall know that I the Lord have spoken it in my zeal, when I shall have accomplished my indignation in them.

"And I will make thee desolate, and a reproach amongst the nations that are round about thee, in the sight of every one that passeth by. And thou shalt be a reproach, and a scoff, an example, and an astonishment amongst the nations that are round about thee, when I shall have executed judgments in thee in anger, and in indignation, and in wrathful rebukes. I the Lord have spoken it..." (Ezechiel 5:13-16)

CBS News - Clergy members and others in the Boston Archdiocese likely sexually abused more than 1,000 people over a period of six decades, Massachusetts' attorney general said Wednesday, calling the scandal so massive it "borders on the unbelievable." ... The sheer number of abuse allegations documented by investigators in Boston appears unprecedented, even amid a scandal that has touched dioceses in virtually every state and has prompted about 1,000 people to come forward with new allegations nationwide in the last year. (CBSNews.com, July 23, 2003)

> **ABC NEWS, Sept. 9**— The Boston Archdiocese and lawyers for victims of sex abuse by priests announced today that they reached a settlement of $85 million, <u>the largest known payout</u> **in the child molestation scandal that has rocked the Roman Catholic Church**. (ABCNews.com, Sept. 9, 2003)

Boston was the signal spot where the massive sexual scandal was uncovered, and Boston was the epicenter of the spiritual earthquake. Boston literally became "the scoff," "the reproach," "the astonishment" of the media and of the world! Why is this? The answer is obvious for those who have eyes to see (Ezekiel 5).

The people and the clergy of Boston hated, persecuted and cursed ("excommunicated") the true meaning of the dogma Outside the Church There is No Salvation and the priest faithfully defending it. So God left their house completely desolate and gave it over to a legion of devils. There is no doubt that the scandal in other areas of the counterfeit, non-Catholic, Vatican II sect was and is incredibly widespread and horrible, but Boston (without any doubt) was by far the most notorious. They got their pack of "non-Feeneyite" priests for sure, just as they desired. They got their priests who believed in "baptism of desire" and "invincible ignorance" for sure.

The heretics in Boston didn't want the truth of Our Lord Jesus Christ and His dogma on the absolute necessity of the Catholic Faith and Baptism for salvation, **so God allowed them to have their own pack of apostate priests and perverts – just as they desired**.

This should actually strike fear into the hearts of those – especially many of the "traditionalists" – who claim to oppose this apostasy and yet hate this dogma, despise and mock Fr. Leonard Feeney, and others who faithfully hold Church teaching on this issue. Such people make themselves hateful to God and were one of the primary causes for this apostasy, an apostasy which is manifested by the incredible scandal among the non-Catholic, counterfeit Vatican II priests. The fact that the **Archdiocese of Boston had to mortgage its very Cathedral and the Archbishop's residence because of the sexual abuse of its priests is highly symbolic.** It is not an accident. It shows how those who deny the Catholic dogma on salvation forfeit their place in the Church of Christ and have no authority whatsoever. The Lord has spoken, and accomplished in His fury His indignation to rest upon them.

DID FR. FEENEY PREDICT THE LOSS OF THE POPE?

Before I get into this point, I must remind the reader that we are not "Feeneyites" and that I had never heard of Fr. Leonard Feeney when I came to the same conclusion on the absolute necessity of water baptism based on the dogmatic teaching of the Catholic

Church. We don't agree with some of Fr. Feeney's conclusions on Justification (we believe he was mistaken in good faith on these points).

In the following passages from Fr. Feeney's book, *Bread of Life*—which is made up of Fr. Feeney's sermons before Vatican II—he connects the eventual loss of the pope (i.e., what we have experienced with the reign of the Vatican II Antipopes) to the denial of the dogma Outside the Catholic Church There is No Salvation. As I have shown, countless heretics who denied this dogma were entrenched in high positions of the Church before Vatican II, and were teaching that men could be saved in false religions. Fr. Feeney seemed to prophesy that it is because of this heresy that God will allow the Great Apostasy and the loss of the pope (i.e., what we have experienced with the reign of the Vatican II Antipopes) to come to pass.

Fr. Leonard Feeney S.J., *Bread of Life*: "We have Protestants in an arrangement-religion that never knows what to call itself from one week to another, that never knows what its new minister is going to tell it from chapter to chapter of Holy Scripture. We have Unitarians who have no faith in the assured Jesus, getting more indefinite about what Christianity meant to say. And, of course, we have Jews evading the Faith, running away from it, pretending they do not hear the name of Jesus – pretending Christmas is not the birth of Jesus Christ, and getting civic leaders to remove 'Merry Christmas' from in front of City Hall and to substitute for it 'Seasons Greetings,' because the word 'Christ' in 'Christmas' annoys them. All this, horrible as it is, I am prepared to cope with.

"But imagine a priest in the Holy Roman Catholic Church, ordained by the successors of the Apostles – dedicated to the Name and purpose and Blood and robes of Jesus – sitting at Harvard College week after week and listening to religion being lectured about in invisible terms. **And imagine their going back, then, to their people and telling them about the 'soul of the Church,' of 'salvation outside the Church through sincerity' – apart from the teachings and Sacraments of Jesus Christ; and calling this arrangement 'Baptism of Desire'**... What kind of teaching is that? That is Christmas without the manger: <u>Good Friday without any God bleeding</u>; Easter Sunday without any Flesh and Blood coming out of the tomb. **<u>That is the Christian Faith without any Pope</u>** – the most visible religious leader in the World!" (Chap. II, pp. 32-33.)

Fr. Feeney, writing the above passage before the Second Vatican Council, predicted the eventual loss of the pope because of the great number of heretics within the structures of the Church who denied the necessity of the Church for salvation. This is an amazing insight!

Fr. Feeney also notes that this heresy against the salvation dogma and the necessity of Baptism leads to "Good Friday without any God bleeding." Just take a look at the

Novus Ordo churches to see if that has been fulfilled. Fr. Feeney goes on to say in the same chapter:

> Fr. Feeney S.J., *Bread of Life*: "When the Vatican Council reconvenes, I humbly plead with our Holy Father, the Pope (Pius XII), that he will immediately gather his plenipotentiary powers of infallible pronouncement to clear up the wild confusion of visible orating (on the part of his priests and bishops) about an invisible Church – or else the gates of Hell will have all but prevailed against us. The most visible ruler in the world, our **Holy Father**, in his white robe and white zuchetto, **may as well take off his triple tiara and get down from his golden throne**, and leave Christianity to the kind of committee arrangements to which it is committed in the present-day America, if we keep on preaching 'Baptism of Desire.'" (Chap. II, p. 42.)

As can be seen on our video *Vatican II: Council of Apostasy*, **this statement underlined above—the loss of the papal tiara—actually took place when Antipope Paul VI gleefully surrendered the papal tiara and papal pectoral cross to the representatives of the United Nations who in turn sold it to a Jewish merchant!**

When Antipope Paul VI gave away the Papal Tiara, it was symbolic of the giving away of Papal authority (although he had none to give away since he was an Antipope). But it was symbolic of how the enemies of the Church, and the non-Catholic heretics, had been allowed to take over the churches' physical structures and create a counterfeit, non-Catholic sect (the Vatican II sect). This insight of Fr. Feeney on the Papal Tiara is so accurate that God must have put these words into his mouth. But it just demonstrates again that once the necessity of the Church is denied the rest of the Faith becomes meaningless. This is why those who think that the Mass issue is the main issue, and where the battle really lies, are mistaken. The battle begins and is centered around this dogma, because once the necessity of the Catholic Faith is denied then everything else becomes meaningless.

Furthermore, notice that Fr. Feeney not only said that the Pope might as well take off the tiara if the heresy against the salvation dogma continued to be preached, but he also said the Pope might as well get down from his golden throne! This also happened! The Vatican II Antipopes not only repudiated the Papal Tiara, as Fr. Feeney predicted, but they repudiated the Papal Throne (the *Sedia Gestatoria*), just as Fr. Feeney said!

In warning of the dire punishments and fatal results that would arise from denial of this dogma, Fr. Feeney was only repeating the warnings of past popes such as Pope Gregory XVI.

Pope Gregory XVI, *Mirari Vos* (#14), Aug. 15, 1832: "This shameful font of <u>indifferentism gives rise</u> to that absurd and erroneous proposition which claims that liberty of conscience must be maintained for everyone."[569]

A certain writer who considers himself a "traditional Catholic," but denies the true meaning of the dogma Outside the Church There is No Salvation, has stated that *the teaching on invincible ignorance didn't kill the missions; Vatican II's teaching on ecumenism and religious liberty did.* What this heretic fails to realize is that the heresy of salvation for non-Catholics through "invincible ignorance" <u>gave rise</u> to the heretical teaching of freedom of religion and conscience, as Pope Gregory XVI points out above. Vatican II's heretical documents on religious liberty, ecumenism and freedom of conscience were not the beginning of the heresy, but <u>the result</u> of the denial of the true meaning of the salvation dogma.

But whereas Pope Gregory XVI had warned of this, Fr. Feeney was living through the beginning stages of its fulfillment, the latter stages culminating with, among other things, the massive priestly scandal documented above in the counterfeit Vatican II sect. Fr. Feeney was the person that God used to announce to the world before the Vatican II revolution that this issue was central and that if it continued to be denied, the end would be at hand and the Great Apostasy would come to pass. Fr. Feeney added the following forward to the 1974 printing of his book *Bread of Life*.

Fr. Feeney S.J., *Bread of Life*: FORWARD TO THE 1974 PRINTING: "The sad situation of the Faith in America and in the whole world is breaking the hearts of true Catholics. The gates of hell have all but prevailed against the Church. <u>It is because Catholics have let go of the Church's doctrine on salvation that all else is being taken away from us</u>. This is what is causing the sickness of the world, and it is even more true to say so today than when I said so twenty-five years ago.

"My message today is identically the same as the one I have been giving for the past quarter of a century. It is perpetually part of the infallible teaching of the Roman Catholic Church, against which Our Lord has promised the gates of hell will never prevail."

Fr. Feeney, in 1974, sees all these things being taken away from Catholics, primarily because they denied the dogma Outside the Church There is No Salvation and didn't care about the divinely revealed truths of the Faith. We see this today not only in the Vatican II sect, but in the traditional Catholic movement. Many of the people attending the Latin Mass today don't care about what the priest actually believes; they only care that he says a valid Mass and not the invalid Novus Ordo. They don't care that the priest holds that Jews who reject Jesus Christ Himself can be saved, while they pretend to have a great devotion to the Mass Christ instituted. These persons are in grave disobedience to God's truth and their sacrifice at the Mass bears no fruit, since they are in rebellion to His divinely revealed word.

1 Kings 15:22-23: "And Samuel said: **Doth the Lord desire holocausts and victims, <u>and not rather that the voice of the Lord should be obeyed</u>? For obedience is better than sacrifices**: and to hearken rather than to offer the fat of rams. **Because it is like the sin of witchcraft to rebel: and like the crime of idolatry, to refuse to obey. <u>Forasmuch as thou hast rejected the word of the Lord, the Lord hath also rejected thee from being king</u>**."

This passage of scripture does not concern obedience to a reputed authority in the Church; **it concerns obedience to the Word of God – Faith in His revealed word**. And the chilling admonition above in 1 Kings 15 was made by the prophet Samuel to King Saul, who had offered sacrifice in direct violation of God's word. Saul had attempted to please God with his sacrifice, while he was simultaneously contravening God's spoken word. King Saul's sacrifice, therefore, was completely rejected by God and Saul himself was cast off by the Lord. **The words spoken by Samuel to King Saul could be said to the multitude of phony "Catholics," who reject God's voice (His revealed dogma that there is no salvation outside the Catholic Church). And because they don't accept His Word on this matter, while they think they can please Him by offering sacrifice at the traditional Latin Mass,** their sacrifice at the Traditional Latin Mass will not profit them and will be rejected by God. Because they reject the "voice of the Lord" – the true and defined meaning of Outside the Church There is No Salvation – God rejects their sacrifices and offerings.

And it is precisely for this reason that God allowed the Catholic Buildings, Seminaries and Schools to be taken away and confiscated by a counterfeit non-Catholic sect (the Vatican II/Novus Ordo sect), with apostate priests, perverts, a phony "Mass" (the New Mass) and an apostate Antipope (John Paul II) – who heads a Vatican which considers all religions true; declares that Jews don't need to convert to Christ to be saved; that Eastern Schismatics should not be converted; that the Council of Trent doesn't condemn Lutherans anymore; that Islam should be protected; etc., etc. etc. God cast off the multitude of professing "Catholics" because they cast off and condemned His truth on salvation; and He gave their possessions over to a legion of devils, just as he cast off Saul from being King.

32. The Heretics Testify

In the foregoing sections, I have traced out the history of the Fr. Feeney controversy in the late 1940's and 1950's, which was preceded by an apostasy from the dogma Outside the Church There is No Salvation which began in the 19th century – on the heels of misinterpreted and fallible statements of Pope Pius IX on "invincible ignorance" and the explosion of the false doctrine of "baptism of desire." I have pointed out that this heresy (of salvation outside the Church/"invincible ignorance" saving those who die as non-Catholics) is now held almost universally by so-called Catholics and "traditionalists." And this heresy is leading countless souls to Hell. Below, the reader will find a few testimonies made by certain enemies of the Faith who readily admit that the new, heretical "understanding" of Outside the Church There is No Salvation that became widespread in the 20th century before Vatican II was contrary to Catholic dogmatic teaching and 2000 years of Catholic Tradition.

A PROTESTANT TESTIFIES

The following quote is from a Protestant author. Please note carefully how this Protestant heretic links the ultimate success of false ecumenism with Pope Pius IX and what he believes to be his teaching that there can be salvation outside the Catholic Church. The Protestant also, of course, praises John XXIII (the initiator of Vatican II) and Paul VI who brought it to completion. Not surprisingly, his ultimate praise goes to the apostate John Paul II, the finisher of the work of the false Second Vatican Council, who now heads the counterfeit Vatican II sect.

John McManners, A Protestant Author, *The Oxford Illustrated History of Christianity:* "Nevertheless the ecumenical mood had consequences in the European churches. They were far readier to share their altars with each other, and even their church buildings, and to co-operate in common social ventures. This difference was most marked in the Roman Catholic Church. Since the Counter-Reformation Rome taught that it alone was the church... **In the nineteenth century, when Catholicism was centralizing itself ever more in Rome, Pope Pius IX admitted that men might be saved outside the church by reason of 'invincible ignorance' of the true faith. This was a large concession of charity in the tradition of thought.** When the ecumenical movement grew strong, Pope Pius XI formally refused to take part (1928), lest participation imply a recognition that the Roman Catholic Church was but one of a number of denominations. The same encyclical forbade Roman Catholics to take part in conferences with non-Roman Catholics. All this began to change after the Second World War. But it was the ascension of Pope John XXIII in 1958 which began to transform the atmosphere. Part of his object in summoning the Second Vatican Council was to heal the separations in the East and West, and he continued to recognize the Protestants of the West as brothers. An encyclical of 1959 greeted non-Catholics as 'separated brethren and sons'. In 1960 the pope set up a Secretariat for Christian Unity. In the same year he received Archbishop Fisher of Canterbury. In 1961 he allowed Roman Catholic observers to attend the meeting of the World Council at Delhi. His successor Paul VI carried this new and far more charitable attitude much further. In 1965 he and the Patriarch of Constantinople Athenagoras agreed to a joint declaration deploring the mutual excommunications of 1054 which had stained their past histories as churches. In 1967 he met the Patriarch again the year after he had met Archbishop Ramsey of Canterbury. The doctrine that Roman Catholics cannot share in worship with other Christians was finally **killed by the Polish Pope John Paul II** when in 1982 he went to Canterbury Cathedral with the Anglican Archbishop Runcie of Canterbury... All this was part of the coming out of the papacy towards the world."[570]

Here you have it directly from the Protestant's mouth. He links the teaching that there is salvation outside the Catholic Church to the future success of the false ecumenical movement (the movement to respect and unite with false religions). This Protestant heretic also commends Pope Pius IX, because he believes that Pope Pius IX introduced the novel heresy of salvation outside the Catholic Church into the minds and souls of Catholics. (Remember, in the section on Pope Pius IX we pointed out how all the modern heretics attempt to use his two fallible statements – which did not teach that non-Catholics can be saved without the Catholic Faith – as the justification for their complete denial of this dogma.) Thus, even the Protestants can see that the allowance of the idea of "invincible ignorance" was "a large concession" (a new idea contrary to Traditional dogma) in the tradition of thought.

A JEW TESTIFIES

The Jewish Week, "Three Faiths and a Glimmer of Hope," Gary Rosenblatt - Editor and Publisher, 8/29/2003: "During the interactive discussions I came to realize how painful and difficult it has been for the Catholic Church, starting with Vatican II in the early 1960s, to face up to its shameful treatment of the Jews and, as a result, **reverse a centuries-old position that salvation for mankind can only come through Jesus.**

"...**In a lesser-known case, Richard Cardinal Cushing excommunicated a Boston priest, Leonard Feeney, in 1953, for preaching that all non-Catholics would go to Hell. Even though Father Feeney's words were based on the Gospel, Cardinal Cushing found them offensive**, in large part because his sister had married a Jew, said Carroll, and the Cardinal had grown close to the family, sensitizing him to the Jewish perspective toward proselytization."

Here we see that the Jew, Gary Rosenblatt, acknowledges that the Fr. Feeney controversy concerned whether or not it is necessary to be Catholic to be saved. He explains that Fr. Feeney was "condemned" for teaching (the dogmatic truth) that all who die as non-Catholics will go to hell. This corroborates the fact that those who opposed Fr. Feeney held that there can be salvation outside the Church, while those who defended Fr. Feeney defended the Catholic dogma Outside the Church There is No Salvation.

A "JESUIT" PRIEST OF THE NEW VATICAN II RELIGION TESTIFIES

What follows is a quote from a heretical priest who is a member of the Vatican II sect. His name is Fr. Mark Massa, "S.J." He is a so-called Jesuit of the new Vatican II sect and **he admits that the new, heretical understanding of the dogma** *Outside the Church There is No Salvation* **that became widespread starting around 1900, is a new revelation that was not accepted as normal until the twentieth century.** Fr. Massa's testimony is particularly interesting simply because he is a blunt heretic who believes that dogmas can change, so he has no problem giving a fair account of what the Fr. Feeney controversy was about: the denial of the traditional dogma Outside the Church There is No Salvation. The other heretics who deny this dogma are forced into all kinds of crafty explanations, since they *claim* to believe that dogmas cannot change. But Fr. Massa has no problem admitting what has really occurred with this issue.

> Fr. Mark S. Massa, "S.J.", *Catholics and American Culture*, p. 21: "'The first sign of your approaching damnation is that Notre Dame has Protestants on its football team.' - A Feeneyite at a Notre Dame Football game, 1953 -
> "On the afternoon of September 4, 1952, the readers of the *Boston Pilot*—the voice of the Roman Catholic archdiocese—found on the front page of their usually staid [sober] weekly the text of the trenchant letter from the Holy Office in Rome. **The text, dated August 8, addressed a group of Boston Catholics who had kicked up quite a fuss over the ancient theological dictum** *extra ecclesiam nulla salus* **("outside the church there is no salvation")**—a phrase going back to St. Cyprian in the third century and <u>one of the pillars of orthodoxy for Christian believers</u>.
> "The letter itself was actually an ambivalent affair… it allowed that a person might be 'in the church' by a more than 'implicit desire'—**<u>an interpretation that had achieved almost normative status among Catholic theologians by the mid-twentieth century, although it has never been officially interpreted as such by Rome</u>**."[571]

Fr. Massa is referring here to Protocol 122/49, the letter written against Fr. Feeney in 1949, published in *The Pilot*, and which I have discussed in detail. Fr. Massa admits that Protocol 122/49 (which is the norm of belief of almost all so-called "traditionalists" today) "was actually an ambivalent affair." Ambivalent means *having two contradictory meanings or notions*. And he is quite correct. The letter claimed to affirm Outside the

Church There is No Salvation while completely denying it. Fr. Massa further admits that this (heretical) understanding of Outside the Church There is No Salvation as expressed in the Protocol (namely, that non-Catholics can be saved by "invincible ignorance"), had achieved <u>normative status</u> in the minds of "Catholic theologians" in the mid-twentieth century before Vatican II. I continue with his testimony.

Fr. Mark S. Massa, "S.J.", *Catholics and American Culture*, p. 27: "Feeney's message—that the Catholic tradition stood over and against a bankrupt post-Protestant culture teetering on the brink of intellectual anarchy and physical annihilation—reached ready ears. **By the late 1940's the center [Fr. Feeney's center] boasted two hundred converts...**"[572]

Fr. Mark S. Massa, "S.J.", *Catholics and American Culture*, pp. 32-33: "**On strictly theological grounds, Feeney's teaching was not as outrageous or pathological as might appear from the vantage of post-Vatican II Catholic reality.** Catholic propagandists in Counter-Reformation Europe had certainly believed their Protestant opponents, no less than Moslem infidels, to be beyond the reach of grace [sanctifying grace], and a rigorist interpretation of Cyprian's phrase clearly uncovers the motives undergirding much of the missionary activity between the sixteenth and twentieth centuries. The urgency of 'snatching souls' from the jaws of hell inspired Jesuit Francis Xavier in India... to go out and preach the good news to the 'people that walked in darkness' (Isa. 9:2)...

"**Long before 1965, however—certainly by the end of the decade following the Second World War—<u>most North American Catholics had ceased to believe that their good Protestant and Jewish neighbors were going to eternal ruin at death</u>, invincibly ignorant or not. <u>Leonard Feeney had recognized as early as 1945 this quiet but quite important revolution in Catholic thinking</u> about boundaries between Catholics and North American culture.** Indeed, Feeney's insight saves the Boston Heresy Case from comic opera and makes it an important episode in the North American experience."[573]

Fr. Massa is admitting here that most "Catholics" <u>well before Vatican II</u> had ceased believing that there is no salvation outside the Catholic Church (i.e., that those who die as non-Catholics cannot be saved), and that this is why Fr. Feeney met with such resistance in reaffirming this dogmatic truth.

Fr. Mark S. Massa, "S.J.", *Catholics and American Culture*, p. 34: "**Feeney's rigorist interpretation of *extra ecclesiam nulla salus* [outside the Church there is no salvation] arguably stood closer to its meaning held by Pope Innocent III in the thirteenth and St. Francis Xavier in the sixteenth centuries than did that of his 'liberal' Catholic opponents who found his teaching abhorrent.** Indeed, in the era **between the Reformation and Vatican II, <u>'the church' in official dogmatic statements had meant precisely what Feeney said it did</u>**..."[574]

Here we see Fr. Massa admitting that "Fr. Feeney's teaching" was exactly what the Church had stated in official dogmatic pronouncements.

> Fr. Mark S. Massa, "S.J.", *Catholics and American Culture*, p. 35: "The church found itself in a no win situation, trying to hold on to its claims to unequivocal truth even while censuring one who had proclaimed that truth a little too literally… The boundary line marking those saved from those condemned had moved (or perhaps been moved) to include others (that is, most Americans) who had no desire, implicit or otherwise, to join the Roman communion."[575]

Fr. Massa admits here that the boundary line of those who could be part of the Church (and therefore could be saved) had been moved; he further admits that the new (heretical) boundary definition (of Protocol 122/49, etc.) included people who had no desire or intention to become Roman Catholics (i.e., non-Catholics).

> Fr. Mark S. Massa, "S.J.", *Catholics and American Culture*, p. 35: "…**Doctrinal positions that had been considered rigorous but nonetheless orthodox at an earlier moment in North American Catholic history were now perceived to be beyond the pale**—beliefs that the collective now declared to be deviant and even dangerous to the community. The collective conscience had changed, the boundary between what constituted 'inside' and 'outside' had moved or been scaled down, and the official interpretation of what it meant to be 'outside the church' had changed with it. …"[576]

> Fr. Mark S. Massa, "S.J.", *Catholics and American Culture*, p. 37: "The Boston Heresy Case foreshadowed a Catholic future that would take the route charted by those whom Feeney termed 'accommodationist liberals.' This may seem like a penetrating glimpse of the obvious today, now safely on the other side of Vatican II, but it was not always so obvious. There was a time, before Knute Rockne's day, when one expected everyone on Notre Dame's football team to be a good Catholic."[577]

Fr. Massa concludes his chapter on the Fr. Feeney controversy by admitting that it foreshadowed a new "Catholic future" that was fulfilled after Vatican II. He is thus corroborating our point: that without the denial of this dogma Vatican II could never have occurred.

33. A Note to Those Who Believe in Baptism of Desire

In discussing this crucial dogma of the faith, I felt that it was important to address something to those of you who believe in baptism of desire, in order to sum up certain points.

First, when the facts are laid on the table, you must admit that baptism of desire has never been infallibly taught. The only two quotations from the infallible Magisterium that you even *try* to bring forward (Sess. 6, Chap. 4 of Trent and Sess. 7, Can. 4 of Trent) do not favor the theory of baptism of desire, as I have shown in this document. And that leaves you with nothing. In fact, your "best" piece of evidence (Sess. 6, Chap. 4) actually contradicts the theory of baptism of desire, by defining **that John 3:5 is to be understood as it is written**.

Yet, despite this fact, many of you (in fact, most of you "traditional" priests) continue to affirm that baptism of desire is something that every Catholic must believe. Many of you even withhold the sacraments from those who don't accept it. Now that you know that you cannot prove that baptism of desire is a dogma, you must stop making this false assertion. **You must cease condemning the Church's understanding that John 3:5 is to be taken as it is written, and that there is only one baptism of water, or you will surely go to Hell.**

And those who continue to make statements or publish books or tracts on baptism of desire, <u>obstinately telling people that men can be saved without the Sacrament of Baptism</u>, are heretics and can feel the brunt of the anathema of Can. 5.

> Pope Paul III, *The Council of Trent*, Can. 5 on the <u>Sacrament </u>of Baptism, Sess. 7, 1547, *ex cathedra*: **"If anyone says that baptism [the Sacrament] is optional, that is, not necessary for salvation (cf. Jn. 3:5): <u>let him be anathema</u>.**"[578]

Secondly, almost all of you who believe in baptism of desire hold that it applies to those who don't know Christ, the Trinity or the Catholic Church. **Most of you come right out and admit that this "baptism of desire" saves members of non-Catholic religions, including Protestants**. This is completely heretical and to continue to hold it or preach it is a mortal sin.

This perverted version of baptism of desire was never held by any saint, which is why you cannot quote saints who taught that members of non-Catholic religions can be saved or that baptism of desire applies to those who don't know Christ and the Trinity. This perverted version of baptism of desire is totally heretical and was an invention of liberal heretics of the 19th and 20th century. It has been perpetuated by heretical catechisms and Protocol 122/49, which have been exposed in this document.

> Pope Eugene IV, *Council of Florence*, Sess. 8, Nov. 22, 1439:
> "**Whoever *wishes* to be saved, needs above all to hold the Catholic faith; unless each one preserves this whole and inviolate, he will without a doubt perish in eternity.**"[579]

Finally, I address all who believe in baptism of desire, both the version held by saints and the version invented by modernists. **The teaching of Pope St. Leo the Great, the Council of Florence, the Canons on the Sacrament of Baptism, and the Church's understanding of John 3:5 prove that the theory of baptism of desire is contrary to Catholic dogma and cannot be taught under any form**. Since obstinacy is the key to heresy, there is no doubt that belief in the *saints' version* of baptism of desire (for catechumens only) has been held in good faith by many of you, as well as many other clerics and laypeople throughout history. No one can dispute this. But once the facts are shown to be clear and undeniable, as they are, so that the theory of *baptism of desire* can be shown to be undeniably at variance with Catholic dogma, one cannot continue to hold it and teach it lawfully.

> Pope St. Leo the Great, **dogmatic** letter to Flavian, *Council of Chalcedon*, 451:
> "**Let him heed what the blessed apostle Peter preaches, that sanctification by the Spirit is effected by the sprinkling of Christ's blood** (1 Pet. 1:2)… *It is He, Jesus Christ, who has come through water and blood, not in water only, but in water and blood. And because the Spirit is truth, it is the Spirit who testifies. For there are three who give testimony – Spirit and water and blood. And the three are one.* (1 Jn. 5:4-8)
> **IN OTHER WORDS, <u>THE SPIRIT OF SANCTIFICATION</u> AND <u>THE BLOOD OF REDEMPTION</u> AND <u>THE WATER OF BAPTISM</u>. THESE THREE ARE ONE AND REMAIN INDIVISIBLE. <u>NONE OF THEM IS SEPARABLE FROM ITS LINK WITH THE OTHERS</u>.**"[580]

As stated already, this is the famous dogmatic letter of Leo the Great to Flavian that was accepted by the dogmatic *Council of Chalcedon*, and received by the fathers of this great council with the famous cry: "*This is the faith of the Fathers, the faith of the Apostles; Peter has spoken through the mouth of Leo.*" It teaches that Justification from sin (the Spirit of Sanctification) is inseparable from water baptism. But to cling to "baptism of desire" is to hold the opposite: that sanctification is separable from the water of baptism. To hold to baptism of desire, therefore, is to contradict the dogmatic pronouncement of Pope Leo the Great. And those who obstinately contradict Leo's pronouncement, even in regard to one iota, will become anathematized heretics.

Pope St. Gelasius, *Decretal*, 495: "**Also the epistle of blessed Leo the Pope to Flavian… if anyone argues concerning the text of this one even in regard to one iota,** and does not receive it in all respects reverently, **let him be anathema.**"[581]

Pope Eugene IV, *The Council of Florence*, "Exultate Deo," Nov. 22, 1439, *ex cathedra*: "**And since death entered the universe through the first man, 'unless we are born of water and the Spirit, we cannot,' as the Truth says, 'enter into the kingdom of heaven' [John 3:5].** The matter of this sacrament is real and natural water."[582]

The following eleven arguments from <u>the infallible</u> teaching of the Chair of St. Peter (besides others) have been presented in this document. Every single one of the following points is a divinely revealed truth of Faith (a dogma), not a fallible opinion of some theologian. These points refute the idea of baptism of desire. And not one baptism of desire advocate can answer any of them.

1) The Catholic Church teaches that the <u>Sacrament</u> of Baptism is necessary for salvation (*de fide, Trent, Sess. 7, Can. 5*).
2) Unless we are born again of water and the Spirit, we cannot enter heaven (*de fide, Florence, Exultate Deo*).
3) The Church understands John 3:5 literally every time, *as it is written (de fide, Trent Sess. 6, Chap. 4)*, and with no exceptions (*de fide, Florence: Denz 696; and Trent: Denz. 791, 858, 861*).
4) The Spirit of Sanctification, the Water of Baptism and the Blood of Redemption are inseparable (*de fide, Pope St. Leo the Great*).
5) All Catholics must profess only one baptism of water (*de fide, Clement V, Council of Vienne*).
6) There is absolutely no salvation outside the one Church of <u>*the faithful*</u> (*de fide, Innocent III, Fourth Lateran Council*), which only includes the water baptized.
7) Every human creature must be subject to the Roman Pontiff to be saved (*de fide, Boniface VIII, Unam Sanctam*), and it is impossible to be subject to the Roman Pontiff without the Sacrament of Baptism (*de fide, Trent, Sess. 14, Chap. 2*).
8) One must belong to <u>the Body</u> of the Church to be saved (*de fide, Eugene IV and Pius XI*), and only the water baptized belong to the Body of the Church.
9) The Church is defined as a union of sacraments (*de fide, Eugene IV, Cantate Domino; Boniface VIII, Unam Sanctam*), which means that only those who have received the Sacrament of Baptism can be inside the unity of the Church.
10) All true Justification meets up with the Sacraments (*de fide, Sess. 7, Foreword to the Decree on the Sacraments*).

11) The Sacraments as such are necessary for salvation though <u>all</u> are not necessary for each individual (*de fide, Profession of Faith at Trent and Vatican I; and the Profession of Faith for converts*), which means that one must at least receive one Sacrament (Baptism) to be saved but one doesn't need to receive them all.

34. The Degenerate Result of Heresy against this Dogma

The heresy that "invincible ignorance" saves those who die as non-Catholics and that non-Catholics can be saved by "baptism of desire" often quickly results in an apostasy from Christ Himself. The famous Irish priest, Fr. Denis Fahey, is a case in point.

> Fr. Denis Fahey, *The Kingship of Christ and the Conversion of the Jewish Nation* (1953), p. 52: "The Jews, as a nation, are objectively aiming at giving society a direction which is in complete opposition to the order God wants. **It is possible that a member of the Jewish Nation, who rejects Our Lord, may have the supernatural life which God wishes to see in every soul**, and so be good with the goodness God wants, but objectively, the direction he is seeking to give to the world is opposed to God and to that life, and therefore is not good. **If a Jew who rejects our Lord is good in the way God demands**, it is in spite of the movement in which he and his nation are engaged."

Here we see the famous Irish priest Fr. Denis Fahey, whose writings are praised by many who call themselves "traditional Catholics," teaching that Jews <u>who reject Our Lord Jesus Christ</u> may "have the supernatural life which God wants to see in every soul" (i.e., the state of grace) and therefore can be saved. This is truly an abomination. Notice how Fr. Fahey's statement directly contradicts the word of God.

> 1 John 5:11-12: "And this is the testimony, that God hath given to us eternal life. **And this life is in his Son. He that hath the Son, hath life. He that hath not the Son, hath not life**."

The word of God tells us that he that hath not the Son *hath not life*. Fr. Denis Fahey tells us that a Jew who <u>rejects the Son</u> *hath life*: "*a member of the Jewish Nation, <u>who rejects Our Lord</u>, may have the supernatural life…*" By making such a statement, Fr. Fahey reveals (unfortunately) that he wasn't a Catholic, but a blatant heretic. Perhaps if Fr. Fahey had spent more time getting to know the truth of Jesus Christ, His Gospel and His dogmas, rather than writing large volumes on "the forces of organized naturalism," he would have discovered that the core focus of the entire Gospel – and the very central truth of the universe along with the dogma of the Trinity – is that **Jesus Christ is the Son of God, and that you must believe in Him to have eternal life.**

"For God so loved the world, as to give His only begotten Son: *that whosoever believeth in Him*, may not perish, but may have life everlasting." (John 3:16)

"He that believeth in the Son hath life everlasting: but <u>he that believeth not the Son, shall not see life</u>, but the wrath of God abideth on him." (John 3:36)

To assert that one can attain salvation while rejecting Jesus Christ is to say that one can attain salvation while rejecting salvation itself. It is one of the worst heresies that one could utter.

"Now <u>this is life everlasting, that they may know thee, the only true God, and Jesus Christ</u>, whom thou hast sent." (John 17:3)

"And he said to them [the Jews]: You are from beneath, I am from above. You are of this world, I am not of this world. Therefore, I said to you, that you shall die in your sins: <u>for if you believe not that I am he, you shall die in your sin</u>." (John 8:23-24)

"Amen, Amen, I say to you: <u>he that entereth not by the door into the sheepfold, but climbeth up another way, the same is a thief and a robber… I am the door</u>." (John 10:1, 9)

"Jesus saith to them: I am the way, and the truth, and the life. <u>No man cometh to the Father, but by me</u>." (John 14:6)

"And when he [the Paraclete] is come, he will convince the world of sin, and of justice, and of judgment. <u>Of sin indeed: because they have not believed in me</u>." (John 15:8-9)

"For this was I born, and for this came I into the world, that I should give testimony to the truth: <u>every one who is of the truth, heareth my voice</u>." (John 18:37)

Pope Eugene IV, *Council of Florence*, Sess. 8, Nov. 22, 1439, *ex cathedra*: "Whoever *wishes* to be saved, needs above all to hold the Catholic faith; unless each one preserves this whole and inviolate, he will without a doubt perish in eternity.– But the Catholic faith is this, that we worship one God in the Trinity, and the Trinity in unity… Therefore let him who wishes to be saved, think thus concerning the Trinity.

"<u>But it is necessary for eternal salvation that he faithfully believe also in the incarnation of our Lord Jesus Christ</u>…the Son of God is God and man…– This is the Catholic faith; unless each one believes this faithfully and firmly, he cannot be saved."

But Fr. Fahey had imbibed the heresy that those who die as non-Catholics can be saved, which was rampant at the turn of the century, as I have shown. He had already imbibed the heresy that Outside the Church There is No Salvation doesn't actually mean outside the Church there is no salvation. By rejecting the true meaning of the dogma, and by holding that non-Catholics can be saved, it was only a short time before Fr. Fahey concluded (as he did above) that persons can be saved in any religion whatsoever – including Jews who reject the Savior Himself. This demonstrates that those who see this dogma and believe that even one pagan, Buddhist, Muslim, Jew, etc. can be saved without conversion to Christ actually hold that a non-Catholic can possibly be saved in *any religion whatsoever*, as the following statement of Archbishop Lefebvre confirms.

> Archbishop Marcel Lefebvre, *Against the Heresies*, p. 216: "Evidently, certain distinctions must be made. **Souls can be saved in a religion other than the Catholic religion (Protestantism, Islam, Buddhism, etc.),** but not by this religion. There may be souls who, not knowing Our Lord, have by the grace of the good Lord, good interior dispositions, who submit to God...But some of these persons make an act of love which implicitly is equivalent to baptism of desire. It is uniquely by this means that they are able to be saved."[583]

Notice the "etc." The word "etc." means "*and the rest, and so on*"! Bishop Lefebvre is saying that there are *many other religions* in which people can be saved. This is complete and utter heresy. Bishop Lefebvre believed that men can be saved while worshipping false gods and many gods (Buddhism, Hinduism). But this simply illustrates that all those who believe that salvation is possible for members of non-Christian religions without the principal mysteries of the Catholic Faith (the Trinity and Incarnation) are admitting that a soul can be saved in any religion whatsoever: Islam, Buddhism, etc. It shows how those who reject the true meaning of Outside the Church There is No Salvation and the necessity of faith in Christ and the Trinity reject all faith and actually have no faith.

> Pope Leo XIII, *Satis Cognitum* (# 9), June 29, 1896:
> "… **can it be lawful for anyone to reject any one of those truths without by that very fact falling into heresy? – without separating himself from the Church? – without repudiating in one sweeping act the whole of Christian teaching?** For such is the nature of faith that nothing can be more absurd than to accept some things and reject others… **But he who dissents even in one point from divinely revealed truth absolutely rejects all faith,** since he thereby refuses to honor God as the supreme truth and the *formal motive of faith*."[584]

Fr. Fahey and Bishop Lefebvre couldn't tell you that one who dies a Satanist is definitely lost. They clearly held that it is possible for <u>anyone else</u> (including Jews who reject the Savior Himself) to be saved without the Catholic Faith and in false religions. **If Jews, Buddhists, Hindus and Muslims can be saved in their false religions and without the Catholic Faith – as they say – then, according to them, a Satanist *could* also be saved without the Catholic Faith and in his false religion**; they would have to admit that we just don't know since he could be in good faith also.

Thus, by holding that salvation is possible for those who die as members of non-Catholic religions, Fr. Fahey, Bishop Lefebvre and every other person who clings to this heresy believes that salvation *is possible in any <u>and every</u> religion*.

Pope Pius IX, *Qui Pluribus* (# 15), Nov. 9, 1846:
"Also perverse is that shocking theory that it makes no difference to which religion one belongs, a theory greatly at variance even with reason. By means of this theory, those crafty men remove all distinction between virtue and vice, truth and error, honorable and vile action. <u>**They pretend that men can gain eternal salvation by the practice of any religion**</u>**, as if there could ever be any sharing between justice and iniquity, any collaboration between light and darkness, <u>or any agreement between Christ and Belial</u>.**"[585]

Bishop Lefebvre, Address given at Rennes, France: "**If men are saved in Protestantism, Buddhism or Islam,** they are saved by the Catholic Church, by the grace of Our Lord, by the prayers of those in the Church, by the blood of Our Lord as individuals, *perhaps through the practice of their religion*, **perhaps of what they understand in their religion**, but not by their religion…"[586]

This should give a message to those who call this issue merely "academic." This issue is not merely "academic"; it influences a person's spiritual life in countless ways. The denial of this dogma corrupts one's faith to the core, and totally perverts a person's belief in Jesus Christ Himself as the savior of the world. It corrupts the entire way one views the supernatural world.

(Acts 4:12): "*… the name of Our Lord Jesus Christ… Nor is there salvation in any other. For there is no other name under heaven, given to men, whereby we must be saved.*"

BY THEIR FRUITS YOU SHALL KNOW THEM – THE FRUITS OF BAPTISM OF DESIRE

At Most Holy Family Monastery, we have personally conversed with hundreds of people on the issue of baptism of desire and *Outside the Church There is No Salvation* and we've been contacted by thousands. Out of the many hundreds of people with whom we've spoken on the issue of baptism of desire, I can honestly say that <u>approximately 5 to 10</u> actually affirmed that it only applies to those who desire water baptism (catechumens). The rest (almost 100%) believed that "baptism of desire" saves Jews, Buddhists, Hindus, Muslims, pagans and even non-Catholics who reject Christ. Why is it that basically every person who believes in baptism of desire rejects the Catholic Church's teaching (Pope Eugene IV, *Council of Florence*, de fide) that all who die as non-Catholics are not saved?

And out of the approximately 5 to 10 persons that I can recall believing in baptism of desire only for catechumens, basically all of those persons were forced to admit that unbaptized catechumens are "outside the Church." So, even those 5 to 10 persons were embracing a position that there is salvation "outside" the Church or salvation for persons who are not in the Church's "bosom and unity," which is heretical. This shows that any good-willed person, who is faithful to Catholic dogmatic teaching, will see that the Catholic Church does not teach baptism of desire at all when all the facts are presented to him.

In fact, a person who attends the Society of St. Pius X recently called us and told me that his Methodist Grandmother was saved by "baptism of desire." I told the man that even if baptism of desire were true (which it isn't), it wouldn't save Methodists (heretics) <u>who are already baptized</u>. But he did not agree, and he fought even more vigorously for his heresy. He then proceeded to tell me that I was in heresy for asserting that there is no salvation outside the Church! And the heretical position of this man only reflects the common position of many heretical "traditionalists" who frequent the Latin Masses around the world, as well as basically every member of the Novus Ordo.

35. Recent Attacks

Recently, there have been a number of specific attacks against the teaching of the Catholic Church on the necessity of baptism and the Catholic Faith for salvation. A refutation of the arguments put forward in these attacks, as well as the relevant dogmas to which these attacks are opposed, are found in this document. However, I felt that it was important to discuss a few groups in particular, and their errors regarding this topic.

THE ERRORS OF THE CURRENT ST. BENEDICT CENTER

The St. Benedict Center was founded by Fr. Feeney before Vatican II. As I have documented, it was a beacon of truth on the salvation dogma when the Fr. Feeney controversy erupted in Boston. But the fact that Fr. Feeney staunchly defended this truth on salvation during his day does not mean, of course, that everything he said on the topic was cogent or correct. He was, in fact, mistaken in his belief that catechumens could be justified (put in a state of grace) by the desire for water baptism. Fr. Feeney knew that the Catholic Church infallibly teaches that no catechumen can be saved without water baptism (Council of Trent, Can. 5 on the Sacrament), but he erroneously thought that the Council of Trent taught that catechumens could be justified by the desire for baptism, when it didn't (See the section on Sess. 6, Chap. 4.). This mistaken position, which I believe was held by him in good faith and which he would have changed if he were today presented with the evidence and the argument showing that Trent does not teach that catechumens can be justified, caused him to be unable to explain the situation of the so-called "justified" catechumen who hadn't been baptized.

Father Feeney, *Bread of Life*, p. 137:

"Q. Can anyone now be saved without Baptism of Water?
A. No one can be saved without Baptism of Water.
Q. Are the souls of those who die in the state of justification saved, if they have not received Baptism of Water?
A. No. They are not saved.
Q. Where do these souls go if they die in the state of justification but have not received Baptism of Water?
A. **I do not know.**
Q. Do they go to Hell?
A. No.
Q. Do they go to Heaven?
A. No.
Q. Are there any such souls?
A. I do not know! Neither do you!
Q. What are we to say to those who believe there are such souls?
A. We must say to them that they are making reason prevail over Faith, and the laws of probability over the Providence of God."

Fr. Feeney was caught in an insoluble dilemma because of his <u>mistaken and incorrect position</u> that a catechumen can be justified without water baptism. And the liberal heretics have a field day with this passage of his book, and they literally spill pages worth of ink gleefully pointing out that Fr. Feeney was inconsistent on this point. By doing so, however, they only demonstrate their profound bad will and their inclination to evil; for whereas Fr. Feeney did make a mistake on this point of Justification (I believe in good faith), the liberal heretics who feign concern for doctrinal integrity in pointing out this mistake **don't even believe that one needs to be a Catholic or believe in Christ to be saved!** They hold that Jews, pagans, heretics, schismatics can all be saved without baptism or the Catholic Faith. Thus, to put it simply: the liberal heretics try to cover up for their own heretical belief that non-Catholics can be saved by focusing page after page after page after page on this one mistake of Fr. Feeney, while they dishonestly fail to address Fr. Feeney's main point, which was that they are denying the dogma Outside the Church There is No Salvation and are complete heretics and doctrinal perverts.

So, don't be fooled by the heretical priests and bishops who pretend to give an entire course on Fr. Feeney's Justification error <u>without addressing their own beliefs on whether non-Catholics can be saved</u> – they are just covering up for their own horrible heresy. Bishop Clarence Kelly of the Society of St. Pius V, for example, produced a long document and gave a lengthy presentation focusing only on the Justification error of Fr. Feeney, while never once addressing his own abominable and heretical belief that Jews, Buddhists, Hindus, Muslims and Protestants can be saved without the Catholic Faith (but more on the SSPV later)!

Fr. Feeney's error on Justification, however, has become a major problem for some; namely, the current members of the St. Benedict Center in New Hampshire. The current members of both St. Benedict Centers affirm communion with the Vatican II sect and bishops who completely reject Outside the Church There is No Salvation. They are, therefore (and most unfortunately) in heresy for obstinately affirming communion with heretics who deny this and other dogmas. Besides this, the Richmond, NH St. Benedict Center obstinately refuses to correct Fr. Feeney's error on Justification and even condemns us as "heretical" for our position!

In May of 1999, the St. Benedict Center (Richmond, NH) accused us in their newsletter of holding a "strange heresy." **They hold that while baptism is absolutely necessary for salvation by divine law, one can be regenerated (justified/born again) by the mere desire for baptism.** They follow Fr. Feeney's own erroneous conclusion in this regard. They believe in a baptism of desire that justifies but does not save, and they call our view that there is no justification at all without baptism heretical. The falsity of such an assertion by the modern-day St. Benedict Center in New Hampshire becomes very clear when this topic is examined more deeply. For example, they accuse us of holding a "strange heresy" when this was the teaching of St. Ambrose (not to mention Catholic dogma, as we will see).

> St. Ambrose, *De mysteriis*, 390-391 A.D.:
> "You have read, therefore, that the three witnesses in Baptism are one: water, blood, and the spirit; and if you withdraw any one of these, the Sacrament of Baptism is not valid. For what is water without the cross of Christ? A common element without any sacramental effect. <u>Nor on the other hand is there any</u>

mystery of regeneration without water: for 'unless a man be born again of water and the Spirit, he cannot enter the kingdom of God.' [John 3:5] Even a *catechumen* believes in the cross of the Lord Jesus, by which also he is signed; but, unless he be baptized in the name of the Father and of the Son and of the Holy Spirit, *he cannot receive the remission of sins* nor be recipient of the gift of spiritual grace."[587]

What's amazing about this is that the St. Benedict Center (Richmond, NH) even quotes this very passage from St. Ambrose in their book to prove **their** position (e.g., *Father Feeney and the Truth about Salvation*, p. 132). So this position – that one cannot be justified without baptism – is put forward as true by the St. Benedict Center when they quote St. Ambrose; but in their newsletter they call this very same position a "strange heresy" because they feel like attacking Most Holy Family Monastery. What incredible hypocrisy!

This means that the St. Benedict Center holds that, by the mere desire for baptism, one can: be born again; be adopted as a son of God; be regenerated; have his original sin remitted; have his actual sins remitted; be united with Christ; possess the infused virtues of faith, hope and charity; receive the application of the Blood of Christ; and receive the Spirit of Sanctification. This is what Justification brings about in a soul, according to the infallible teaching of the Catholic Church. And all of this can occur by the mere desire for baptism, according to the St. Benedict Center, even though they hold that this same person must receive the Sacrament of Baptism in order to be saved.

As stated already, there is no doubt that many members of the St. Benedict Center, including Father Feeney himself, held this erroneous position in good faith in the past. They misunderstood the Council of Trent's teaching in Sess. 6, Chap. 4 on Justification. They thought that this Chapter was teaching that Justification can take place by the desire for baptism (and they knew that Trent excluded the possibility of *salvation* without actually receiving baptism), so they concluded that *justification* can take place by the desire for the Sacrament of Baptism, but that *salvation* can only come from actually receiving Baptism. Their writings are filled with the distinction between *justification* and *salvation*.

Even though this erroneous position may have been a sincere attempt to uphold the Church's teaching on the necessity of Baptism for *salvation* (in the face of what they mistakenly thought was the Church's teaching on desire being sufficient for *justification*), there are many problems with this explanation.

1) Trent doesn't teach that the desire for baptism is sufficient for Justification. This has been shown in this document. And this was the root cause of their erroneous belief.

2) ***In Justification, the Spirit of Sanctification and the Blood of Redemption cannot be separated from the water of baptism (de fide).*** As has been shown already, Pope St. Leo the Great **eliminates** the St. Benedict Center's entire theory.

> Pope St. Leo the Great, **dogmatic** letter to Flavian, *Council of Chalcedon*, 451: "Let him heed what the blessed apostle Peter preaches, that sanctification by the Spirit is effected by the sprinkling of Christ's blood (1 Pet. 1:2)… *It is He, Jesus Christ, who has come through water and blood, not in water only, but in water and blood. And because the Spirit is truth, it is the Spirit who testifies. For there are three who give testimony – Spirit and water and blood. And the three are one.* (1 Jn. 5:4-8) IN OTHER WORDS, THE SPIRIT OF SANCTIFICATION AND THE BLOOD OF REDEMPTION AND THE WATER OF BAPTISM. THESE THREE ARE ONE AND REMAIN INDIVISIBLE. NONE OF THEM IS SEPARABLE FROM ITS LINK WITH THE OTHERS."[588]

It is defined dogma that no one can be Justified without the Blood of Redemption (Trent, Sess. 5 and 6, Denz. 790; 795). Pope St. Leo defines that in Sanctification, **the Spirit of Sanctification (Justification) and the Blood of Redemption** *are inseparable* **from the water of baptism.** This means that there can be no Justification – no application of the Blood of Redemption – without water baptism (*de fide*). There can be no Justification by desire.

The St. Benedict Center holds that a sinner can have the Spirit of Sanctification and the Blood of Redemption by desire, *without water baptism,* and are therefore expressly contradicting this dogmatic pronouncement. If the St. Benedict Center's affiliates refuse to change their position after seeing this pronouncement they are clinging to heresy.

3) ***Outside the Church there is no remission of sins (de fide).*** The St. Benedict Center holds that an unbaptized catechumen is outside the Catholic Church (which is correct, since only Baptism makes one a member). Proof that this is their belief is found on page 77 of their book, *Father Feeney and the Truth about Salvation.* But while they profess that it is only through Baptism that one can be inside the Church, **they hold that an unbaptized catechumen can have Justification (remission of sins and sanctifying grace) by his desire for baptism, while he is still outside the Church.** This is directly contrary to the *ex cathedra* definition of Pope Boniface VIII below. It is therefore heresy to say, as they do, that one who is outside the Church can have his sins remitted.

> Pope Boniface VIII, *Unam Sanctam,* Nov. 18, 1302, *ex cathedra*: "With Faith urging us we are forced to believe and to hold the one, holy, Catholic Church and that, apostolic, and we firmly believe and simply confess **this Church outside of which there is no salvation NOR REMISSION OF SIN**…"[589]

Some of the defenders of the St. Benedict Center have argued that only the end of the Bull *Unam Sanctam* is solemn (and therefore infallible), not the part quoted above. This is a desperate attempt to defend their false position on Justification, and it is proven wrong by Pope Pius XII.

> Pope Pius XII, *Mystici Corporis Christi* (# 40), June 29, 1943: **"That Christ and His Vicar constitute one only Head is the <u>solemn</u> teaching of Our predecessor of immortal memory Boniface VIII in the Apostolic Letter *Unam Sanctam*;** and his predecessors have never ceased to repeat the same."[590]

Pope Pius XII is referring to the part of *Unam Sanctam* which the defenders of the St. Benedict Center argue is not solemn (infallible), and he says that it is "solemn" (infallible). This demonstrates that the part of the Bull quoted above is indeed solemn and infallible. In fact, the paragraph of *Unam Sanctam* that Pius XII is referring to in *Mystici Corporis* incorporates even less solemn language than the paragraph quoted above on outside the Church there is no remission of sins. The bottom-line is that the teaching of the Bull on Faith is an *ex cathedra* pronouncement which no one can deny. The St. Benedict Center denies it by their position that catechumens can be justified outside the Church.

4) The Justified are heirs according to hope of life everlasting (de fide). The Church teaches that one who is justified is an heir to heaven. This means that if one dies in a state of Justification he will go to heaven. The St. Benedict Center teaches that one can be justified without baptism, but such a person <u>still isn't an heir to heaven</u> because he hasn't received baptism yet. This position contradicts dogma.

> Pope Paul III, *Council of Trent*, Session 6, Chap. 7 on Justification, *ex cathedra*: **"Justification** … is not merely remission of sins, but also the sanctification and renewal of the interior man through the voluntary reception of the grace and gifts, **whereby an unjust man becomes a just man**, and from being an enemy becomes a friend, that he may be '**<u>an heir according to hope of life everlasting</u>**' [Tit. 3:7]."[591]

The true position is that every truly justified person is indeed an heir to heaven (*de fide*) and will go to heaven if he dies in that state, **because only the baptized are truly justified from sin.**

5) The Justified have fully satisfied the divine law and have merited heaven according to their state in life (de fide). This one really crushes the St. Benedict Center's position.

Pope Paul III, *Council of Trent*, Sess. 6, Chap. 16: "… **hence IT MUST BE BELIEVED THAT NOTHING MORE IS NEEDED FOR THE JUSTIFIED TO BE CONSIDERED TO HAVE FULLY SATISFIED THE DIVINE LAW,** according to this state in life, by the deeds they have wrought in him **and to have truly merited eternal life to be obtained in its own time** (if they shall have departed this life in grace)…"[592]

The St. Benedict Center's position is that a person *justified* without baptism is not yet in a state worthy of *salvation and has not yet merited heaven*. He still needs to fulfill the divine law requiring baptism, according to them. Remember, they constantly focus on the distinction between *justification* and *salvation*. But the Council of Trent contradicts this by asserting that *the justified have fully satisfied the divine law and have merited eternal life* to be obtained in its own time (if they shall have departed this life in grace). Nothing more is needed for the justified to get to heaven; they need only to maintain the state of Justification and die in it. This is not consistent with the St. Benedict Center's position, but it is consistent with the teaching of the Church (e.g., Pope St. Leo the Great) that no sinner can be justified without the Sacrament of Baptism. This quotation from Trent actually blows the St. Benedict Center's position away.

6) The possession of faith, hope and charity makes one a member of Christ's Body (de fide). From Trent's definition on the Justification of the sinner, one learns that it is not possible for a sinner to possess the infused, supernatural virtues of faith, hope and charity without being a member of Christ's Body. These virtues are infused at the time of Justification.

Pope Paul III, *Council of Trent*, Sess. 6, Chap. 7 on Justification: "Hence man through Jesus Christ, into whom he is ingrafted, *receives in the said justification together with the remission of sins all these gifts infused at the same time: faith, hope and charity.* **For faith, unless hope and charity be added to it, neither unites one perfectly with Christ, nor makes him a living *member of his body*.**"[593]

This means that *if* hope and charity are added to faith, faith does unite one perfectly with Christ *and* make him a living member of Christ's body. This is not consistent with the St. Benedict Center's position, because they hold that it's possible for hope and charity to be united with faith in a justified catechumen who is not a member of Christ's body.

Since these errors that I have described deal with finer points of this issue, there is no doubt that many supporters of the St. Benedict Center have held – and some still may hold – these errors in good faith, while affirming the dogma that the Catholic Faith and Baptism are necessary for salvation. However, they cannot lawfully hold these errors after they have been pointed out to them. And unfortunately, the current day leaders of the St. Benedict Center, as well as many of its affiliates, members and writers, *refuse* to correct themselves, and must be considered heretical. Further, they bring down on their heads definite condemnation when they condemn the teaching of the Church described above as a "strange heresy," as they did in their newsletter. We pray that the affiliates of the St. Benedict Center will change their position on these matters, as well as their heretical allegiance to the Vatican II sect, because they have endured unjust persecution from heretics who hate the dogma Outside the Catholic Church There is No Salvation and Our Lord Jesus Christ's doctrine on the necessity of Baptism.

THE SOCIETY OF ST. PIUS X

OBJECTION- The Society of Saint Pius X has published numerous books and articles which show that baptism of desire is the teaching of the Catholic Church, such as *Baptism of Desire* by Fr. Jean-Marc Rulleau and *Is Feeneyism Catholic?* by Fr. Francois Laisney.

ANSWER- I have already shown that the teaching of Pope St. Leo the Great, the Council of Florence on John 3:5, and the Council of Trent on John 3:5 and the Sacrament of Baptism (among many other things) disprove any claim that salvation can be attained without water baptism. But I will address the books of the Society of St. Pius X in this regard. The Society of Saint Pius X (SSPX), founded by the late Archbishop Marcel Lefebvre, has spread heresy publicly on the necessity of the Catholic Church for salvation, and has attacked with heretical tenacity Catholics who defend the Church's infallible teaching on the necessity of Baptism. The arguments that the Society of St. Pius X brings forward are refuted in this book. But to fully expose the heresy – and shocking dishonesty – which is easily detected in their works, I will examine a few of their books in detail.

I will give a brief overview of the heresies present in the writings of Archbishop Lefebvre, followed by a more in-depth exposé of the SSPX's recent works.

- ## *Against the Heresies,* by Archbishop Marcel Lefebvre:

1. Page 216: "Evidently, certain distinctions must be made. **Souls can be saved in a religion other than the Catholic religion (Protestantism, Islam, Buddhism, etc.), but not by this religion.** There may be souls who, <u>not knowing Our Lord</u>, have by the grace of the good Lord, good interior dispositions, who submit to God...But some of these persons make an act of love which implicitly is equivalent to baptism of desire. It is uniquely by this means that they are able to be saved."[594]

2. Page 217: "<u>One cannot say</u>, then, that no one is saved in these religions..."[595]

3. Pages 217-218: "This is then what Pius IX said and what he condemned. It is necessary to **understand** the formulation that was so often employed by the Fathers of the Church: 'Outside the Church there is no salvation.' **When we say that, it is incorrectly believed that we think that all the Protestants, all the Moslems, all the Buddhists, all those who do not publicly belong to the Catholic Church go to hell. Now, I repeat, it is possible for someone to be saved in these religions**, but they are saved by the Church, and so the formulation is true: Extra Ecclesiam Nulla Salus. This must be preached."[596]

What we see here from the founder of the Society of St. Pius X is blatant heresy. He directly contradicts the solemnly defined dogma that Outside the Catholic Church There is No Salvation. Some adherents of the Society of St. Pius X have tried to defend these heretical words of Archbishop Lefebvre by pointing out that, although he did say that men can be saved <u>in</u> other religions, he emphasized that it is <u>*by*</u> the Catholic Church.

This response is a pathetic attempt to defend the indefensible. In fact, those who attempt to defend Lefebvre in this way actually mock God. I could say that all men go to heaven (universal salvation), but all men go to heaven "by the Catholic Church." Does this change the heresy? No, of course not. Thus, it doesn't matter how Lefebvre tried to explain away or justify his heresy; he was still teaching that souls can be saved <u>in non-Catholic religions,</u> which is heresy!

The dogma of the Catholic Church does not merely affirm that *"no one is saved <u>except</u> <u>by</u> the Catholic Church"*; it states that no one is saved *outside* the Catholic Church and that no one is saved without the Catholic Faith. This means that no one can be saved inside non-Catholic religions. The defenders of the SSPX need to get that through their heads. The dogma of the Catholic Church <u>excludes</u> the idea that anyone is saved <u>in another</u> <u>religion</u>.

> Pope Gregory XVI, *Summo Iugiter Studio* (# 2), May 27, 1832:
> "<u>**Finally some of these misguided people attempt to persuade themselves and others that men are not saved only in the Catholic religion**</u>, but that even heretics may attain eternal life."[597]

Since he was teaching that people can be saved *in* another religion, Lefebvre's emphasis that everyone is saved <u>*by*</u> the Catholic Church has no relevance. The words of Pope Gregory XVI in *Summo Iugiter Studio* cited above could have been addressed specifically to Bishop Lefebvre and the Society of St. Pius X.

Bishop Lefebvre, Sermon at first Mass of a newly ordained priest (Geneva: 1976): "We are Catholics; we affirm our faith in the divinity of Our Lord Jesus Christ; we affirm our faith in the divinity of the Holy Catholic Church; we <u>think</u> that Jesus Christ is the sole way, the sole truth, the sole life, and that one cannot be saved outside Our Lord Jesus Christ and consequently outside His Mystical Spouse, the Holy Catholic Church. No doubt, the graces of God are distributed outside the Catholic Church, **but those who are saved, even outside the Catholic Church**, are saved by the Catholic Church, by Our Lord Jesus Christ, even if they do not know it. even if they are unaware of it...”[598]

Here Lefebvre denies the dogma <u>word for word</u>.

> Bishop Lefebvre, Address given at Rennes, France: “**If men are saved in Protestantism, Buddhism or Islam,** they are saved by the Catholic Church, by the grace of Our Lord, by the prayers of those in the Church, by the blood of Our Lord as individuals, *perhaps through the practice of their religion*, **perhaps of what they understand in their religion**, but not by their religion...”[599]

Notice again, in fact, how Bishop Lefebvre stated that men can be saved by the practice of false religions.

> Pope Pius IX, *Qui Pluribus* (# 15), Nov. 9, 1846:
> **"Also perverse is that shocking theory that it makes no difference to which religion one belongs, a theory greatly at variance even with reason**. By means of this theory, those crafty men remove all distinction between virtue and vice, truth and error, honorable and vile action. **They pretend that men can gain eternal salvation <u>by the practice of any religion</u>**, as if there could ever be any sharing between justice and iniquity, any collaboration between light and darkness, <u>or any agreement between Christ and Belial</u>."[600]

- *Open Letter to Confused Catholics*, by Archbishop Marcel Lefebvre:

> Pages 73-74: “**<u>Does this mean that no Protestant, no Muslim, no Buddhist or animist will be saved? No, it would be a second error to think that</u>**. Those who cry for intolerance in interpreting St. Cyprian's formula *Outside the Church there is no salvation*, also reject the Creed, “I accept one baptism for the remission of sins,” and are insufficiently instructed as to what baptism is. There are three ways of receiving it: the baptism of water; the baptism of blood (that of martyrs who confessed their faith while still catechumens); and baptism of desire. Baptism can be explicit. **Many times in Africa I heard one of our catechumens say to me, “Father, baptize me straightaway because if I die before you come again, I shall go to hell.” I told him, “No, if you have no mortal sin on your conscience and if you desire baptism, then you already have the grace in you**...”[601]

Here we find more heresy against the dogma Outside the Catholic Church There is No Salvation from Bishop Lefebvre.

- *Baptism of Desire,* by Fr. Jean-Marc Rulleau (SSPX):

Recently, the Society of St. Pius X (SSPX – Lefebvrists) published two books attacking the teaching of the Church on Baptism. They spend their time trying to figure out ways for people to be saved without baptism – but to no avail. **Baptism of Desire by Fr. Jean-Marc Rulleau** was published by the SSPX in 1999, while *Is Feeneyism Catholic?* **by Fr. Francois Laisney** was published in 2001. I will examine both of these books in detail. I will break up the examination of these books into separate topics of omissions, lies, contradictions and heresies. This will enable the reader to identify the dishonesty and unorthodoxy of these authors and the group they represent.

I will begin with the book *Baptism of Desire* by Fr. Rulleau.

OMISSIONS:

- The book *Baptism of Desire* by Fr. Jean-Marc Rulleau pretends to be an examination of the Church's teaching on what is necessary for salvation: the necessity of baptism, the necessity of faith in Jesus Christ, etc. Yet amazingly, **in the entire book, the author does not quote one (I repeat, not one) of the *ex cathedra* (infallible) Papal statements on Outside the Church There is No Salvation!** I guess he didn't feel they were relevant? He probably didn't feel that they were relevant because he does not believe in them.

- Despite having an entire section on the necessity of explicit vs. implicit faith in Jesus Christ (pp. 53-62), Fr. Rulleaus fails to quote, in the entire book, the *Athanasian Creed*, the dogmatic symbol of faith which defined that faith in Jesus Christ and the Trinity is necessary for all who wish to be saved. If he had simply quoted this creed, Fr. Rulleau could have settled the whole issue which he spends pages examining. Unfortunately, he does not quote the Creed, probably because he does not believe in it.

- Canons 2 and 5 from the Council of Trent's Canons on the Sacrament of Baptism are not quoted anywhere in the book. This is interesting, because **one would think that what the Council of Trent defined about the necessity of baptism might come up in a book about the necessity of baptism**.

Notice that the major omissions of Father Rulleau concern the Church's **dogmatic** teaching: on no salvation outside the Church, on faith in Jesus Christ and the Trinity, on the necessity of the Sacrament of Baptism. The Society of St. Pius X, unfortunately, is not interested in what the Church teaches dogmatically.

HERESIES:

While failing to quote key dogmas, Fr. Rulleau did feel it important to mention that:

- *it is an error to attribute infallibility to every document of the Magisterium* (p. 9). – heresy.
- *justifying faith can come from the Christian elements present in false religions* (p. 61).- heresy.
- *it is difficult to say whether belief in God who rewards is all that is necessary to be saved (p. 63)* – heresy.
- *it cannot be granted that justifying faith occurs <u>normally</u> in every religious tradition (p. 63), which implies that it can occur <u>in every religious tradition</u>, just not normally.* – heresy.
- *Baptism of Desire can occur among paganism* (p. 64). – heresy.

LIES:

- Fr. Rulleau, *Baptism of Desire*, p. 63: "This baptism of desire makes up for the want of sacramental baptism… The existence of this mode of salvation is a truth taught by the Magisterium of the Church and held from the first centuries <u>by all the Fathers</u>. **No Catholic theologian has contested it**."[602]

This is an utter lie! As I have shown, the whole early Church **rejected** the idea that an unbaptized catechumen could be saved by his desire for baptism, including the 1 or 2 fathers who seemed to contradict themselves on the matter. This is why, throughout the whole early Church, prayer, sacrifice and Christian burial were not allowed for catechumens who died without baptism. To assert, in the face of these facts, that "no theologian has contested it" is outrageous – as proven in the large section on "Baptism of Desire and Baptism of Blood: Erroneous Traditions of Man."

- On page 39, Fr. Rulleau misquotes the crucial passage from the fourth chapter of the Council of Trent's Decree on Justification: "and this translation after the promulgation of the Gospel cannot be effected *<u>except through</u>* the laver of regeneration or a desire for it…"[603] The Latin original of this passage from Trent does not translate to, "except through the laver of regeneration or a desire for it…" It translates to, "… <u>without</u> the laver of regeneration or a desire for it…"

Introducing "except through" in the place of "without" changes the entire meaning of the passage to favor baptism of desire (as shown in the Section on Sess. 6, Chap. 4 of the Council of Trent). To do it deliberately is a mortal sin. Fr. Rulleau may have made an innocent mistake (by quoting this horribly misleading translation from Denzinger), but the point is that the Society of St. Pius X as a whole continues to use this horribly misleading translation all the time to deceive their readers even after they have been made aware of it. Fr. Peter Scott, former United States District Superior of the SSPX, in a recent *Regina Coeli Report*, misquoted this passage again in the same way to favor baptism of desire. This type of obstinate misrepresentation of Church teaching is mortally sinful.

CONTRADICTIONS:

Fr. Rulleau's treatment of St. Thomas Aquinas is where his dishonesty really begins to shine through.

- On page 11, Fr. Rulleau makes the absurd statement: *"Quite simply, to refuse St. Thomas Aquinas is to refuse the Magisterium of the Church."*[604]

St. Thomas is one of the greatest doctors in the history of the Church and one of the most brilliant men to have ever lived; but it is well known that he erred on a number of points, as discussed in the section on "St. Thomas Aquinas." **St. Thomas did not believe that Mary was conceived immaculately** (cf. *Summa Theologica*, Pt. III, Q. 14, Art. 3, Reply to Obj. 1). According to the absolutely ridiculous assertion of Fr. Rulleau, to believe in the dogma of the Immaculate Conception is to refuse the Magisterium, because St. Thomas didn't believe in it! Such a position is equivalent to heresy. Why does Fr. Rulleau assert such nonsense? Simply because St. Thomas believed in baptism of desire and Fr. Rulleau wants to prove that *that fact alone* requires Catholics to submit to it. But notice how, when presented with a doctrine of St. Thomas which Fr. Rulleau is not ready to accept, he quickly abandons his ridiculous principle that *"to refuse St. Thomas Aquinas is to refuse the Magisterium of the Church."*

- Fr. Rulleau, *Baptism of Desire*, pp. 56-57: "**From this survey it appears that St. Thomas opts for the necessity of an act of explicit faith in the Incarnation and the Trinity**, and, more generally, in the mysteries of faith. To the question of how a man can be saved if he has not been evangelized by missionaries, he replies that God sees to it by giving an interior inspiration or by sending a missionary. **How should this doctrine of St. Thomas be interpreted? What weight should it be given**. The theologians have not been unanimous."[605]

In this paragraph, Fr. Rulleau is analyzing St. Thomas' clear teaching that no one can be saved without explicit faith in Jesus Christ and the Trinity – in other words, no salvation for the invincibly ignorant and no salvation for those of non-Catholic religions.

St. Thomas, *Summa Theologica*: "After grace had been revealed, **both the learned and simple folk are bound to explicit faith in the mysteries of Christ**, chiefly as regards those which are observed throughout the Church, and publicly proclaimed, **such as** the articles which refer to **the Incarnation**, of which we have spoken above."[606]

Saint Thomas, *Summa Theologica*: "And consequently, when once grace had been revealed, **all were bound to explicit faith in the mystery of the Trinity.**"[607]

In regard to the objection about one who had never heard of Christ, St. Thomas replies:

St. Thomas Aquinas, *Sent. II*, 28, Q. 1, A. 4, ad 4: "If a man, born among barbarian nations, does what he can, **God himself will show him what is necessary for salvation, either by inspiration or by sending a teacher to him.**"[608]

St. Thomas Aquinas, *Sent. III*, 25, Q. 2, A. 2, solut. 2: "If a man should have no one to instruct him, **God will show him**, unless he culpably wishes to remain where he is."[609]

St. Thomas Aquinas, *De Veritate*, 14, A. 11, ad 1: objection- "**It is possible that someone may be brought up in the forest, or among wolves; such a man cannot explicitly know anything about the faith. Reply-** It is the characteristic of Divine Providence to provide every man with what is necessary for salvation… provided on his part there is no hindrance. In the case of a man who seeks good and shuns evil, by the leading of natural reason, **God would either reveal to him through internal inspiration what had to be believed, or would send some preacher of the faith to him…**"[610]

St. Thomas repeatedly and unambiguously <u>refuted</u> the heresy that "invincible ignorance" saves. He affirmed that explicit faith in the mysteries of the Trinity and the Incarnation is absolutely necessary. If Fr. Rulleau is honest, he should not refuse this position of St. Thomas, for that would be, according to his own words, **"*to refuse the Magisterium of the Church.*"** But no, Fr. Rulleau demonstrates remarkable dishonesty by asking:

"**How should this doctrine of St. Thomas be interpreted? What weight should it be given.** The theologians have not been unanimous."[611]

So much for "*to refuse St. Thomas Aquinas is to refuse the Magisterium of the Church*"! Fr. Rulleau quickly abandons this position when presented with a doctrine from St. Thomas with which he and his heretical cohorts don't agree. The Society of St. Pius X rejects the necessity of explicit faith in the Trinity and Incarnation – as the quotes from Lefebvre prove – so, in an act of astounding hypocrisy, they abandon St. Thomas when he teaches this, and bind others to St. Thomas' opinion when he teaches baptism of desire!

- ## *Is Feeneyism Catholic?*, by Fr. Francois Laisney (SSPX)

Published in 2001, Fr. Laisney's book was a masterpiece in deceit. There are startling and shockingly dishonest things in his book, which will be exposed in the "Lies" section.

HERESY:

- On page 21, Fr. Laisney comments on the necessity of explicit faith in Jesus Christ: "*… how much is exactly necessary to know explicitly has not been settled.*" This statement clearly implies that it has not been settled whether it is necessary for salvation to believe in the Most Holy Trinity and that Jesus Christ is God and man, which is a denial of the Athanasian Creed, not to mention the teaching of St. Thomas Aquinas which they claim to love so much.

LIES:

- Fr. Laisney, *Is Feeneyism Catholic?*, p. 47: "*Moreover, **the very Council of Florence**, in the very same decree for the Jacobites (part of the bull Cantate Domino) **mentions baptism of desire**.*"[612] This is a complete lie! The Council of Florence makes no mention at all of baptism of desire and Fr. Laisney knows this! The fact that Laisney can write such a thing – and the fact that the Society of St. Pius X prints it – is abominable. This is a horrible sign for the SSPX. Deceit of this magnitude reveals that they are on the side of the devil.

- As if his horrible lie above weren't bad enough, Fr. Laisney commits another equally horrendous lie on the next page regarding the Council of Florence: "*Thus far from being against Baptism of Desire, the very Council of Florence, the very bull Cantate Domino, teaches it as being 'another remedy' permitting a delay for adult catechumens for the reasons given by St. Thomas.*"[613] **This borders on a sin that cries to heaven**. Not only does Laisney again assert <u>the blatant untruth</u> that baptism of desire is taught by the Council of Florence, but he even adds that Florence teaches it as being another remedy, putting "another remedy" in quotation marks! This is a complete lie! This type of dishonesty is mind-boggling. And then Fr. Laisney proceeds to write that Florence permitted a delay in baptizing adult catechumens for the reasons given by St. Thomas. **But the Council of Florence mentions nothing of adult catechumens**! Fr. Laisney is <u>*literally*</u> adding things to the Council that aren't there. Wake up, you supporters of the SSPX!

- After quoting the document *Quanto Conficiamur Moerore* of Pope Pius IX (treated in the section "The Dogma, Pope Pius IX and Invincible Ignorance"), Fr. Laisney writes: "*This passage of Pope Pius IX shows clearly: 1) baptism of desire is not opposed to the dogma outside the Catholic Church there is no salvation, 2) baptism of desire is not without*

divine light and grace… 3) baptism of desire is incompatible with indifference to God…"[614]
The document *Quanto Conficiamur Moerore* mentions nothing at all about baptism of desire. It mentions neither the concept nor the term. Yet Laisney, having no shame (and apparently not much of a conscience), does not hesitate to lie on three different counts, by asserting that Pius IX reveals three different aspects of baptism of desire. This type of lying has truly diabolical effects, because the lax readers of Fr. Laisney's books, who don't possess the resources to check his sources, will come away with the impression that *Fr. Laisney must be right*. This is how heretics kill souls.

- On page 38, Fr. Laisney says: *"**Ex ipso voto, the very term used by the Council of Trent**, thereby giving to St. Thomas Aquinas the approbation of an infallible Council. Some followers of Father Feeney claim that the Council of Trent did not uphold this teaching of St. Thomas on baptism of desire… We see here how false this claim is."*[615]

Fr. Laisney's argument here is that the Council of Trent used the same term that St. Thomas did (*ex ipso voto*) when defining on the necessity of baptism. Thus, according to him, it embraced St. Thomas' teaching on baptism of desire. The problem for Fr. Laisney, however, is that **nowhere does the Council of Trent use the term** *"ex ipso voto"* in regard to baptism or justification (and, to my knowledge, nowhere at all)! The term used in Sess. 6, Chap. 4 (the passage Laisney wrongly believes favors his view) is not *ex ipso voto*, but *"aut eius voto."* Also, the term used in Sess. 7, Can. 4 (which Laisney also wrongly believes favors his view) is not *ex ipso voto* either, but *"aut eorum voto."* Does the fact that he attributes a term to Trent, which is not to be found in Trent, matter to him at all? Apparently not.

As they are used in their respective contexts, the terms that Trent did employ do not favor baptism of desire, as shown in the sections on Trent's teaching in this document. But this is another example of how Fr. Laisney feels that he can just add terms to Trent according to his own whim. He remains oblivious to the fact that it is a mortal sin to knowingly attribute things to infallible documents which most certainly aren't there. Laisney's knowledge of Latin and familiarity with the topic are such that there is no excuse for him on the basis of an innocent mistake.

- Similar to the last lie, on page 49, Fr. Laisney writes: *"**The very famous expression 're aut voto – in deed or in desire' was used twice by the Council of Trent**, once in the explanation ('chapter') explicitly applied to the necessity of baptism and once even in an ex cathedra canon on the very necessity of sacraments in general."*[616]

In the last lie that we exposed, Fr. Laisney was claiming that the term used by Trent was *ex ipso voto*. Here he decides to say that Trent used the expression *"re aut voto* ("in deed or in desire") in Sess. 6, Chap. 4 and Sess. 7, Can. 4. Which one is it, Father Laisney?

Is it "re aut voto" or "ex ipso voto"? I guess the answer is: whatever is more convenient for Fr. Laisney. The problem for Fr. Laisney – and this seems to be a consistent problem – **is that Trent also does not use the term "re aut voto" in either of these passages!** Fr. Laisney has again added to an infallible document and deliberately misrepresented its teaching.

- On pages 85-86, Fr. Laisney writes: *"**The doctrine of baptism of blood and baptism of desire is inseparably linked by the Church to the dogma outside the Church there is no salvation**. It belongs to the very proper understanding of that dogma, so much that if one denies it, he no longer holds that dogma in the same sense and the same words as the Church holds it."*[617]

First of all, it's ironic that Fr. Laisney uses the term "inseparably linked," because it was Pope St. Leo the Great who defined that the sanctification of a sinner is *inseparably linked* to water baptism!

> Pope St. Leo the Great, **dogmatic** letter to Flavian, *Council of Chalcedon*, 451: *"For there are three who give testimony – Spirit and water and blood. And the three are one.* (1 Jn. 5:4-8) IN OTHER WORDS, THE SPIRIT OF SANCTIFICATION AND THE BLOOD OF REDEMPTION AND THE WATER OF BAPTISM. THESE THREE ARE ONE AND REMAIN INDIVISIBLE. NONE OF THEM IS SEPARABLE FROM ITS LINK WITH THE OTHERS."[618]

So while Fr. Laisney raves about how inseparably linked baptism of desire and baptism of blood are to the dogma Outside the Church There is No Salvation, **he actually uses the same language that the pronouncement of Pope St. Leo did, but with precisely the opposite meaning.** He asserts that the idea that the Spirit of Sanctification *can be separated from the water of baptism* is "inseparably linked" to Catholic dogma; whereas Pope St. Leo defines *dogmatically* that the Spirit of Sanctification *is inseparably linked to water baptism.*

Besides this, what else can be said about the assertion, *"**The doctrine of baptism of blood and baptism of desire is inseparably linked by the Church to the dogma outside the Church there is no salvation**"*? The only thing that I can think of is, "Oh really?" Is that why in no less than seven *ex cathedra* pronouncements on "the dogma outside the Church there is no salvation," the "doctrine of baptism of desire/blood" is not mentioned even once? Is that why in all the Councils in the history of the Church not one mention is made of either term? Is that why in no encyclical in the history of the Catholic Church was this "doctrine" taught? Yes, the "doctrines" of baptism of desire and baptism of blood are so inseparably linked to the dogma Outside the Catholic Church There is No Salvation that none of the many Popes who defined this dogma bothered to mention them. Fr. Laisney's statement is just another lie.

- On page 87, Laisney asserts that *"not a single one"* opposed baptism of desire, apparently referring to saints and Popes.

In other words, according to Fr. Laisney, not a single saint or Pope in the history of the Church denied the existence of baptism of desire! This is the same lie that Fr. Rulleau asserted in his book. So my question is: Do these men have consciences? **Fr. Laisney knows that St. Gregory Nazianz specifically denied the concept of baptism of desire** (See "Baptism of Desire and Baptism of Blood: Erroneous Traditions of Man"), which makes his statement another lie. And we know for a fact that Fr. Laisney knows this, **because the passage from St. Gregory is quoted on pages 64-65 of his book!**

CONTRADICTIONS:

Father Laisney justifies his belief in baptism of desire exclusively on the teaching of saints. It is on this same authority that he attempts to justify binding others to baptism of desire.

- In his book (pp. 58-60), Fr. Laisney asserts that to deny St. Cyprian's acceptance of baptism of blood is to distort the dogma Outside the Catholic Church There is No Salvation. Hence, he quotes St. Cyprian to "prove" his position. Yet, as I have shown in the section on the Fathers, in the same document of St. Cyprian, which Laisney quotes to justify his claim, **St. Cyprian teaches that baptisms performed by heretics are invalid – an idea that has been infallibly condemned**.

Hence, if Fr. Laisney were logical, he must teach that Catholics are bound to believe that baptisms performed by heretics are invalid, since St. Cyprian teaches this in the same document in which he teaches baptism of blood. But no, Fr. Laisney does not teach this and therefore contradicts his own line of reasoning. In fact, Cyprian's rejection of the validity of baptisms performed by heretics is not the only error that he makes in the aforementioned document. He also teaches that baptism of blood is a sacrament,[619] a position that is denied universally by all modern baptism of desire apologists, including Laisney himself.[620]

- On page 68, Fr. Laisney quotes St. Bernard to justify baptism of desire. But, as I have shown, in the same document quoted by Laisney, St. Bernard not only admits that he may be wrong, but says this: "This intimated that sometimes **faith alone would suffice for salvation**, and that without it, nothing would be sufficient."[621]

But being the remarkable hypocrite that he is, Fr. Laisney does not dogmatize St. Bernard's erroneous statement above, but only those passages from St. Bernard which he likes: the few on baptism of desire. And Laisney **cuts out of the quotation** the part

where St. Bernard admitted that he may have been wrong (see section on St. Bernard in this document for the full discussion). Likewise, when the incredibly dishonest Fr. Laisney quotes St. Alphonsus, **he does not include** St. Alphonsus' erroneous reference to Sess. 14, Chap. 4 because he knows that St. Alphonsus was dead wrong on this point.[622] Further, when he quotes St. Robert Bellarmine on the Church, **Laisney does not include** where St. Robert Bellarmine says that catechumens are <u>not</u> part of the Church![623]

As I've said, in studying the quotations from saints and theologians which Laisney brings forward as "proof texts" for baptism of desire, **I have found that in almost every single instance, the same saint or theologian makes another significant error in the same document**. For example:

- On page 34 of his book, Fr. Laisney quotes Cornelius a Lapide's commentary on John 3:5: "He who is contrite over his sins, wants baptism, and cannot receive it because of lack of water or minister, is reborn through resolution and desire of baptism. **The Council of Trent explains this verse <u>expressly</u> so in Session 7, Canon 4 about the Sacraments in General.**"[624]

Here Cornelius a Lapide makes a <u>major error.</u> He says that the Council of Trent "expressly" explains John 3:5 in Sess. 7, Can. 4 to favor the idea of baptism of desire. But Sess. 7, Can. 4 does not mention John 3:5 at all. John 3:5 is not even *mentioned* in the entire decree on the Sacraments in General, so it most certainly does not explain John 3:5 "expressly" to favor baptism of desire.

But this instance is very useful for this discussion for this reason: If Lapide makes a <u>major blunder</u> about Trent's teaching on John 3:5 (in fact, Lapide's statement wasn't even in the ballpark), then obviously he is vulnerable to other errors. To quote such passages from theologians as if they "confirm"[625] the so-called baptism of desire, as Laisney does, is ridiculous. Lapide **wasn't even in the ballpark** on what he was trying to convey; yet, according to the Society of St. Pius X, we are supposed to assent to his every sentence as an expression of infallible dogma.

I believe that there is a reason why God allowed these saints and theologians to err repeatedly and on various matters when explaining baptism of desire: to let people know that they are not infallible. Fr. Laisney and the SSPX most certainly do not get this message. They continue on in their diabolical campaign to denounce those who understand John 3:5 "as it is written" (Trent, Sess. 6, Chap. 4) and that the Sacrament of Baptism is necessary for salvation (Trent, Sess. 7, Can. 5 on the Sacrament of Baptism).

AMAZING CONTRADICTIONS:

Besides the contradictions already exposed, there are others that must be considered in the SSPX book *Is Feeneyism Catholic?* The fact that a self-proclaimed "traditional

Catholic priest," Fr. Laisney, can lie about the Council of Florence the way that he does, makes it not that surprising when we find him contradicting himself all over the place.

- On page 22, Laisney states the following: "**Note that an infant, not having yet the use of his reason, has no other possibility to be saved than through the actual reception of the sacrament of baptism, i.e., baptism of water.**"[626]

This statement is quite true, founded on solemnly defined dogma (See the section "Infants Cannot Be Saved Without Baptism"). But look at this:

- Fr. Laisney, *Is Feeneyism Catholic?*, p. 77: "*He interestingly exposes at length **the common teaching that baptism of blood applies also to infants** (e.g., those who are martyred with their parents).*"[627]

Need I say more to prove that Fr. Laisney is a liar and an astounding hypocrite, who contradicts himself blatantly within just a few pages? Page 22 of his book says that there is "no other possibility" for infants' salvation than through water baptism. Page 77 teaches quite clearly that "baptism of blood" applies to infants. So much for his statement on page 22! But it gets worse when we consider what Laisney had to say about the definition from the Council of Florence which declares that no infant can possibly be justified without the Sacrament of Baptism.

- On page 47, Fr. Laisney quotes the dogmatic definition from the Council of Florence: "**Regarding children**, indeed, because of danger of death, which can often take place, **when no help can be brought to them by another remedy than through the sacrament of baptism**, **through which they are snatched from the domination of the Devil** and adopted among the sons of God, it advises that holy baptism ought not be deferred for forty or eighty days, or any time according to the observance of certain people..."[628]

A number of things are significant about Fr. Laisney's treatment of this dogmatic definition. First is the fact that Fr. Laisney makes it a special point to note that Florence <u>only mentioned children</u> in this passage. He concludes that while there is *no other remedy* for children other than the Sacrament of Baptism, there is another remedy for original sin for adults (baptism of desire). He tries to bolster this position by pointing out that the above passage from Florence is a quotation from St. Thomas Aquinas, who (in the document quoted) goes on to teach that there is another remedy for adults. The problem for Fr. Laisney is that the Council of Florence did not incorporate St. Thomas' paragraph on there being another remedy for adults, but **stopped the quotation from him after stating that there is no other remedy for infants**.

This fact should make Fr. Laisney think. Why did the Holy Ghost only allow Pope Eugene IV and the Council of Florence to incorporate the passage from St. Thomas on infants, and not his teaching *in the very next paragraph* on baptism of desire? Why didn't God allow the Council to simply continue with the quotation only one more short paragraph, which would have made it clear once and for all that baptism of desire is a teaching of the Church? **It's obvious that the Holy Ghost wanted St. Thomas' teaching on the Sacrament of Baptism being the only remedy for infants in the Council, and that He did not want St. Thomas' teaching that baptism of desire is another remedy for adults in the Council. This is why the one paragraph appears and the other does not.**

But what actually appears in the Council of Florence **and what doesn't** *is not a concern to Fr. Laisney*, because when he finds that something is not in a Council which he wants to be there, he just adds it himself. In this case, Laisney decides to create his own definition by adding the paragraph of St. Thomas which *Florence very specifically did not incorporate*. I quote him again:

- Fr. Laisney, *Is Feeneyism Catholic?*, p. 47: "*Moreover, **the very Council of Florence**, in the very same decree for the Jacobites (part of the bull Cantate Domino) **mentions** baptism of desire.*"[629]

- Fr. Laisney, *Is Feeneyism Catholic?*, p. 48: "*Thus far from being against Baptism of Desire, the very Council of Florence, the very bull Cantate Domino, **teaches it as being 'another remedy' permitting a delay for adult catechumens for the reasons given by St. Thomas.**"[630]

Sorry Fr. Laisney, but the Council of Florence did not mention baptism of desire, and it did not permit a delay for catechumens for the reasons given by St. Thomas. And it most certainly did not teach that baptism of desire is "another remedy" for adult catechumens. These thoughts of St. Thomas were *not* incorporated into the Council; but because you want them to be there so badly, you just couldn't refrain from adding them in. Hence, you do not honestly report the teaching of the Church on the subject of Baptism, as you claim, but you lie about the content of the highest Magisterial pronouncements, because you are ***uncontrollably biased and obsessed*** in your quest to prove that people can be saved without baptism. What Florence did define, in fact, denies any possibility of salvation without water baptism.

Pope Eugene IV, *The Council of Florence*, "Exultate Deo," Nov. 22, 1439, *ex cathedra*: "Holy baptism, which is the gateway to the spiritual life, holds the first place among all the sacraments; through it we are made members of Christ and of the body of the Church. **And since death entered the universe through the first man, 'unless we are born again of water and the Spirit, we cannot,' as the Truth says, 'enter into the kingdom of heaven' [John 3:5].** The matter of this sacrament is real and natural water."[631]

So, let's reconsider Fr. Laisney's astounding contradictions on whether an infant can be saved without the Sacrament of Baptism. If Fr. Laisney made it a *special point* to lie that Florence taught that there is another remedy for adults, based (albeit illogically) on the fact that Florence did teach that there is no other remedy for infants, then at least one would expect that Fr. Laisney is going to be consistent with the fact that there is no other remedy for infants other than the Sacrament of Baptism, right? In other words, *there is no way in the world* that Fr. Laisney, if he is honest, could teach that there is another remedy for infants other than the Sacrament of Baptism. After all, this fact (that infants have no other remedy other than the Sacrament) is the basis upon which his lie (that there is another remedy for adults) is founded. But no! Fr. Laisney doesn't even believe that infants have no other remedy, but rather holds that infants can be saved without the Sacrament of Baptism, according to page 77 of his book.

This proves that Fr. Laisney's emphasis (on pages 47-48 of his book) that Florence defined that for children there is "no other remedy" other than the Sacrament of Baptism was made for one calculated reason. It was made in the hope of being able to prove that there is another remedy for adults – baptism of desire. His emphasis on this point was solely because he thought it would favor baptism of desire. His whole discussion about how Catholics must be faithful to the definition of Florence was a sham and a deception. Listen to this hypocrite explain how no one can deny the passage of Florence on there being no other remedy for infants other than baptism, which he himself denies in his book!

- Fr. Laisney, *Is Feeneyism Catholic?*, p. 48: "*Thus far from being against Baptism of Desire, the very Council of Florence, the very bull Cantate Domino, teaches it as being 'another remedy' permitting a delay for adult catechumens for the reasons given by St. Thomas.* **And lest some follower of Fr. Feeney say that this passage is not infallible, let him consider that the paragraph on baptism from which it is taken starts with the very same words as the one on the Church: '[The Holy Roman Church] firmly believes, professes, and teaches that…' Hence both paragraphs have the very same degree of authority.**"[632]

"*Woe to you scribes and Pharisees, hypocrites… Wherefore you are witnesses against yourselves… You serpents, generations of vipers, how will you flee from the judgment of hell?*" (Mt. 23: 23,31,33). Fr. Laisney's activity is that of a serpent, the same serpent who is responsible for the appalling deception in his book. Fr. Laisney is condemned by his own words. He contradicts that to which he admits he is bound, and which he took great pains to emphasize. But the pains taken to emphasize this dogma – that infants have no other remedy than water baptism – were not taken out of a spirit of fidelity to the teaching of the Church, but only in the hopeless endeavor of trying to prove the false doctrine of baptism of desire.

And ironically, while Laisney claims his false position as the teaching of Tradition, it is Tradition which shows that water baptism is the only help (i.e., the only remedy) to salvation for everyone, even adults who desire it.

> Pope St. Siricius, *Letter to Himerius*, 385:
> "As we maintain that the observance of the holy Paschal time should in no way be relaxed, in the same way we desire that infants who, on account of their age, cannot yet speak, or those who, in any necessity, are in want of **the water of holy baptism**, be succored with all possible speed, for fear that, **if those who leave this world should be deprived of the life of the Kingdom <u>for having been refused the source of salvation which they desired</u>**, this may lead to the ruin of *our* souls. **If those threatened with shipwreck, or the attack of enemies, or the uncertainties of a siege, or those put in a hopeless condition due to some bodily sickness, <u>ASK FOR WHAT IN THEIR FAITH IS THEIR ONLY HELP</u>, let them receive at the very moment of their request the reward of regeneration they beg for. Enough of past mistakes! From now on, let all the priests observe the aforesaid rule if they do not want to be separated from the solid apostolic rock on which Christ has built his universal Church."**[633]

One could go on exposing the books of the Society of St. Pius X, but what has been shown thus far should suffice to establish that they do not uphold Church teaching, to put it nicely. **No one can give a penny of financial support to this heretical Society or the St. Benedict Center or any other priest or group who does not uphold the Church's teaching on the absolute necessity of baptism and the absolute necessity of the Catholic Faith for salvation, which unfortunately includes almost every priest today.** One who would obstinately support such a priest, after becoming aware of his heretical position, would partake in his heresy and place himself on the road to Hell.

Furthermore, in light of Pope St. Leo the Great's dogmatic pronouncement against the concepts of baptism of desire and baptism of blood, the teaching of the Council of Florence on John 3:5, and the teaching of the Council of Trent that the Sacrament of Baptism is necessary for salvation (Sess. 7, Can. 5), **no one could even support a priest who believes in the theory of** *explicit baptism of desire* **(even if that priest may be in good faith until the Church's teaching is pointed out to him).** The first duty of any Catholic is to uphold the faith. One cannot compromise any point of the faith by supporting a priest who does not hold the faith whole and undefiled.

Unfortunately, the Society of St. Pius X is not alone among heretical "traditionalists". It is a fact that almost every priest in the world today, including almost every "traditional" priest, denies the necessity of baptism for salvation, and holds that people who die as non-Catholics can attain salvation. This lack of faith is explained by the fact that we are living in the last days of the world, the times of the Great Apostasy predicted in Sacred Scripture.

THE SOCIETY OF ST. PIUS V

In our previous magazines we have pointed out the unfortunate fact that the priests of the Society of St. Pius V hold to the heresy that non-Catholics can be saved without the Catholic Faith. They adhere to the same heresy as expressed by Archbishop Lefebvre and the books of the SSPX, as well as the heresy articulated in the 1949 Protocol 122/49 against Fr. Leonard Feeney (exposed already in this document). The SSPV's priests are also vigorous defenders of the false doctrine of baptism of desire. They consider baptism of desire to be a defined dogma. Fr. Baumberger of the Society of St. Pius V (SSPV) stated in the presence of the superior of our Monastery that Buddhists can be united to the Catholic Church. This is what their priests obstinately hold and believe; it is unfortunate, yet undeniably true. And because of this, we have pointed out that no Catholic aware of this can financially contribute to them under pain of mortal sin.

It had been our position in the past (a position rooted in the principle of *Epieikeia* and St. Thomas, among other things) that, despite the grave problems with the SSPV, a Catholic could avail himself of the sacraments of the SSPV <u>if the Catholic did not agree with them (of course) or support them in any way</u> (of course). However, this is no longer an option. <u>The SSPV Masses should no longer be attended even when one doesn't give them any support</u> because beginning some time in 2003 the priests of the SSPV consistently began making announcements before their traditional Masses (and it seems to be occurring at all of their chapels almost every week!) that no one who holds to the "errors of Fr. Feeney" should receive Holy Communion. They are referring to Fr. Feeney's belief, which is the infallible teaching of the Roman Catholic Church, that no one can be saved without the Sacrament of Baptism.

> Pope Paul III, *The Council of Trent,* canons on the <u>Sacrament </u>of Baptism, canon 5, *ex cathedra*: **"If anyone says that baptism [the Sacrament] is optional, that is, not necessary for salvation (cf. Jn. 3:5): let him be anathema."**[634]

> Pope Eugene IV, *The Council of Florence,* "Exultate Deo," Nov. 22, 1439, *ex cathedra*: **"Holy baptism, which is the gateway to the spiritual life, holds the first place among all the sacraments; through it we are made members of Christ and of the body of the Church. And since death entered the universe through the first man, 'unless we are born again of water and the Spirit, we cannot,' as the Truth says, 'enter into the kingdom of heaven' [John 3:5]. The matter of this sacrament is real and natural water."**[635]

The SSPV is therefore <u>publicly and notoriously announcing to everyone</u> that if they believe in the above infallible dogma of the Catholic Faith that they are not Catholic and cannot receive Holy Communion. When priests make public announcements that are heretical, <u>which impose the heretical belief upon the people attending the Mass,</u> then a Catholic must not attend the Mass or receive Holy Communion from such a priest. To do so would be a denial of the Catholic Faith. By receiving Communion from an SSPV priest who has made such an announcement, one would be tacitly (silently) indicating that he or she agrees with the priest's heretical position.

This is not necessarily the case with other heretical independent "traditionalist" priests who have not made announcements such as this and hold to their heretical positions more privately; and in fact, many of the heretical independent "traditionalist" priests are not notorious about their heresies, so that receiving Communion from them (as long as one does not support them or agree with them) is not a denial or a compromise of the Faith. But the SSPV has placed itself in another category – the category of notorious heretics who impose their heresy upon the people attending their Masses – which puts their Masses and their sacraments off limits. We posted this warning about the SSPV in the Summer of 2003 and they responded in the Fall 2003 issue of their magazine. Their response was very revealing and confirmed exactly what we said about them.

THE SSPV RESPONDS

The SSPV responded to us in the Fall, 2003 edition of their publication. Referring to Brother Michael Dimond and myself as "Brothers Grim" on the introductory page of their issue, Fr. Jenkins of the SSPV writes:

> The SSPV, The Roman Catholic, Fall, 2003, introductory page: "The controversy surrounds the Church's teaching regarding 'Baptism of Desire.' **The Brothers Grim try to make it look as though traditional Catholic priests are denying the Catholic doctrine that outside of the Church there is no salvation, but no traditional Catholic priest is disputing the necessity of membership in the Church for salvation.**"

Oh really? Remember that claim ("*no traditional Catholic priest is disputing the necessity of membership in the Church for salvation*") dear reader. And remember how I have pointed out that the thing which most characterizes the denial of *Outside the Church There is No Salvation* is dishonesty. Remember how we have seen that the heretics on this issue speak out of both sides of their mouth with a satanic double-tongue: one minute they tell you that the Church is necessary and the next they deny it; one minute they tell you that there is no salvation outside the Church and the next they explain it away. So now watch the heretics at work. Watch how the heretics of the SSPV teach on page 1 of their Fall, 2003 issue the exact thing they deny on the introductory page. On pages 1-8 of this same issue, the SSPV carries an article by Francis Fenton explaining what they consider the real meaning of *Outside the Church There is No Salvation*.

> The SSPV, *The Roman Catholic*, Fenton Article, Fall, 2003, p. 1: "It is a doctrine of our faith that 'outside the Church there is no salvation.' **This does not mean,**

however, either that an individual is assured eternal salvation simply because he is a member of the Roman Catholic Church or **that he cannot be saved because he is not an actual member of the body of the Church.**"

Did you get that? *Outside the Church There is No Salvation* "**does not mean… that he cannot be saved because he is not an actual member of the body of the Church.**" But on the introductory page of this issue, Fr. Jenkins told us on behalf of the SSPV that no traditional priest "is disputing the necessity of membership in the Church for salvation"! They assert here the exact heresy – word for word – which they claimed to reject on the introductory page! The statement here on page 1 of their publication (*that persons who are not members of the Church can be saved*) **thus proves that their statement on the introductory page** (*that no one is disputing the necessity of membership in the Church for salvation*) **was a complete lie!** It confirms what we have been saying all along about these dishonest heretics. The heretical Society of St. Pius V priests are so blinded by their denial of this truth that they cannot see that they are word for word contradicting themselves, in a matter of a few pages and in the very issue in which they purport to clarify their belief as in accord with Catholic teaching.

Thus, as I have said, it is a fact that the SSPV rejects the dogma Outside the Catholic Church There is No Salvation and they lie every time they say they uphold Catholic teaching on the necessity of Church membership for salvation. They indeed believe and obstinately hold that Buddhists, Jews, Hindus, etc. can be saved without the Catholic Faith. In fact, the same article in their Fall, 2003 issue proceeds to deny the dogma in bold fashion <u>over and over again</u>.

> The SSPV, *The Roman Catholic*, Fenton Article, Fall 2003, p. 5: "**A non-Catholic, then, who, through no grave fault of his own, is not a formal member of the Church at the moment of death, is certainly not going to lose his soul on that score.**"

> The SSPV, *The Roman Catholic*, Fenton Article, Fall 2003, p. 6: "**So, is it true and an article of faith that 'outside the Church there is no salvation'? Yes, it is. <u>Does this mean that a person, no matter how praiseworthy a life</u> he may have led, <u>will be eternally lost who</u>, through no grave fault of his own, <u>is not an actual member of the Church at the moment of death</u>? No, it does not.**"

Here again they assert word for word the heresy they claimed to reject on the introductory page. It is most appropriate here, in view of this horribly heretical statement, to quote the teaching of Pope Gregory XVI in *Mirari Vos* to condemn this awful and widespread heresy.

Pope Gregory XVI, *Mirari Vos* (# 13), Aug. 15, 1832: "Now we consider another abundant source of the evils with which the Church is afflicted at present: indifferentism. **This perverse opinion is spread on all sides by the fraud of the wicked who claim that it is possible to obtain the eternal salvation of the soul by the profession of any kind of religion, <u>as long as morality is maintained</u>.** Surely, in so clear a matter, you will drive this deadly error far from the people committed to your care. With the admonition of the apostle, that 'there is one God, one faith, one baptism' (Eph. 4:5), may those fear who contrive the notion that the safe harbor of salvation is open to persons of any religion whatever. They should consider the testimony of Christ Himself that 'those who are not with Christ are against Him,' (Lk. 11:23) and that they disperse unhappily <u>who do not gather with Him</u>. **Therefore, '<u>without a doubt, they will perish forever, unless they hold the Catholic faith</u> whole and inviolate (Athanasian Creed)."[636]**

But the SSPV's Fall, 2003 issue is not yet finished denying this dogma.

The SSPV, *The Roman Catholic*, Fenton Article, Fall 2003, p. 7: "<u>With the strict, literal interpretation of this doctrine, however, I must take issue</u>, for if I read and understand the strict interpreters correctly, nowhere is allowance made for invincible ignorance, conscience, or good faith on the part of those who are not actual or formal members of the Church at the moment of death. <u>It is inconceivable to me that, of all the billions of non-Catholics who have died in the past nineteen and one-half centuries, none of them were in good faith in this matter and, if they were, I simply refuse to believe that hell is their eternal destiny</u>."

This is brazen heresy against the dogma Outside the Church There is No Salvation. Allow me to briefly summarize, therefore, their Fall 2003 issue on this point:

- In response to our warning about them, the SSPV asserts on the introductory page that they have been misrepresented and that no one is "disputing the necessity of Church membership for salvation," while in the self-same issue of their magazine they run an article which proceeds to explicitly assert no less than 3 times that persons can be saved who are not members of the Catholic Church.
- The SSPV, according to page 5 of the Fenton Article in their publication, holds that non-Catholics can be saved.
- They find it "inconceivable" and "refuse to believe" that all who die as non-Catholics go to hell (p. 7), which is exactly what the Catholic Church has infallibly defined.
- They "take issue" with the "strict, literal" interpretation of this dogma (p. 7), which is to say, they reject the dogma as holy Mother Church has declared it (Vatican I).

> Pope Pius IX, First Vatican Council, Sess. 3, Chap. 2 on Revelation, 1870, ex cathedra: "Hence, also, that understanding of its sacred dogmas must be perpetually retained, which Holy Mother Church has once declared; and there must never be a recession from that meaning under the specious name of a deeper understanding."[637]

For these reasons only, we are glad that the SSPV attempted to respond to our charges of heresy against them; for in doing so they proved that our charges are 100% accurate and condemned themselves out of their own mouth.

> Pope Eugene IV, *Council of Florence*, "Cantate Domino," 1441, *ex cathedra*: **"The Holy Roman Church firmly believes, professes and preaches that all those who are outside the Catholic Church, not only pagans but also Jews or heretics and schismatics, cannot share in eternal life and will go into the everlasting fire which was prepared for the devil and his angels, unless they are joined to the Church before the end of their lives**; that the unity of this ecclesiastical body is of such importance that only those who abide in it do the Church's sacraments contribute to salvation and do fasts, almsgiving and other works of piety and practices of the Christian militia productive of eternal rewards; and that **nobody can be saved, no matter how much he has given away in alms and even if he has shed blood in the name of Christ, unless he has persevered in the bosom and unity of the Catholic Church."**[638]

Bishop Kelly (the leader of the SSPV), who also holds that members of non-Catholic religions (Protestants, Buddhists, Jews, etc.) can be saved without the Catholic Faith, is so heretical, in fact, that he wrote the following to someone we know on Sept. 25, 2003.

> Bishop Clarence Kelly of the SSPV, *Letter to Tim Whalen*, Sept. 25, 2003: "Contrary to what many think, the controversy stirred up by Fr. Feeney and now by the Diamonds (sic) is really not about the dogma that outside the Church there is no salvation. That is the cover for what they are really teaching which is **their own dogma that outside Baptism of Water there is no Salvation**."

Bishop Kelly calls the dogma that one must be baptized with water for salvation our own dogma!

> John 3:5,7 – "[Jesus saith] Amen, amen I say to thee, *unless a man be born again of water and the Holy Ghost, he cannot enter into the kingdom of God... wonder not, that I said to thee, you must be born again.*"

Bishop Kelly is such a heretic that he is refuted even by Dr. Ludwig Ott, as quoted already.

Dr. Ludwig Ott, *Fundamentals of Catholic Dogma*, p. 354: "1. Necessity of Baptism for Salvation- **Baptism by water** (Baptismus Fluminis) **is**, since the promulgation of the Gospel, **necessary for all** men **without exception**, for salvation. (*de fide*.)"[639]

Bishop Kelly is an abomination.

Pope Paul III, *The Council of Trent*, canons on the <u>Sacrament</u> of Baptism, canon 5, *ex cathedra*: **"If anyone says that baptism is optional, that is, not necessary for salvation (cf. Jn. 3:5): let him be anathema."**[640]

Pope Eugene IV, *The Council of Florence*, "Exultate Deo," Nov. 22, 1439, *ex cathedra*: **"Holy baptism, which is the gateway to the spiritual life, holds the first place among all the sacraments; through it we are made members of Christ and of the body of the Church. And since death entered the universe through the first man, 'unless we are born of water and the Spirit, we cannot,' as the Truth says, 'enter into the kingdom of heaven' [John 3:5].** The matter of this sacrament is real and natural water."[641]

Since the SSPV priests <u>notoriously preach and impose their heresy</u> by way of announcements at their chapels, no Catholic should receive any sacraments from them or attend their Masses at all (and of course no one can support them in any way under pain of grave sin).

THE CMRI

Unfortunately, the priests of the CMRI (Congregation of Mary Immaculate Queen) also reject the true meaning of the dogma Outside the Church There is No Salvation. They also adhere to and promote the heretical Protocol 122/49 and hold that those who die as non-Catholics can be saved.

In the Winter 1992 issue of *The Reign of Mary* (the CMRI's publication), the CMRI ran an article called "The Salvation of Those Outside the Church."[642] This is a word for word denial of the dogma Outside the Church There is No Salvation. It is equivalent to publishing an article called "The Original Sin Mary Had." The article, of course, inculcates the heresy that non-Catholics can be saved without the Catholic Faith. And this is their position to this day.

In the Winter of 1996, *The Reign of Mary* (publication of the CMRI) featured another heretical article called "The Boston Snare," by Bishop Robert McKenna.[643] Bishop McKenna believes that souls who die as non-Catholics can be saved; **he also believes that it is not heretical to believe that Jews who reject Christ can be in the state of grace**, as confirmed in an exchange of letters that I had with him in the Spring of 2004. Ironically, Bishop McKenna's thesis in the article is that this "heresy" of denying "baptism of desire" and "invincible ignorance" was the devil's snare which was sown in Boston, when the truth is actually just the opposite. Bishop McKenna and the CMRI (who printed his heretical article because they believe just as he does) are eating their words ["the Boston Snare"] right now by the scandal in Boston. But let's look at an excerpt from his article.

> Bishop Robert McKenna, "The Boston Snare," printed in the CMRI's Magazine *The Reign of Mary*, Vol. XXVI, No. 83: "**The doctrine, then, of no salvation outside the Church is to be understood in the sense of *knowingly* outside the Church**… But, they may object, if such be the sense of the dogma in question, why is the word 'knowingly' not part of the formula, 'Outside the Church no salvation'? **For the simple reason that the addition is unnecessary.** How could anyone know of the dogma and not be knowingly outside the Church? **The 'dogma' is not so much a doctrine intended for the instruction of Catholics,** since it is but a logical consequence of the Church's claim to be the true Church, **but rather a solemn and material warning or declaration for the benefit of those outside the one ark of salvation**." [644]

Frankly, this has to be one of the more heretical statements ever made by a person purporting to be a traditional Catholic Bishop. As can be seen clearly from these words, Bishop McKenna (like almost every modern priest) rejects the true meaning of this dogma and holds that non-Catholics can be saved without the Catholic Faith. In a desperate attempt to defend his heretical version of Outside the Church There is No Salvation, McKenna admittedly must change the understanding of the dogmatic formula proclaimed by the Popes. He tells us that the "true" meaning of the dogma is that only those who are "*knowingly*" outside the Church cannot be saved. Oh really? Where was that qualification ever mentioned in the dogmatic definitions on this topic? Nowhere!

> Pope Innocent III, *Fourth Lateran Council*, Constitution 1, 1215, *ex cathedra*: "There is indeed one universal Church of the faithful, outside of which nobody at all is saved, in which Jesus Christ is both priest and sacrifice." [345]

> Pope Boniface VIII, *Unam Sanctam*, Nov. 18, 1302, *ex cathedra*:
> "With Faith urging us we are forced to believe and to hold the one, holy, Catholic Church and that, apostolic, and we firmly believe and simply confess this Church outside of which there is no salvation nor remission of sin… Furthermore, we declare, say, define, and proclaim to every human creature that they by absolute necessity for salvation are entirely subject to the Roman Pontiff." [646]

> Pope Clement V, *Council of Vienne*, Decree # 30, 1311-1312, *ex cathedra*:" Since however there is for both regulars and seculars, for superiors and subjects, for exempt and non-exempt, *one universal Church, outside of which there is no salvation*, for all of whom there is *one Lord, one faith, and one baptism*…" [647]

> Pope Eugene IV, *Council of Florence*, Sess. 8, Nov. 22, 1439:
> "Whoever *wishes* to be saved, needs above all to hold the Catholic faith; unless each one preserves this whole and inviolate, he will without a doubt perish in eternity." [648]

Pope Eugene IV, *Council of Florence*, "Cantate Domino," 1441, *ex cathedra*:
"The Holy Roman Church firmly believes, professes and preaches that <u>all those who are outside</u> the Catholic Church, not only <u>pagans</u> but also Jews or <u>heretics</u> and <u>schismatics</u>, cannot share in eternal life and will go into the everlasting fire which was prepared for the devil and his angels, unless they are joined to the Church before the end of their lives; that the unity of this ecclesiastical body is of such importance that <u>only those who abide in it</u> do the Church's sacraments contribute to salvation and do fasts, almsgiving and other works of piety and practices of the Christian militia productive of eternal rewards; and that <u>nobody</u> can be saved, no matter how much he has given away in alms and even if he has shed blood in the name of Christ, unless he has persevered in the bosom and unity of the Catholic Church."[649]

Pope Leo X, *Fifth Lateran Council*, Session 11, Dec. 19, 1516, *ex cathedra*: "For, regulars and seculars, prelates and subjects, exempt and non-exempt, belong to the one universal Church, outside of which <u>no one at all is saved</u>, and they all have *one Lord and one faith*."[650]

Pope Pius IV, Council of Trent, *Iniunctum nobis*, Nov. 13, 1565, *ex cathedra*: *"This true Catholic faith, outside of which <u>no one</u> can be saved… I now profess and truly hold…"*[651]

Pope Benedict XIV, *Nuper ad nos*, March 16, 1743, Profession of Faith: **"**This faith of the Catholic Church, without which <u>no one</u> can be saved, and which of my own accord I now profess and truly hold…"[652]

Pope Pius IX, *Vatican Council I*, Session 2, Profession of Faith, 1870, *ex cathedra*: "This true Catholic faith, outside of which <u>none</u> can be saved, which I now freely profess and truly hold…"[653]

Recognizing that his understanding runs contrary to the clear words of the dogmatic definitions on the topic – none of which ever mentioned "knowingly" <u>and all of which eliminated all exceptions</u> – Bishop McKenna attempts to explain away the problem.

Bishop Robert McKenna, "The Boston Snare," printed in the CMRI's Magazine *The Reign of Mary*, Vol. XXVI, No. 83*:* "The 'dogma' is <u>not so much a doctrine intended for the instruction of Catholics</u>… **but rather a solemn and material warning or declaration for the benefit of those outside the one ark of salvation**."[654]

The dogma Outside the Catholic Church There is No Salvation, according to McKenna and the heretical CMRI which printed this article in their magazine (Vol. XXIV, No. 83), is not a truth from heaven, but a warning or admonition written for non-Catholics! This is nonsense and flat out heresy.

Pope Pius X, *Lamentabile*, The Errors of the Modernists, July 3, 1907, #22: "**The dogmas which the Church professes as revealed <u>are not truths fallen from heaven</u>**, but they are a kind of interpretation of religious facts, which the human mind by a laborious effort prepared for itself."[655]- **Condemned**

<u>**Dogmas are truths fallen from heaven which cannot possibly contain error**</u>. They are not merely human statements, written to warn non-Catholics, which are subject to correction and qualification. Dogmas are infallible definitions of the truth which can

never be changed or corrected, and have no need to be changed or corrected since they cannot possibly contain error. Dogmas are defined so that Catholics must know <u>what they must believe as true from divine revelation</u> without any possibility of error, which is exactly the opposite of what McKenna and the CMRI assert.

And this is perhaps what is most important about the heresy of Bishop McKenna and the CMRI: the dogma deniers are revealing by such ridiculous argumentation that *their* "version" of this dogma is incompatible <u>with the words of the dogmatic definitions</u>; for if their version were compatible with the dogmatic definitions <u>they would never be forced into heretical statements such as those above</u>.

The CMRI has printed other heretical articles on this issue, including in the Winter of 2004. In this article, they compile basically all of the dishonest and/or invalid arguments usually brought forward by baptism of desire advocates, all of which have been refuted in this document. Worst of all, they misquote the Council of Trent, Sess. 6, Chap. 4 (as discussed in Section 16 of this document). And ironically, the priests of the CMRI don't actually believe in baptism of desire because they don't believe that one must desire baptism to be saved. They hold that members of false religions can be saved without the Catholic Faith and are complete heretics. It is a demonstrable fact, easily ascertained by just asking any of their priests, that the priests of the CMRI adhere to the heretical Protocol 122/49 and believe that invincible ignorance can save members of false, non-Catholic religions and persons who don't believe in Jesus Christ. This heresy is held by almost all priests today.

36. Conclusion

In this document I have shown that it is the infallible teaching of the Catholic Church – and therefore the true teaching of Jesus Christ – that only those who die as baptized Catholics can be saved. Anyone who refuses to accept this teaching is not a Catholic. The fact that most of the world refuses to accept this teaching must not get us discouraged. This has been predicted and God is still with His Church, even though it has been reduced to a remnant of faithful Catholics.

Fr. William Jurgens: "At one point in the Church's history, only a few years before Gregory's [Nazianz] present preaching (+380 A.D.), <u>perhaps the number of Catholic bishops in possession of sees, as opposed to Arian bishops in possession of sees, was no greater than something between 1% and 3% of the total</u>. **Had doctrine been determined by popularity, today we should all be deniers of Christ and opponents of the Spirit.**"[656]

Fr. William Jurgens: "In the time of the Emperor Valens (4ᵗʰ century), Basil was virtually the only orthodox Bishop in all the East who succeeded in retaining charge of his see… If it has no other importance for modern man, **a knowledge of the history of Arianism should demonstrate at least that the Catholic Church takes no account of popularity and numbers in shaping and maintaining doctrine**: else, we should long since have had to abandon Basil and Hilary and Athanasius and Liberius and Ossius and call ourselves after Arius."[657]

If the Arian heresy in the 4ᵗʰ century was so bad that approximately 1% of the jurisdictional bishops remained Catholic and 99% became Arian, and the Great Apostasy preceding the Second Coming of Christ is predicted to be even worse – the worst apostasy of all time (2 Thess. 2) – then one should not be incredulous at the fact that there are barely any authentically Catholic priests in the world today who believe in the true meaning of Outside the Church There is No Salvation and the necessity of the Sacrament of Baptism.

Luke 18:8 "But yet the Son of man, when he cometh, shall he find, think you, faith on earth?"

We must surge forward in defense of this faith and preserve it undefiled. We must inform in charity those non-Catholics whom God puts on our path that they must embrace the Catholic Faith – the traditional, historical Catholic Faith – if they want to be saved. And we must inform those professing to be Catholic, but who don't believe in these dogmas, how they are in error so that they can be corrected.

We believe in this dogma only because it is the truth of Jesus Christ. And because we love non-Catholics and have true concern for their eternal happiness as their true friends, we tell them that they cannot obtain eternal happiness except in the Catholic Church (the traditional Catholic Church, not the Novus Ordo/Vatican II sect).

Luke 12:4-5: "[Jesus saith] And I say to you, my friends: **Be not afraid of them who kill the body**, and after that have no more that they can do. But I will shew you whom you shall fear: fear ye him, who after he hath killed, hath power to cast into hell. Yea, I say to you, fear him."

Finally, one cannot compromise this faith at any cost. One cannot financially support any priest who does not hold that only baptized Catholics can be saved, which includes almost every priest today. **One cannot financially support or give Mass stipends to any priest who accepts baptism of desire or the heresy of salvation for the "invincibly ignorant."** One cannot join or be affiliated with any religious society which does not preserve and publicly defend this dogma and *all* the teachings of the Church.

A Catholic should not attend funerals of deceased non-Catholics, since this implies that non-Catholics can be saved, which is heresy. A Catholic also should not attend the funerals of "Catholics" who were known to deny this dogma or who were known to obstinately support those who denied it. Further, a Catholic should not attend the Weddings of non-Catholics or members of the Novus Ordo, since this gives scandal and it gives the non-Catholics getting married the impression that you approve of them where they are. Nor should a Catholic attend the Wedding of a person who claims to be a "traditional Catholic" yet obstinately supports the heretical positions or heretical groups exposed in this document. To do so would be a scandal and a compromise of the Faith.

On Judgment Day, God will separate those who have preserved the true faith and the state of grace from those who have not. Those who have defiled this faith will have to line up with the reprobate. So those who, knowing these facts, continue to financially support, even in the slightest way, groups which believe in baptism of desire or salvation for the "invincibly ignorant" or which deny any other teaching of the Church, can expect to line up behind the reprobate who have defiled the faith on Judgment Day.

The Church teaches that one may receive the Sacraments from a validly ordained priest who holds a heretical position (if the priest does not notoriously preach or impose that heresy), but one may not support him financially or compromise the faith. To *put money in the collection basket* of a priest or a group who does not uphold the faith is to deny the faith. To give them donations is to deny the faith. Obviously, the Catholic Faith does not forbid us to buy Catholic books (etc.) from a group which may be heretical, but one must not donate to such a group or even give them Mass stipends. If it comes down to compromising the faith or attending Mass and receiving Communion, one must stop attending Mass and receiving Communion, because one can be saved without attending Mass and receiving Communion, especially in a state of necessity; but one cannot ever be saved without the true faith.

Apoc. 2:10 "Be thou faithful until death: and I will give thee the crown of life."

Apoc. 14:12 "Here is the patience of the saints, who keep the commandments of God, and the faith of Jesus."

Apoc. 3:11 "Behold, I come quickly: hold fast that which thou hast, that no man take thy crown."

Permission is granted to make copies of this book or to quote sections from it, but the author's name must be given.

Extra copies of this book are available from Most Holy Family Monastery.

Copyright © 2004: Most Holy Family Monastery

Most Holy Family Monastery
4425 Schneider Rd.
Fillmore, NY 14735
(800) 275-1126
(585) 567-4433
www.mostholyfamilymonastery.com

Endnotes

* The first time any source is cited in these endnotes, its complete information is given, including publisher, year, etc. The second and following times a given source is cited, only the title and page number are given.

[1] *Decrees of the Ecumenical Councils*, Sheed & Ward and Georgetown University Press, 1990, Vol. 1, p. 230; Denzinger 430.

[2] Denzinger, *The Sources of Catholic Dogma*, B. Herder Book. Co., Thirtieth Edition, 1957, 468-469.

[3] *Decrees of the Ecumenical Councils*, Vol. 1, p. 386.

[4] *Decrees of the Ecumenical Councils*, Vol. 1, pp. 550-553; Denzinger 39-40.

[5] *Decrees of the Ecumenical Councils*, Vol. 1, p. 578; Denzinger 714.

[6] *Decrees of the Ecumenical Councils*, Vol. 1, p. 646.

[7] Denzinger 1000.

[8] Denzinger 1473.

[9] *Decrees of the Ecumenical Councils*, Vol. 2, p. 803.

[10] Denzinger 1837.

[11] Denzinger 1836.

[12] Denzinger 163.

[13] Denzinger 1839.

[14] *The Papal Encyclicals*, by Claudia Carlen, Raleigh: The Pierian Press, 1990, Vol. 2 (1878-1903), p. 394.

[15] Denzinger 2021.

[16] *The Papal Encyclicals*, Vol. 2 (1878-1903), p. 394.

[17] Fr. Christopher Rengers, *The 33 Doctors of the Church*, Rockford: IL, Tan Books, 2000, p. 273.

[18] Denzinger 1800.

[19] Denzinger 2022.

[20] Denzinger 2054.

[21] *The Papal Encyclicals*, Vol. 1 (1740-1878), p. 236.

[22] Denzinger 1792.

[23] *The Papal Encyclicals*, Vol. 1 (1740-1878), p. 230.

[24] Denzinger 423.

[25] Denzinger 570b.

[26] *The Papal Encyclicals*, Vol. 1 (1740-1878), p. 201.

[27] *The Papal Encyclicals*, Vol. 1 (1740-1878), p. 207.

[28] *The Papal Encyclicals*, Vol. 1 (1740-1878), pp. 237-238.

[29] *The Papal Encyclicals*, Vol. 1 (1740-1878), p. 229.

[30] *The Papal Encyclicals*, Vol. 1 (1740-1878), p. 289.

[31] *The Papal Encyclicals*, Vol. 1 (1740-1878), p. 297 and footnote 4.

[32] Denzinger 1716.

[33] *The Papal Encyclicals*, Vol. 2 (1878-1903), p. 474.

[34] *The Papal Encyclicals*, Vol. 3 (1903-1939), p. 22.

[35] *The Papal Encyclicals*, Vol. 3 (1903-1939), pp. 121-122.

[36] *The Papal Encyclicals*, Vol. 3 (1903-1939), p. 318.

[37] Denzinger 895; *Decrees of the Ecumenical Councils*, Vol. 2, p. 704.

[38] Denzinger 696; *Decrees of the Ecumenical Councils*, Vol. 1, p. 542.

[39] Denzinger 2286.

[40] *The Papal Encyclicals*, Vol. 4 (1939-1958). p. 42.

[41] *The Papal Encyclicals*, Vol. 4 (1939-1958). p. 127.

[42] Denzinger 430.

[43] Fr. Casimir Kucharek, *The Byzantine-Slav Liturgy of St. John Chrysostom*, Combermere, Ontario, Canada: Alleluia Press, 1971, p. 475.

[44] Fr. Casimir Kucharek, *The Byzantine-Slav Liturgy of St. John Chrysostom*, p. 326.

[45] Fr. Casimir Kucharek, *The Byzantine-Slav Liturgy of St. John Chrysostom*, p. 100.

[46] *The Catholic Encyclopedia*, "Faithful," Volume 5, Robert Appleton Company, 1909, p. 769.

[47] *The Catholic Encyclopedia*, "Catechumen," Volume 3, 1908, p. 430.

[48] Fr. Casimir Kucharek, *The Byzantine-Slav Liturgy of St. John Chrysostom*, p. 458.

[49] *The Papal Encyclicals*, Vol. 3 (1903-1939), p. 273.

[50] *The Sunday Sermons of the Great Fathers*. Regnery, Co: Chicago, IL, 1963, Vol. 4, p. 5.

[51] *Catechism of the Council of Trent*, Tan Books: Rockford, IL, 1982, p. 184.

[52] *Catechism of the Council of Trent*, p. 159.

[53] Denzinger 570a.

[54] Denzinger 799-800.

[55] Denzinger 468-469.

[56] *The Papal Encyclicals*, Vol. 2 (1878-1903), pp. 86-87.

[57] Denzinger 895; *Decrees of the Ecumenical Councils*, Vol. 2, p. 704.

[58] Denzinger 861; *Decrees of the Ecumenical Councils*, Vol. 2, p. 685.

[59] Denzinger 792.

[60] Denzinger 696; *Decrees of the Ecumenical Councils*, Vol. 1, p. 542.

[61] *Decrees of the Ecumenical Councils*, Vol. 1, p. 230; Denzinger 430.

[62] Denzinger 1470.

[63] Denzinger 2195; *The Papal Encyclicals*, Vol. 3 (1903-1939), p. 274.

[64] Denzinger 1788.

[65] Denzinger 696; *Decrees of the Ecumenical Councils*, Vol. 1, p. 542.

[66] Denzinger 858.

[67] Denzinger 861; *Decrees of the Ecumenical Councils*, Vol. 2, p. 685.

[68] Denzinger 791; *Decrees of the Ecumenical Councils*, Vol. 2, pp. 666-667.

[69] Denzinger 102, authentic addition to Can. 3.

[70] Denzinger 447.

[71] Denzinger 712; *Decrees of the Ecumenical Councils*, Vol. 1, p. 576.

[72] *Decrees of the Ecumenical Councils*, Vol. 1, p. 422.

[73] *Decrees of the Ecumenical Councils*, Vol. 1, pp. 421-422.

[74] Denzinger 102, authentic addition to Can. 2.

[75] Denzinger 791.

[76] *Decrees of the Ecumenical Councils*, Vol. 1, p. 528; Denzinger 693.

[77] Denzinger 1526.

[78] *The Papal Encyclicals*, Vol. 3 (1903-1939), p. 530.

[79] *The Papal Encyclicals*, Vol. 3 (1903-1939), p. 273.

[80] *Decrees of the Ecumenical Councils*, Vol. 1, p. 24.

[81] *Decrees of the Ecumenical Councils*, Vol. 1, p. 70.

[82] Denzinger 347.

[83] Denzinger 468.

[84] *Decrees of the Ecumenical Councils*, Vol. 1, p. 386.

[85] *The Papal Encyclicals*, Vol. 1 (1740-1878), p. 174.

[86] *The Papal Encyclicals*, Vol. 1 (1740-1878), p. 201.

[87] *The Papal Encyclicals*, Vol. 1 (1740-1878), p. 222.

[88] *The Papal Encyclicals*, Vol. 1 (1740-1878), pp. 237-238.

[89] *The Papal Encyclicals*, Vol. 2 (1878-1903), p. 481.

[90] Denzinger 482.

[91] *Decrees of the Ecumenical Councils*, Vol. 1, pp. 550-553; Denzinger 39-40.

[92] Denzinger 1349a.

[93] Denzinger 1349b.

[94] St. Thomas Aquinas, *Summa Theologica*, Pt. II-II, Q. 2., A. 7.

[95] St. Thomas Aquinas, *Summa Theologica*, Pt. II-II, Q. 2., A. 8.

[96] *The Papal Encyclicals*, Vol. 1 (1740-1878), p. 45.

[97] *The Papal Encyclicals*, Vol. 1 (1740-1878), p. 46.

[98] *The Papal Encyclicals*, Vol. 3 (1903-1939), p. 30.

[99] Tixeront, *Handbook of Patrology*, St. Louis, MO: B. Herder Book Co., 1951.

[100] Jurgens, *The Faith of the Early Fathers*, Collegeville, MN, The Liturgical Press, 1970, Vol. 1: 34.

[101] Jurgens, *The Faith of the Early Fathers*, Vol. 1: 92.

[102] Jurgens, *The Faith of the Early Fathers*, Vol. 1: 126.

[103] Jurgens, *The Faith of the Early Fathers*, Vol. 1: 135a.

[104] Jurgens, *The Faith of the Early Fathers*, Vol. 1: 219; 220.

[105] Jurgens, *The Faith of the Early Fathers*, Vol. 1: 181.

[106] Jurgens, *The Faith of the Early Fathers*, Vol. 1: 306.

[107] Jurgens, *The Faith of the Early Fathers*, Vol. 1: 302

[108] Jurgens, *The Faith of the Early Fathers*, Vol. 1: 92.

[109] Jurgens, *The Faith of the Early Fathers*, Vol. 1: 712.

[110] *Patrologiae Cursus Completus*: Series Graecae, 46:417b, Fr. J.P. Migne, Paris: 1866; quoted in Michael Malone, *The Only-Begotten*, Monrovia, CA: Catholic Treasures, 1999, p. 175.

[111] Jurgens, *The Faith of the Early Fathers*, Vol. 1: 407.

[112] Jurgens, *The Faith of the Early Fathers*, Vol. 1: 501.

[113] Jurgens, *The Faith of the Early Fathers*, Vol. 1: 681.

[114] Jurgens, *The Faith of the Early Fathers*, Vol. 1: 683.

[115] Jurgens, *The Faith of the Early Fathers*, Vol. 1: 810a.

[116] *The Sunday Sermons of the Great Fathers*, Vol. 3, p. 10.

[117] Jurgens, *The Faith of the Early Fathers*, Vol. 1: 899.

[118] *The Sunday Sermons of the Great Fathers*, Vol. 2, p. 51.

[119] Jurgens, *The Faith of the Early Fathers*, Vol. 1: 910r.

[120] Jurgens, *The Faith of the Early Fathers*, Vol. 2: 1323.

[121] Jurgens, *The Faith of the Early Fathers*, Vol. 2: 1324.

[122] Jurgens, *The Faith of the Early Fathers*, Vol. 2: 1330.

[123] Jurgens, *The Faith of the Early Fathers*, Vol. 2: 1206; *The Nicene and Post-Nicene Fathers*, New York: Charles Scribner's Sons, 1905, Vol. XIII, p. 197.

[124] Jurgens, *The Faith of the Early Fathers*, Vol. 3: 1536.

[125] Jurgens, *The Faith of the Early Fathers*, Vol. 3: 2016.

[126] *The Sunday Sermons of the Great Fathers*, Vol. 1, p. 89.

[127] *The Sunday Sermons of the Great Fathers*, Vol. 2, p. 412.

[128] Jurgens, *The Faith of the Early Fathers*, Vol. 3, pp. 14-15 footnote 31.

[129] Denzinger 861; *Decrees of the Ecumenical Councils*, Vol. 2, p. 685.

[130] Jurgens, *The Faith of the Early Fathers*, Vol. 1, p. 413.

[131] Jurgens, *The Faith of the Early Fathers*, Vol. 2 940 .

[132] Denzinger 1526.

[133] *The Catholic Encyclopedia*, Volume 9, "Limbo," 1910, p. 257.

[134] *The Papal Encyclicals*, Vol. 1 (1740-1878), p. 29.

[135] Denzinger 1320.

[136] *The Papal Encyclicals*, Vol. 4 (1939-1958), pp. 178-179.

[137] Jurgens, *The Faith of the Early Fathers*, Vol. 1 811.

[138] Jurgens, *The Faith of the Early Fathers*, Vol. 3: 2269.

[139] Jurgens, *The Faith of the Early Fathers*, Vol. 3: 2251a.

[140] Jurgens, *The Faith of the Early Fathers*, Vol. 3: 2275.

[141] Jurgens, *The Faith of the Early Fathers*, Vol. 3: 2271.

[142] Denzinger 1526.

[143] Jurgens, *The Faith of the Early Fathers*, Vol. 2: 1139.

[144] Barlam and Josaphat, Woodward & Heineman, trans., pp. 169-171.

[145] Denzinger 714.

[146] Jurgens, *The Faith of the Early Fathers*, Vol. 1: 598

[147] Jurgens, *The Faith of the Early Fathers*, Vol. 1: 593 .

[148] Jurgens, *The Faith of the Early Fathers*, Vol. 1: 591 .

[149] Denzinger 1837.

[150] Jurgens, *The Faith of the Early Fathers*, Vol. 1: 309 .

[151] Jurgens, *The Faith of the Early Fathers*, Vol. 1: 310a .

[152] Denzinger 712; *Decrees of the Ecumenical Councils*, Vol. 1, p. 576.

[153] Jurgens, *The Faith of the Early Fathers*, Vol. 1: 306.

[154] Bro. Robert Mary, *Father Feeney and The Truth About Salvation*, p. 176.

[155] Denzinger 165.

[156] Abbot Giuseppe Ricciotti, *The Age of Martyrs – Christianity from Diocletian to Constantine*, Tan Books, Originally published 1959, reprinted 1999, p. 90.

[157] Denzinger 696; *Decrees of the Ecumenical Councils*, Vol. 1, p. 542.

[158] *Decrees of the Ecumenical Councils*, Vol. 1, p. 6.

[159] *The Catholic Encyclopedia*, "Baptism," Volume 2, 1907, p. 265.

[160] Donald Attwater, *A Catholic Dictionary*, Tan Books, 1997, p. 310.

[161] Denzinger 861; *Decrees of the Ecumenical Councils*, Vol. 2, p. 685.

[162] Quoted by Bro. Robert Mary, *Father Feeney and The Truth About Salvation*, Winchester, NH: St. Benedict Center, 1995, pp. 184-186.

[163] Denzinger 714.

[164] Denzinger 895; *Decrees of the Ecumenical Councils*, Vol. 2, p. 704.

[165] Denzinger 2286.

[166] *The Papal Encyclicals*, Vol. 4 (1939-1958), p. 127.

[167] Fr. Jean-Marc Rulleau, *Baptism of Desire* Kansas City, MO: Angelus Press, 1999, p. 36; Sulpicius Severus, *Life of St. Martin*, 7, 1-7.

[168] Father Albert J. Herbert, *Raised From The Dead*, Rockford, IL: Tan Books, 1986, footnote adjacent to p. 93.

[169] Michael Malone, *The Only-Begotten*, p. 384.

[170] Michael Malone, *The Only-Begotten*, p. 385.

[171] Michael Malone, *The Only-Begotten*, p. 386.

[172] Fr. E. Laveille, S.J., *The Life of Fr. De Smet*, Rockford, IL: Tan Books, 2000, p. 93.

[173] Fr. E. Laveille, S.J., *The Life of Fr. De Smet*, p. 172.

[174] Quoted by Michael Malone, *The Only-Begotten*, p. 364; Malone is quoting *The Catechist*, by Rev. Canon Howe, cf. 9th ed., London: Burns, Oates, and Washbourne, 1922, vol. 1, p. 63.

[175] Fr. E. Laveille, S.J., *The Life of Fr. De Smet*, pp. 165-166, footnote 7.

[176] Introduction to *The Catholic Controversy* by St. Francis De Sales, Tan Books, 1989, p. lv.

[177] St. Francis De Sales, *The Catholic Controversy*, pp. 156-157.

[178] Quoted by Michael Malone, The Only-Begotten, p. 386; taken from Rev. Canon Howe, *The Catechist*, London: Burns, Oates, and Washbourne, Tenth Edition, 1922, Vol. 2, cf. pp. 596-597.

[179] Denzinger 1784.

[180] Denzinger 530

[181] Fr. Jean-Marc Rulleau, *Baptism of Desire*, p. 63.

[182] Fr. Francois Laisney, *Is Feeneyism Catholic?*, Angelus Press, 2001, p. 79.

[183] Jurgens, *The Faith of the Early Fathers*, Vol. 3: 1630.

[184] *The Catechism of the Council of Trent*, p. 171.

[185] Jurgens, *The Faith of the Early Fathers*, Vol. 3: 1536.

[186] Jurgens, *The Faith of the Early Fathers*, Vol. 3: 1717.

[187] Jurgens, *The Faith of the Early Fathers*, Vol. 3: 1496.

[188] Quoted by Fr. Jean-Marc Rulleau, *Baptism of Desire*, p. 33.

[189] Quoted by Fr. Jean-Marc Rulleau, *Baptism of Desire*, pp. 30-31.

[190] Bro. Robert Mary, *Fr. Feeney and the Truth About Salvation*, p. 132.

[191] Bro. Robert Mary, *Fr. Feeney and the Truth About Salvation*, p. 133.

[192] Fr. Jean-Marc Rulleau, *Baptism of Desire*, p. 37.

[193] Jurgens, *The Faith of the Early Fathers*, Vol. 2: 1330.

[194] Jurgens, *The Faith of the Early Fathers*, Vol. 2: 1323.

[195] Jurgens, *The Faith of the Early Fathers*, Vol. 2: 1324.

[196] Michael Malone, *The Only-Begotten*, p. 404.

[197] Jurgens, *The Faith of the Early Fathers*, Vol. 2: 1330.

[198] Jurgens, *The Faith of the Early Fathers*, Vol. 3, pp. 14-15 footnote 31.

[199] Jurgens, *The Faith of the Early Fathers*, Vol. 2: 1012.

[200] Dom Prosper Gueranger, *The Liturgical Year*, Fitzwilliam, NH: Loreto Publications, 2000, Vol. 8, p. 478.

[201] Dom Prosper Gueranger, *The Liturgical Year*, Vol. 8, p. 475.

[202] Saint John Chrysostom, "The Consolation of Death," *Sunday Sermons of the Great Fathers*, vol. IV, p. 363.

[203] Saint John Chrysostom, "The Consolation of Death," *Sunday Sermons of the Great Fathers*, vol. IV, p. 363.

[204] *Hom. in Io.* 25, 3 = PG 59 151-152; quoted by Fr. Jean-Marc Rulleau, *Baptism of Desire*, p. 34.

[205] *The Nicene and Post-Nicene Fathers*, Vol. XIII, p. 197.

[206] St. John Chrysostom, *Homily XXV*, on the Gospel of John 3:5.

[207] *The Catholic Encyclopedia*, "Baptism," Volume 2, 1907, p. 265.

[208] J. Corblet, *Histoire du sacrement de bapteme*, (Paris: Palme, 1881), pp. 155-56; quoted by Fr. Jean-Marc Rulleau, *Baptism of Desire*, p. 36.

[209] Dr. Ludwig Ott, *Fundamentals of Catholic Dogma*, St. Louis, MO: B. Herder Book, Co., 1954, p. 309.

[210] *The Papal Encyclicals*, Vol. 1 (1740-1878), p. 230.

[211] Fr. Jacques Dupuis, S.J. and Fr. Josef Neuner, S.J., *The Christian Faith*, Sixth Revised and Enlarged Edition, Staten Island, NY: Alba House, 1996, p. 540.

[212] Quoted by Fr. Jean-Marc Rulleau, *Baptism of Desire*, p. 37.

[213] Quoted by Fr. Jean-Marc Rulleau, *Baptism of Desire*, p. 37.

[214] Quoted by Fr. Jean-Marc Rulleau, *Baptism of Desire*, p. 37.

[215] Denzinger 1784.

[216] Jurgens, *The Faith of the Early Fathers*, Vol. 3: 1496.

[217] Denzinger 696; *Decrees of the Ecumenical Councils*, Vol. 1, p. 542.

[218] St. Thomas Aquinas, *Summa Theologica*, Pt. III, Q. 14, Art. 3, Reply to Obj. 1.

[219] Michael Malone, *The Only-Begotten*, p. 395.

[220] Michael Malone, *The Only-Begotten*, p. 70.

[221] Denzinger 1837.

[222] Fr. Francois Laisney, *Is Feeneyism Catholic?*, p. 9.

[223] Denzinger 861; *Decrees of the Ecumenical Councils*, Vol. 2, p. 685.

[224] Denzinger 861; *Decrees of the Ecumenical Councils*, Vol. 2, p. 685.

[225] *The Papal Encyclicals*, Vol. 1 (1740-1878), p. 29.

[226] *The Papal Encyclicals*, Vol. 4 (1939-1958), pp. 178-179.

[227] *The Papal Encyclicals*, Vol. 3 (1903-1939), p. 92.

[228] Denzinger 858.

[229] Denzinger 482.

[230] Quoted by Fr. Jean-Marc Rulleau, *Baptism of Desire*, pp. 55-56.

[231] Quoted by Fr. Jean-Marc Rulleau, *Baptism of Desire*, p. 55.

[232] Quoted by Fr. Jean-Marc Rulleau, *Baptism of Desire*, p. 55.

[233] St. Thomas Aquinas, *Summa Theologica*, Pt. II-II, Q. 2., A. 7.

[234] St. Thomas Aquinas, *Summa Theologica*, Pt. II-II, Q. 2., A. 8.

[235] *Decrees of the Ecumenical Councils*, Vol. 1, p. 81.

[236] *Decrees of the Ecumenical Councils*, Vol. 1, p. 112.

[237] *Decrees of the Ecumenical Councils*, Vol. 1, p. 127.

[238] Denzinger 165.

[239] Denzinger 246.

[240] Denzinger 1463.

[241] Denzinger 165.

[242] Denzinger 790.

[243] Denzinger 795.

[244] *Decrees of the Ecumenical Councils*, Vol. 1, p. 81.

[245] *Decrees of the Ecumenical Councils*, Vol. 1, p. 81.

[246] Denzinger 790.

[247] Denzinger 696; *Decrees of the Ecumenical Councils*, Vol. 1, p. 542.

[248] Denzinger 791; *Decrees of the Ecumenical Councils*, Vol. 2, pp. 666-667.

[249] Denzinger 858.

[250] Denzinger 861; *Decrees of the Ecumenical Councils*, Vol. 2, p. 685.

[251] Denzinger 796; *Decrees of the Ecumenical Councils*, Vol. 2, p. 672.

[252] *Decrees of the Ecumenical Councils*, Vol. 1, p. 578; Denzinger 714.

[253] Denzinger 792a.

[254] Denzinger 931.

[255] *The Catechism of the Council of Trent*, p. 180.

[256] Denzinger 796; *Decrees of the Ecumenical Councils*, Vol. 2, p. 672.

[257] Denzinger 861; *Decrees of the Ecumenical Councils*, Vol. 2, p. 685.

[258] Denzinger 791; *Decrees of the Ecumenical Councils*, Vol. 2, pp. 666-667.

[259] Denzinger 858.

[260] Denzinger 696; *Decrees of the Ecumenical Councils*, Vol. 1, p. 542.

[261] Denzinger 799-800.

[262] Denzinger 1800.

[263] *The Papal Encyclicals*, Vol. 2 (1878-1903), p. 402.

[264] *Decrees of the Ecumenical Councils*, Vol. 1, p. 230; Denzinger 430.

[265] Denzinger 468-469.

[266] *Decrees of the Ecumenical Councils*, Vol. 1, p. 386.

[267] *Decrees of the Ecumenical Councils*, Vol. 1, pp. 550-553; Denzinger 39-40.

[268] *Decrees of the Ecumenical Councils*, Vol. 1, p. 578; Denzinger 714.

[269] *Decrees of the Ecumenical Councils*, Vol. 1, p. 646.

[270] Denzinger 1000.

[271] Denzinger 1473.

[272] *Decrees of the Ecumenical Councils*, Vol. 2, p. 803.

[273] *The Papal Encyclicals*, Vol. 1 (1740-1878), p. 229.

[274] *The Papal Encyclicals*, Vol. 3 (1903-1939), p. 157.

[275] Denzinger 377.

[276] St. Thomas Aquinas, *Summa Theologica*, Pt. II-II, Q. 10., A. 1.

[277] Quoted by Fr. Jean-Marc Rulleau, *Baptism of Desire*, pp. 55-56.

[278] Quoted by Fr. Jean-Marc Rulleau, *Baptism of Desire*, p. 55.

[279] Quoted by Fr. Jean-Marc Rulleau, *Baptism of Desire*, p. 55.

[280] *Sermons of St. Alphonsus Liguori*, Tan Books, 1982, p. 219.

[281] Michael Malone, *The Apostolic Digest*, Monrovia, CA: Catholic Treasures, Abridged Edition, 1994, p. 159.

[282] Saint Alphonsus Maria De Liguori, *Preparation for Death*, unabridged version, Redemptorist Fathers: Brooklyn, NY, 1926, p. 339.

[283] Denzinger 1647.

[284] *The Papal Encyclicals*, Vol. 1 (1740-1878), p. 369.

[285] *The Papal Encyclicals*, Vol. 1 (1740-1878), p. 370.

[286] Denzinger 1791.

[287] *The Papal Encyclicals*, Vol. 1 (1740-1878), p. 297 and footnote 4.

[288] *The Papal Encyclicals*, Vol. 1 (1740-1878), p. 289.

[289] Denzinger 1716.

[290] Fr. Michael Muller, C.SS.R., *The Catholic Dogma*, New York: Benzinger Bros., 1888, pp. 217-218.

[291] Fr. Leonard Feeney, *Bread of Life*, Cambridge, MA: St. Benedict Center, 1952, p. 53.

[292] *The Sunday Sermons of the Great Fathers*, Vol. 1, p. 42.

[293] Denzinger 1806.

[294] Jurgens, *The Faith of the Early Fathers*, Vol. 3: 1997.

[295] Denzinger 2195; *The Papal Encyclicals*, Vol. 3 (1903-1939), p. 274.

[296] Jurgens, *The Faith of the Early Fathers*, Vol. 3: 1946.

[297] Jurgens, *The Faith of the Early Fathers*, Vol. 3: 2047.

[298] *The Papal Encyclicals*, Vol. 1 (1740-1878), p. 46.

[299] *The Papal Encyclicals*, Vol. 3 (1903-1939), p. 30.

[300] *The Papal Encyclicals*, Vol. 1 (1740-1878), p. 260.

[301] Fr. E. Laveille, S.J., *The Life of Fr. De Smet*, p. 80.

[302] Fr. E. Laveille, S.J., *The Life of Fr. De Smet*, pp. 139-140.

[303] Fr. E. Laveille, S.J., *The Life of Fr. De Smet*, pp. 139-140.

[304] St. Louis De Montfort, *True Devotion to Mary*, Bay Shore, NY: The Montfort Fathers, 1946, # 61.

[305] St. Francis De Sales, *The Catholic Controversy*, p. 59.

[306] St. Francis De Sales, *The Catholic Controversy*, p. 74.

[307] St. Francis De Sales, *The Catholic Controversy*, p. 200.

[308] *The Papal Encyclicals*, Vol. 2 (1878-1903), p. 285.

[309] Denzinger 228a.

[310] Michael Malone, *The Only-Begotten*, p. 329.

[311] Denzinger 1793.

[312] Denzinger 1000.

[313] *The Catholic Encyclopedia*, "Brendan," Volume 2, 1907, p. 758.

[314] St. Louis De Montfort, *The Secret of the Rosary*, Tan Books, p. 65.

[315] Denzinger 1800.

[316] St. Francis De Sales, *The Catholic Controversy*, p. 228.

[317] *The Devil's Final Battle*, compiled by Paul Kramer, Good Counsel Publications, 2002, p. 183.

[318] Denzinger 2022.

[319] Denzinger 2054.

[320] *The Papal Encyclicals*, Vol. 1 (1740-1878), p. 236.

[321] *The Catechism of the Council of Trent*, p. 179.

[322] *The Catechism of The Council Of Trent*, Introduction, XXXVI.

[323] *The Catechism of The Council Of Trent*, p. 243.

[324] Denzinger 1379.

[325] Denzinger 468-469.

[326] *Decrees of the Ecumenical Councils*, Vol. 2, p. 806; Denzinger 1784.

[327] Denzinger 804.

[328] *The Catechism of the Council of Trent*, p. 154.

[329] *The Catechism of the Council of Trent*, pp. 176-177.

[330] *The Catechism of the Council of Trent*, p. 163.

[331] *The Catechism of the Council of Trent*, p. 180.

[332] *The Catechism of the Council of Trent*, p. 171.

[333] *The Catechism of the Council of Trent*, p. 165.

[334] *The Catechism of the Council of Trent*, p. 159.

[335] *The Catechism of the Council of Trent*, p. 165.

[336] *Decrees of the Ecumenical Councils*, Vol. 2, p. 684; Denzinger 847.

[337] Denzinger 388.

[338] Denzinger 413.

[339] Denzinger 410.

[340] Denzinger 793.

[341] Denzinger 793.

[342] *Decrees of the Ecumenical Councils*, Vol. 1, p. 230; Denzinger 430.

[343] *Decrees of the Ecumenical Councils*, Vol. 1, p. 230; Denzinger 430.

[344] Denzinger 412.

[345] Fr. Christopher Rengers, *The 33 Doctors of the Church*, p. 504.

[346] *The Catholic Encyclopedia*, Volume 9, "Limbo," 1910, p. 258.

[347] Jurgens, *The Faith of the Early Fathers*, Vol. 1: 591 .

[348] Fr. Jean-Marc Rulleau, *Baptism of Desire*, p. 43.

[349] Denzinger 898.

[350] Fr. Francois Laisney, *Is Feeneyism Catholic*, p. 77.

[351] *Sermons of St. Alphonsus Liguori*, Tan Books, 1982, p. 219.

[352] Saint Alphonsus Marie De Liguori, *Instructions On The Commandments And Sacraments*, G. P. Warren Co., 1846. Trans. Fr. P. M'Auley, Dublin, p. 57.

[353] Michael Malone, *The Apostolic Digest*, p. 159.

[354] Saint Alphonsus Maria De Liguori, *Preparation for Death*, unabridged version, p. 339.

[355] Denzinger 712; *Decrees of the Ecumenical Councils*, Vol. 1, p. 576.

[356] *The Catechism of the Council of Trent*, p. 171.

[357] *Decrees of the Ecumenical Councils*, Vol. 1, p. 422.

[358] *Decrees of the Ecumenical Councils*, Vol. 1, pp. 421-422.

[359] Fr. Christopher Rengers, *The 33 Doctors of the Church*, pp. 623-624.

[360] Denzinger 861; *Decrees of the Ecumenical Councils*, Vol. 2, p. 685.

[361] Denzinger 861; *Decrees of the Ecumenical Councils*, Vol. 2, p. 685.

[362] Denzinger 916; also *The Canons and Decrees of the Council of Trent*, Tan Books, 1978, p. 102.

[363] *Decrees of the Ecumenical Councils*, Vol. 2, p. 712

[364] Denzinger 895.

[365] Denzinger 898.

[366] Denzinger 807.

[367] Denzinger 839.

[368] Denzinger 861; *Decrees of the Ecumenical Councils*, Vol. 2, p. 685.

[369] St. Thomas Aquinas, *Summa Theologica*, Pt. III, Q. 14, A. 3, Reply to Obj. 1.

[370] *The Catholic Encyclopedia*, "Baptism," Volume 2, 1907, p. 265.

[371] *The Catholic Encyclopedia*, "Baptism," Volume 2, 1907, p. 267.

[372] *The Papal Encyclicals*, Vol. 4 (1939-1958), p. 50.

[373] *Decrees of the Ecumenical Councils*, Vol. 1, p. 74.

[374] Denzinger 714.

[375] *The Papal Encyclicals*, Vol. 1 (1740-1878), p. 229.

[376] Denzinger 861; *Decrees of the Ecumenical Councils*, Vol. 2, p. 685.

[377] Denzinger 804.

[378] Denzinger 1031.

[379] Denzinger 1033.

[380] Denzinger 799-800.

[381] Denzinger 468-469.

[382] Denzinger 646.

[383] Denzinger 423.

[384] St. Francis De Sales, *The Catholic Controversy, pp. 305-306*

[385] *The Papal Encyclicals*, Vol. 2 (1878-1903), p. 401.

[386] *The Catechism of the Council of Trent*, p. 171.

[387] *Decrees of the Ecumenical Councils*, Vol. 1, p. 578; Denzinger 714.

[388] *The Life and Letters of St. Francis Xavier* by Henry James Coleridge, S.J. (Originally published: London: Burns and Oates, 1874) Second Reprint, New Delhi: Asian Educational Services, 2004, Vol. 2, p. 281.

[389] Denzinger 2022.

[390] Denzinger 2026.

[391] *Decrees of the Ecumenical Councils*, Vol. 1, p. 578; Denzinger 714.

[392] *The Devil's Final Battle*, compiled and edited by Paul Kramer, p. 69.

[393] *Our Lady of the Roses (Blue Book)*, the "messages" of Bayside, published by Apostles of Our Lady, Inc. Lansing, MI, 1993, p. 81.

[394] *The Papal Encyclicals*, Vol. 1 (1740-1878), p. 201.

[395] *The Apparitions of Our Lady of Medjugorje*, Franciscan Herald Press, 1984.

[396] *The Apparitions of Our Lady of Medjugorje*, Franciscan Herald Press, 1984.

[397] Janice T. Connell, *The Visions of the Children, The Apparitions of the Blessed Mother at Medjugorje*, St. Martin's Press, August, 1992.

[398] Denzinger 2288.

[399] *Decrees of the Ecumenical Councils*, Vol. 1, p. 639.

[400] *The Papal Encyclicals*, Vol. 3 (1903-1939), p. 117.

[401] *The Papal Encyclicals*, Vol. 1 (1740-1878), p. 205.

[402] *The Papal Encyclicals*, Vol. 2 (1878-1903), p. 388.

[403] Pope Pius XI, *Mortalium Animos* (# 10), Jan. 6, 1928.

[404] Pope Pius XII, *Mystici Corporis Christi* (# 64), June 29, 1943.

[405] Denzinger 714; *Decrees of the Ecumenical Councils*, Vol. 1, p. 578.

[406] *The Papal Encyclicals*, Vol. 3 (1903-1939), p. 317.

[407] *Decrees of the Ecumenical Councils*, Vol. 1, p. 646.

[408] *The Papal Encyclicals*, Vol. 1 (1740-1878), p. 160.

[409] Denzinger 1683.

[410] Jurgens, *The Faith of the Early Fathers*, Vol. 3, pp. 14-15 footnote 31.

[411] *The Catholic Encyclopedia*, Volume 9, "Limbo," 1910, p. 257.

[412] *The Catechism of the Council of Trent*, p. 171.

[413] Archbishop Patrick Kenrick, *Treatise on Baptism*, Baltimore: Hedian and O'Brien, 1852, pp. 84-85; quoted by Michael Malone, *The Only-Begotten*, p. 394.

[414] Jurgens, *The Faith of the Early Fathers*, Vol. 2, p. 39.

[415] Jurgens, *The Faith of the Early Fathers*, Vol. 2, p. 3.

[416] *The Papal Encyclicals*, Vol. 4 (1939-1958), pp. 178-179.

[417] Dr. Ludwig Ott, *Fundamentals of Catholic Dogma*, p. 354.

[418] Fr. Francis Spirago and Fr. Richard Clarke, *The Catechism Explained*, Rockford: IL, Tan Books, p. 579.

[419] Fr. Francis Spirago and Fr. Richard Clarke, *The Catechism Explained*, p. 579.

[420] Dr. Ludwig Ott, *Fundamentals of Catholic Dogma*, p. 309.

[421] Denzinger 714; *Decrees of the Ecumenical Councils*, Vol. 1, p. 578.

[422] Dr. Ludwig Ott, *Fundamentals of Catholic Dogma*, p. 309.

[423] Denzinger 468-469.

[424] Denzinger 895; *Decrees of the Ecumenical Councils*, Vol. 2, p. 704.

[425] Dr. Ludwig Ott, *Fundamentals of Catholic Dogma*, p. 309.

[426] *Decrees of the Ecumenical Councils*, Vol. 1, p. 230; Denzinger 430.

[427] Dr. Ludwig Ott, *Fundamentals of Catholic Dogma*, p. 309.

[428] *De Ecclesia Militante*, Book III, Ch. 2, *opera omnia*, Naples 1872, p. 75; partially quoted by Fr. Laisney, *Is Feeneyism Catholic?*, p. 76.

[429] *The Catholic Encyclopedia*, Volume 9, "Limbo," 1910, p. 258.

[430] Denzinger 468.

[431] Denzinger 714; *Decrees of the Ecumenical Councils*, Vol. 1, p. 578.

[432] St. Francis De Sales, *The Catholic Controversy*, p. 161.

[433] *The Catechism of the Council of Trent*, pp. 99-100.

[434] *The Catechism of the Council of Trent*, p. 159.

[435] *De Ecclesia Militante*, Book III, Ch. 3, *opera omnia*, Naples 1872, p. 75; quoted by Fr. Laisney, *Is Feeneyism Catholic?*, p. 76.

[436] *De Ecclesia Militante*, Book III, Ch. 2, *opera omnia*, Naples 1872, p. 75; partially quoted by Fr. Laisney, *Is Feeneyism Catholic?*, p. 76.

[437] Dr. Ludwig Ott, *Fundamentals of Catholic Dogma*, p. 309.

[438] *The Catechism of the Council of Trent*, p. 110

[439] Jurgens, *The Faith of the Early Fathers*, Vol. 2: 1012.

[440] *The New St. Joseph Baltimore Catechism. No. 2*, New York: Catholic Book Publishing Co., 1962-1969, p. 153.

[441] Jurgens, *The Faith of the Early Fathers*, Vol. 1: 92.

[442] Jurgens, *The Faith of the Early Fathers*, Vol. 1: 126.

[443] *The New St. Joseph Baltimore Catechism*, No. 2, 1962-1969, p. 153.

[444] *The New St. Joseph Baltimore Catechism*, No. 2, p. 153.

[445] *Decrees of the Ecumenical Councils*, Vol. 1, p. 230; Denzinger 430.

[446] The Catechism of Pope St. Pius X, Angelus Press, 1993, p. 71.

[447] The Catechism of Pope St. Pius X, Angelus Press, 1993, p. 71.

[448] The Catechism of Pope St. Pius X, Angelus Press, 1993, p. 31.

[449] The Catechism of Pope St. Pius X, Angelus Press, 1993, pp. 31-32.

[450] *The Papal Encyclicals*, Vol. 3 (1903-1939), p. 317.

[451] Denzinger 1647.

[452] Denzinger 861; *Decrees of the Ecumenical Councils*, Vol. 2, p. 685.

[453] Denzinger 696; *Decrees of the Ecumenical Councils*, Vol. 1, p. 542.

[454] *The Papal Encyclicals*, Vol. 2 (1878-1903), p. 188.

[455] *Decrees of the Ecumenical Councils*, Vol. 1, pp. 580-581.

[456] *Decrees of the Ecumenical Councils*, Vol. 1, p. 589.

[457] *Decrees of the Ecumenical Councils*, Vol. 1, p. 541; Denzinger 695.

[458] Denzinger 696; *Decrees of the Ecumenical Councils*, Vol. 1, p. 542.

[459] *The Life and Letters of St. Francis Xavier* by Henry James Coleridge, Vol. 1, p. 162.

[460] Denzinger 791-792.

[461] Denzinger 324.

[462] Denzinger 895; *Decrees of the Ecumenical Councils*, Vol. 2, p. 704.

[463] Denzinger 468-469.

[464] *The Papal Encyclicals*, Vol. 2 (1878-1903), pp. 86-87.

[465] *The Sunday Sermons of the Great Fathers*, Vol. 4, p. 5.

[466] Jurgens, *The Faith of the Early Fathers*, Vol. 3:1424.

[467] Jurgens, *The Faith of the Early Fathers*, Vol. 3:1425.

[468] Denzinger 799-800.

[469] *Decrees of the Ecumenical Councils*, Vol. 1, p. 230; Denzinger 430.

470 Jurgens, *The Faith of the Early Fathers*, Vol. 3:1717.

471 Jurgens, *The Faith of the Early Fathers*, Vol. 3:2251a.

472 Jurgens, *The Faith of the Early Fathers*, Vol. 2: 1368.

473 Jurgens, *The Faith of the Early Fathers*, Vol. 1: 681.

474 *Decrees of the Ecumenical Councils*, Vol. 1, p. 386.

475 Denzinger 482.

476 *Decrees of the Ecumenical Councils*, Vol. 1, p. 24.

477 Denzinger 468.

478 *The Sunday Sermons of the Great Fathers*, Vol. 2, p. 93.

479 Denzinger 796.

480 *The Sunday Sermons of the Great Fathers*, Vol. 2, p. 151.

481 Denzinger 843a.

482 *The Sunday Sermons of the Great Fathers*, Vol. 4, p. 8.

483 Denzinger 799.

484 Denzinger 792.

485 Denzinger 799.

486 Denzinger 996.

487 *Decrees of the Ecumenical Councils*, Vol. 2, p. 803.

488 Francis Talbot, *Saint Among Savages: The Life of St. Isaac Jogues* (Original Edition: Harper and Brothers, New York and London, 1935), New Edition, San Francisco: Ignatius Press, 2002, pp. 219, 221.

489 Francis Talbot, *Saint Among Savages: The Life of St. Isaac Jogues*, p. 197.

490 Francis Talbot, *Saint Among Savages: The Life of St. Isaac Jogues*, pp. 267-268.

491 Francis Talbot, *Saint Among Savages: The Life of St. Isaac Jogues*, p. 300.

492 Francis Talbot, *Saint Among Savages: The Life of St. Isaac Jogues*, pp. 145-146.

493 Francis Talbot, *Saint Among Savages: The Life of St. Isaac Jogues*, p. 141.

494 *The Life and Letters of St. Francis Xavier* by Henry James Coleridge, Vol. 1, pp. 155-156.

495 *The Life and Letters of St. Francis Xavier* by Henry James Coleridge, Vol. 1, p. 265.

496 *The Life and Letters of St. Francis Xavier* by Henry James Coleridge, Vol. 1, p. 380.

497 *The Life and Letters of St. Francis Xavier* by Henry James Coleridge, Vol. 2, p. 87.

498 *The Life and Letters of St. Francis Xavier* by Henry James Coleridge, Vol. 2, p. 348.

499 Francis Talbot, *Saint Among Savages: The Life of St. Isaac Jogues*, p. 92.

500 Francis Talbot, *Saint Among Savages: The Life of St. Isaac Jogues*, p. 136.

501 Francis Talbot, *Saint Among Savages: The Life of St. Isaac Jogues*, pp. 97-98.

502 Francis Talbot, *Saint Among Savages: The Life of St. Isaac Jogues*, p. 142.

503 Francis Talbot, *Saint Among Savages: The Life of St. Isaac Jogues*, p. 279.

504 Francis Talbot, *Saint Among Savages: The Life of St. Isaac Jogues*, p. 199.

505 Francis Talbot, *Saint Among Savages: The Life of St. Isaac Jogues*, pp. 122-123.

506 Francis Talbot, *Saint Among Savages: The Life of St. Isaac Jogues*, pp. 298-299.

507 Francis Talbot, *Saint Among Savages: The Life of St. Isaac Jogues*, p. 272.

508 Francis Talbot, *Saint Among Savages: The Life of St. Isaac Jogues*, p. 225.

509 Francis Talbot, *Saint Among Savages: The Life of St. Isaac Jogues*, p. 205.

510 Francis Talbot, *Saint Among Savages: The Life of St. Isaac Jogues*, p. 168.

511 *The Life and Letters of St. Francis Xavier* by Henry James Coleridge, Vol. 1, p. 375.

512 *The Life and Letters of St. Francis Xavier* by Henry James Coleridge, Vol. 2, p. 23.

513 Francis Talbot, *Saint Among Savages: The Life of St. Isaac Jogues*, p. 94.

514 *The Papal Encyclicals*, Vol. 2 (1878-1903), p. 394.

515 Bro. Robert Mary, *Father Feeney and The Truth About Salvation*, p. 13.

516 Bro. Robert Mary, *Father Feeney and The Truth About Salvation*, p. 13.

517 Bro. Robert Mary, *Father Feeney and The Truth About Salvation*, p. 14.

518 *The Papal Encyclicals*, Vol. 1 (1740-1878), p. 297 and footnote 4.

519 Bro. Robert Mary, *Father Feeney and The Truth About Salvation*, p. 16.

520 Bro. Robert Mary, *Father Feeney and The Truth About Salvation*, p. 16.

[521] *The Papal Encyclicals*, Vol. 1 (1740-1878), p. 229.

[522] Fr. Mark Massa, *Catholics and American Culture*, New York: The Crossroad Publishing, Co., 1999, p. 31.

[523] Bro. Robert Mary, *Father Feeney and The Truth About Salvation*, p. 18.

[524] Bro. Robert Mary, *Father Feeney and The Truth About Salvation*, p. 21.

[525] The Official English Translation of Protocol 122/49, quoted by Fr. Jean-Marc Rulleau, *Baptism of Desire*, p. 69.

[526] *The Papal Encyclicals*, Vol. 1 (1740-1878), pp. 229-230.

[527] Denzinger 1800.

[528] The Official English Translation of Protocol 122/49, quoted by Fr. Jean-Marc Rulleau, *Baptism of Desire*, p. 70.

[529] Denzinger 468-469.

[530] The Official English Translation of Protocol 122/49, quoted by Fr. Jean-Marc Rulleau, *Baptism of Desire*, p. 70.

[531] The Official English Translation of Protocol 122/49, quoted by Fr. Jean-Marc Rulleau, *Baptism of Desire*, p. 70.

[532] Denzinger 714; *Decrees of the Ecumenical Councils*, Vol. 1, p. 578.

[533] The Official English Translation of Protocol 122/49, quoted by Fr. Jean-Marc Rulleau, *Baptism of Desire*, p. 71.

[534] Fr. Michael Muller, C.SS.R., *The Catholic Dogma*, pp. 217-218.

[535] *Decrees of the Ecumenical Councils*, Vol. 1, p. 551.

[536] Denzinger 1000.

[537] Denzinger 1473.

[538] *Decrees of the Ecumenical Councils*, Vol. 2, p. 803.

[539] Quoted by St. Robert Bellarmine, *De Romano Pontifice*, II, 30.

[540] *The Catholic Encyclopedia*, Vol. 3, 1908, "Church," pp. 752-753.

[541] *The Papal Encyclicals*, Vol. 2 (1878-1903), p. 474.

[542] *The Papal Encyclicals*, Vol. 1 (1740-1878), pp. 229-230.

[543] *My Catholic Faith*, a Catechism by Bishop Louis LaRavoire, Kenosha, WI: My Mission House, 1949, p. 272.

[544] Denzinger 570b.

[545] *The Papal Encyclicals*, Vol. 1 (1740-1878), pp. 237-238.

[546] Dr. Ludwig Ott, *Fundamentals of Catholic Dogma*, p. 310.

[547] Dr. Ludwig Ott, *Fundamentals of Catholic Dogma*, pp. 310-311.

[548] *Decrees of the Ecumenical Councils*, Vol. 1, p. 386.

[549] Rev. Spirago and Rev. Clark, *The Catechism Explained*, p. 246.

[550] *The Papal Encyclicals*, Vol. 1 (1740-1878), pp. 237-238.

[551] Bro. Robert Mary, *Father Feeney and The Truth About Salvation*, p. 153.

[552] Denzinger 802.

[553] Bro. Robert Mary, *Father Feeney and The Truth About Salvation*, p. 154.

[554] *The Papal Encyclicals*, Vol. 1 (1740-1878), p. 207.

[555] *The Papal Encyclicals*, Vol. 1 (1740-1878), p. 238.

[556] Denzinger 2286.

[557] *The Papal Encyclicals*, Vol. 4 (1939-1958), p. 127.

[558] *The Papal Encyclicals*, Vol. 4 (1939-1958), p. 179; Denzinger 2319.

[559] For example, *Second Council of Nicaea (787), Decrees of the Ecumenical Councils*, Vol. 1, p. 135; and the *Fourth Council of Constantinople (869-870), Decrees of the Ecumenical Councils*, Vol. 1, p. 162.

[560] Bro. Robert Mary, *Father Feeney and The Truth About Salvation*, p. 37.

[561] Bro. Robert Mary, *Father Feeney and The Truth About Salvation*, p. 22.

[562] Bro. Robert Mary, *Father Feeney and The Truth About Salvation*, p. 23.

[563] Bro. Robert Mary, *Father Feeney and The Truth About Salvation*, p. 23.

[564] Bro. Robert Mary, *Father Feeney and The Truth About Salvation*, p. 25.

[565] Bro. Robert Mary, *Father Feeney and The Truth About Salvation*, p. 25.

[566] Denzinger 2026.

567 *Decrees of the Ecumenical Councils*, Vol. 1, p. 578; Denzinger 714.
568 Fr. Mark Massa, *Catholics and American Culture*, p. 31.
569 *The Papal Encyclicals*, Vol. 1 (1740-1878), pp. 239.
570 *The Oxford Illustrated History of Christianity*, by John McManners, cap. 10, "The Ecumenical Movement," Oxford, NY: Oxford University Press, 1990, p., 373.
571 Fr. Mark Massa, *Catholics and American Culture*, p. 21.
572 Fr. Mark Massa, *Catholics and American Culture*, p. 27.
573 Fr. Mark Massa, *Catholics and American Culture*, pp. 32-33.
574 Fr. Mark Massa, *Catholics and American Culture*, p. 34.
575 Fr. Mark Massa, *Catholics and American Culture*, p. 35.
576 Fr. Mark Massa, *Catholics and American Culture*, p. 35.
577 Fr. Mark Massa, *Catholics and American Culture*, p. 38.
578 Denzinger 861; *Decrees of the Ecumenical Councils*, Vol. 2, p. 685.
579 *Decrees of the Ecumenical Councils*, Vol. 1, pp. 550-553; Denzinger 39-40.
580 *Decrees of the Ecumenical Councils*, Vol. 1, p. 81.
581 Denzinger 165.
582 Denzinger 696; *Decrees of the Ecumenical Councils*, Vol. 1, p. 542.
583 Archbishop Marcel Lefebvre, *Against the Heresies,* Angelus Press, 1997, p. 216.
584 *The Papal Encyclicals*, Vol. 2 (1878-1903), p. 394.
585 *The Papal Encyclicals*, Vol. 1 (1740-1878), p. 280.
586 Quoted in Bro. Robert Mary, *Fr. Feeney and the Truth About Salvation*, p. 213.
587 Jurgens, *The Faith of the Early Fathers*, Vol. 2: 1330.
588 *Decrees of the Ecumenical Councils*, Vol. 1, p. 81.
589 Denzinger 468-469.
590 *The Papal Encyclicals*, Vol. 4 (1939-1958), p. 45.
591 Denzinger 799.
592 *Decrees of the Ecumenical Councils*, Vol. 2, p. 678; Denz. 809.
593 Denzinger 800.
594 Archbishop Marcel Lefebvre, *Against the Heresies*, p. 216.
595 Archbishop Marcel Lefebvre, *Against the Heresies*, p. 217.
596 Archbishop Marcel Lefebvre, *Against the Heresies*, pp. 217-218.
597 *The Papal Encyclicals*, Vol. 1 (1740-1878), p. 229.
598 Brother Robert Mary, *Father Feeney and The Truth About Salvation*, pp. 213-214.
599 Quoted in Bro. Robert Mary, *Fr. Feeney and the Truth About Salvation*, p. 213.
600 *The Papal Encyclicals*, Vol. 1 (1740-1878), p. 280.
601 Archbishop Marcel Lefebvre, *Open Letter to Confused Catholics*, Angelus Press, pp. 73-74.
602 Fr. Jean-Marc Rulleau, *Baptism of Desire*, p. 63.
603 Fr. Jean-Marc Rulleau, *Baptism of Desire*, p. 39.
604 Fr. Jean-Marc Rulleau, *Baptism of Desire*, p. 11.
605 Fr. Jean-Marc Rulleau, *Baptism of Desire*, pp. 56-57.
606 St. Thomas Aquinas, *Summa Theologica*, Pt. II-II, Q. 2., A. 7.
607 St. Thomas Aquinas, *Summa Theologica*, Pt. II-II, Q. 2., A. 8.
608 St. Thomas Aquinas, Sent. II, 28, Q. 1, A. 4, ad 4; quoted by Fr. Jean-Marc Rulleau, *Baptism of Desire*, p. 55.
609 St. Thomas Aquinas, *Sent.* III, 25, Q. 2, A. 2, solut. 2; quoted by Fr. Jean-Marc Rulleau, *Baptism of Desire*, p. 55.
610 St. Thomas Aquinas, *De Veritate*, 14, A. 11, ad 1; quoted by Fr. Jean-Marc Rulleau, *Baptism of Desire*, pp. 55-56.
611 Fr. Jean-Marc Rulleau, *Baptism of Desire*, pp. 56-57.
612 Fr. Francois Laisney, *Is Feeneyism Catholic*, p. 47.
613 Fr. Francois Laisney, *Is Feeneyism Catholic*, p. 48.
614 Fr. Francois Laisney, *Is Feeneyism Catholic*, p. 52.
615 Fr. Francois Laisney, *Is Feeneyism Catholic*, p. 38.

[616] Fr. Francois Laisney, *Is Feeneyism Catholic*, p. 49.

[617] Fr. Francois Laisney, *Is Feeneyism Catholic*, pp. 85-86.

[618] *Decrees of the Ecumenical Councils*, Vol. 1, p. 81.

[619] Fr. Francois Laisney, *Is Feeneyism Catholic*, p. 59.

[620] Fr. Francois Laisney, *Is Feeneyism Catholic*, p. 9.

[621] Fr. Francois Laisney, *Is Feeneyism Catholic*, p. 68.

[622] Fr. Francois Laisney, *Is Feeneyism Catholic*, p. 77.

[623] Fr. Francois Laisney, *Is Feeneyism Catholic*, p. 76.

[624] Fr. Francois Laisney, *Is Feeneyism Catholic*, p. 34.

[625] Fr. Francois Laisney, *Is Feeneyism Catholic*, p. 34.

[626] Fr. Francois Laisney, *Is Feeneyism Catholic*, p. 22.

[627] Fr. Francois Laisney, *Is Feeneyism Catholic*, p. 77.

[628] Fr. Francois Laisney, *Is Feeneyism Catholic*, p. 47.

[629] Fr. Francois Laisney, *Is Feeneyism Catholic*, p. 47.

[630] Fr. Francois Laisney, *Is Feeneyism Catholic*, p. 48.

[631] Denzinger 696; *Decrees of the Ecumenical Councils*, Vol. 1, p. 542.

[632] Fr. Francois Laisney, *Is Feeneyism Catholic*, pp. 48-49.

[633] Fr. Jacques Dupuis, S.J. and Fr. Josef Neuner, S.J., *The Christian Faith*, p. 540.

[634] Denzinger 861.

[635] Denzinger 696.

[636] *The Papal Encyclicals*, Vol. 1 (1740-1878), pp. 237-238.

[637] Denzinger 1800.

[638] Denzinger 714.

[639] Dr. Ludwig Ott, *Fundamentals of Catholic Dogma*, p. 354.

[640] Denzinger 861.

[641] Denzinger 696.

[642] *The Reign of Mary*, Vol. XXIV, No. 70, Spokane, WA, Winter, 1992, p. 10 ff.

[643] *The Reign of Mary*, Vol. XXVI, No. 83, pp. 4-5.

[644] *The Reign of Mary*, Vol. XXVI, No. 83, pp. 4-5.

[645] *Decrees of the Ecumenical Councils*, Vol. 1, p. 230; Denzinger 430.

[646] Denzinger 468-469.

[647] *Decrees of the Ecumenical Councils*, Vol. 1, p. 386.

[648] *Decrees of the Ecumenical Councils*, Vol. 1, pp. 550-553; Denzinger 39-40.

[649] *Decrees of the Ecumenical Councils*, Vol. 1, p. 578; Denzinger 714.

[650] *Decrees of the Ecumenical Councils*, Vol. 1, p. 646.

[651] Denzinger 1000.

[652] Denzinger 1473.

[653] *Decrees of the Ecumenical Councils*, Vol. 2, p. 803.

[654] *The Reign of Mary*, Vol. XXVI, No. 83, pp. 4-5.

[655] Denzinger 2022.

[656] Jurgens, *The Faith of the Early Fathers*, Vol. 2, p. 39.

[657] Jurgens, *The Faith of the Early Fathers*, Vol. 2, p. 3.

Outside the Catholic Church There is Absolutely No Salvation
by Bro. Peter Dimond O.S.B.

By far the best and most in-depth book that has ever been written on the Catholic Church's infallible teaching on the necessity of the Catholic Faith and the Sacrament of Baptism for salvation." (*From many who have read it*)

1 copy for $8.00 *1 copy to a Canadian or Foreign address = $10.00*	**8 copies for $25.00** (please include street address, No PO Boxes) *8 copies to a Canadian or Foreign address = $40.00*
15 copies for $45.00 (please include street address, No PO Boxes) *15 copies to a Canadian or Foreign address = $65.00*	**30 copies for $85.00** (please include street address, No PO Boxes) *30 copies to a Canadian or Foreign address = $110.00*

* For larger quantity orders please call us at 585-567-4433

Book List	AMOUNT	COST
Outside the Catholic Church There is Absolutely No Salvation (299 page book)		
Name:	Shipping:	Included
Address:	**Total:**	
City /St /Zip:	email address:	
Visa /MC /Discover:	Exp Date:	

Most Holy Family Monastery * 4425 Schneider Rd. Fillmore, NY. 14735 * 800-275-1126 / 585-567-4433 (24 hour fax 585-567-8352) www.mostholyfamilymonastery.com

SPECIAL OFFERS
www.mostholyfamilymonastery.com

In order to provide as many souls as possible with the critical information they need to be Faithful Catholics in our day, we are now offering the following special offe

VIDEO TAPE and DVD List	#of Videos	Cost for Videos	#of DVDs	Cost for DVDs
1) *Antipope John Paul II: Final Antichrist Revealed*				
2) *Why Antipope John Paul II Cannot be the Pope*				
3) *Vatican II: Council of Apostasy*				
4) *Death, and the Journey Into Hell*				
5) *Creation and Miracles, Past and Present*				
6) *End Times Prophecies II: Agents of Antichrist*				
7) *Communist Infiltration of the Catholic Church*				

VIDEO TAPE SPECIALS FOR THOSE IN US: *All 7 videos listed above for $15.00, or $3.00 a video tape, or any 12 video tapes for $20.00, or any 24 video tapes for $24.00, or any 46 video tapes for $46.00 (all prices include shipping)*

VIDEO TAPE SPECIALS FOR THOSE OUTSIDE THE US: *All 7 videos listed above for $30.00, or $6.00 a video tape, or any 12 video tapes for $40.00, or any 24 video tapes for $70.00, or any 46 video tapes for 120.00 (all prices include shipping)*

DVD SPECIALS FOR THOSE IN US: *All 7 DVDs listed above for $15.00, or $3.00 a DVD, or any 12 DVDs for $20.00, or any 24 DVDs for $36.00, or any 46 DVDs tapes for $65.00 (all prices include shipping)*

DVD SPECIALS FOR THOSE OUTSIDE THE US: *All 7 DVDs listed above for $30.00, or $6.00 a DVD, or any 12 DVDs for $40.00, or any 24 DVDs for $60.00, or any 46 DVDs tapes for $75.00 (all prices include shipping)*

Shipping: Included
Total:

PAL OR SECAM TAPE List (FOREIGN COUNTRIES)	#of PAL Tapes	#of SECAM Tapes	Cost
1) Antipope John Paul II: Final Antichrist Revealed			
2) Why Antipope John Paul II Cannot be the Pope			
3) Vatican II: Council of Apostasy			
4) Death, and the Journey Into Hell			
5) Creation and Miracles, Past and Present			
6) End Times Prophecies II: Exposing Agents of Antichrist			
7) Communist Infiltration of the Catholic Church			

Shipping: Included
Total:

(PAL AND SECAM are the sam price) for those in US: $5.00 a tape, 3 or more copies are $4.00 a copy
(PAL AND SECAM are the sam price) outside US: $10.00 a tape or 3 or more for $8.00 a copy,

AUDIO TAPE List	#of Audio Tapes	Cost
1) Antipope John Paul II: Final Antichrist Revealed		
2) Why Antipope John Paul II Cannot be the Pope		
3) Vatican II: Council of Apostasy		
4) Death, and the Journey Into Hell		
5) Creation and Miracles, Past and Present		
6) End Times Prophecies II: Exposing Agents of Antichrist		
7) Communist Infiltration of the Catholic Church		
8) A Soldier Encounters an Angel and the story of Claude Neuman		
9) Prayer, the Great Means of Grace		
10) Hell, and the Brown Scapular by Fr. Marcel Naught		

Shipping: Included
Total:

AUDIO TAPE SPECIALS FOR THOSE IN US: *All 10 audios listed to the left, including binder and color cover for $10.00 or $2.00 an audio tape, or any 10 audio tapes for $10.00, or any 25 audio tapes for $15.00, or any 50 audio tapes for $27.00, or any 75 audio tapes for $35.00 (all prices include shipping)*

AUDIO TAPE SPECIALSFOR THOSE OUTSIDE THE US: *All 10 audios listed to the left, including binder and color cover for $22.00, or $4.00 an audio tape, or any 10 audio tapes for $25.00, or any 25 audio tapes for $45.00, or any 50 audio tapes for $55.00, or any 75 audio tapes for $63.00 (all prices include shipping)*

Best video ever produced exposing Rock music!

	#of Copies	Cost	Shipping:	Total:
1) Rock-n-Roll Sorcerers of the New Age Revolution 3 1/2 hour video (not available in DVD)		$15.00 a copy in US $22.00 a copy outside US	Included	

Other Items (available in both video and DVD)

	#of Videos	Cost for Videos	#of DVDs	Cost for DVDs	Shipping:	Total:
1) Jesus and the Shroud of Turin (1 hour) The best video produced on the Shroud of Turin		$7.00 a copy in US $12.00 a copy outside US		$7.00 a copy in US $12.00 a copy outside US	Included	
2) The Exodus Revealed (1 hour) Shows incredible evidence of Moses's crossing of the Red Sea		$7.00 a copy in US $12.00 a copy outside US		$7.00 a copy in US $12.00 a copy outside US	Included	

Name:

Address:

City /St /Zip:

Visa /MC /Discover: *Exp Date:*

Email(so that you will be put on our email list)

Most Holy Family Monastery * 4425 Schneider Rd. Fillmore, NY. 14735 * 800-275-1126 / 585-567-4433 (24 hour fax 585-567-8352)

Outside the Catholic Church There is Absolutely No Salvation
by Bro. Peter Dimond O.S.B.

"By far the best and most in-depth book that has ever been written on the Catholic Church's infallible teaching on the necessity of the Catholic Faith and the Sacrament of Baptism for salvation." (*From many who have read it*)

1 copy for $8.00	**8 copies for $25.00** (please include street address, No PO Boxes)
1 copy to a Canadian or Foreign address = $10.00	*8 copies to a Canadian or Foreign address = $40.00*
15 copies for $45.00 please include street address, No PO Boxes	**30 copies for $85.00** (please include street address, No PO Boxes)
15 copies to a Canadian or Foreign address = $65.00	*30 copies to a Canadian or Foreign address = $110.00*

* For larger quantity orders please call us at 585-567-4433

Book List		AMOUNT	COST
Outside the Catholic Church There is Absolutely No Salvation (299 page book)			
Name:		Shipping:	Included
Address:		**Total:**	
City /St /Zip:		email address:	
Visa /MC /Discover:			Exp Date:

Most Holy Family Monastery * 4425 Schneider Rd. Fillmore, NY. 14735 * 800-275-1126 / 585-567-4433 (24 hour fax 585-567-8352) www.mostholyfamilymonastery.com

SPECIAL OFFERS
www.mostholyfamilymonastery.com

In order to provide as many souls as possible with the critical information they need to be Faithful Catholics in our day, we are now offering the following special offe

VIDEO TAPE and DVD List	#of Videos	Cost for Videos	#of DVDs	Cost for DVDs
1) Antipope John Paul II: Final Antichrist Revealed				
2) Why Antipope John Paul II Cannot be the Pope				
3) Vatican II: Council of Apostasy				
4) Death, and the Journey Into Hell				
5) Creation and Miracles, Past and Present				
6) End Times Prophecies II: Agents of Antichrist				
7) Communist Infiltration of the Catholic Church				

VIDEO TAPE SPECIALS FOR THOSE IN US: All 7 videos listed above for $15.00, or $3.00 a video tape, or any 12 video tapes for $20.00, or any 24 video tapes for $24.00, or any 46 video tapes for $46.00 (all prices include shipping)

VIDEO TAPE SPECIALS FOR THOSE OUTSIDE THE US: All 7 videos listed above for $30.00, or $6.00 a video tape, or any 12 video tapes for $40.00, or any 24 video tapes for $70.00, or any 46 video tapes for 120.00 (all prices include shipping)

DVD SPECIALS FOR THOSE IN US: All 7 DVDs listed above for $15.00, or $3.00 a DVD, or any 12 DVDs for $20.00, or any 24 DVDs for $36.00, or any 46 DVDs tapes for $65.00 (all prices include shipping)

DVD SPECIALS FOR THOSE OUTSIDE THE US: All 7 DVDs listed above for $30.00, or $6.00 a DVD, or any 12 DVDs for $40.00, or any 24 DVDs for $60.00, or any 46 DVDs tapes for $75.00 (all prices include shipping)

		Shipping:	Included
		Total:	

PAL OR SECAM TAPE List (FOREIGN COUNTRIES)	#of PAL Tapes	#of SECAM Tapes	Cost
1) Antipope John Paul II: Final Antichrist Revealed			
2) Why Antipope John Paul II Cannot be the Pope			
3) Vatican II: Council of Apostasy			
4) Death, and the Journey Into Hell			
5) Creation and Miracles, Past and Present			
6) End Times Prophecies II: Exposing Agents of Antichrist			
7) Communist Infiltration of the Catholic Church			

(PAL AND SECAM are the sam price) for those in US: $5.00 a tape, 3 or more copies are $4.00 a copy

(PAL AND SECAM are the sam price) outside US: $10.00 a tape or 3 or more for $8.00 a copy,

	Shipping:	Included
	Total:	

AUDIO TAPE List

	#of Audio Tapes	Cost
1) Antipope John Paul II: Final Antichrist Revealed		
2) Why Antipope John Paul II Cannot be the Pope		
3) Vatican II: Council of Apostasy		
4) Death, and the Journey Into Hell		
5) Creation and Miracles, Past and Present		
6) End Times Prophecies II: Exposing Agents of Antichrist		
7) Communist Infiltration of the Catholic Church		
8) A Soldier Encounters an Angel and the story of Claude Neuman		
9) Prayer, the Great Means of Grace		
10) Hell, and the Brown Scapular by Fr. Marcel Naught		

AUDIO TAPE SPECIALS FOR THOSE IN US: All 10 audios listed to the left, including binder and color cover for $10.00 or $2.00 an audio tape, or any 10 audio tapes for $10.00, or any 25 audio tapes for $15.00, or any 50 audio tapes for $27.00, or any 75 audio tapes for $35.00 (all prices include shipping)

AUDIO TAPE SPECIALSFOR THOSE OUTSIDE THE US: All 10 audios listed to the left, including binder and color cover for $22.00, or $4.00 an audio tape, or any 10 audio tapes for $25.00, or any 25 audio tapes for $45.00, or any 50 audio tapes for $55.00, or any 75 audio tapes for $63.00 (all prices include shipping)

	Shipping:	Included
	Total:	

Best video ever produced exposing Rock music!

	#of Copies	Cost	Shipping:	**Total:**
1) Rock-n-Roll Sorcerers of the New Age Revolution 3 1/2 hour video (not available in DVD)		$15.00 a copy in US $22.00 a copy outside US	Included	

Other Items (available in both video and DVD)

	#of Videos	Cost for Videos	#of DVDs	Cost for DVDs	Shipping:	**Total:**
1) Jesus and the Shroud of Turin (1 hour) The best video produced on the Shroud of Turin		$7.00 a copy in US $12.00 a copy outside US		$7.00 a copy in US $12.00 a copy outside US	Included	
2) The Exodus Revealed (1 hour) Shows incredible evidence of Moses's crossing of the Red Sea		$7.00 a copy in US $12.00 a copy outside US		$7.00 a copy in US $12.00 a copy outside US	Included	

Name: _____

Address: _____

City /St /Zip: _____

Visa /MC /Discover: _____ *Exp Date:* _____

Email(so that you will be put on our email list)

Most Holy Family Monastery * 4425 Schneider Rd. Fillmore, NY. 14735 * 800-275-1126 / 585-567-4433 (24 hour fax 585-567-8352)